Secular Conversions

Why does secularization proceed differently in otherwise similar countries? Secular Conversions demonstrates that the institutional structure of the state is a key factor shaping the course of secularization. Drawing upon detailed historical analysis of religious education policy in the United States and Australia, Damon Mayrl details how administrative structures, legal procedures, and electoral systems have shaped political opportunities and even helped create constituencies for secular policies. In so doing, he also shows how a decentralized, readily accessible American state acts as an engine for religious conflict, encouraging religious differences to spill into law and politics at every turn. This book provides a vivid picture of how political conflicts interacted with the state over the long span of American and Australian history to shape religion's role in public life. Ultimately, it reveals that taken-for-granted political structures have powerfully shaped the fate of religion in modern societies.

Damon Mayrl is Assistant Professor of Sociology at Universidad Carlos III de Madrid. His recent publications include writings in *Sociological Theory, Social Forces, Social Science Research, Journal for the Scientific Study of Religion, European Journal of Sociology,* and *Sociological Inquiry*.

Cambridge Studies in Social Theory, Religion and Politics

Editors

David C. Leege, University of Notre Dame
Kenneth D. Wald, University of Florida, Gainesville
Richard L. Wood, University of New Mexico

The most enduring and illuminating bodies of late nineteenth-century social theory – by Marx, Weber, Durkheim, and others – emphasized the integration of religion, polity, and economy through time and place. Once a staple of classic social theory, however, religion gradually lost the interest of many social scientists during the twentieth century. The recent emergence of phenomena such as Solidarity in Poland, the dissolution of the Soviet empire, various South American, Southern African, and South Asian liberation movements, the Christian Right in the United States, and Al Qaeda have reawakened scholarly interest in religiously based political conflict. At the same time, fundamental questions are once again being asked about the role of religion in stable political regimes, public policies, and constitutional orders. The series *Cambridge Studies in Social Theory, Religion, and Politics* will produce volumes that study religion and politics by drawing upon classic social theory and more recent social scientific research traditions. Books in the series offer theoretically grounded, comparative, empirical studies that raise "big" questions about a timely subject that has long engaged the best minds in social science.

Titles in the series

Luke Bretherton, *Resurrecting Democracy: Faith, Citizenship, and the Politics of a Common Life*

David E. Campbell, John C. Green, and J. Quin Monson, *Seeking the Promised Land: Mormons and American Politics*

Ryan L. Claassen, *Godless Democrats and Pious Republicans? Party Activists, Party Capture, and the "God Gap"*

Paul A. Djupe and Christopher P. Gilbert, *The Political Influence of Churches*

Joel S. Fetzer and J. Christopher Soper, *Muslims and the State in Britain, France, and Germany*

François Foret, *Religion and Politics in the European Union: The Secular Canopy*

Jonathan Fox, *A World Survey of Religion and the State*

Anthony Gill, *The Political Origins of Religious Liberty*

Brian J. Grim and Roger Finke, *The Price of Freedom Denied: Religious Persecution and Conflict in the 21st Century*

Kees van Kersbergen and Philip Manow, editors, *Religion, Class Coalitions, and Welfare States*

Karrie J. Koesel, *Religion and Authoritarianism: Cooperation, Conflict, and the Consequences*

Ahmet T. Kuru, *Secularism and State Policies toward Religion: The United States, France, and Turkey*

Damon Mayrl, *Secular Conversions: Political Institutions and Religious Education in the United States and Australia, 1800–2000*

Jeremy Menchik, *Islam and Democracy in Indonesia: Tolerance without Liberalism*

Pippa Norris and Ronald Inglehart, *Sacred and Secular: Religion and Politics Worldwide*

Amy Reynolds, *Free Trade and Faithful Globalization: Saving the Market*

Peter Stamatov, *The Origins of Global Humanitarianism: Religion, Empires, and Advocacy*

Secular Conversions

Political Institutions and Religious Education in the United States and Australia, 1800–2000

DAMON MAYRL

Universidad Carlos III de Madrid

CAMBRIDGE
UNIVERSITY PRESS

University Printing House, Cambridge CB2 8BS, United Kingdom

One Liberty Plaza, 20th Floor, New York, NY 10006, USA

477 Williamstown Road, Port Melbourne, VIC 3207, Australia

4843/24, 2nd Floor, Ansari Road, Daryaganj, Delhi – 110002, India

79 Anson Road, #06-04/06, Singapore 079906

Cambridge University Press is part of the University of Cambridge.

It furthers the University's mission by disseminating knowledge in the pursuit of education, learning, and research at the highest international levels of excellence.

www.cambridge.org
Information on this title: www.cambridge.org/9781107503236

© Cambridge University Press 2016

First published 2016

Printed in the United States of America by Sheridan Books, Inc.

A catalogue record for this publication is available from the British Library.

Library of Congress Cataloguing in Publication Data
Names: Mayrl, Damon, 1977– author.
Title: Secular conversions : political institutions and religious
education in the United States and Australia, 1800–2000 / Damon Mayrl,
Universidad Carlos III de Madrid.
Description: New York : Cambridge University Press, 2016. |
Includes bibliographical references and index.
Identifiers: LCCN 2016014634| ISBN 9781107103719 (hardback) |
ISBN 9781107503236 (pbk)
Subjects: LCSH: United States–Religion. | Secularism–United States. |
Secularization. | Religion and politics–United States. |
Religious education–United States. | Australia–Religion. | Secularism–Australia. |
Religion and politics–Australia. | Religious education–Australia.
Classification: LCC BL2525.M385 2016 | DDC 322/.10973–dc23
LC record available at https://lccn.loc.gov/2016014634

ISBN 978-1-107-10371-9 Hardback
ISBN 978-1-107-50323-6 Paperback

Contents

Figures and Tables

Acknowledgments

I have amassed many debts writing this book. The book began as a dissertation at the University of California, Berkeley, where I had the immense benefit of being advised by a stellar committee. Margaret Weir has been an amazing mentor, responsive and generous with her time and incisive and thorough in her feedback. My many intellectual debts to her are readily apparent throughout the manuscript. Marion Fourcade pushed me toward greater conceptual precision and helped me see how my research spoke to broader sociological debates. Phil Gorski believed in this project from the outset, advising it from afar and offering agile guidance through the thicket of secularization theory. David Hollinger provided a sharp historian's eye and a number of early leads that paid important theoretical dividends.

I am also grateful for the influential exchanges I had while at Berkeley in a series of dissertation support groups with increasingly ridiculous acronyms. Early on, Shannon Gleeson, Angelo Gonzales, Matt Grossman, Bruce Huber, Ben Moodie, Rachel Robinson, Aliya Saperstein, and Laurel Westbrook helped me hone the design of the project. Later, Ryan Calder, Sarah Garrett, Lynne Gerber, Kristen Jafflin, Laura Mangels, Sarah Quinn, Sarah Staveteig, Nick Wilson, and Ariane Zambiras sustained and inspired me through the writing process. Farther afield, Ben Manning offered indispensable guidance to Australian culture and politics during my time in Australia.

Universidad Carlos III has been a wonderfully supportive home in which to teach, think, and write over the past several years. Peter Stamatov and Juan Fernández generously provided detailed readings and stimulating conversations about this project that have, I hope, substantially improved it. Juan Díez Medrano, Roberto Garvía, Javier Polavieja, Marga Torre, and Antonio Veira also read chapter drafts and offered exceptionally helpful feedback.

I have benefited from the collective wisdom of the larger academic community in many ways. Nick Wilson has been an enthusiastic supporter, sounding board, and critic since this project's earliest beginnings, providing trenchant commentary upon multiple drafts of multiple chapters. Lori Beaman, Lynne Gerber, Bill Mayrl, Rebecca Sager, and an anonymous reviewer read the entire manuscript and offered detailed, invaluable feedback. Ateş Altınordu, Siri Colom, Laura Mangels, Carol Nguyen, Sarah Quinn, Tim Ruckle, and Aliya Saperstein also read and provided helpful comments on shorter sections of the manuscript, sometimes more than once. Many others, including Jerome Baggett, Rogers Brubaker, Cathy Byrne, José Casanova, Benjamin Edwards, Barry Eidlin, Carolyn Evans, Neil Fligstein, Anna Halafoff, John Hall, Heather Haveman, Matthias Koenig, Marion Maddox, Dawne Moon, Sam Nelson, Freeden Oeur, Steve Pfaff, Dylan Riley, Suzanne Rutland, Christian Smith, Lyn Spillman, Sarah Valdez, Melissa Wilde, and Gene Zubovich, contributed to the book through conversations that stuck with me, helped me see a problem in a new light, or gently diverted me away from saying something truly embarrassing.

This book could not have been written without more tangible forms of support. I thank Margaret Avard, Marianne Dacy, Kate Musgrave, Edmund Perrin, Pennie Pemberton, and the other archivists at the National Library of Australia, State Records New South Wales, Noel Butlin Labour Archives, Uniting Church Archive, and Lyndon B. Johnson Presidential Library for their assistance in identifying and locating documents. The National Science Foundation (Dissertation Improvement Grant #0727814), the University of California Office of the President Pacific Rim Research Program, and the Institute of International Studies and Department of Sociology at the University of California, Berkeley provided me with grants and fellowships that enabled me to conduct the research for this book. Bob Goodin and the Philosophy Department in the Research School of Social Sciences at the Australian National University were gracious hosts during my first round of archival work in 2007; and Jan Burgers and Laura Guichard opened their homes to me on subsequent archival trips to Canberra and Austin. I completed the manuscript as a visiting scholar at the Berkeley Center for the Study of Religion, and thank Jonathan Sheehan and Mark Csikszentmihalyi for inviting me to visit and for their hospitality during my stay.

Portions of Chapters 3 and 4 previously appeared in substantially different form in the *European Journal of Sociology* ("Administering Secularization: Religious Education in New South Wales since 1960" [April 2011] and "How Does the State Structure Secularization?" [September 2015]). I gratefully acknowledge permission to reproduce that material.

At Cambridge University Press, Rich Wood championed this book from a very early date, and I thank him for shepherding it through the publication process and patiently managing the anxieties and confusion of a first-time author with grace and humor. Thanks too to the rest of the editorial and production teams at Cambridge, including David Leege, Ken Wald, Lew Bateman, Claudia Bona-Cohen, Ellena Moriarty, David Mackenzie, Christofere Fila,

Aimée Feenan, and Richard Hutchinson, for their work making this book a reality; and to Jim Diggins for compiling the index.

Finally, my family has been incredibly supportive throughout this lengthy process. My brother, Matthew; my sisters- and brothers-in-law; and my nieces and nephews not only cheered me on, but also supplied me with a steady stream of happy distractions over the years. My parents, Robin and Bill Mayrl, continue to inspire me in ways large and small. I am grateful for their many sacrifices and unconditional support. Last but not least, Luis Barcena has lived this book the entire way alongside me, enduring lengthy separations, unpredictable schedules, and epic meltdowns. Through it all, he has provided me with constant encouragement and boundless faith in both me and my research. I could not have completed this book without his love, support, and patience, and I dedicate it to him.

Acronyms

ACER	Australian Council for Educational Research
ACLU	American Civil Liberties Union
ADL	Anti-Defamation League of B'Nai B'rith
AEF	Association for Educational Freedom
AHMS	American Home Missionary Society
AII	American Institute of Instruction
AISV	Association of Independent Schools in Victoria
AJC	American Jewish Congress
AJCommittee	American Jewish Committee
ALP	Australian Labor Party
CCES	Council for Christian Education in Schools
CIO	Congress of Industrial Organizations
CSB	Common Schools Board
DLP	Democratic Labor Party
DOGS	Council for the Defence of Government Schools
FCSC	Federal Catholic Schools Committee
HMC	Protestant Headmasters Conference of Independent Schools in Australia
IJ	Institute for Justice
INB	Irish National Board
NAE	National Association of Evangelicals
NBPE	National Board of Popular Education
NCC	National Civic Council
NCWC	National Catholic Welfare Conference
NEA	National Education Association
NSWTF	New South Wales Teachers' Federation
P&C	Parents and Citizens Association

POAU	Protestants and Other Americans United for the Separation of Church and State
PSS	Public School Society
REA	Religious Education Association
SES	Secular Education Society

ARCHIVES

NBLA	Noel Butlin Labour Archive
NLA	National Library of Australia
SRNSW	State Records New South Wales
UCA	Uniting Church Archive

OTHER

ESEA	Elementary and Secondary Education Act
GRME	General Religious and Moral Education
GRT	General religious teaching
KJV	King James Version
NDEA	National Defense Education Act
SRI/SRE	Special religious instruction/education

Introduction

On 17 June, 1963, the United States Supreme Court banned the devotional reading of the Bible and the saying of the Lord's Prayer in American public schools. Finding that the practices unequivocally constituted "religious exercises," it declared that they were "required by the States in violation of the command of the First Amendment that the Government maintain strict neutrality, neither aiding nor opposing religion."[1] The decision, coming on the heels of a decision the previous year prohibiting nondenominational prayers in the public schools,[2] firmly closed the door on nearly two hundred years of religious exercises in American schools. It also fed a strong backlash. Religious and political leaders denounced the decision, school officials around the country defiantly vowed to continue the practices irrespective of the decision, and scores of federal legislators introduced Constitutional amendments to reverse the decision.[3] Nevertheless, these efforts ultimately failed, and within twenty years official Bible reading and school prayer had virtually vanished from schools outside the South, while even in the South their frequency had declined substantially.[4]

Just five months later, half a world away, Australian Prime Minister Robert Menzies shocked political observers by announcing in a campaign speech that he intended to begin to provide federal funding for science education, to be made "available to all secondary schools, government or independent, without discrimination."[5] The proposal represented a marked departure from

---

[1] *School District of Abington Township* v. *Schempp*, 374 US 203 (1963), pp. 225–26.

[2] *Engel* v. *Vitale*, 370 US 421 (1962).

[3] Joan DelFattore. 2004. *The Fourth R: Conflicts over Religion in America's Public Schools*. New Haven: Yale University Press, pp. 98–126.

[4] Richard B. Dierenfield. 1986. "Religious Influence in American Public Schools." *The Clearing House* 59(9): 390–92, p. 391.

[5] R.G. Menzies. 1963. *Federal Election, 1963: Policy Speech of the Prime Minister*. Sydney: Government Printer, p. 22.

Australia's longstanding policy, dating to the late nineteenth century, against providing funding to religious schools. Following his reelection, Menzies implemented his proposal over his opponents' accusations that he was trying to buy Catholic votes. The legislation was "conceived in chicanery, born in duplicity, and nurtured on deceit," declared the opposition leader; while another Member of Parliament lamented that "the political bribery" the bill represented had "never been surpassed in Australia's history."[6] Nevertheless, the legislation passed easily, and was quickly followed by a spate of additional subsidies that cemented "state aid" to religious schools as a permanent feature of the Australian educational landscape.[7]

Separated by space but not by time, these two scenes are important moments that heralded the arrival of new *secular settlements* – that is, relatively stable sets of policies governing the role of religion in particular social domains – in each country. Secular settlements have become an important focus of research on secularization in recent years.[8] Responding to the persistent vitality of religion around the world, scholars have increasingly abandoned the classic "secularization thesis," which predicted that religion would decline as societies became more modern.[9] As the fortunes of the secularization thesis have waned, scholars across the humanities and social sciences have become increasingly attuned to the varied arrangements that govern religious life in the contemporary world, and have begun to catalog, interpret, and analyze this diversity.[10]

[6] Australia. House of Representatives. 1964. *Commonwealth Parliamentary Debates*. Canberra: Government Printer, 14 May, pp. 1980, 1930.

[7] Ian R. Wilkinson, Brian J. Caldwell, R.J.W. Selleck, Jessica Harris, and Pam Dettman. 2006. *A History of State Aid to Non-Government Schools in Australia*. Canberra: Department of Education, Science, and Training.

[8] Philip S. Gorski and Ateş Altınordu. 2008. "After Secularization?" *Annual Review of Sociology* 34: 55–85, p. 76.

[9] E.g., Peter Berger. 1969. *The Sacred Canopy: Elements of a Sociological Theory of Religion*. New York: Anchor Books.

[10] This literature is large and growing. For a sampling of recent contributions, see Birol Başkan. 2014. *From Religious Empires to Secular States: State Secularization in Turkey, Iran, and Russia*. New York: Routledge; Peter Berger, Grace Davie, and Effie Fokas. 2008. *Religious America, Secular Europe? A Theme and Variations*. Burlington, VT: Ashgate Press; Linell E. Cady and Elizabeth Shakman Hurd, eds. 2010. *Comparative Secularisms in a Global Age*. New York: Palgrave Macmillan; Craig Calhoun, Mark Juergensmeyer, and Jonathan VanAntwerpen, eds. 2011. *Rethinking Secularism*. New York: Oxford University Press; François Foret and Xabier Itçaina, eds. 2011. *Politics of Religion in Western Europe: Modernities in Conflict?* New York: Routledge; Daphne Halikiopoulou. 2011. *Patterns of Secularization: Church, State, and Nation in Greece and the Republic of Ireland*. Burlington, VT: Ashgate; Janet R. Jakobsen and Ann Pellegrini, eds. 2008. *Secularisms*. Durham, NC: Duke University Press; Hans Joas and Klaus Wiegandt, eds. 2009. *Secularization and the World Religions*. Liverpool: Liverpool University Press; Monika Wohlrab-Sahr and Marian Burchardt. 2012. "Multiple Secularities: Toward a Cultural Sociology of Secular Modernities." *Comparative Sociology* 11: 875–909. It should be noted that, while all of these works seek to understand and analyze the varied forms of religion in public life, they

This research demonstrates that apparently subtle differences in how religion is incorporated into or excluded from public life can have major consequences for important social outcomes. Differences in secular settlements can affect a society's religious vitality and degree of religious diversity.[11] They can also affect political life, by governing access to the public sphere, spurring popular mobilization, and contributing to political conflict.[12] The particular features of secular settlements have even been linked to such disparate and seemingly unrelated outcomes as patterns of economic development, the incorporation of migrant populations, and educational stratification.[13] Understanding where secular settlements come from and why they persist or change is therefore an important question.

Despite this profusion of scholarship, our understanding of why different countries adopt the secular settlements that they do remains limited. Classic explanations, following the secularization thesis, have emphasized the effect of large-scale structural shifts, such as the rise of the state or increasing economic

can adopt quite different objects of study, among them discourses, ideologies, and policies. This book, with its focus on secular settlements, adopts a more narrow definition than some of these works. For good overviews of these conceptual distinctions, see the introduction to Calhoun et al., *Rethinking Secularism*; and José Casanova. 2009. "The Secular and Secularisms." *Social Research* 76(4): 1049–66.

[11] Roger Finke and Rodney Stark. 2005 [1992]. *The Churching of America, 1776–2005: Winners and Losers in Our Religious Economy*. 2nd edn. New Brunswick, NJ: Rutgers University Press; Anthony Gill. 1998. *Rendering unto Caesar: The Catholic Church and the State in Latin America*. Chicago: University of Chicago Press; Steven Pfaff. 2008. "The Religious Divide: Why Religion Seems to Be Thriving in the United States and Waning in Europe." Pp. 24–52 in *Growing Apart? America and Europe in the Twenty-First Century*, edited by Jeffrey Kopstein and Sven Steinmo. Cambridge: Cambridge University Press; Rodney Stark and Roger Finke. 2000. *Acts of Faith: Explaining the Human Side of Religion*. Berkeley: University of California Press.

[12] Talal Asad. 2006. "French Secularism and the 'Islamic Veil Affair.'" *Hedgehog Review* 8(1/2): 93–106; Craig Calhoun. 2011. "Secularism, Citizenship, and the Public Sphere." Pp. 75–91 in Calhoun et al., *Rethinking Secularism*; José Casanova. 1994. *Public Religions in the Modern World*. Chicago: University of Chicago Press; James Davison Hunter. 1991. *Culture Wars: The Struggle to Define America*. New York: Basic Books; Ted G. Jelen. 1998. "Research in Religion and Mass Political Behavior in the United States: Looking Both Ways after Two Decades of Scholarship." *American Politics Quarterly* 26(1): 110–34; William Martin. 1996. *With God on Our Side: The Rise of the Religious Right in America*. New York: Broadway Books; Zehra Fareen Parvez. 2011. "Politicizing Islam: State, Gender, Class, and Piety in France and India." Ph.D. Dissertation, Department of Sociology, University of California, Berkeley.

[13] Robert J. Barro and Rachel M. McCleary. 2003. "Religion and Economic Growth across Countries." *American Sociological Review* 68: 760–81; Joel S. Fetzer and J. Christopher Soper. 2005. *Muslims and the State in Britain, France, and Germany*. Cambridge: Cambridge University Press; Matthias Koenig. 2005. "Incorporating Muslim Migrants in Western Nation States: A Comparison of the United Kingdom, France, and Germany." *Journal of International Migration and Integration* 6(2): 219–34; Steven Pfaff and Anthony J. Gill. 2006. "Will a Million Muslims March? Muslim Interest Organizations and Political Integration in Europe." *Comparative Political Studies* 39: 803–29; Louise Watson and Chris Ryan. 2009. "Choice, Vouchers and the Consequences for Public High Schools: Lessons from Australia." Unpublished manuscript, Faculty of Education, University of Canberra.

development.[14] Yet these explanations have proven too broad to account for fine-grained, yet demonstrably significant, variations in secular settlements. More promisingly, a number of recent works have focused on secularization as a political project.[15] Recognizing that a more secular society advantages some actors and disadvantages others, these accounts have placed interests, conflict, and strategic action at the center of our understanding of secularization. At the same time, however, these accounts have tended to focus so intently upon secularizing actors' interests and strategies that the broader context of their political struggles often fades from view. In particular, the most important political context of all – the state – is often a mere shadow in these accounts.

This book tells the story of how secularizing (and anti-secularizing) actors encounter the state, and how those encounters contribute to the ultimate development of secular settlements. The central contention of this book is that political institutions matter to the course of secularization. Secularization may be fundamentally political at its core, but those political struggles are conceived and carried out within institutional contexts that shape both how they unfold, and whether they unfold at all. Explaining variation in secular settlements requires integrating those contexts more centrally into our theories of religious change.

In bringing the role the state plays in secularization into sharper focus, I seek to answer both a particular historical question and a general theoretical one. The historical question is why the United States and Australia developed such dramatically different secular settlements after 1960 despite their many demographic, constitutional, and historical commonalities. For most of their histories, Australia and the United States featured quite similar secular settlements, permitting religion in the public schools while prohibiting public aid to religious schools. Yet in the wake of World War II, the two nations diverged, ultimately creating new settlements that redefined the appropriate relationship between religion and the state in education. The direction and timing of these settlements is peculiar, to say the least. Ironically, it was the United States, with

---

[14] Steve Bruce. 2011. *Secularization: In Defence of an Unfashionable Theory.* New York: Oxford University Press; Pippa Norris and Ronald Inglehart. 2004. *Sacred and Secular: Religion and Politics Worldwide.* Cambridge: Cambridge University Press.

[15] Anthony Gill. 2008. *The Political Origins of Religious Liberty.* Cambridge: Cambridge University Press; Philip S. Gorski. 2003. "Historicizing the Secularization Debate: An Agenda for Research." Pp. 110–22 in *Handbook of the Sociology of Religion,* edited by Michele Dillon. Cambridge: Cambridge University Press; Philip S. Gorski. 2005. "The Return of the Repressed: Religion and the Political Unconscious of Historical Sociology." Pp. 161–89 in *Remaking Modernity: Politics, History, and Sociology,* edited by Julia Adams, Elisabeth S. Clemens, and Ann Shola Orloff. Durham: Duke University Press; Ahmet T. Kuru. 2009. *Secularism and State Policies toward Religion: The United States, France, and Turkey.* Cambridge: Cambridge University Press; David Martin. 1978. *A General Theory of Secularization.* New York: Harper & Row; Christian Smith, ed. 2003. *The Secular Revolution: Power, Interests, and Conflict in the Secularization of American Public Life.* Berkeley: University of California Press.

its unusually pious and God-fearing citizenry,[16] which adopted one of the *most* secular educational systems in the world. More surprising still, it did so near the height of the Cold War, when geopolitical considerations had otherwise amplified the already strongly religious timbre of American political culture.[17] In Australia, meanwhile, the new settlement drew the state and religious schools into a closer embrace just as Australians' personal religiosity began a precipitous decline.[18] Over the ensuing years, religion and education would become ever more intertwined even as increasing numbers of Australians drifted away from their churches.[19]

The answer to this question lies in how the state structured a series of political conflicts over religious education that began in the mid-nineteenth century. In the United States, political institutions created a *permeable state*, characterized by decentralized and democratically accessible institutions that granted widespread access to decision-makers and posed relatively few barriers to actors who sought to challenge the religion-friendly settlement of the nineteenth century. America's decentralized system of educational administration facilitated challenges to pan-Protestant religious exercises in the public schools by religious minorities and educational professionals, which led to a slow attenuation of religion's position in public education over the early twentieth century. Further, America's highly democratic approach to public law enabled a coalition of Protestants, Jews, and civil libertarians to wage a campaign through the courts to define the First Amendment in uncompromising terms.

By contrast, Australian political institutions created an *insulated state*, characterized by a centralized structure and elaborate gatekeeping mechanisms that buffered state officials and neutralized a variety of parallel political challenges. Australia's centralized educational systems and relatively inaccessible approach to public law offered religious minorities and professionals none of the advantages that the American system provided. However, Australia's system of preference-voting and flexible party structure did facilitate a political campaign by Catholics to obtain funding for their school system in the postwar era, a goal American Catholics were unable to attain thanks to unfavorable coalition dynamics within America's rigid two-party system. In short, political conflicts were the driving force behind the policy changes of the 1960s, but these conflicts produced different settlements because they were waged in different kinds of states.

---

[16] Norris and Inglehart, *Sacred and Secular*, pp. 83–95.

[17] Jonathan P. Herzog. 2011. *The Spiritual–Industrial Complex: America's Religious Battle against Communism in the Early Cold War*. New York: Oxford University Press.

[18] Gary Bouma. 2006. *Australian Soul: Religion and Spirituality in the Twenty-First Century*. Cambridge: Cambridge University Press, p. 53.

[19] Marion Maddox. 2014. *Taking God to School: The End of Australia's Egalitarian Education?* Sydney: Allen & Unwin.

This explanation suggests a new answer to a more general theoretical question: why do states adopt particular policies governing religion in public life? By focusing on the state, I seek to develop an account of the emergence and transformation of secular settlements that takes both political *conflicts* and political *contexts* seriously. I call this a *political-institutional approach* to secularization. I argue that secularization is primarily driven by multiple forms of political conflict. These conflicts involve different sets of stakes, engage different groups of actors, and play out over time as political processes. Throughout this book, I focus on three primary processes that were dispositive in the American and Australian cases: state-building, professionalization, and religious conflict. These processes are general – that is, each process engages similar actors, deals with similar stakes, and is otherwise recognizably patterned – and each contributes in its own way to a decline in religious authority in the educational sector. At the same time, however, the ultimate outcome of any given process is neither preordained nor identical. Instead, they vary in their strength and influence thanks to the way they interact with other processes and with a nation's distinctive institutional terrain. In sum, therefore, I argue that secular settlements emerge from the interaction of common secularizing processes and specific political institutions.

Focusing on the interaction of processes and institutions lays the foundation for a broader comparative theory of secularization. By identifying the political processes behind the emergence of secular settlements in Australia and the United States, this study develops a set of analytical tools that can be extrapolated to other contexts where secularization has occurred. While this focus on processes does not promise to yield a new "grand theory" of secularization, it does permit us to identify patterns in the politics of secularization, and to develop some bounded generalizations about the conditions of possibility for the emergence and transformation of new secular settlements elsewhere in the developed world.

Similarly, by examining how these processes interact with their institutional contexts, this study provides some general insights into how institutions shape the course of secularization. Political institutions play two key structuring roles in secularization: (1) they structure the conflicts between religious, professional, and political actors over the role of religion in public life; and (2) they contribute to the formation of actors motivated to alter settlements in more or less secular directions. This dual role played by institutions – mediating and constitutive – makes them indispensable to understanding the emergence of new secular settlements. They act as essential links between macro-level social change and the strategies of individual actors and social groups in ways that cannot be accounted for in existing theories that focus on one or the other alone. By placing them at the center of its analysis, this study reclaims political institutions as an important focus for research into comparative secularization.

My political-institutional approach also improves our understanding of the politics of secularization in a number of ways. First, it broadens our understanding of the actors behind secularization, their motives, and their origins. Existing political theories of secularization tend to focus on actors with a fairly narrow range of anticlerical and self-aggrandizing interests.[20] Rational-choice variants in fact explicitly assume a fixed and narrow set of preferences that are presumed to motivate all secularizing actors.[21] But the politics of secularization are far more complex and multiple than this. Some secularizing actors are motivated by the defense of religious tenets; others by collective interests; and still others by practical motives that are orthogonal to religion but that nevertheless have secularizing effects. Thinking about secularization as the outcome of multiple political processes that capture different kinds of political conflict allows us to relate this diversity of motives and interests to the secular settlements that result.

Further, thinking institutionally allows us to see how secularizing actors' interests may have been constituted, in whole or in part, by the demands and incentives of the state. Scholars have long acknowledged that state churches help to generate anticlerical actors, and this insight has informed many of our newer political theories of secularization.[22] But the constitution of interests is a general institutional phenomenon that extends far beyond state churches.[23] We should expect other political institutions to generate actors with specific interests, including pragmatic or professional interests that incline them toward more secular policies. By adopting a political-institutional approach, we gain the ability to explain where some of these secularizing actors and interests come from in the first place.

A political-institutional approach also acts as a brake against the tendency to view secularization as primarily a project of intellectual elites, undertaken from above and imposed upon an unsuspecting pious population.[24] While secularization does at times take this form, it may also occur from below, through

---

[20] E.g., Gill, *Political Origins*; Kuru, *Secularism and State Policies*; Smith, *Secular Revolution*.

[21] Gill, *Political Origins*.

[22] Casanova, *Public Religions*; Gorski, "Return of the Repressed"; Martin, *General Theory of Secularization*. This observation is often traced back to Alexis de Tocqueville. 1988 [1835–1840]. *Democracy in America*. New York: HarperPerennial, pp. 300–01.

[23] Drew Halfmann. 2011. *Doctors and Demonstrators: How Political Institutions Shape Abortion Law in the United States, Britain, and Canada*. Chicago: University of Chicago Press, pp. 16–18, 211–12; Ira Katznelson. 2003. "Periodization and Preferences: Reflections on Purposive Action in Comparative Historical Social Science." Pp. 270–301 in *Comparative Historical Analysis in the Social Sciences*, edited by James Mahoney and Dietrich Rueschemeyer. New York: Cambridge University Press, p. 280; Kathleen Thelen and Sven Steinmo. 1992. "Historical Institutionalism in Comparative Politics." Pp. 1–32 in *Structuring Politics: Historical Institutionalism in Comparative Analysis*, edited by Sven Steinmo, Kathleen Thelen, and Frank Longstreth. New York: Cambridge University Press, pp. 8–9.

[24] E.g., Berger et al., *Religious America, Secular Europe*, pp. 12, 18, 54–56; David Martin. 2005. *On Secularization: Towards a Revised General Theory*. Burlington, VT: Ashgate, pp. 69–72; Christian Smith. 2003. "Introduction: Rethinking the Secularization of American Public Life." Pp. 1–96 in Smith, *The Secular Revolution*, pp. 1, 33, 37.

grassroots campaigns animated largely by conflict among competing religious groups. Theoretically, secularization from below emerges from different processes and benefits from different institutional arrangements than secularization from above. By overemphasizing secularization as an elite project, we have neglected important grassroots dynamics that can propel secularization forward. Further, thinking about secularization as being driven in part by religious conflict complicates any binary characterization of "secular" actors acting against a "religious" population. Ironically, many of the actors promoting more strongly secular settlements have themselves been religious. By incorporating religious conflict as a secularizing process, the political-institutional approach takes these "religious secularists" seriously, and reveals the profound influence they have sometimes had on generating and sustaining new secular settlements.

Finally, by "bringing the state back in" to the study of secularization, this study also provides some interesting insights into the role of religion in American public life, and into American political culture more generally. Specifically, it sheds new light on how the permeable character of the American state – and in particular, its decentralized administrative bodies and broadly accessible legal system – has facilitated, and continues to facilitate, ongoing conflict over religion in public life. Ironically, the root of America's secular education system lies in the strength and vitality of its highly religious people. It is not news that Americans' devotion to their religious beliefs frequently drives conflict with others who hold other, equally powerfully held, beliefs. What I hope will be clearer from this study, however, is the extent to which America's political institutions actively encourage these conflicts. The decentralized, readily accessible American state is, in fact, an engine for religious conflict, allowing religious differences to spill into law and politics at every turn. The contrast with the more centralized and insulated Australian state, where religious differences roil beneath the surface but far less often disturb the gaze of public officials, is striking. This suggests that religious controversies should be thought of as a structural feature of American politics, deeply connected to its institutional design. The specific issues over which battles are fought may change (and have changed), but *conflict* over religion is (and will remain) endemic to American public life.

PLAN OF THE BOOK

Chapter 1 lays out the political-institutional approach to secularization in greater detail, situating it in dialogue with existing theories of secularization and identifying how political processes and institutional contexts work together to produce secular settlements. The remainder of the book is organized in four parts, each of which examines how political processes and institutions interacted to create or transform secular settlements at different points in time.

Part I examines the emergence of the parallel secular settlements that developed in each country in the mid-nineteenth century. In Chapter 2, I demonstrate that variations in the state-building process resulted in similar secular settlements, but vastly different administrative structures, in the two nations. In the United States, common schools developed organically at the local level, often with the assistance of evangelical clergy. In Australia, by contrast, national schools were created through the conscious displacement of an existing and inadequate system of denominational schools. Although in both cases, the resulting settlement permitted public school religion while prohibiting funding for religious schools, the administrative structure of education that resulted was centralized in Australia, but radically decentralized in the United States.

Part II turns specifically to the question of how institutions affected the trajectory – and politics – of secularization in each country before World War II. Like most complex historical phenomena, the emergence of new secular settlements in the 1960s cannot be reduced to the proximate events that surrounded their immediate fashioning.[25] They were not sudden transformations, in other words, but instead emerged from developments that occurred over the course of the preceding century. Part II examines these developments. Chapter 3 shows how decentralized administrative control in the United States facilitated both professionalization and religious conflict before 1945, leading to the slow decline of religious devotionals over the late nineteenth and early twentieth centuries. America's local school boards provided multiple sites where religious exercises could be challenged by religious outsiders, and facilitated the rise of progressive educational ideas and associations that transformed educational practice in ways that undermined traditional religious education. Squeezed from below by religious conflict, and from above by the spread of progressive education, religious exercises declined in American public schools between 1870 and 1950. Chapter 4, by contrast, demonstrates how the highly centralized Australian system of educational administration inhibited these secularizing processes before 1960. Tight centralized control effectively eliminated local influence over policy and discouraged professionalization among teachers. Accordingly, religious education in public schools persisted, and even grew more widespread, until the 1960s. The chapter concludes with a case study of events in New South Wales since 1960, which vividly demonstrates the impact that centralization had on religious education. Efforts to decentralize curricular decision-making contributed to a rapid partial secularization of public education in that state.

Part III turns to developments since World War II, focusing on the contrasting campaigns that dominated each country's renegotiation of its secular settlement at midcentury, and how those campaigns took advantage of openings provided by different political institutions to craft a new settlement. Chapter 5 examines the effect of legal institutions on secularization in the postwar era. The combination of relatively easy access to the legal system and a favorable

---

[25] Paul Pierson. 2004. *Politics in Time: History, Institutions, and Social Analysis.* Princeton: Princeton University Press, pp. 16, 79–102.

realist hermeneutic approach made American courts an attractive and receptive target for a campaign by Protestants, Jews, and civil libertarians to exclude devotional exercises from the public schools. In Australia, by contrast, parallel lawsuits were compromised by restrictive standing rules, the absence of state-level constitutional religious freedom provisions, and an unfavorable textualist hermeneutic. Chapter 6, by contrast, examines how political parties and voting systems shaped religious policy after 1945. In Australia, the politics of the Cold War fractured traditional party coalitions, leading to the creation of a new party dominated by conservative Catholics who advocated for state aid. Australia's preference-voting system provided incentives for politicians to pursue Catholic votes, and the ensuing contest for Catholic votes led to the introduction and entrenchment of aid to religious schools. In the United States, by contrast, the rigid two-party system and the anticommunist fervor of the Cold War locked Catholics into a partisan alliance with conservative Southerners, who were opposed to public aid. The stalemate between Southern Democrats and Catholics held up legislation that would have granted public aid to Catholic schools through the early 1960s.

Part IV considers the theoretical and political implications of this analysis. Chapter 7 draws the threads from these chapters together and unpacks their implications both for the study of secularization, and for our understanding of the dynamics of religion in American public life. Finally, in the Epilogue, I consider how my political-institutional approach helps to make sense of the current flux in American church–state jurisprudence. I argue that the political and institutional foundations on which strict separation rests have been undermined in recent years, and that a new settlement, similar in some respects to the contemporary Australian settlement, may be emerging. Drawing lessons from recent Australian history, I consider how an "Australian" settlement might function within the American context, and how such a system might affect American religion, education, and politics.

I

Politics, Institutions, and Secularization

INTRODUCTION

The United States poses significant problems for orthodox theories of secularization. While secularization theorists for years anticipated the inevitable demise of religion at the hands of modernization, religious pluralism, and scientific progress,[1] the United States – a modern, religiously pluralistic, and scientifically advanced country if ever there was one – flummoxed their every prediction. In nearly every respect, relative to other modern, Western countries, it is saturated with religion: churches overflowing with congregants, sky-high rates of belief in God, and a public political culture that begins with prayer breakfasts between clergy and politicians, and ends with speeches ritualistically declaiming "God bless America!" "That the reigning theory [of secularization] does not seem to work has become an open secret," confessed Stephen Warner en route to proclaiming a "new paradigm" for the study of religion that gave American developments pride of place.[2]

Yet in at least one important respect, the United States *does* in fact approximate the predictions of sociology's classical secularization theorists. America's educational system is extremely – one might say *resolutely* – secular. In fact, it is secular even in comparison to those other modern, Western countries that otherwise cast America's religiousness in such high relief. Unlike nearly every other Western nation, religious exercises and religious instruction are excluded

---

[1] Most classical sociological theorists embraced some version of this approach. See Peter Berger. 1969. *The Sacred Canopy: Elements of a Sociological Theory of Religion.* New York: Anchor Books; Emile Durkheim. 1995 [1912]. *The Elementary Forms of Religious Life,* trans. Karen E. Fields. New York: The Free Press; Max Weber. 1946. "Science as a Vocation." Pp. 129–56 in *From Max Weber: Essays in Sociology,* edited by H.H. Gerth and C. Wright Mills. Oxford: Oxford University Press.

[2] R. Stephen Warner. 1993. "Work in Progress toward a New Paradigm for the Sociological Study of Religion in the United States." *American Journal of Sociology* 98: 1044–93, p. 1048.

from American public schools. More striking still, the United States is virtually alone in refusing to provide public support for religious schools; even hyper-secular France funds its system of Catholic schools.[3] How did this paradoxical situation come to pass?

American anomalies are often explained by resorting to one American "exceptionalism" or another, yet in this case no obvious candidate suffices. Appeals to national culture might suggest that America's secular educational system reflects a longstanding desire to keep religion voluntary and separated from state support.[4] But American education has *not* always been so secular. In fact, for most of American history, religious instruction and devotional exercises held a prominent place in American public schools, and it is only since the 1960s that religion and education have experienced such a total divorce. Others have suggested that America's unusual religious diversity required it to adopt "a school system which keeps religious plurality out."[5] America's high degree of religious pluralism has certainly contributed to considerable contestation over the relationship between religion and education. Yet other highly religiously diverse countries, such as Canada and Australia, permit far greater ties between religion and education.[6] Perhaps America's secular educational system reflects its strong constitutional language disestablishing religion?[7] America's Constitution clearly matters, but it is far from determinative. Although the text of the First Amendment has remained constant since 1791, its interpretation has varied wildly over that time, and the contemporary understanding of disestablishment as "separation of church and state" in a holistic sense, disallowing all ties, is less than seventy years old.[8] Moreover, "separation" is often observed much less strictly – if at all – in other domains, such as social welfare.[9] Nor, finally, is America's secular educational system entirely attributable to "judicial activism," as popular accounts would have it.[10] The Supreme Court certainly played its part, but it was not the only actor with a say in events.

---

[3] Jonathan Fox. 2008. *A World Survey of Religion and the State.* Cambridge: Cambridge University Press, p. 112.

[4] E.g., Seymour Martin Lipset. 1990. *Continental Divide: The Values and Institutions of the United States and Canada.* New York: Routledge, p. 75.

[5] David Martin. 1978. *A General Theory of Secularization.* New York: Harper & Row, p. 36.

[6] On Australian and Canadian pluralism, see Gary Bouma. 2006. *Australian Soul: Religion and Spirituality in the Twenty-First Century.* Cambridge: Cambridge University Press, pp. 75–76.

[7] Fox, *World Survey*, pp. 134–35.

[8] Philip Hamburger. 2002. *Separation of Church and State.* Cambridge: Harvard University Press.

[9] See, e.g., Stephen V. Monsma and J. Christopher Soper. 1997. *The Challenge of Pluralism: Church and State in Five Democracies.* Lanham, MD: Rowman and Littlefield; and Rebecca Sager. 2010. *Faith, Politics, and Power: The Politics of Faith-Based Initiatives.* New York: Oxford University Press.

[10] E.g., Jane Lampmann. 2005. "Bringing the Case against Judges." *Christian Science Monitor,* 13 April. For a more scholarly version of this argument, see Barbara M. Yarnold. 1998. "The U.S. Supreme Court in Religious Freedom Cases, 1970–1990: Champion to the Anti-Religion Forces." *Journal of Church and State* 40: 661–72.

Courts cannot call their caseloads into existence, for one thing,[11] and secularizing trends were already well underway by the late 1940s when the Court began to rule against religion in education.[12] Indeed, the closer one looks, the more puzzling it becomes. What accounts for America's strict secularism in the educational domain?

In this book, I argue that the secularization of American education can only be understood in terms of certain peculiarities of its administrative, electoral, and judicial *institutions*; and in terms of the *political campaigns* through which its religiously and epistemologically diverse constituencies realized a particular understanding of secularism. Moreover, it is an outcome that was perhaps uniquely achievable in the United States thanks to its specific institutional features. In particular, its decentralized system of education, its democratic and expansive vision of public law, and its rigid two-party system created an institutional infrastructure favorable to those actors who sought more secular outcomes. Ultimately, I argue that America's uniquely secular educational system owes as much to its permeable institutional structure as it does to its religious pluralism or constitutional guarantees.

Secular Antipodes? Australia and the United States in Comparative Perspective

I develop this argument through a comparison with Australia. By comparing the United States against a highly similar country, I am able to identify subtle differences that had an important impact on the development of religious education policy in each country. For the purposes of this study, Australia provides an excellent comparative case. As former British colonies, the two nations share many similar traits, such as a common language, a common-law legal system empowered with judicial review, and democratic systems of government organized on a federal model.[13] Moreover, Australia is uncannily similar to the United States in terms of the supposed "exceptionalisms" outlined above. Table 1.1 shows that both nations are highly religiously pluralistic. While not as riotously diverse as the United States, Australia is nevertheless home to a wide array of denominations; neither today nor during the pivotal 1960s did any single religious group hold a majority market share in either nation.[14] Historically, moreover, the Protestant majority in each country has

---

[11] Charles R. Epp. 1998. *The Rights Revolution: Lawyers, Activists, and Supreme Courts in Comparative Perspective*. Chicago: University of Chicago Press, pp. 18, 37–38.

[12] See below, Chapter 3.

[13] Gerald Baier. 2006. *Courts and Federalism: Judicial Doctrine in the United States, Canada, and Australia*. Vancouver: UBC Press.

[14] The statistics for Australia in Table 1.1 reflect official census data; the 1961 data is drawn from Commonwealth Bureau of Census and Statistics. 1962. *Census Bulletin No. 23: Summary of Population for Australia*. Canberra: Government Printer, Table 16, p. 21; while the 2011 data can be found in Australian Bureau of Statistics. 2012. *Reflecting a Nation: Stories from the 2011*

TABLE 1.1. *Religious diversity in Australia and the United States*

	Australia		United States	
	1961	2011	1958	2008
Catholic	24.9%	25.3%	25.7%	25.1%
Anglican	34.9%	17.1%	—	1.1%
Baptist	1.4%	1.6%	19.7%	15.8%
Methodist/Congregationalist/Uniting Church	10.9%	5.0%	14.0%	5.3%
Lutheran	1.5%	1.2%	7.1%	3.8%
Presbyterian	9.3%	2.8%	5.6%	2.1%
Nondenominational Protestant	—	—	19.8%	14.2%
Pentecostal/Charismatic/Holiness	—	1.1%	—	3.5%
Latter-Day Saints	—	0.3%	—	1.4%
Orthodox	1.5%	2.6%	—	—
Other Christian	3.7%	4.2%	—	3.1%
Buddhist	—	2.5%	—	0.5%
Muslim	—	2.2%	—	0.6%
Jewish	0.6%	0.5%	3.2%	1.2%
Other non-Christian	0.1%	2.0%	1.3%	1.6%
None/No answer	11.1%	30.9%	3.6%	20.2%

shared space with a sizable Catholic minority. As Figure 1.1 shows, Catholics have been a significant minority in both nations since the mid-nineteenth century, and the Catholic proportion of each country's population has been roughly equivalent since the 1930s.[15]

Census. Canberra: Australian Bureau of Statistics. Data for the United States are from a 1958 United States Census Sample Survey, as reported in William Petersen. 1962. "Religious Statistics in the United States." *Journal for the Scientific Study of Religion* 1(2): 165–78, p. 169; and from the 2008 American Religious Identification Survey, available in Barry A. Kosmin and Ariela Keysar. 2009. *American Religious Identification Survey (ARIS 2008)*. Hartford, CT: Trinity College, p. 5. Because the United States Census does not track information on religion, religious statistics in the United States before 1970 are notoriously fragmented. Accordingly, the data for Table 1.1 and Figure 1.1 are drawn from different sources. The slight discrepancy between the percentage Catholic reported in Table 1.1 (approximately twenty-six percent) and that reported in Figure 1.1 for 1958 (approximately twenty-three percent) reflects the different estimates in each data series.

[15] Catholics formed a larger proportion of the Australian population in the nineteenth century thanks to extensive convict transportation from Ireland. Notably, however, as I discuss below, this did not translate into greater political power for Australian Catholics; if anything, American Catholics were more successful in obtaining their preferred education policies during the nineteenth century. Population estimates for Australia in Figure 1.1 are drawn from Australian Bureau of Statistics. 2006. *Year Book Australia, 2006*. Canberra: Government Printer, Table 12.26, p. 376; and W.W. Phillips. 1986. "Religion." Pp. 418–35 in *Australian*

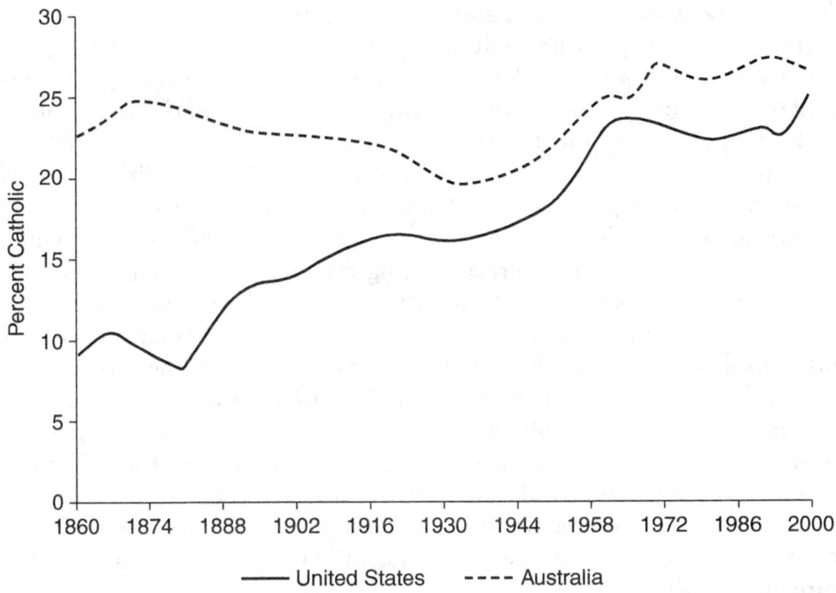

FIGURE I.I. Catholic population, 1860–2000

Also like the United States, Australia's Constitution contains a disestablishment clause. In fact, Section 116 of the Australian Constitution was modeled explicitly after the United States' First Amendment, in what one Australian legal scholar has called a "fairly blatant piece of transcription."[16] Accordingly, the two countries share nearly identical constitutional language regarding the relationship between church and state.[17] Moreover, Australia also has a longstanding tradition of ties between religion and education. In fact, between

Historical Statistics, edited by Wray Vamplew. Sydney: Fairfax, Syme, and Weldon, pp. 421–26. Figures for the United States are drawn from Susan B. Carter, Scott Sigmund Gartner, Michael R. Haines, Alan L. Olmstead, Richard Sutch, and Gavin Wright. 2006. *Historical Statistics of the United States*. Millennial Edition Online. Cambridge: Cambridge University Press, Tables Aa6–8, Bg334–348; James Hennesey. 1981. *American Catholics: A History of the Roman Catholic Community in the United States*. New York: Oxford University Press, p. 173; and Toby J. Heytens. 2000. "School Choice and State Constitutions." *Virginia Law Review* 86 (1): 117–62, p. 135.

[16] Clifford L. Pannam. 1963. "Travelling Section 116 with a U.S. Road Map." *Melbourne University Law Review* 4: 41–90, p. 41.

[17] Compare the United States Constitution, Amendment I ("Congress shall make no law respecting an establishment of religion, or prohibiting the free exercise thereof"), and the Australian Constitution, Section 116 ("The Commonwealth shall not make any law for establishing any religion, or for imposing any religious observance, or for prohibiting the free exercise of any religion, and no religious test shall be required as a qualification for any office or public trust under the Commonwealth"). The "no religious test" portion of Section 116 is derived from Article V of the American Constitution.

roughly 1880 and 1960, Australia and the United States shared nearly identical policies toward religion and education. Each nation permitted religious instruction in its public schools, although the different states of each federation embraced this possibility to a different extent; and each nation broadly prohibited any kind of direct support for religious schools.[18]

Despite these similarities, however, Australia today looks quite different from the United States. Whereas the United States, largely through a series of court rulings, moved to exclude religious exercises from the public schools while maintaining its barriers against direct funding for religious schools, Australia moved in the opposite direction. Through a series of federal and state legislative initiatives, Australia began to provide massive direct financial support for religious schools beginning in the 1960s.[19] Overall, nongovernment schools in Australia now rely on government subsidies for more than half of their annual income;[20] in some schools, public financing underwrites up to eighty percent of operating costs.[21] At the same time, Australia retained a place for religion in the public school curriculum. Today, most government schools permit clergy or lay representatives to teach regularly timetabled "special religious instruction" (SRI) classes; and collective worship, prayers, and even Bible reading continue to feature in the curriculum.[22]

This situation obviously contrasts greatly with the American situation, where prayer, Bible reading, religious instruction, and even moments of silence are forbidden; and only indirect funding (such as tax credits, transportation subsidies, and loans of supplies and services) is permitted.[23] The type of direct support either for religious education or for religious schools that Australia embraces would be inconceivable in the United States. Viewed in comparative perspective against Australia, then, our puzzle deepens still further. Why did the United States come to embrace a supremely secular approach to religion and education *even as* an extremely similar country with which it once

---

[18] See below, Chapter 2.

[19] Ian R. Wilkinson, Brian J. Caldwell, R.J.W. Selleck, Jessica Harris, and Pam Dettman. 2006. *A History of State Aid to Non-Government Schools in Australia*. Canberra: Department of Education, Science, and Training.

[20] Ministerial Council on Education, Employment, Training, and Youth Affairs. 2007. *National Report on Schooling in Australia 2007*. Carlton, Vic.: Ministerial Council on Education, Employment, and Youth Affairs, p. 27.

[21] John Luttrell. 2008. "Come to Our Aid: Funding Catholic Schools in NSW since 1800." Unpublished manuscript, Catholic Education Office Sydney, p. 1; Marion Maddox. 2014. *Taking God to School: The End of Australia's Egalitarian Education?* Sydney: Allen & Unwin, p. 92.

[22] Cathy Byrne. 2014. *Religion in Secular Education: What, in Heaven's Name, Are We Teaching Our Children?* Leiden: Brill.

[23] See generally John Witte, Jr. 2005 [2000]. *Religion and the American Constitutional Experiment*. 2nd edn. Boulder, CO: Westview Press. It should be noted, however, that restrictions on public school devotionals apply to the schools and not to the students; there are no prohibitions on voluntary student-initiated religious activities that do not disrupt the functioning of the school day.

shared nearly identical policies moved in the *opposite* direction, toward greater church–state collaboration?

AMERICAN EDUCATION AND SECULARIZATION THEORY

These puzzles, while interesting in their own right, are also useful for helping us to think about secularization and religious change more generally. Secularization theory is currently undergoing a period of great intellectual ferment, as scholars attempt to come to terms with the collapse of the classical paradigm. As the persistence of religious belief and activism has undermined longstanding assumptions about the relationship between modernity and religion, social scientists have begun to reexamine and refine secularization theory, to clarify in what respects it may continue to hold. It is now widely understood that secularization may occur (or not) along multiple dimensions. Declines in individual belief and practice (*micro-level secularization*) are analytically distinct from internal changes to religious organizations that bring them into closer conformity with the secular world (*meso-level secularization*), which in turn are to be distinguished from the differentiation of social spheres in ways that render them autonomous of religious authority (*macro-level secularization*).[24] These forms of secularization are potentially independent of one another, such that meso- and macro-level secularization may occur even if micro-level secularization does not.[25]

While much of the original scholarship challenging the classic secularization thesis focused on micro-level secularization,[26] scholars have recently taken a renewed interest in understanding how secularization, understood as a macro-level process of institutional differentiation, takes place.[27] Rather than asking why people stop believing in God or going to church, these studies instead ask why religion comes to take a less and less prominent role in various social spheres over time. In so doing, scholars have largely abandoned the search for a transhistorical, teleological account of the position of religion in society. Instead, recognizing that secularization appears to be both widely

[24] Karel Dobbelaere. 1981. "Secularization: A Multi-Dimensional Concept." *Current Sociology* 29: 1–216.

[25] José Casanova. 2006. "Rethinking Secularization: A Global Comparative Perspective." *Hedgehog Review* 8: 7–22; Mark Chaves. 1994. "Secularization as Declining Religious Authority." *Social Forces* 72: 749–74; Dobbelaere, "Secularization"; Anne Mark Nielsen. 2014. "Accommodating Religious Pluralism in Denmark." *European Journal of Sociology* 55(2): 245–74.

[26] See, e.g., Rodney Stark and Roger Finke. 2000. *Acts of Faith: Explaining the Human Side of Religion*. Berkeley: University of California Press.

[27] In addition to those studies detailed below, see also José Casanova. 1994. *Public Religions in the Modern World*. Chicago: University of Chicago Press; Philip S. Gorski. 2000. "Historicizing the Secularization Debate: Church, States, and Society in Late Medieval and Early Modern Europe, ca. 1300 to 1700." *American Sociological Review* 65: 138–67; and Olivier Tschannen. 1991. "The Secularization Paradigm: A Systematization." *Journal for the Scientific Study of Religion* 30(4): 395–415.

variable and even reversible,[28] secularization theorists have instead begun to ask what accounts for the variety of "secular settlements" – or relatively stable sets of policies governing the role of religion in public life – that are visible in the contemporary world.[29]

In this context, the American and Australian cases should be understood as but two possible "secular settlements" among many. Indeed, studying them as historical outcomes can teach us a great deal about secularization and religious change more generally. In addition to helping to shed light on why America adopted its particularly strict secular settlement in education, a comparative study such as this permits us to ask more general questions about why different states adopt different policies toward religion; what processes and mechanisms lie at the heart of secularization and desecularization; and how secular settlements relate to broader social, political, and religious dynamics. Accordingly, the goal of this book is twofold: First, to provide a better explanation for the divergent paths and secular settlements of Australia and the United States; and second, to identify common processes and mechanisms in the two countries' histories that have the potential to contribute to our understanding of secularization in other settings.

Accounting for Variations in Secular Settlements: Existing Approaches

What accounts for the secular settlements we see today? Secularization theorists have offered up four primary approaches to explain why states adopt particular secular settlements. Two of them, the modernization approach and the *ancien régimes* approach, focus primarily on structural features of a society. Another two, the rational choice approach and the secular movements approach, focus instead on the agents advancing particular settlements (and their interests and motives). While each approach has certain strengths, none ultimately allows us to make satisfactory sense of the American–Australian comparison.

The Modernization Approach

As the contemporary successor to classical secularization theory, the modernization approach attributes religious change to broad structural shifts associated with modernity, such as the growth of the state, economic development, urbanization, or the rise of science. Some, like Steve Bruce, argue that these modernizing trends promote secularization by undermining the communal and cognitive foundations of religious belief and practice.[30] Others, like

---

[28] E.g., Gorski, "Historicizing the Secularization Debate: Church, States, and Society."

[29] Philip S. Gorski and Ateş Altınordu. 2008. "After Secularization?" *Annual Review of Sociology* 34: 55–85, p. 76.

[30] Steve Bruce. 2002. *God Is Dead: Secularization in the West*. Oxford: Blackwell Books; Steve Bruce. 2011. *Secularization: In Defence of an Unfashionable Theory*. New York: Oxford University Press.

Pippa Norris and Ronald Inglehart, argue that modernity drives secularization by increasing a society's level of "existential security." The more broadly
prosperous a nation becomes, in their view, the more secular it is likely to
become.[31] Most relevant for our purposes, Phillip Hammond has argued that
the American trend toward strict separation of church and state was driven
by "structural features of modern-day America – especially religious pluralism and government's inevitable involvement in our lives," which made strict
separation more or less inevitable irrespective of any political interventions pro
or con.[32]

The modernization approach would therefore explain divergence in secular settlements by reference to variations in how "modern" each country is.
However, this does not enable us to explain the divergent policies of Australia
and the United States, since both countries are modern, highly developed
nations.[33] Indeed, the Australian trajectory is particularly problematic. The
postwar era was a period of massive economic growth in Australia, accompanied by rapid religious and ethnic diversification and the dramatic expansion
of the welfare state.[34] Yet even as these quintessentially modernizing trends
were operating at full force, Australian educational policy was drawing church
and state into a closer embrace. Modernization approaches alone cannot
account for the variations between the United States and Australia, nor can
they account for why Australian policy desecularized even as it modernized in
the postwar era.

The Ancien Régimes *Approach*

A second approach links secular settlements to the historical presence or
absence of an *"ancien régime"* – that is, a political establishment with tight,
often formal, ties with a particular church. In his classic comparative analysis of secular settlements in the Christian West, David Martin argues that
secularization proceeded differently depending on whether a country was
primarily Catholic or Protestant; whether it was religiously homogeneous or

---

[31] Pippa Norris and Ronald Inglehart. 2004. *Sacred and Secular: Religion and Politics Worldwide.*
Cambridge: Cambridge University Press.

[32] Phillip E. Hammond. 1997. *With Liberty for All: Freedom of Religion in the United States.*
Louisville, KY: Westminster John Knox Press, pp. 14, 27.

[33] Indeed, Australia and the United States have been comparably modern along multiple metrics
for quite some time. In the late nineteenth century, Australia was more urbanized and had
a higher GDP than the United States; enrolled a comparable number of children in primary
education; and enjoyed flourishing democratic political institutions, a market economy, labor
unions, and a developed transportation network. See generally Robin Archer. 2007. *Why Is
There No Labor Party in the United States?* Princeton: Princeton University Press; for educational enrollment statistics, see Aaron Benavot and Phyllis Riddle. 1988. "The Expansion of
Primary Education, 1870–1940: Trends and Issues." *Sociology of Education* 61(3): 191–210,
p. 205.

[34] Geoffrey Bolton. 2006 [1990]. *The Oxford History of Australia.* Vol. 5, *The Middle Way,
1942–1995.* 2nd edn. South Melbourne, Vic.: Oxford University Press, pp. 89–110, 139–62.

pluralistic; and – crucially – whether or not it had a state church.[35] In countries with a strong established church, political reforms often required a simultaneous overthrow of church and state; consequently, established churches tend to promote more strongly secular outcomes by encouraging anticlericalism. In a similar vein, Philip Gorski has suggested a "sociopolitical conflict model" of secularization, where secularization arises from conflicts between religious and secularist movements. These conflicts take on a particular character depending on how closely connected church and state are at any given time; separationist (and anticlerical) movements emerge in contexts where church and state are closely aligned, while combinationist movements may emerge in contexts where church and state are separate.[36]

Most recently, Ahmet Kuru has put forward a related argument to explain why modern, secular states pursue different policies toward religion.[37] Comparing American, French, and Turkish educational systems, Kuru argues that ideology is the key factor explaining different state policies toward religion. Kuru distinguishes between ideologies of "passive secularism," seen in the United States and generally permissive of student religious expression and the invocation of God in the Pledge of Allegiance; and "assertive secularism," seen in France and Turkey and associated with bans on headscarves and no such pledges. These ideologies are, in turn, the result of whether each nation needed to overthrow an *ancien régime* in order to establish itself. In both France and Turkey, the need to overthrow the established order and its religious supporters led to an ideology of assertive secularism and more aggressively secular policies, whereas the United States' lack of such a *régime* meant that a more conciliatory ideology of passive secularism came to predominate.[38]

The *ancien régimes* approach would therefore explain divergence in terms of the political dynamics unleashed by the degree of religious pluralism and the presence or absence of an *ancien régime*. Yet these factors too do not permit us to distinguish between the United States and Australia. Both nations are

---

[35] Martin, *General Theory of Secularization*; see also David Martin. 2005. *On Secularization: Towards a Revised General Theory*. Burlington, VT: Ashgate Press.

[36] Philip S. Gorski. 2005. "The Return of the Repressed: Religion and the Political Unconscious of Historical Sociology." Pp. 161–89 in *Remaking Modernity: Politics, History, and Sociology*, edited by Julia Adams, Elisabeth S. Clemens, and Ann Shola Orloff. Durham: Duke University Press, pp. 177–78.

[37] Ahmet T. Kuru. 2009. *Secularism and State Policies toward Religion: The United States, France, and Turkey*. Cambridge: Cambridge University Press.

[38] Kuru's depiction of American education is obviously somewhat at odds with that expressed here: his vision is of an American education system less resolutely secular than its European neighbors, whereas mine is of a system in some respects more secular than European systems. In part, this has to do with which policies are emphasized; he emphasizes student dress codes and pledges of allegiance, whereas I emphasize devotional practices and funding for religious schools. Both sets of distinctions are legitimate, and reflect both the complexity of America's "secular" policies, and the difficulty of developing holistic yet meaningful criteria for cross-national comparisons of secularization.

predominantly Protestant yet highly pluralistic, and neither nation featured an established church or *ancien régime* that required its citizens to choose between religion and reform. And both countries are, as Kuru observes, ones in which a passive secularist ideology holds sway.[39] This approach also has difficulty explaining policy variation within the same country over time. Kuru explains America's historical variations in part as the result of battles between "separationist" and "accommodationist" interpretations of passive secularism, but these categories (derived from American jurisprudence) do not travel well to Australia, where such legal camps have not developed. Moreover, the separationist–accommodationist dichotomy itself conceals, in both countries, important aspects of the historical trajectory, such as how those positions were themselves shaped and taken up differently by different religious and nonreligious groups in response to religious competition. In short, the focus on *ancien régimes* and ideological variation cannot explain the Australian–American divergence, and potentially obscures, rather than reveals, how religious and ideological cleavages intersected and overlapped in changing configurations over time.

The Rational Choice Approach

Whereas the modernization and *ancien régimes* approaches focus on the structural determinants of secularization, the rational choice approach focuses instead on how actors contribute to secularization by pursuing their interests and preferences. In its most direct application to macro-level secularization, Anthony Gill argues that state policies governing "religious liberty" reflect the calculations of political actors attempting to preserve their political power, maximize economic resources, and ensure social stability. State policies toward religion are means to these ends, and change as necessary to grow and maintain political power. Thus, Gill concludes, "when restrictions on religious liberty have a high opportunity cost as measured in terms of political survival, government revenue, and/or economic growth, deregulation of the religious market results."[40] Given these preferences, Gill argues that democratic and religiously pluralistic political environments tend toward less cooperation between church and state because they make such cooperation less appealing to politicians.

The rational choice approach would therefore explain divergence in secular settlements in terms of the strategic behavior of self-interested political actors. This approach has definite applications; political calculation was an important factor behind the reintroduction of state aid in Australia, for instance. Yet at the same time, because the rational choice approach assumes that actors are

---

[39] Kuru, *Secularism and State Policies*, p. 27.

[40] Anthony Gill. 2008. *The Political Origins of Religious Liberty.* Cambridge: Cambridge University Press, p. 52. See also Roger Finke. 1990. "Religious Deregulation: Origins and Consequences." *Journal of Church and State* 32: 609–26; and Anthony Gill and Arang Keshavarzian. 1999. "State Building and Religious Resources: An Institutional Theory of Church–State Relations in Iran and Mexico." *Politics & Society* 27(3): 430–64.

motivated by a predetermined and delimited set of preferences, it has difficulty accounting for actors with other motivations. In the United States, however, these sorts of actors are an important part of the story. America's Supreme Court justices, for instance, played a key role in advancing strict separation, yet their positions were consciously insulated from the demands of maintaining power or extracting revenues.[41] Similarly, the rational choice approach has little place for actors motivated (at least in part) by interests such as group allegiance, legitimacy, or the pragmatic desire to solve problems.[42] Yet as we shall see, educational administrators embraced a more secular curriculum in part in response to the practical difficulties of teaching religion to a diversifying student body, and President Kennedy's decision to oppose federal aid to religious schools was motivated at least in part out of desires to preserve the political viability of future Catholic presidents. While these actions may be "self-interested" in some sense, the interests and preferences behind them seem not to accord with the assumed preferences of the rational choice approach.

Moreover, while it may be generally true that dominant religions "prefer a regulatory regime that discriminates against religious minorities" while minority religions "favor regulations that make it easier for their clergy and members to openly practice their faith and proselytize,"[43] these assumed preferences cannot make sense of the strange and shifting positions taken by American religious groups. During the mid-twentieth century, for instance, the campaign for strict separation drew support from both dominant mainline Protestants *and* the quintessential religious minority, Jews. The rational choice approach's assumption of fixed preferences cannot capture the important ecumenical and nativist motives that help explain these positions. Thus, the rational choice approach is incomplete. While it points us toward important dynamics in the evolution of secular settlements, its rigid focus on political calculation based on fixed preferences does not provide sufficient explanatory power to account for the policies that eventually developed, especially in the United States.

The Secular Movements Approach

A final approach is the "secular movements" approach pioneered by Christian Smith.[44] This approach argues that secularization is the result of a deliberate

---

[41] For a parallel critique, see Kuru, *Secularism and State Policies*, p. 21.

[42] On group allegiance, see Julia Adams. 1999. "Culture in Rational-Choice Theories of State-Formation." Pp. 98–122 in *State/Culture: State-Formation after the Cultural Turn*, edited by George Steinmetz. Ithaca, NY: Cornell University Press, pp. 107–09. On legitimacy, see Melissa Wilde. 2007. *Vatican II: A Sociological Analysis of Religious Change*. Princeton: Princeton University Press, pp. 45–46. On the distinction between preference maximization and problem solving, see Neil Gross. 2009. "A Pragmatist Theory of Social Mechanisms." *American Sociological Review* 74: 358–79, p. 367.

[43] Gill, *Political Origins*, p. 8.

[44] Christian Smith, ed. 2003. *The Secular Revolution: Power, Interests, and Conflict in the Secularization of American Public Life*. Berkeley: University of California Press.

campaign by rising intellectual elites to enhance their social position at the expense of established religious elites. Through a series of analyses of Victorian- and Progressive-Era America, the contributors to Smith's volume *The Secular Revolution* forcefully argue that public life was strategically secularized by actors whose interests lay in delegitimizing the Protestant Establishment and asserting the primacy of academic and nonreligious knowledge in public culture. The key figures in this account are cultural elites, especially intellectuals, who developed new, nonreligious forms of knowledge in order to "increase their own cultural authority and class autonomy – and to reinforce their own intellectual identities."[45]

The secular movements approach would therefore explain divergent secular settlements by reference to differential access to resources and political opportunities encountered by campaigns by intellectual elites to enhance their social status.[46] Yet this can only provide a partial explanation for the Australian–American divergence. Like the rational choice approach, the secular movements approach focuses on a narrow set of actors with a particular set of interests – though in this case, the actors are cultural elites and their motives are largely a mixture of self-aggrandizement and antipathy toward religion. Similarly, it focuses narrowly on cultural institutions as the venues for secularization. This focus yields important insights, but it does so at the cost of leaving out the important electoral and legal campaigns waged by nonintellectual and nonelite actors, including religiously motivated actors who actively campaigned for secular educational policies in more traditional political contexts, such as school boards and courtrooms.[47]

Further, while its focus on political opportunities is important, the secular movements approach tends to view those opportunities primarily in terms of divisions within the dominant religious establishment.[48] Yet while this operationalization may be useful for explaining the success or failure of any particular secularizing campaign, shifting elite alignments may be less relevant in explaining cross-national variation than more durable political structures.[49] Similarly, the secular movements approach provides few theoretical tools to

---

[45] Christian Smith. 2003. "Introduction: Rethinking the Secularization of American Public Life." Pp. 1–96 in *The Secular Revolution: Power, Interests, and Conflict in the Secularization of American Public Life.* Berkeley: University of California Press, p. 37.

[46] Smith, "Introduction," p. 61.

[47] An important exception is George M. Thomas, Lisa R. Peck, and Channin G. De Haan. 2003. "Reforming Education, Transforming Religion, 1876–1931." Pp. 355–94 in *The Secular Revolution: Power, Interests, and Conflict in the Secularization of American Public Life,* edited by Christian Smith. Berkeley: University of California Press.

[48] See, e.g., Smith, "Introduction," pp. 60–73.

[49] Herbert P. Kitschelt. 1986. "Political Opportunity Structures and Political Protest: Anti-Nuclear Movements in Four Democracies." *British Journal of Political Science* 16: 57–85; Hanspeter Kriesi. 2004. "Political Context and Opportunity." Pp. 67–90 in *The Blackwell Companion to Social Movements,* edited by David A. Snow, Sarah A. Soule, and Hanspeter Kriesi. Malden, MA: Blackwell Publishing, pp. 70–71; David S. Meyer. 2004. "Protest and Political Opportunities."

explain why actors with objectively similar positions nevertheless develop different sets of interests in different countries. Educators, for instance, were an important secularizing force in American education, but not in Australia. In short, the secular movements approach can take us partway to an explanation of the Australia–America divergence, but its theoretical apparatus does not easily lend itself to comparative analysis, and its narrow focus on cultural elites obscures the role of other actors – often religious actors – who played decisive roles in secularization.

Beyond Existing Approaches: Reclaiming the Role of Institutions

I propose that a better explanation can be developed by attending to political action *within the context of political institutions*. Institutions have been largely overlooked by secularization theorists. To the extent that scholars have considered institutions at all, they have tended to treat them primarily as mechanisms of, or targets for, mobilization, rather than as important political constraints and resources in and of themselves. Educational systems, for example, are sometimes treated as systems through which secular ideas are disseminated to the population at large,[50] and sometimes as a set of institutions that religious and nonreligious actors compete over for influence.[51] In neither case is the actual administrative and bureaucratic structure of the state treated as a serious independent factor that constrains and shapes the activities of contesting parties. Yet it is precisely these *institutional* factors that help to determine whether and to what extent political contests over religion's position in social domains are resolved in a more secular direction. While scholars have yet to consider how institutions affect the course of secularization, recent scholarship suggests the relevance of institutions to studies of religion and politics. An emerging literature on the "judicialization of religious freedom" suggests that courts play a uniquely important role in protecting religious liberties,[52]

Annual Review of Sociology 30: 125–45, pp. 134–35; Miriam Smith. 2008. *Political Institutions and Lesbian and Gay Rights in the United States and Canada*. New York: Routledge, pp. 8–9.

[50] Peter Berger, Grace Davie, and Effie Fokas. 2008. *Religious America, Secular Europe? A Theme and Variations*. Burlington, VT: Ashgate Press, pp. 19–20.

[51] See, e.g., Kraig Beyerlein. 2003. "Educational Elites and the Movement to Secularize Public Education: The Case of the National Education Association." Pp. 160–96 in *The Secular Revolution: Power, Interests, and Conflict in the Secularization of American Public Life*, edited by Christian Smith. Berkeley: University of California Press; and Christian Smith. 2003. "Secularizing American Higher Education: The Case of Early American Sociology." Pp. 97–159 in *The Secular Revolution: Power, Interests, and Conflict in the Secularization of American Public Life*, edited by Christian Smith. Berkeley: University of California Press.

[52] James T. Richardson. 2015. "Managing Religion and the Judicialization of Religious Freedom." *Journal for the Scientific Study of Religion* 54(1): 1–19. See also Roger Finke. 2013. "Origins and Consequences of Religious Freedoms: A Global Overview." *Sociology of Religion* 74(3): 297–313; Roger Finke and Robert R. Martin. 2014. "Ensuring Liberties: Understanding State Restrictions on Religious Freedoms." *Journal for the Scientific Study of Religion* 53(4): 687–705; Matthias

for instance, while other scholarship suggests that institutional arrangements influence the steps states take to manage religious pluralism.[53]

There is, therefore, a real opportunity to expand our understanding of how institutions contribute to the development of diverse secular settlements. I do this by bringing to bear insights and concepts from the literature on historical institutionalism.[54] Over the past several decades, scholars working under the banner of historical institutionalism have demonstrated that variation in national political institutions has affected the development of social policy in fields as diverse as social welfare, health care, taxation, immigration, gay rights, and abortion.[55] It stands to reason that political institutions may have affected the development of policies toward religion as well. To date, however, historical institutionalism has had little influence on secularization debates – or on the sociology of religion more generally. By bringing in insights from this literature, I show how institutions – by constraining, enabling, and constituting actors – can have an important independent effect on secularization.

Thus, what is needed is a political-institutional approach to secularization. In setting forth such an approach, I argue that the development of secular settlements is fundamentally driven by political struggles among interested actors. However, those actors' interests and strategies must be understood as having been indelibly shaped by the institutional contexts in which they must operate. To understand the emergence and transformation of secular settlements, in other words, we must pay attention to how political conflicts and institutional contexts interact.

Koenig. 2015. "Governance of Religious Diversity at the European Court of Human Rights." Pp. 51–78 in *International Approaches to Governing Ethnic Diversity*, edited by Jane Bolden and Will Kymlicka. New York: Oxford University Press.

[53] Karen Barkey. 2008. *Empire of Difference: The Ottomans in Comparative Perspective.* Cambridge: Cambridge University Press; Joel S. Fetzer and J. Christopher Soper. 2005. *Muslims and the State in Britain, France, and Germany.* Cambridge: Cambridge University Press; Claus Hofhansel. 2015. "Recognition Regimes for Religious Minorities in Europe: Institutional Change and Reproduction." *Journal of Church and State* 57(1): 90–118; Steven Pfaff and Anthony J. Gill. 2006. "Will a Million Muslims March? Muslim Interest Organizations and Political Integration in Europe." *Comparative Political Studies* 39: 803–29.

[54] For reviews, see Peter A. Hall and Rosemary C.R. Taylor. 1996. "Political Science and the Three New Institutionalisms." *Political Studies* 44: 936–57; and Kathleen Thelen. 1999. "Historical Institutionalism in Comparative Politics." *Annual Review of Political Science* 2: 369–404.

[55] Fetzer and Soper, *Muslims and the State*; Drew Halfmann. 2011. *Doctors and Demonstrators: How Political Institutions Shape Abortion Law in the United States, Britain, and Canada.* Chicago: University of Chicago Press; Ellen M. Immergut. 1992. "The Rules of the Game: The Logic of Health Policy-Making in France, Switzerland, and Sweden." Pp. 57–89 in *Structuring Politics: Historical Institutionalism in Comparative Analysis*, edited by Sven Steinmo, Kathleen Thelen, and Frank Longstreth. New York: Cambridge University Press; Smith, *Political Institutions and Lesbian and Gay Rights*; Sven Steinmo. 1993. *Taxation and Democracy.* New Haven: Yale University Press; Margaret Weir and Theda Skocpol. 1985. "State Structures and the Possibilities for 'Keynesian' Responses to the Great Depression in Sweden, Britain, and the United States." Pp. 107–67 in *Bringing the State Back In*, edited by Peter Evans, Dietrich Rueschemeyer, and Theda Skocpol. New York: Cambridge University Press.

A POLITICAL-INSTITUTIONAL APPROACH TO SECULARIZATION

The approach advanced here takes the central contention of the agent-centered approaches to secularization – namely, that secularization is fundamentally a political project – as its starting point, but it situates this insight firmly in specific institutional contexts by focusing on the interaction of political actors and political institutions. This political-institutional approach to secularization argues that secularization occurs through the working out of a set of common *political processes*, but that specific outcomes will vary depending on the *institutional contexts* in which they play out. Analytically, this entails breaking down "secularization" into a number of component processes, and identifying how those processes articulate with and are transformed by the specific institutional features of each country. In short, we cannot understand how secularization occurs, or the secular settlements that result, without paying close attention to *both* the actors who pursue particular policies governing religion *and* the structure of the state, and how it shapes the goals and strategies of those actors.

Common Secularizing Processes

Australia and the United States currently feature very different secular settlements, but their histories are not idiosyncratic. Instead, a close examination of the histories of the two countries reveals a number of commonalities in the political dynamics at work in each country. These similarities become intelligible when they are understood as common secularizing processes. Although secularization is sometimes treated as a single, unitary process, it is actually better understood as a contingent *outcome* generated by the action and interaction of *multiple secularizing processes*. Each process works at different speeds, engages different actors, and articulates with institutions in different ways, but all ultimately tend toward more secular outcomes.

These secularizing processes are fundamentally political – that is to say, the ultimate driving force behind each of them has to do with conflicts among various groups for status, resources, or power – but the character and political stakes of each process differ. This multiprocess approach reflects the fact that the politics of secularization are varied. We should not necessarily expect any single group of actors to be the driving force behind secularization. Instead, we must begin by recognizing that secularization has its roots in multiple conflicts. Similarly, there is nothing inevitable about these processes. The strength and success of each process will depend on the encounters and strategic decisions made by the actors who drive each process forward.

In the United States and Australia, secularization was driven forward by at least three separate political processes: state-building, professionalization, and religious conflict. Each process is analytically distinct, although as we will see, they sometimes operate in combination in historical reality. The key features of these processes are presented in Table 1.2.

TABLE 1.2. *Secularizing political processes*

	State-building	Professionalization	Religious conflict
Major conflict	Political elites vs. religious actors	Religious actors vs. professional actors	Religious actors vs. one another
Stakes	Institutional dominance	Authoritative knowledge claims	Inclusion and representation
Character	Jurisdictional	Epistemological	Symbolic/ Representational

State-Building

The state-building process contains within it the potential for *conflict between political elites and religious actors for control over domains of social life*. It is a process of jurisdictional conflict over whether church or state will be the dominant institutional actor in a particular sector.[56] The quintessential example of this process is the creation of state education systems. Today, education is nearly universally provided by the state, yet it was largely in the hands of the churches until the nineteenth century. As state education systems were created, religious authority over education decreased accordingly, as churches' control over education policy was transferred to state agents, elected boards, and politicians. Political actors may attempt to expand the reach of the state into new social domains for a variety of reasons, including expanding state capacity, securing social control, promoting democracy, or constructing a more unified national polity.[57] As the state expands into new social domains, jurisdictional conflicts may emerge as state-provided services begin to compete with or displace religious providers, and religious actors attempt to halt or redirect these moves.

The state-building process itself can take a variety of forms. State-building always occurs on a preexisting terrain of institutional practice in a given social domain,[58] and states may engage with those existing institutions in several

---

[56] These jurisdictional conflicts may contribute to the broader process of "differentiation" to the extent that states contribute to the development of new logics and authority structures in the course of developing new administrative infrastructure. For a forceful argument that state-building necessarily requires secularization, see Birol Başkan. 2014. *From Religious Empires to Secular States: State Secularization in Turkey, Iran, and Russia*. New York: Routledge.

[57] Ben Ansell and Johannes Lindvall. 2013. "The Political Origins of Primary Education Systems: Ideology, Institutions, and Interdenominational Conflict in an Era of Nation-Building." *American Political Science Review* 107(3): 505–22; David T. Buckley and Luis Felipe Mantilla. 2013. "God and Governance: Development, State Capacity, and the Regulation of Religion." *Journal for the Scientific Study of Religion* 52: 328–48; Gill and Keshavardzian, "State-Building and Religious Resources"; Francisco O. Ramirez and John Boli. 1987. "The Political Construction of Mass Schooling: European Origins and Worldwide Institutionalization." *Sociology of Education* 60(1): 2–17.

[58] Nancy Beadie. 2010. "Education, Social Capital, and State Formation in Comparative Historical Perspective: Preliminary Investigations." *Paedagogica Historica* 46(1/2): 15–32, p. 19.

different ways. Margaret Archer distinguishes between two state-building strategies: "substitution," in which states attempt to take control of a domain by building new institutions and allowing them to compete against existing ones; and "restriction," in which states coercively suppress existing institutions and replace them with state ones.[59] In addition to these strategies, states may also engage in "cooptation," in which states work through or take over existing institutions, incorporating them into the state's administrative machinery.[60] Which strategy state actors pursue depends both on the existing institutional terrain and on the response of religious actors to the state-building process. Where religious actors support the state-building process, cooptation is a more likely outcome; where they actively oppose it, restriction is more likely.

While all of these strategies are likely to displace religious control of a given social domain, the different strategies can have important institutional consequences, shaping the ultimate administrative form and cultural content of the new state institutions. Strategies of cooptation and substitution may provide incentives for religious cultural elements to linger on in the new state institutions. Similarly, restriction strategies may require a more forceful administrative structure and incentives to sever ties with religious bodies. In many respects, state-building, by removing a domain from religious control, is an essential precondition for the subsequent negotiation of secular settlements. And the administrative and cultural dynamics that shape the state-formation process may reverberate into the settlement that eventually emerges.

The development of Australian and American common schools in the nineteenth and twentieth centuries, detailed in Chapter 2, offers a paradigmatic example of the state-building process at work. State-building took a different form in each country: American common schools were constructed in cooperation with religious leaders in a relatively open educational environment, whereas Australian state schools were established by displacing an established system of denominational schools, often over the protests of clergy. In both cases, the churches eventually largely (though not completely) yielded control of education to the state, but the systems that emerged differed considerably in their organization and tone. America's system was decentralized and, until the late nineteenth century, featured a heavily and identifiably Protestant curriculum. The Australian system, by contrast, was highly centralized, and – while it usually retained Protestant religious education – somewhat less saturated with Protestant content.

---

[59] Margaret Archer. 1979. *The Social Origins of Educational Systems*. London: Sage, pp. 106–07.
[60] Philip S. Gorski. 2003. *The Disciplinary Revolution: Calvinism and the Rise of the State in Early Modern Europe*. Chicago: University of Chicago Press, p. 166. This was often a preferred strategy in education for states with an established church; see Yasemin Nuhoğlu Soysal and David Strang. 1989. "Construction of the First Mass Education Systems in Nineteenth-Century Europe." *Sociology of Education* 62(4): 277–88, p. 279.

Professionalization

A second secularizing process is professionalization, which contains within it the potential for *conflict between religious and professional actors for control over authoritative forms of knowledge in particular social domains.* Professionalization is fundamentally a process of epistemological conflict. As sociologist Andrew Abbott has shown, one of the key characteristics of a profession is the development of specialized, abstract, and authoritative forms of knowledge. Members of a profession draw upon this technical knowledge to justify their claim to control the rules and practices governing their chosen line of work. Further, they may also use these claims to technical expertise to defend their control over and against competing claims by other would-be practitioners.[61] Professionalization as a process thus reflects the development of both these occupational groups and the bodies of knowledge that legitimate their control over the work that they do.

Professionalization drives secularization by supplanting religiously based forms of knowledge and replacing them with novel ones not based in religion. Because the claim that one body of knowledge is superior is by its nature an exclusive claim, the rise of a new professional knowledge typically entails the marginalization of those epistemologies previously used to understand and justify a social phenomenon.[62] In social domains governed by religious knowledge, professionalization requires the displacement of the religiously grounded forms of knowledge previously used to understand social phenomena. This epistemological struggle is often realized practically in the reorganization of institutions and procedures, the marginalization of religious ideas, and overt conflict over organizational ethics and goals.[63] Secularization theorists have previously noted the close links between professionalization and secularization.[64] Indeed, *The Secular Revolution*, the magnum opus of the secular movements approach, is in many respects an extended meditation on how the development of professional knowledge, norms, and practices during late nineteenth- and early twentieth-century America displaced the Protestant establishment from its cultural and intellectual perch in education, law, journalism, and social welfare.[65]

Professionalization as a secularizing process can be seen vividly in education. This process involved the development of new educational theories, often based on developmental psychology, which reoriented the practice of teaching from "instruction" (or the transmission of knowledge) to "education" (or the encouragement of learning). It also entailed the expansion of education, both formally (e.g., the development of high schools) and thematically (e.g., the

---

[61] Andrew Abbott. 1988. *The System of Professions: An Essay on the Division of Expert Labor*. Chicago: University of Chicago Press, pp. 8–9.

[62] Abbott, *System of Professions*, pp. 2, 34.

[63] Dobbelaere, "Secularization," pp. 67–68.

[64] Chaves, "Secularization as Declining Religious Authority," pp. 770–71.

[65] Smith, *Secular Revolution*.

development of social studies, sex education, etc.) according to a professional rationale. Professionalization thus altered the purpose, form, and content of education in ways that undercut traditional religious content and practices. In the United States, education professionalized earlier and had a more immediate impact on school districts, in large part thanks to a highly developed professional infrastructure that encouraged the development and dissemination of novel educational theories, as discussed in Chapter 3. In Australia, however, a tightly controlled system of centralized administration discouraged the development of an independent educational infrastructure until the mid-twentieth century. As discussed in Chapter 4, this stunted the professional development of education and allowed the traditional "instructional" model (with its associated religious content) to go largely unchallenged until the 1960s.

Religious Conflict

Finally, there is religious conflict, which refers to *symbolic conflicts between different religious and/or nonreligious groups over inclusion and representation in civil institutions and the public sphere.* In any religiously pluralistic society, the policies embedded in civil institutions typically vary in how closely aligned they are with different religious groups. A state that establishes a church, adopts blasphemy laws, regulates religious garb, or requires devotionals in its civic institutions must simultaneously decide which church to establish, which statements are blasphemous, which garb to suppress or permit, and which prayers to read. In making those decisions, state actors symbolically embrace some religious parties and exclude others.[66] These decisions have high stakes for religious groups, because symbolic inclusion in the polity touches on a wide array of political and religious concerns. Some, like the distribution of government benefits, are basely political, but others run far deeper. Existential concerns like the conditions of cultural reproduction, and deep moral concerns such as whether public and private life is to be governed according to theological principles, are often implicated in whose religion is recognized in social policy, and how.[67] Religious conflict is thus readily activated by policy decisions that are not perceived to be equally inclusive or representative.[68] When states act to privilege one side of a dominant cleavage over another, the excluded may

---

[66] Ted G. Jelen and Clyde Wilcox. 2002. "Religion: The One, the Few, and the Many." Pp. 1–24 in *Religion and Politics in Comparative Perspective*, edited by Ted Gerard Jelen and Clyde Wilcox. Cambridge: Cambridge University Press, p. 11.

[67] For instance, Catholic requests for public aid were on one level about the fair distribution of resources, but they were also intimately tied up with concerns about transmitting the faith to the next generation, and with deeply held beliefs about the conditions under which education had to be conducted for it to be moral. On the varied stakes of religious conflict, see Rogers Brubaker. 2015. "Religious Dimensions of Political Conflict and Violence." *Sociological Theory* 33(1): 1–19, pp. 4–5.

[68] N.J. Demerath III. 1991. "Religious Capital and Capital Religions: Cross-Cultural and Non-Legal Factors in the Separation of Church and State." *Daedalus* 120(3): 21–40, pp. 35–36.

mobilize to advance their own substantive visions through symbolic inclusion in the policy realm.[69]

To an extent, religious conflict differs from the other two processes in that it is not *necessarily* secularizing. The type of secular settlement that religious conflict may promote depends both on the relationship among the religious parties in conflict, and also – crucially – on the nature of the existing secular settlement. State-building and professionalization tend to be zero-sum games (that is, political or professional elites gain in power at the expense of religious elites). Religious conflict, by contrast, is not just oriented to the question of *whether* religion will control or rule a given sphere, but also *whose* religion will be recognized in public life. Different religious groups will adopt different positions depending on whether they see themselves and their concerns reflected in the specific content of a policy. The dynamics of religious conflict thus change constantly as new political and theological conditions create new and destabilize old coalitions.

At the same time, the existing secular settlement also matters. In settings where a settlement permits considerable ties between religion and the state – and particularly when those ties are with one religious group – religious conflict may tend in a secularizing direction. In more starkly secular settlements, however, religious conflict may instead tend toward desecularization. This is because religious groups interact with one another within the context of existing settlements, and develop their own positions based on their own theological and political interests, their perceived alliances, and the nature of the existing settlement. When previously conflicting groups reach détente over points of disagreement, or when new, common goals are identified among former adversaries, new, ecumenical arrangements can develop that can have a *desecularizing* effect. Religious conflict thus promotes *settlement change* above all else; it is the great churning motor of secularization and desecularization alike.

As the substantive chapters that follow demonstrate, religious conflict was (and remains) a central feature of the politics of religion and education in both countries. During the nineteenth and early twentieth centuries, religious minorities in each country (especially Catholics) were at the forefront of campaigns challenging the policies with respect to religion that had been enshrined into law by the Protestant establishment. They used a variety of methods, from local school board campaigns to legal challenges, to attempt to remove Protestant religious exercises from the public schools. Protestants in turn passed laws and waged court challenges to prevent any supports for Catholic schools from being enacted. In the twentieth-century United States, religious minorities – especially Jews – once again helped to lead the litigation campaign to persuade the Supreme Court to ban those practices that symbolically

---

[69] Philip S. Gorski. 2003. "Historicizing the Secularization Debate: An Agenda for Research." Pp. 110–22 in *Handbook of the Sociology of Religion*, edited by Michele Dillon. Cambridge: Cambridge University Press, p. 116.

excluded them from America's public schools. But when sectarian divisions faded, *desecularization* could also result. In Australia, ecumenical trends in the 1960s allowed Catholics and Protestants to join forces in favor of a policy that provided funding for all religious schools, as desecularization became a means of symbolically including Catholics in the polity.

These three processes should not be understood as inevitable or unidirectional, but instead as general impulses and common conflicts that take particular historical shapes and character depending on the actors involved, their strategies, and the institutional structures in which they work themselves out. Nor should this list be read as necessarily exhaustive; other processes may play an important role at other times and in other settings. However, these three processes were central to the development of secular settlements in the United States and Australia. These three processes are *general* – that is, they should occur in multiple settings beyond the two cases analyzed in this book, when and where the conditions are right for them. But at the same time, I do not argue that they must always and everywhere lead to the same outcomes. Instead, they advance (or fail to advance) largely *contingent upon* the way that they interact with specific political institutions.

Institutions as Contexts for Secularizing Processes

Political institutions are those "formal or informal procedures, routines, norms and conventions embedded in the organizational structure of the polity or political economy."[70] Institutions in and of themselves are not secularizing agents; as Kathleen Thelen and Sven Steinmo have noted, "institutions constrain and refract politics but they are never the sole 'cause' of outcomes."[71] However, by shaping how political processes unfold, they do decisively shape the speed and force of secularization. Political institutions work in two primary ways to shape the course of secularization: by *mediating* political contests among secularizing and anti-secularizing actors, and by actively *constituting* those actors by shaping their identities and worldviews.

The Mediating Role of Political Institutions
One way that institutions structure secularization is by acting as a mediator of political conflicts. Institutions disperse power unevenly among competing actors and grant political advantages to some and not others. Because different political institutions feature different rules for entry and participation, they

---

[70] Hall and Taylor, "Political Science and the Three New Institutionalisms," p. 938.
[71] Kathleen Thelen and Sven Steinmo. 1992. "Historical Institutionalism in Comparative Politics." Pp. 1–32 in *Structuring Politics: Historical Institutionalism in Comparative Analysis*, edited by Sven Steinmo, Kathleen Thelen, and Frank Longstreth. New York: Cambridge University Press, p. 3.

vary in terms of their *accessibility*.[72] Some institutions provide ready access to decision-makers, while others sequester decision-makers within administrative barriers. These institutional differences govern whether and how political claimants may engage with policy-makers, and how responsive those policy-makers are likely to be.

The degree of institutional accessibility is often inversely related to institutional *scope*. Local institutions may be smaller in scope, but are often more accessible. National institutions, by contrast, have a much broader scope but are usually less accessible. These differences in institutional scope generate distinct dynamics of institutional capture. Although fragmentation is often seen as an impediment to policy change at the national level because it makes concerted action more difficult,[73] fragmented or decentralized political systems can also at times enable policy change at subnational levels. The multiple "venues"[74] in which political action can take place in a decentralized state can provide access routes that are unavailable in more centralized polities. Decentralized states can increase challengers' influence on policy by enabling them to triumph in some locales even if they do not triumph everywhere,[75] but it also makes it much harder for challengers to successfully implement their policies on a nationwide scale. By contrast, highly centralized states require the capture of the entire state apparatus to effect policy change, but once achieved, that change will be broadly disseminated.

Political institutions can also have an important effect on the development of political coalitions. Institutions create space or foreclose opportunities for actors to pursue their interests independently. As a result, they bundle actors into and out of coalitions with other actors who may or may not share their interests. At times, this can prevent groups with objectively similar interests from joining forces, but at other times it can force groups with diametrically opposed interests together, compromising political strategies.[76]

Institutions thus vary substantially in how favorable they are as terrain for secularizing campaigns. This shapes actors' strategic decision-making. The existing institutional terrain strongly conditions would-be secularizing actors' decisions about where – and even whether – to pursue more secular policies, how to engage with potential allies and adversaries, and whether to temper

---

[72] E.g., Theda Skocpol. 1992. *Protecting Soldiers and Mothers: The Political Origins of Social Policy in the United States.* Cambridge: Belknap Press, p. 54; see also Weir and Skocpol, "State Structures."

[73] E.g., Edwin Amenta. 1998. *Bold Relief: Institutional Politics and the Origins of Modern American Social Policy.* Princeton: Princeton University Press.

[74] E.E. Schattschneider. 1960. *The Semi-Sovereign People.* New York: Holt, Reinhart, and Winston.

[75] For examples where religious claimants' political influence appears to have been enhanced by decentralized polities, see Fetzer and Soper, *Muslims and the State*, pp. 11–12, 53, 149; Gill, *Political Origins*, pp. 207–12.

[76] Margaret Weir. 1992. *Politics and Jobs: The Boundaries of Employment Policy in the United States.* Princeton: Princeton University Press.

their demands in order to navigate coalitional dynamics. However, while political actors are subject to institutional constraints, institutions can also act as enabling resources for them.[77] Within the overall political order, certain institutions may prove to be more forgiving than others. In these circumstances, actors may engage in venue-shifting, moving their campaigns to another institutional venue to evade obstacles and find more favorable terrain.[78] Similarly, faced with favorable terrain, actors may work to develop or enlarge the power of those institutions, or to cultivate certain institutions to maximize their advantage. In short, actors' chances for success and the strategies they pursue will not just depend on their interests, ideologies, or access to resources, but also on the institutional terrain that they need to navigate in pursuit of their goals.

The Constitutive Role of Institutions

Political institutions also have a second effect: they can help to constitute secularizing actors by shaping the interests and behavior of groups in ways that lead them to adopt more or less favorable stances toward secular policies. Interests and preferences are not always immediately evident from one's social position. Instead, as John Zysman has noted, "the definition of interests and objectives is created in institutional contexts and is not separable from them."[79] Political institutions contain within them relations of authority, rules, regulations, and normative content. These institutional features combine to create a system of incentives and punishments, which inclines the actors who inhabit and interact with it to construe their interests in particular ways. Similarly, actors may also define their options in terms of the practices and constraints of existing institutions.[80] As a result, similarly positioned actors may develop very different sets of interests and goals, and may consequently act differently, in response to the institutional environments in which they exist.[81]

Institutions can also help to shape worldviews and objectives by reinforcing public sentiments, norms, and identities over time, making certain issues salient, and creating principled beliefs about what constitutes appropriate or noble behavior.[82] Institutions are bearers and promoters of ideals, and actors interacting with those institutions may imbibe those ideals and take them on as

[77] Kathleen Thelen. 2003. "How Institutions Evolve: Insights from Comparative Historical Analysis." Pp. 208–40 in *Comparative Historical Analysis in the Social Sciences*, edited by James Mahoney and Dietrich Rueschemeyer. New York: Cambridge University Press, p. 213.

[78] Halfmann, *Doctors and Demonstrators*, p. 22.

[79] John Zysman. 1994. "How Institutions Create Historically Rooted Trajectories of Growth." *Industrial and Corporate Change* 3(1): 243–83, p. 244.

[80] Weir and Skocpol, "State Structures," pp. 120–21.

[81] Marion Fourcade. 2009. *Economists and Societies: Discipline and Profession in the United States, Britain, and France, 1890s to 1990s*. Princeton: Princeton University Press; Halfmann, *Doctors and Demonstrators*, p. 203.

[82] John L. Campbell. 2004. *Institutional Change and Globalization*. Princeton: Princeton University Press, p. 112.

their own. In fact, the dissemination of ideals can contribute to the emergence of actors whose interests and goals are oriented to those ideals. In other words, because actors form around particular issues and interests, institutional norms can create the issues and interests around which influential groups come to mobilize.

This constitutive effect is important because analyses that take the existence of secularizing groups for granted miss an important part of the story. Secularization theorists acknowledge that established churches can produce anticlerical actors with strong secularizing interests. But this is just a prominent example of a wider set of institutional effects. Other aspects of the state similarly provide incentives and shape interests in ways that make actors more or less likely to take up secularizing campaigns. Secularizing actors are not always exogenous forces; instead, some of the most vocal advocates for a more secular public sphere may be in a very real sense the creature of those political institutions themselves. The very existence of strong, secularizing actors, in other words, may be in part attributable to the incentives and cultural norms of political institutions.

Pulling these pieces together, one arrives at a political-institutional approach to secularization. Secular settlements emerge over time as political conflicts (of various sorts) are carried forward through institutional contexts, which may frustrate, facilitate, or amplify them. It is in this interaction of general secularizing processes and specific political institutions that we find an explanation for the varied secular settlements we see today.

In the cases at hand, while all three political processes were at work in both countries, American political institutions provided a more favorable environment for secularization. The United States, with its decentralized, widely dispersed administrative system and open, democratic legal system, amounted to a *permeable state*, featuring many access points where political challenges could take place and new ideas could take root. Further, these institutions helped constitute the interests and goals of important secularizing actors, including professional educators, civil libertarians, and Jews. By contrast, Australia's highly centralized policy-setting structures and strong gatekeeping mechanisms amounted to an *insulated state*, where any changes or challenges required the persuasion or cooptation of the entire state government. Accordingly, religious minorities and professionalizing educators had an easier time penetrating American institutions and dislodging traditional religious exercises in the United States. Meanwhile, Catholics took advantage of the relatively more accessible structure of the Australian party system to leverage ecumenical developments into a system of wholescale funding for religious schools. Thus, while institutions were not determinative, their influence decisively shaped the trajectory of each secularizing process, and thus the ultimate secular settlement that emerged.

The Scope of this Argument

While the argument presented here possesses some degree of generalizability, I do not intend for it to function as a universal or general covering law. Instead, it takes its cue from recent developments in historical sociology and advances more modest claims. Inspired by advances in the study of temporality on the one hand, and the influence of critical realism on the other,[83] historical sociologists have increasingly abandoned the search for "covering laws" presumed to be valid across time and space and applicable in all contexts. These are now thought to be effectively impossible to derive, since the social world constitutes an "open system" embedded in time, space, and constantly shifting cultural meanings.[84]

Consequently, many historical sociologists now seek instead to identify particular processes and mechanisms that inhere across some, but not necessarily all, cases. This is done with the awareness of the possibility that broad social phenomena may have multiple variants, in which some processes and mechanisms may have stronger or weaker effects.[85] And it is done without the expectation that the same process must necessarily lead everywhere to the same outcome. Indeed, the same process, under different circumstances or in conjunction with other processes, can yield different outcomes; while the same outcome, under different circumstances or in conjunction with other processes, may be attributable to different causal processes.[86] The point of comparative analysis, therefore, is to isolate patterns in terms of contexts, processes, and mechanisms that transcend specific cases and may inform analyses elsewhere without assuming that they will apply universally; to "understand the interpenetration of general processes and local settings as played out in world historical time."[87] The goal of social scientific inquiry, then, is not universal explanation, but instead *epistemic gain*; progress occurs "through the construction of

[83] See, e.g., Andrew Abbott. 2001. *Time Matters: On Theory and Method.* Chicago: University of Chicago Press; William H. Sewell. 2005. *Logics of History: Social Theory and Social Transformation.* Chicago: University of Chicago Press; George Steinmetz. 1998. "Critical Realism and Historical Sociology: A Review Article." *Comparative Studies in Society and History* 40: 170–86.

[84] Andrew Collier. 1994. *Critical Realism: An Introduction to Roy Bhaskar's Philosophy.* New York: Verso.

[85] S.N. Eisenstadt. 2000. "Multiple Modernities." *Daedalus* 129: 1–30; Charles Taylor. 2004. *Modern Social Imaginaries.* Durham, NC: Duke University Press; Peter Wagner. 2004. "Modernity—One or Many?" Pp. 30–42 in *The Blackwell Companion to Sociology*, edited by Judith R. Blau. Oxford: Blackwell.

[86] Christian Smith. 2008. "Future Directions in the Sociology of Religion." *Social Forces* 86: 1561–89, p. 1579.

[87] Julia Adams, Elisabeth S. Clemens, and Ann Shola Orloff. 2005. "Introduction: Social Theory, Modernity, and the Three Waves of Historical Sociology." Pp. 1–72 in *Remaking Modernity: Politics, History, and Sociology*, edited by Julia Adams, Elisabeth S. Clemens, and Ann Shola Orloff. Durham, NC: Duke University Press, p. 66.

better and better explanatory models rather than the falsification of bolder and bolder theories."[88]

In this regard, this study adopts the approach taken by several scholars who have examined secularization at the level of individual beliefs. David Martin has made the case for "rival patterns of secularization,"[89] while José Casanova and Christian Smith have likewise urged that we use the concept of "multiple modernities" to improve our ability to understand variations in secularization and religious deprivatization in a global context.[90] Philip Gorski's "sociopolitical conflict model" of secularization explains the "variations in secularity" that one finds in Europe and the United States in reference to religious pluralism and church–state relations,[91] while Peter Berger, Grace Davie, and Effie Fokas account for that same divergence through a multi-layered analysis of the boundedness of churches in territories, Enlightenment traditions, institutional carriers, and ethnic diversity.[92]

This study follows the lead of these scholars in the sociology of religion and applies their approach and method to the study of secularization as a structural process. The processes and mechanisms that I identify here should be thought of as the building blocks for a broader theory of secularization. They were decisive in the cases at hand, and they also have potentially broad applicability to the study of the emergence of secular settlements in other countries. However, I also expect that these processes may be more or less determinative in other cases. Religiously pluralist countries in the Anglo-American ambit, such as Canada and New Zealand, are likely to have the most similarities, whereas those countries with established churches, Catholic majorities, or low levels of religious pluralism, such as France or Sweden, may have histories of secularization that are more strongly governed by other processes not considered here.[93]

Limitations of time, space, and resources preclude me from definitively canvassing and evaluating these possibilities here. All scholarship, but perhaps especially historical-comparative scholarship, is a communal enterprise, and

---

[88] Philip S. Gorski. 2004. "The Poverty of Deductivism: A Constructive Realist Approach to Sociological Explanation." *Sociological Methodology* 34(1): 1–33, p. 22.

[89] Martin, *On Secularization*, p. 47.

[90] Casanova, "Rethinking Secularization"; Smith, "Future Directions."

[91] Gorski, "Return of the Repressed," pp. 176–78.

[92] Berger et al., *Religious America*.

[93] As several scholars have observed, secularization appears to have markedly different "Catholic" and "Protestant" variants, to say nothing of potential Muslim, Buddhist, or Hindu ones. See Casanova, "Rethinking Secularization," pp. 11–14; Martin, *General Theory of Secularization*, *passim*. For thoughtful attempts to extend these typologies beyond the Christian West, see Casanova, "Rethinking Secularization"; Martin, *On Secularization*; Hans Joas and Klaus Wiegandt, eds. 2009. *Secularization and the World Religions*. Liverpool: Liverpool University Press; and Alfred Stepan. 2011. "The Multiple Secularisms of Modern Democratic and Non-Democratic Regimes." Pp. 114–44 in *Rethinking Secularism*, edited by Craig Calhoun, Mark Juergensmeyer, and Jonathan VanAntwerpen. New York: Oxford University Press.

the true scope and power of arguments and theories depend on revisitations and comparisons across an expanding number of settings.[94] My hope is that this study will inspire others to test its broader applicability in other cases. Meanwhile, the rest of this book will demonstrate how this approach helps to explain the American and Australian cases – a task which takes us back to the mid-nineteenth century.

[94] Paul Pierson and Theda Skocpol. 2002. "Historical Institutionalism in Contemporary Political Science." Pp. 693–721 in *Political Science: The State of the Discipline,* edited by Ira Katznelson and Helen V. Milner. New York: W.W. Norton & Company, p. 715.

PART I

FORGING THE NINETEENTH-CENTURY SETTLEMENT

State-Building and Secularization, 1800–1880

2

State-Building and Secularization in Comparative Perspective

INTRODUCTION

In the nineteenth century, jurisdiction over education shifted from the churches to the state in both Australia and the United States. In the United States, the diverse array of private, denominational, and town schools that prevailed in the early national era were slowly gathered together into a coherent system of "common schools." In Australia, the mostly denominational system that grew out of the convict garrisons was edged out by a new system of government schools after the colonies were granted responsible government in the 1850s. By 1880, the two nations had settled on remarkably similar secular settlements. The state dominated schooling in both countries, providing free education to all children irrespective of class or religious background. Each nation had erected strong legal barriers against funding for denominational schools ("public aid" or "state aid"), but were remarkably open to religious instruction in the public schools – especially instruction in a "nondenominational" Christianity heavily colored by Protestant assumptions. Yet although their settlements were similar, each nation's system of educational administration differed dramatically. In the United States, common schools were governed through a decentralized network of thousands of local school boards, while in Australia, government schools were run out of highly centralized state ministries of education.

Why did Australia and the United States arrive at nineteenth-century settlements that were so similar in their approach to religious education, yet so different in their administrative structure? I argue that the nearly complete shift in control from church to state in each country was driven primarily by the state-building process. In both countries, an organized campaign, led by actors determined to make education universal and subject to state control, succeeded in relocating the primary responsibility for education from the churches to the state. Yet state-building interacted differently with religious conflict in the two nations, in ways that shaped the administrative structures that ultimately developed. In the United States, the state-building process was driven largely from the bottom up with the avid participation of evangelical Protestant clergy. As a result, it was able to coopt the existing educational infrastructure, leading to an administratively decentralized school system that harmoniously fused state education with a strongly Protestant curriculum. In Australia, by contrast, the state-building process was driven largely by actors within the state, often over the active opposition of those denominations with an extensive system of denominational schools. As a result, state-building was only accomplished by imposing sharp restrictions on the existing denominational sector. This antagonistic dynamic yielded a strongly centralized administrative structure, and generated unstable alliances among the various denominations that ultimately led to substantial variation in the religious content of the state schools.

STATE-BUILDING, RELIGION, AND EDUCATION IN AMERICA, 1800–1880

American education took a variety of forms at the turn of the nineteenth century. Over the course of the nineteenth century, however, this diverse educational sector was synthesized and homogenized through the action of a grassroots campaign for "common schools." This campaign helped spread a locally organized, decentralized, district-based educational system across the rapidly expanding frontier. By the 1880s, this decentralized system, whose vibrant religious curriculum reflected the beliefs and assumptions of the Protestants who played a key role in its formation, attained a dominant position in the United States.

The Rise of the American Common School: An Overview

At the turn of the nineteenth century, American education was provided through a mix of private and denominational schools. Denominational schooling was strongest in the settled regions near the coast. In New England, education was provided through an established system of town schools. While technically civic institutions, town schools had their origins in the theocratic Puritan colonial governments of the seventeenth century and were, for all intents and purposes, "Congregational parochial schools."[1] Local Congregationalist ministers served as teachers, schoolmasters, and inspectors who monitored the schools' moral tone and occasionally examined students on the content of the Sunday sermons.[2] Outside of New England, the provision of education was

---

[1] Richard J. Gabel. 1937. *Public Funds for Church and Private Schools.* Washington, DC: Catholic University of America, pp. 28, 51.

[2] Gabel, *Public Funds*, pp. 55–56, 61; Mary Paul Mason. 1953. *Church–State Relationships in Education in Connecticut, 1633–1953.* Washington, DC: Catholic University of America Press, pp. 106–09.

much more varied, although the churches did control substantial portions of it. Denominational schooling was the rule in the middle colonies, where it had emerged early on as the solution to religious diversity.[3] Southern states also retained some schools founded by the Church of England during its time as the established church in those colonies, as well as a substantial number of denominational academies sponsored by Presbyterian and other Dissenting sects.[4] Religious schooling was also common in the growing cities of the eastern seaboard, where it typically took the form of interdenominational charity schooling aimed at poor urban children.[5]

In more rural areas and along the frontier, by contrast, schools were often entirely free from ecclesiastical control. In the rural North, as historian Carl Kaestle has observed, "the characteristic school was the district school, organized and controlled by a small locality and financed by some combination of property taxes, fuel contributions, tuition payments, and state aid."[6] Early district schools were held in barns, living rooms, or churches – wherever suitable shelter could be found – and were often organized along "nonsectarian" Protestant lines to make them amenable to children from multiple denominations.[7] The South had its own version of the rural district school, the "old-field" school, which was typically set up on fallow land on private initiative to provide education for a group of rate-paying parents.[8] Finally, in the cities, individual teachers often established private schools. "Dame schools" run by women in their homes, schools offering classical education by trained Latin scholars, and a variety of other independent private teachers were all common in the early national period.[9]

Thus, in 1800, formal church "control" of education was strong but far from universal. Churches obviously controlled education in their denominational schools, and the town schools in New England were also effectively under the control of the Congregational church. Still, considerable schooling took place outside of church auspices. Despite this varied pattern of control, nearly all education at the turn of the nineteenth century was thoroughly religious in its content and goals. Religious and moral training was generally understood to

[3] R. Freeman Butts and Lawrence A. Cremin. 1953. *A History of Education in American Culture*. New York: Holt, Rinehart, and Winston, pp. 98, 111; Gabel, *Public Funds*, pp. 127–38.

[4] Sadie Bell. 1969 [1930]. *The Church, the State, and Education in Virginia*. New York: Arno Press & the New York Times, pp. 144–46, 214, 219, 242.

[5] Carl F. Kaestle. 1983. *Pillars of the Republic: Common Schools and American Society, 1780–1860*. New York: Hill and Wang, pp. 32, 37.

[6] Kaestle, *Pillars of the Republic*, p. 13.

[7] William J. Reese. 2005. *America's Public Schools: From the Common School to "No Child Left Behind."* Baltimore: Johns Hopkins University Press, p. 29; James Pyle Wickersham. 1886. *A History of Education in Pennsylvania: Private and Public, Elementary and Higher, from the Time the Swedes Settled on the Delaware to the Present Day*. Lancaster, PA: Inquirer Publishing Company, p. 185.

[8] Kaestle, *Pillars of the Republic*, p. 13.

[9] Butts and Cremin, *History of Education*, p. 113.

be a key component of education, and nearly all schools – denominational and private – engaged in it. Although educational legislation was uncommon, those laws that did exist on the subject – such as Massachusetts' 1789 Education Act and the Northwest Ordinance – stressed the promotion of religion and morality as a preeminent goal of education.[10] The Old and New Testaments were common reading books in all schools, and some schools continued to use denominational catechisms.[11]

The Rise of State Schooling, 1800–1870

Between 1830 and 1860, control of education in the United States shifted decisively to the state. Gradually, the disparate educational institutions that prevailed at the beginning of the nineteenth century were absorbed into or replaced by a new system of "common schools" whose control and finance were entrusted to public agencies rather than any church or private group. Throughout the North,[12] as historian Timothy Smith has written, the common school was built "upon previous efforts of a private and denominational character ... [and] stemmed from efforts to harmonize these conflicting traditions."[13] In New England, where public education had the strongest roots, the town schools shifted completely from ecclesiastical to civic control after the disestablishment of the Congregational Church in the early nineteenth century. In Massachusetts, the state legislature forbade schools in 1827 from using books "calculated to favor any particular religious sect or tenet."[14] By the Civil War, the New England town schools had become wholly civic, rather than hybrid civic–ecclesiastical, institutions. Similarly, the interdenominational charity schools became the backbone of urban public schooling. In many cities, including New York, Philadelphia, and Baltimore, the charity schools literally became the public schools, initially expanding to take in non-indigent children, and eventually gaining a monopoly on public funding in the cities.[15] In the

[10] Leo Pfeffer. 1953. *Church, State, and Freedom.* Boston: Beacon Press, pp. 121, 282.

[11] Kaestle, *Pillars of the Republic*, p. 17.

[12] The South resisted the common school movement for a number of reasons, including a greater unwillingness to assess taxes for education, but also, prominently, because the common school was seen as a Northern institution—and it was therefore opposed for this reason. State schooling was ultimately imposed upon the South during Reconstruction. See Kaestle, *Pillars of the Republic*, pp. 192–216.

[13] Timothy L. Smith. 1970. "Parochial Education and American Culture." Pp. 192–211 in *History and Education: The Educational Uses of the Past*, edited by Paul Nash. New York: Random House, pp. 194–95.

[14] Quoted in Tracy Fessenden. 2005. "The Nineteenth-Century Bible Wars and the Separation of Church and State." *Church History* 74(4): 784–811, p. 788.

[15] Kaestle, *Pillars of the Republic*, pp. 52, 57–59. See also David L. Angus. 1990. "The Origins of Urban Schools in Comparative Perspective." Pp. 59–78 in *Southern Cities, Southern Schools: Public Education in the Urban South*, edited by David N. Plank and Rick Ginsberg. Westport, CT: Greenwood Press, p. 66.

Mid-Atlantic states, many other denominational schools – the Protestant ones, at least – were simply absorbed into the evolving common school system.[16]

However, the common school movement had its greatest success in the Midwest. The movement to build common schools coincided with the settlement of the Midwest, to the advantage of educational reformers. Because there were fewer private, parochial, or subscription schools on the frontier, common school advocates typically faced an open field with little opposition from vested interests.[17] These features allowed the common school to achieve explosive growth, and by 1870 the Midwest had become the most heavily schooled section of the country.[18]

In both the Midwest and the Northeast, district schools became free and publicly controlled in the decades before the Civil War. Most northern states abolished tuition fees in the 1850s and 1860s, and passed laws permitting local taxation for educational purposes. These moves, in turn, greatly increased the appeal of the new public schools, eventually crowding out all but the elite private schools (and the Catholic schools, as discussed below).[19] In Illinois, for example, fully two-thirds of private schools closed their doors or converted to public schools in the two years following the passage of a law making public schools free in 1855.[20] The emergence of state education also coincided with a dramatic sharpening of the line between private and public education – a line that had frequently been blurry in the early nineteenth century – and to the restriction of public financing to schools under public auspices.[21] As the common school spread, this distinction was increasingly embodied in legislation, and ultimately constitutional provisions, that more clearly regulated the form and content of education under public control.[22]

Thus, by 1880, most Protestant denominational schools had closed their doors or been converted to public schools, private education had been largely squeezed out of the market by free public education, and a system of state schooling had risen to dominance across the United States. The only major countervailing trend to this pattern was the expansion of Catholic denominational schooling, which began to grow in earnest starting in the 1840s. As I discuss below, Catholics perceived the emerging state system to be fundamentally

---

[16] Gabel, *Public Funds*, pp. 375–76, 381, 500.

[17] Robert G. Bone. 1957. "Education in Illinois before 1857." *Journal of the Illinois State Historical Society* 50: 119–40, p. 128.

[18] David Tyack and Elizabeth Hansot. 1982. *Managers of Virtue: Public School Leadership in America, 1820–1980.* New York: Basic Books, p. 32.

[19] Kaestle, *Pillars of the Republic*, p. 117.

[20] Daniel W. Kucera. 1955. *Church–State Relationships in Education in Illinois.* Washington DC: Catholic University of America Press, pp. 77–78.

[21] See generally Lloyd P. Jorgenson. 1987. *The State and the Non-Public School, 1825–1925.* Columbia: University of Missouri Press.

[22] David Tyack, Thomas James, and Aaron Benavot. 1987. *Law and the Shaping of Public Education, 1785–1954.* Madison: University of Wisconsin Press, pp. 22, 55–57.

Protestant and hostile to their interests, and set about constructing a network of parochial schools that would permit them to protect their parishioners.

Evangelical Protestantism and State-Building from the Bottom Up

State-building in the United States was a bottom-up project, advanced and organized by a "grass-roots movement" of local communities and voluntary associations.[23] To a great extent, the impetus for the formation of new schools came not from state officials, but instead from civil society – especially the clergy and voluntary associations of America's evangelical Protestant community. In the main, therefore, the common school developed with the explicit blessing of America's dominant religious actors; and it likewise bore the unmistakable imprint of its evangelical champions, featuring a curriculum saturated with Protestant morality, punctuated by devotional Bible reading, and laced with anti-Catholic rhetoric.

Local Initiative and the Rise of the Common School

Local initiative was essential to the emergence and spread of the American common school. Thanks to the weak supervisory powers and inconsistent support that legislation granted state officers, formal state legislation typically meant less than local action to the creation of schools in the mid-nineteenth century.[24] Thus, the development of common schools in the United States was preeminently a local phenomenon, created through a groundswell of support in thousands of towns and neighborhoods across the country.

In part because local action was so important to its founding, American education adopted a radically decentralized administrative structure – the "district system." Under the district system, local neighborhoods created their own schools and incorporated them as separate school districts. In Pennsylvania, for instance, the typical pattern was for a group of neighbors to form a committee or board of trustees who would be entrusted with the creation of a local neighborhood school. The trustees would select a site for the school, erect a schoolhouse, fix tuition, employ a teacher, and otherwise manage the school. Trustees would then be elected at annual meetings of those who patronized the school.[25] The local practice of creating school districts usually preceded the formal recognition of districts in law,[26] but the formal attribution of taxing and supervisory powers to local districts affirmed and encouraged the district pattern.[27]

---

[23] Butts and Cremin, *History of Education*, p. 253.
[24] Lawrence A. Cremin. 1980. *American Education: The National Experience, 1783–1876.* New York: Harper & Row, pp. 171–74.
[25] Wickersham, *History of Education in Pennsylvania*, p. 181.
[26] Kaestle, *Pillars of the Republic*, pp. 13, 26–27.
[27] Bone, "Education in Illinois," pp. 120–21, 125, 131; Benjamin Justice. 2005. *The War That Wasn't: Religious Conflict and Compromise in the Common Schools of New York State, 1865–1900.* Albany: State University of New York Press, p. 29.

The district system proved incredibly popular, and it was quickly extended to the new states of the West as the frontier expanded.[28] Localized control came later to the cities, often in the form of ward schools, as occurred in New York City after the charity schools were fully incorporated into the state system in the 1840s.[29] Under the ward system, neighborhood ward school boards held the authority to levy taxes, hire teachers, and build schools just like rural district schools. Whether urban or rural, local districts were given nearly complete control over curriculum, staffing, and finance.[30]

Building with God: Evangelical Clergy and the Common School Crusade

Religious actors played a crucial role in the common school movement. While the movement attracted men and women from diverse religious and political backgrounds, including many liberal Christians such as the Unitarian Horace Mann in Massachusetts, evangelical Protestants were by far the movement's most important participants.[31] Evangelical Protestantism enjoyed a remarkable efflorescence in the United States at the beginning of the nineteenth century, in a period generally referred to as the Second Great Awakening. Between about 1800 and 1850, American religiosity grew and diversified, expanding in both the settled states of the East and in the new states of the Western frontier.[32] Out of this great religious awakening emerged a new, assertive form of evangelical Protestantism, whose theology synthesized diverse strands of Protestantism as they had developed on the frontier.[33] This new evangelical theology was pragmatic and interdenominational, where "the goal was not right faith, but unity in a common task, becoming co-workers in building the kingdom of God."[34]

Thanks to the Second Great Awakening, as educational historian David Tyack has written, "Almost everywhere, Protestant ministers and prominent churchmen were in the forefront of the common school crusade and took a proprietary interest in the institutions they helped to build."[35] Indeed, they

[28] Kaestle, *Pillars of the Republic*, pp. 24–25, 111–12.

[29] Joan DelFattore. 2004. *The Fourth R: Conflicts over Religion in America's Public Schools*. New Haven: Yale University Press, p. 29.

[30] Tracy L. Steffes. 2012. *School, Society, and State: A New Education to Govern Modern America, 1890–1940*. Chicago: University of Chicago Press, pp. 26, 49–50.

[31] James W. Fraser. 1985. *Pedagogue for God's Kingdom: Lyman Beecher and the Second Great Awakening*. Lanham, MD: University Press of America, pp. 185–86.

[32] Roger Finke and Rodney Stark. 2005 [1992]. *The Churching of America, 1776–2005: Winners and Losers in Our Religious Economy*. 2nd edn. New Brunswick, NJ: Rutgers University Press, pp. 22–23, 55–60.

[33] Sydney E. Ahlstrom. 2004 [1972]. *A Religious History of the American People*. 2nd edn. New Haven: Yale University Press, p. 470.

[34] Fraser, *Pedagogue for God's Kingdom*, p. 28.

[35] David B. Tyack. 1970. "Onward Christian Soldiers: Religion in the American Common School." Pp. 212–55 in *History and Education: The Educational Uses of the Past*, edited by Paul Nash. New York: Random House, p. 217.

styled their activity a "crusade" and used nondenominational voluntary societies as central vehicles for their work.[36] Evangelical reformers saw common schools as the centerpiece of a larger program of building the kingdom of God, which they hoped would usher in the Millennium and the second coming of Jesus Christ. Appeals on behalf of the common schools were thus influential in part because of their "consistency with themes and visions for the future that were already very much in the air in religious circles."[37]

Evangelicals contributed to the common school crusade in two primary ways. First, many evangelicals were prominent leaders of and advocates for the common schools. Lyman Beecher, Congregationalist minister and President of Lane Theological Seminary in Cincinnati, was among the earliest and most vocal advocates of common schooling. In his influential 1835 address, *A Plea for the West*, Beecher declared,

The thing required for the civil and religious prosperity of the West, is universal education, and moral culture, by institutions commensurate to that result – the all pervading influence of schools, and colleges, and seminaries, and pastors, and churches. When the West is well supplied in this respect, though there may be great relative defects, there will be ... the stamina and vitality of a perpetual civil and religious prosperity.[38]

Although Beecher mainly exhorted his fellow Protestants to build up universal education, others took a more direct role in leading the crusade. Many of the first state superintendents, both in the East and on the frontier, were clergymen, as were countless other principals, superintendents, administrators, and educational officials.[39]

Second, evangelical Protestants were responsible for constructing and staffing many of the new common schools on the frontier. Protestant voluntary associations, including the American Home Missionary Society (AHMS) and the National Board of Popular Education (NBPE), were largely responsible for peopling the frontier with capable teachers. Ministers sent out by the AHMS in the late 1820s settled in as frontier schoolmasters after seeing the neglected state of education along the frontier.[40] Later, groups like the NBPE recruited and trained scores of Christian women in the East and sent them to the western states to open schools.[41] Ministers and their wives were essential to the spread

---

[36] Cremin, *American Education: The National Experience*, p. 176; Kaestle, *Pillars of the Republic*, p. 105.

[37] Charles L. Glenn. 2012. *The American Model of State and School: An Historical Inquiry*. New York: Continuum International Publishing Group, p. 2.

[38] Lyman Beecher. 1835. *A Plea for the West*. Cincinnati: Truman & Smith, pp. 9–10, 13.

[39] Gabel, *Public Funds*, pp. 280–81, 419 n.69; Lloyd P. Jorgenson. 1956. *The Founding of Public Education in Wisconsin*. Madison: State Historical Society of Wisconsin, pp. 122–24; Jorgenson, *State and the Non-Public School*, pp. 36–54.

[40] Timothy L. Smith. 1967. "Protestant Schooling and American Nationality, 1800–1850." *Journal of American History* 53(4): 679–95, p. 690.

[41] James W. Fraser. 1999. *Between Church and State: Religion and Public Education in a Multicultural America*. New York: St. Martin's Press, pp. 37–38.

of public education in the western states in the 1830s and 1840s, since public tax laws did not go into effect until around midcentury, and clergy and their families were among the few willing to accept the low salaries and hardship conditions associated with frontier schools.[42] Through these efforts, evangelical Protestants literally helped to build the American common school system.

Protestantism and the Common School Curriculum

As a result of the close links between evangelical Protestantism and the common school movement, Protestant ideas and values deeply permeated the common school curriculum. Under the leadership of evangelical Protestants, a "vast spiritualizing of the educational institutions" took place.[43] Common school advocates advanced what historian Carl Kaestle has termed a "Native Protestant ideology," a mix of republican and evangelical Protestant values that sustained a desire to assimilate and integrate a diverse population into a common political culture.[44] This ideology assumed a close and mutually sustaining fit between republican government and Protestant Christianity, and Protestant leaders believed that this essential fit needed to be aggressively buttressed through the new common schools.[45] Protestant educational leaders, therefore, all agreed that religious and moral training should be an essential aspect of the common school curriculum.

At the same time, there was less agreement on how to integrate religious instruction into schools that were growing more religiously diverse by the day. The solution that eventually emerged was "nonsectarian" religious education based on Bible reading.[46] Nonsectarian religious education's most forceful advocate was Horace Mann, the first Superintendent of Schools in Massachusetts. Mann was charged with interpreting Massachusetts' 1827 law forbidding the use of books "calculated to favor any particular religious sect or tenet." He did so by refusing to permit any books into the schools that were "sectarian," which he defined as containing any theological point "which

[42] Smith, "Protestant Schooling and American Nationality," p. 692.

[43] Cremin, *American Education: The National Experience*, p. 63.

[44] Kaestle, *Pillars of the Republic*, pp. ix–x, 76; see also Mark Noll. 2002. *America's God: From Jonathan Edwards to Abraham Lincoln.* New York: Oxford University Press. Proponents actively sought to use the schools to mold Americans of many religious and ethnic backgrounds into one people. It was taken for granted that Protestantism was a key feature of American culture into which immigrants were to be assimilated, and that Protestant moral and religious instruction was an appropriate means of doing so.

[45] Robert T. Handy. 1984 [1971]. *A Christian America: Protestant Hopes and Historical Realities.* 2nd edn. New York: Oxford University Press, p. 27; Smith, "Protestant Schooling and American Nationality," p. 680.

[46] Although, as I discuss below, "nonsectarianism" eventually became a cudgel to be used against Catholics, in the 1820s and 1830s it developed primarily as an inclusive solution to divisions among Protestant churches. See Noah Feldman. 2002. "Non-sectarianism Reconsidered." *Journal of Law and Politics* 18(1): 65–117, pp. 67, 78.

belongs to a *part*, not to the *whole*."[47] Instead, Mann argued, schools should provide religious education built around the reading of the Bible. By allowing the Bible to *"speak for itself,"* without comment, he thought schools could teach a common religion – i.e., "all the doctrines which the Bible really contains," without any of the "many inventions" that the denominations used to "overlay the text." By making the Bible the centerpiece of religious education, Mann argued that the schools could provide "a religious education for the young upon the most broad and general grounds, purposely leaving it to every individual to add for himself those auxiliary arguments which may result from his own peculiar views of religious truth" through supplementary learning in church, Sunday school, and family.[48]

Mann's faith in the unifying power of Bible reading reflected his somewhat distinctive Unitarian views,[49] but his "nonsectarian" solution had much in common with the emerging religious instruction program evangelicals were developing on the frontier. Theologically, the Second Great Awakening weakened the power of doctrinal distinctions and encouraged interdenominational cooperation among Protestants. Charles Grandison Finney, perhaps the greatest revivalist of the era, advised his converts not "to dwell on sectarian distinctions, or to be sticklish about sectarian points" – a directive that many carried into the classroom.[50] Practically speaking, pioneering educators on the frontier also had to teach a broad, nonsectarian religion, in regions where the population was typically small and denominational diversity relatively wide. Because minister-educators on the frontier were responsible for growing their own schools just as they were responsible for building their own congregations, they typically developed nondenominational practices that would appeal to all Protestant families in the area.[51]

By the 1840s, therefore, something of a consensus had developed among evangelical and liberal Protestants alike, that Bible reading should be the central, "nonsectarian" pillar of religious education in the common school.[52] The theologian Horace Bushnell argued in 1839 that "Nothing is more certain than that no such thing as a sectarian religion is to find a place in our schools. It

---

[47] Horace Mann. Letter to the Editor of the *Witness and Advocate*, 30 March 1844. Pp. 18–21 in Horace Mann and Edward A. Newton. 1844. *The Common School Controversy*. Boston: J.N. Bradley & Co, p. 20.

[48] Horace Mann. 1891 [1848]. "Report for 1848." Pp. 222–340 in *Life and Works of Horace Mann*. Vol. 4, *Annual Reports of the Secretary of the Board of Education of Massachusetts for the Years 1845–1848*. Boston: Lee and Shepard Publishers, pp. 312, 335, 296–97.

[49] Robert Michaelsen. 1970. *Piety in the Public School: Trends and Issues in the Relationship between Religion and the Public School in the United States*. New York: Macmillan, p. 69.

[50] Charles G. Finney. 1868 [1835]. *Lectures on Revivals of Religion*. Rev. edn. Oberlin, OH: E.J. Goodrich, p. 381.

[51] David Tyack. 1966. "The Kingdom of God and the Common School." *Harvard Educational Review* 36: 447–69, pp. 454–55, 463.

[52] Michaelsen, *Piety in the Public School*, pp. 78–79.

must be enough to find a place for the Bible as a book ... containing the true standards of character and the best motives and aids to virtue."[53] Calvin Stowe, son-in-law of Lyman Beecher and common school advocate, declared in 1844 that "The Bible, the whole Bible, and nothing but the Bible, without note or comment, must be taken as the text-book of religious instruction. Instruction in those points which divide the sects from each other must be confined to the family and the Sunday school."[54] Likewise, Rev. Samuel Lewis, the first Superintendent of Schools in Ohio, agreed that "the utmost care should be taken to inculcate sound principles of Christian morality. No creed or catechism of any sect should be introduced into our schools; there is a broad, common ground, where all Christians and lovers of virtue meet."[55] By the mid-nineteenth century, Bible reading had become the central, if not universal, religious practice in American public schools, especially in the Northeast and, later, the South.[56]

In addition to Bible reading, the typical nineteenth-century common school student read from books steeped in Protestant religion and morality. The most popular books, by far, were the McGuffey Readers, which "read more like a theology text than a schoolbook," featured multiple references to God, and were sprinkled liberally throughout with Biblical material.[57] The McGuffey Readers, and other schoolbooks like them, also aggressively and unmistakably advanced an evangelical Protestant worldview. Students in the typical nineteenth-century classroom read from providential histories, theistic science books, and nationalistic geography texts that sang the praises of Protestant countries while casting aspersions on Catholic ones.[58] Indeed, in her study of nineteenth-century textbooks, Ruth Miller Elson observed, "No theme in these schoolbooks before 1870 is more universal than anti-Catholicism."[59] Thus, the curriculum of the nineteenth-century common school was steeped

---

[53] Horace Bushnell. 1839. "Christianity and Common Schools." *Connecticut Common School Journal* 2: 102–03, p. 102.

[54] Calvin Ellis Stowe. 1844. *The Religious Element in Education*. Boston: William D. Ticknor & Co., p. 25.

[55] Quoted in William G.W. Lewis. 1857. *Biography of Samuel Lewis, First Superintendent of Common Schools for the State of Ohio*. Cincinnati: E.P. Thompson, p. 132.

[56] R. Laurence Moore. 2000. "Bible Reading and Nonsectarian Schooling: The Failure of Religious Instruction in Nineteenth-Century Public Education." *Journal of American History* 86(4): 1581–99, pp. 1582–83, 1586. As Moore notes, Bible reading never became as firmly established in the West.

[57] Warren A. Nord. 1995. *Religion and American Education: Rethinking a National Dilemma*. Chapel Hill: University of North Carolina Press, p. 67. Over 120 million copies of the Readers were sold between 1836 and 1920.

[58] William J. Reese. 2007. *History, Education, and the Schools*. New York: Palgrave Macmillan, pp. 84–88.

[59] Ruth Miller Elson. 1964. *Guardians of Tradition: American Schoolbooks of the Nineteenth Century*. Lincoln: University of Nebraska Press, p. 53.

in evangelical Protestantism above and beyond the regular devotional reading of the Bible.

Religious Conflict, "Nonsectarianism," and the Consolidation of Public Finance

Despite the strong synergies between state-building and religious activism, the development of common schools was shot through with religious conflict. These conflicts inflected the state-building process, shaping the contours of the emerging secular settlement. As the common school system grew, first the various Protestant denominations, and then – more consequentially – Protestants and Catholics, strenuously disagreed on the appropriate religious content of the common school curriculum. The resulting conflicts sharpened the public–private divide in education, encouraging stark prohibitions on "public aid" to religious schools.

"Nonsectarianism" and the Common School

Although common school advocates broadly agreed that the common schools should be "nonsectarian," there was substantial controversy over how that term should be defined. Early on, many of these battles took place between liberal and evangelical Protestants. The nonsectarian education advocated by the Unitarian Horace Mann, for instance, was roundly criticized by more conservative Protestants as being essentially irreligious. In 1838, Mann was publicly attacked by Frederick Packard, Secretary of the American Sunday School Union, for refusing to include several of the Union's preferred reading books in Massachusetts school libraries. Packard believed that the books, which had been approved by a multidenominational committee of Protestant clergy, were sufficiently nonsectarian to pass muster under that state's 1827 law. Mann, however, disagreed, arguing that the books were "sectarian" because their references to a judgment day and the possibility of eternal damnation, among others, offended the beliefs of Unitarians and Universalists.[60] To Packard, this definition essentially made the schools irreligious; in a letter to Mann, he acidly inquired, "What 'doctrines of revealed religion' will remain, to be connected with a system of public instruction, after subtracting those about which there are conflicting creeds among men?"[61] Despite receiving similar criticism from orthodox Congregationalists and Episcopalians, Mann remained steadfast in his position that only the reading of the Bible without note or comment could be truly "nonsectarian."[62]

---

[60] Raymond B. Culver. 1929. *Horace Mann and Religion in the Massachusetts Public Schools.* New Haven: Yale University Press, pp. 71–80.

[61] Letter, Frederick J. Packard to Horace Mann, 19 September 1838. Reprinted as pp. 270–84 in Culver, *Horace Mann and Religion*, p. 278.

[62] Charles Leslie Glenn, Jr. 1988. *The Myth of the Common School.* Amherst: University of Massachusetts Press, pp. 180–96.

The controversies in Massachusetts were portentous. As the term "nonsectarian" grew more firmly associated with the common school ideal, common school advocates began to deploy charges of "sectarianism" to marginalize their opponents and solidify their position in the educational domain. One of the earliest instances of this took place in New York City in the early 1820s. For several years, the Free School Society of New York had received an annual grant from the state to provide nondenominational education to poor children. In 1820, however, the Bethel Baptist Church requested a similar subsidy to enable it to expand its own charity school system. Concerned that the Bethel schools might siphon off subsidies and enrolments, the Society petitioned the legislature to end grants to the Baptists, contrasting the "careful preclusion of all sectarian principles" in their schools with the inherent sectarianism of the Bethel schools.[63] Society spokesmen argued that allowing clergy to control public money would lead inexorably to the collapse of common schools in favor of a denominational system. Accordingly, they pleaded that the state must "save untouched the sacred principle of our constitution, that church and state shall not be united."[64] In 1824, the New York City Common Council ruled in favor of the Free School Society, declaring that henceforth no public funds would flow to denominational schools.

The Free School Society's victory would not be the last time a monopoly on public aid was secured by using "sectarianism" as a weapon. Increasingly, religion became a key attribute in determining which schools would be eligible to receive public money, and which would be excluded. Traditionally, the distinction between public and private education had been very fluid, with many private, denominational, and even Sunday schools receiving government funding.[65] As historian Lloyd Jorgenson has written, however, "By the mid-nineteenth century it had become important to differentiate between 'public' and 'non-public' schools because the former were increasingly considered the only legitimate recipients of public financial support."[66] While private, nondenominational schools were similarly excluded from the public purse, the most vitriolic battles took place over funding for religious schools, and in these battles the degree to which religious schools were "sectarian," and the public schools "nonsectarian," became a key point of contention that helped to define the nascent public/private divide. Already by the 1830s, denominational

---

[63] Quoted in Smith, "Protestant Schooling and American Nationality," pp. 685–86.

[64] Quoted in John Webb Pratt. 1967. *Religion, Politics, and Diversity: The Church–State Theme in New York History*. Ithaca, NY: Cornell University Press, p. 167.

[65] See generally Gabel, *Public Funds*.

[66] Jorgenson, *State and the Non-Public School*, p. 7. As legal historian Steven Green notes, this legitimacy in part derived from the belief that public agencies would be more financially accountable than private bodies, and thus more likely to maximize the financial stability of the new schools. These practical motives existed alongside the religious objections discussed below. See Steven K. Green. 2012. *The Bible, the School, and the Constitution: The Clash that Shaped Modern Church–State Doctrine*. New York: Oxford University Press, pp. 45–46.

schools were beginning to be defined as fundamentally alien to the common school project – as the New York City Common Council's law committee concluded in 1831, "if religion be taught in a school, it strips it of one of the characteristics of a common school."[67] Within two decades, the requirement that common schools be "nonsectarian" had begun to be enshrined in law. In an 1851 decision, the New York Supreme Court ruled that "the state ought not, and cannot constitutionally, contribute to" education "of a partial or sectarian character."[68] "Sectarianism," in other words, was increasingly coming to define the rapidly solidifying boundary between public and private education.

"Nonsectarianism" Challenged: Catholics and the Protestant Matrix

Part of the reason that these battles were so fierce was that, after 1840, the notion of "sectarianism" became increasingly intertwined with anti-Catholicism. The arrival of massive numbers of Irish immigrants in the 1830s and 1840s created a substantial Catholic population in the United States for the first time,[69] and the controversies between Catholics and Protestants that had haunted Europe since the Reformation came along with them. Faced with a new, common enemy, Protestants set aside their differences and united behind "nonsectarian" education.[70] Although Protestants found the "nonsectarian" education developing in the emerging common schools to be inoffensive (if imperfect), Catholics found the common school curriculum to be objectionably Protestant and, in fact, "sectarian."

Catholic objections to "nonsectarian" Bible reading were multiple. The Bible typically used was the King James Version (KJV), a Protestant version that Catholics contended represented an inaccurate and incomplete translation "made under sectarian bias."[71] On a deeper level, Catholics also objected to the very idea that children could be allowed to read the Bible "without note or comment" as common school advocates recommended. For Catholics, the idea that students could be allowed to let the Bible "speak for itself" and develop their own interpretation was an inescapably Protestant idea. "The Catholic Church tells her children that they must be taught their religion by AUTHORITY," wrote John Power, a Catholic Vicar-General in New York City, in 1840. "The sects say, Read the Bible, judge for yourselves. The Bible is read

---

[67] Quoted in Green, *Bible, the School, and the Constitution*, p. 51.

[68] *People ex rel. Roman Catholic Orphan Asylum* v. *Board of Education*, 13 Barb. 400 (N.Y. Sup. 1851), p. 411.

[69] Jay P. Dolan. 1985. *The American Catholic Experience: A History from Colonial Times to the Present*. Garden City, NY: Doubleday & Company, pp. 128–29.

[70] Steven K. Green. 2010. *The Second Disestablishment: Church and State in Nineteenth-Century America*. New York: Oxford University Press, p. 265.

[71] "The Pastoral Letter of 1843." 1923 [1843]. Pp. 150–61 in *The National Pastorals of the American Hierarchy (1792–1919)*, edited by Peter Guilday. Washington, DC: National Catholic Welfare Council, p. 152.

in the public schools, the children are allowed to judge for themselves. The Protestant principle is therefore acted upon, silently inculcated, and the schools are Sectarian."[72]

Accordingly, the Catholic hierarchy took a hard line against religious exercises in the public school. In 1840, the Catholic bishops directed pastors to prevent Catholic children from participating in any Protestant school devotionals, and urged them to lobby authorities to eliminate the offensive practices.[73] Three years later, the bishops again decried "efforts made to poison the fountain of public education, by giving it a sectarian hue," and instructed parents to "see that no interference with the faith of their children be used in public schools, and no attempt made to induce conformity in any thing contrary to the laws of the Catholic Church."[74]

As their numbers grew, Catholics spoke out ever more forcefully against the "nonsectarian" religion in the common schools. One of the first, and most consequential, such conflicts took place in New York City in 1840.[75] In that year, Catholic Bishop John Hughes petitioned the Common Council for a share of the school fund, arguing that the teaching in the public schools was sectarian and biased against Catholics, and that only a denominational system could protect the interests of Catholic children. The petition stirred up strong opposition both from the Public School Society (PSS) and from local Protestant clergy. After months of contentious arguing, the Common Council ultimately rejected the petition, justifying its position by stating that the PSS schools were nonsectarian, while the Catholic schools were sectarian. Although the PSS offered to black out much of the anti-Catholic material from its textbooks, it insisted that the Bible should continue to be read. Not satisfied, Catholics continued to protest until 1842, when the New York State legislature stepped in, passing a law declaring that "No school ... in which any religious, sectarian doctrine or tenet shall be taught, inculcated, or practiced, shall receive any portion of the school moneys to be distributed by this act."[76] In so doing, they definitively placed the Catholic schools outside the purview of the public purse.

Catholic protests ultimately failed to dislodge the strong belief among common school advocates that the pan-Protestant common school curriculum was "nonsectarian." In 1844, the New York state legislature passed an additional

[72] John Power. 1974 [1840]. "Rev. John Power, Vicar-General of the Diocese of New York, on the 'Sectarian' Schools of the Public School Society (1840)." Pp. 1137–39 in *Education in the United States: A Documentary History*, edited by Sol Cohen. New York: Random House, p. 1138.

[73] William Kailer Dunn. 1958. *What Happened to Religious Education? The Decline of Religious Teaching in the Public Elementary School, 1776–1861*. Baltimore: The Johns Hopkins Press, p. 211.

[74] "Pastoral Letter of 1843," pp. 152–53.

[75] DelFattore, *Fourth R*, pp. 22–29.

[76] Quoted in Donald E. Boles. 1963. *The Bible, Religion, and the Public Schools*. Ames: Iowa State University Press, p. 29.

act clarifying that the legislation banning the teaching of sectarian doctrine was not to be interpreted by the Board of Education to "exclude the Holy Scriptures without note or comment" from the New York schools, a move that excluded the annotated Catholic Douay–Rheims version of the Bible, but not the Protestant KJV.[77] Elsewhere, too, Protestants argued that the pan-Protestant "nonsectarian" curriculum was sacrosanct. In Detroit, Baptists and Methodists not only convinced the school board that reading of the KJV should be permitted in the schools, but also argued that *not* doing so would be a "sectarian" violation of the rights of Protestants.[78] Even the moralistic, strongly Protestant McGuffey readers were praised by advocates as "excellent for educational purposes" because "their religion is unsectarian, true religion – their morality, the morality of the Gospel."[79]

What Catholic protests did succeed in doing, however, was to feed a growing nativist campaign that viewed Catholic immigrants and their schools as threats to the American republic. Some evangelical leaders already entertained nativist sympathies; indeed, much of the evangelical motivation to build schools in the West was generated by fears of the "multitudes of foreign papists [who] are every year pouring in upon our shores, bringing with them all the passions and prejudices of a foreign education."[80] Lyman Beecher's *Plea for the West* included the apocalyptic declaration that "The conflict which is to decide the destiny of the West will be a conflict of institutions for the education of her sons, for purposes of superstition, or evangelical light; of despotism, or liberty."[81] Nativist societies in the early nineteenth century were already making the case that Catholics were enemies of the Bible. After the events in New York City, this argument was amplified and applied to the schools, as propagandists relentlessly argued that "the school controversy clearly demonstrated Rome's enmity to the Scriptures."[82] Protestant defense of the Bible ratcheted up; in short order, a request by Philadelphia Catholics for exemption from reading the KJV led to riots in that city, while in Maine and Massachusetts, Catholic students who refused to read from the KJV were beaten or expelled.[83]

---

[77] Quoted in DelFattore, *Fourth R*, p. 31.

[78] David L. Angus. 1980. "Detroit's Great School Wars: Religion and Politics in a Frontier City, 1842–1853." *Michigan Academician* 12(3): 261–80, pp. 263–65.

[79] Lyman Beecher, quoted in Fraser, *Pedagogue for God's Kingdom*, p. 190.

[80] W.W. Turner. 1835. "Report of the Connecticut Branch." *American Quarterly Register* 8(1): 93–95, p. 94. Indeed, many of the most active school-building organizations, including the American Education Society and the Western Baptist Educational Association, were motivated by the desire to counter "Romanism" in the West. See also Kucera, *Church–State Relationships in Education in Illinois*, p. 46.

[81] Beecher, *Plea for the West*, p. 12.

[82] Ray Allen Billington. 1963 [1938]. *The Protestant Crusade, 1800–1860: A Study of the Origins of American Nativism*. Gloucester, MA: Peter Smith, pp. 142–43, 157.

[83] Green, *Second Disestablishment*, pp. 266–75.

Catholic Parochial Schools, Nativism, and the Solidification of the Public–Private Divide

Catholics took note of the hardening Protestant line on the public schools, and responded by doubling down on the construction of their own parochial schools. In 1850, Bishop Hughes declared that, in light of the hostile climate of the public schools, "the time has almost come when it will be necessary to build the school-house first, and the Church afterward."[84] Shortly thereafter, he further counseled Catholic parents to withdraw their children from public schools, "where they are certain to learn evil, and probably very little but evil."[85] When the Catholic hierarchy met at the First Plenary Council of Baltimore in 1852, they exhorted their flock to "see that schools be established in connection with all the churches of their diocese; and ... to provide, from the revenues of the church to which the school is attached, for the support of competent teachers."[86] In response, Catholics around the country inaugurated a campaign to build new schools and, fatefully, to seek funding for them. These requests produced another nativist backlash and a rash of laws prohibiting public aid in the decades before and after the Civil War.

During the 1850s, states began to move decisively to limit public expenditures on private and religious schooling. In the West, a robust tradition of aid to private schools never fully developed, and many states constitutionally prohibited public aid quite independently of any nativist agitation.[87] Elsewhere, however, strong new restrictions were enacted through campaigns dominated or strongly influenced by the nativist Know-Nothing Party, whose fortunes surged in the mid-1850s thanks to anti-Catholic hysteria. Proudly wearing their anti-Catholicism on their sleeves, nativist campaigners succeeded in prohibiting public aid in California, Illinois, and Massachusetts, and defeating bills in Michigan and Minnesota that would have permitted some forms of public aid.[88] A second wave of Catholic petitions in the 1870s further cemented the hard line against public aid to religious schools. In 1869, Boss Tweed, head of New York City's Democratic political machine, convinced the state legislature to surreptitiously provide funds for Catholic schools. When Tweed's maneuver was discovered, Protestants around the nation recoiled at what they perceived to be an attack on the public schools. In short order, over a dozen

---

[84] Quoted in John R.G. Hassard. 1866. *The Life of the Most Reverend John Hughes, D.D., First Archbishop of New York*. New York: D. Appleton & Company, p. 338.

[85] Quoted in Jorgenson, *State and the Non-Public School*, p. 85.

[86] Quoted in Francis P. Cassidy. 1949. "Catholic Education in the Third Plenary Council of Baltimore. [Part] II." *Catholic Historical Review* 34(4): 414–36, p. 431. For similar sentiments directed at the laity, see "The Pastoral Letter of 1852." 1923 [1852]. Pp. 181–96 in *The National Pastorals of the American Hierarchy (1792–1919)*, edited by Peter Guilday. Washington, DC: National Catholic Welfare Council, p. 191.

[87] Gabel, *Public Funds*, pp. 455–70; Green, *Second Disestablishment*, pp. 269–70.

[88] Jorgenson, *State and the Non-Public School*, pp. 87–90, 100–06.

states passed constitutional amendments banning or strengthening their bans on public funding for parochial schools.[89]

This strong response helped raise the issue of public aid to the national level for the first time. Leaders in the Republican Party saw anti-Catholicism as a winning issue that could salvage its flagging electoral prospects.[90] Accordingly, in 1875, President Grant gave a speech in which he urged Americans to "Encourage free schools, and resolve that not one dollar, appropriated for their support, shall be appropriated to the support of any sectarian schools."[91] Following Grant's lead, congressional Republicans, led by Maine Representative James Blaine, proposed an amendment to the Constitution that read, in part:

No public property and no public revenue, nor any loan of credit by or under the authority of the United States, or any State, Territory, District, or municipal corporation, shall be appropriated to or made or used for the support of any school, educational or other institution under the control of any religious or anti-religious sect, organization, or denomination, or wherein the particular creed or tenets of any organization, or denomination shall be taught.[92]

After spirited debate, the Blaine Amendment passed both houses, but narrowly fell short of the margin required to be approved.[93] Undeterred, Congress began to require future states to include similar constitutional provisions prohibiting public aid as a condition for statehood, and multiple other states enacted similar laws in the ensuing twenty years.[94]

In the process, prohibitions on public aid came to be understood as an essential part of the longstanding American ideal of "separation of church and state." Famously articulated by Roger Williams and, later, Thomas Jefferson, separation was a familiar, foundational principle of American public life, associated with many early constitutional protections of religion. As the nineteenth-century settlement in education solidified, its Protestant champions celebrated it as the proper realization of "separation," one which prohibited public aid to religious schools but allowed room for the practice of religion

---

[89] Fraser, *Between Church and State*, p. 112; Jorgenson, *State and the Non-Public School*, pp. 113–14. Not all of these amendments were advanced for purely nativist reasons; the Missouri amendment, for instance, was passed with little evidence of nativist rancor. See Aaron E. Schwartz. 2007. "Dusting off the Blaine Amendment: Two Challenges to Missouri's Anti-Establishment Tradition." *Missouri Law Review* 72: 339–86, pp. 369–76.

[90] Ward M. McAfee. 1998. *Religion, Race, and Reconstruction: The Public School in the Politics of the 1870s.* Albany: State University of New York Press, pp. 6–7.

[91] Quoted in Steven K. Green. 1992. "The Blaine Amendment Reconsidered." *American Journal of Legal History* 36: 38–69, p. 47.

[92] Quoted in Green, "Blaine Amendment Reconsidered," p. 60.

[93] Green, "Blaine Amendment Reconsidered," pp. 57–68.

[94] Noah Feldman. 2005. *Divided by God: America's Church-State Problem—and What We Should Do about It.* New York: Farrar, Straus, & Giroux, p. 86; Ursula Hackett. 2014. "Republicans, Catholics, and the West: Explaining the Strength of Religious School Aid Prohibitions." *Politics and Religion* 7: 499–520, p. 507.

in the public schools. This understanding would become the dominant understanding of separation until the mid-twentieth century.[95]

Meanwhile, as their prospects for public aid dimmed, Catholics moved decisively to expand their parochial school system and finance it independently from the state. As early as 1858, bishops in the Midwest decreed that pastors under their jurisdiction were "bound, under pain of mortal sin, to provide a Catholic school."[96] A quarter-century later, this position received the official backing of the American hierarchy. At the Third Plenary Council in 1884, the Catholic bishops decreed that Catholic schools must be established within two years near each church. Pastors who failed to do so faced removal, and parishes who failed to support these efforts faced the threat of sanctions.[97] Parents, meanwhile, were "command[ed] … with all the authority in our power" to "send [their children] to parochial schools or others truly Catholic" unless given an express exemption by a diocesan official.[98] These orders were enforced through both informal and formal sanctions. The Catholic press accused Catholic parents who failed to send their children to Catholic schools of imperiling their mortal souls, and in some dioceses, bishops denied the sacraments to parents who sent their children to public schools. Catholic parents quickly fell into line. By 1894, the Catholic school system had increased in size by more than fifty percent.[99]

Thus, by 1880, the state-building process, led by a grassroots movement of clergy and laymen, had yielded a new secular settlement in American education. This settlement featured a system of free, locally governed, state-controlled "common schools" which dominated the educational domain, laid claim to a monopoly on public funds, and featured a strongly Protestant-inflected "non-sectarian" curriculum, typically including devotional Bible reading. Under this settlement, religious and "sectarian" schools, especially Catholic denominational schools, were cast in opposition to this system, and strong legislative barriers were erected to prevent the distribution of funds to such schools.

STATE-BUILDING, RELIGION, AND EDUCATION IN AUSTRALIA, 1848–1880

Australia was founded as a penal colony for the transportation of British prisoners after the end of the American Revolutionary War, and granted responsible

---

95 Philip Hamburger. 2002. *Separation of Church and State*. Cambridge: Harvard University Press; John Witte, Jr. 2006. "Facts and Fictions about the History of Separation of Church and State." *Journal of Church and State* 48: 15–45.

96 Quoted in J.A. Burns. 1912. *The Growth and Development of the Catholic School System in the United States*. New York: Benziger Brothers, p. 186.

97 Burns, *Growth and Development*, p. 195.

98 Quoted in Cassidy, "Catholic Education in the Third Plenary," pp. 433–34.

99 Robert N. Gross. 2014. "Public Regulation and the Origins of Modern School-Choice Policies in the Progressive Era." *Journal of Policy History* 36(4): 509–33, pp. 511–12.

government – i.e., legislative control over internal affairs – in the mid-1850s.[100] The new colonial governments rapidly began constructing a state-run system of schools.[101] Although not a single government school existed in Australia in 1848, by 1880 state-run education had achieved almost total dominance in the educational domain. This state-building process occurred from the top down, and was accomplished through successive waves of centralization that marginalized both the existing system of denominational education and the incipient local boards that governed the earliest state schools. The net result was a series of tightly controlled, centralized educational systems, organized at the colonial level, which embraced religious education to different degrees. In the analysis that follows, I focus most closely on developments in the two most populous colonies, New South Wales and Victoria, although I bring in developments in other colonies where appropriate.

The Rise of Australian Government Schools: An Overview

Prior to 1848, education in Australia was provided through an "unstable and patchy" system of private and denominational schools.[102] While private schools slightly outnumbered denominational schools (fifty-three percent to forty-seven percent), denominational schools educated the great majority – nearly two-thirds – of all Australian children. Ninety-seven percent of these church schools were under the control of just four denominations: Anglican, Catholic, Presbyterian, and Methodist.[103] Denominational schooling thrived thanks to the close church–state ties that had developed in the period of early convict transportation. Before 1820, religious and moral education was emphasized as a means of countering the "social consequences of convictism," and the Church of England was treated as the sole legitimate provider of education.[104] The Church of England received subsidies to operate schools, governors requested schoolmasters "untainted by Methodism or other sectarian opinion," and Catholic schooling was banned altogether.[105] After 1820, the

---

[100] Stuart Macintyre. 2004. *A Concise History of Australia.* New York: Cambridge University Press, p. 91. Responsible government was granted to New South Wales, Tasmania, and Victoria in 1855; South Australia in 1856; and Queensland in 1859. Western Australia, settled later, was granted responsible government in 1890.

[101] Australian federation and independence was not accomplished until 1901, well after the period covered here. Accordingly, I use the term "colonies" throughout this chapter.

[102] Craig Campbell and Helen Proctor. 2014. *A History of Australian Schooling.* Sydney: Allen & Unwin, p. 61.

[103] Alan Barcan. 1965. *A Short History of Education in New South Wales.* Sydney: Martindale Press, p. 68.

[104] Alan Barcan. 1991. "The Aims of Education in New South Wales, 1788–1867." Pp. 137–153 in *Melbourne Studies in Education, 1991,* edited by David Stockley. Melbourne: University of Melbourne Press, pp. 139–40.

[105] A.G. Austin. 1961. *Australian Education, 1788–1900: Church, State, and Public Education in Colonial Australia.* Melbourne: Sir Isaac Pitman & Sons, Ltd., p. 7; John F. Cleverley. 1971.

Catholic and Presbyterian Churches became eligible for government support, but the Church of England retained a privileged position. Under the short-lived Church and School Corporation (1825–28), colonial lands were set aside for the exclusive support of Anglican clergy and schools. This setup drew loud protests from Australia's large Catholic and Presbyterian communities, and the scheme was quickly dropped. In 1836, the Church Act created a *de facto* system of multiple establishment in which each of the major denominations (Anglican, Catholic, Presbyterian, and Methodist) received government grants to support their churches and schools.[106]

Under the auspices of the Church of England, schools were associated with Anglican parishes and advanced as the parish system expanded. Catholic schools adopted this parish-based pattern after they became eligible for funding in 1820, and the "parish" pattern continued to characterize denominational schooling into the 1860s.[107] As a consequence, church schooling tended to be strong in the cities, where multiple churches congregated and competed for members, but weak or entirely absent in the countryside, where it was more difficult to sustain congregations. The inadequate distribution of schools was a source of frequent concern. A Select Committee on Education in 1844 complained that the "very essence" of the denominational systems was to "leave the majority uneducated," since whenever one denominational school was founded, two or three others would spring up next to it, "not because they [were] wanted, but because it was feared that proselytes [would] be made." Thus, concluded the Committee, "a superfluous activity [was] produced in one place, and a total stagnation in the other."[108]

Under church control, these schools were thoroughly denominational, and featured a curriculum designed to build and maintain students' faith. The curriculum was strongly influenced by the Christian ethic, and "the textbooks of the time were written to compel acceptance of such moral lessons."[109] Children attending denominational schools studied from catechisms, sang hymns, and

---

The First Generation: School and Society in Early Australia. Sydney: Sydney University Press, pp. 23–35, 41, 129.

[106] Michael Hogan. 1987. *The Sectarian Strand: Religion in Australian History.* Ringwood, Vic.: Penguin Books Australia, pp. 32, 36–39. Support for the churches was quickly abolished after the introduction of responsible government, although aid to schools persisted for several years afterwards. Support for public worship was abolished in South Australia (1851), Queensland (1860), New South Wales (1862), Tasmania (1869), Victoria (1870), and Western Australia (1890).

[107] Ronald Fogarty. 1959. *Catholic Education in Australia, 1806–1950.* Vol. 1, *Catholic Schools and the Denominational System.* Melbourne: Melbourne University Press, pp. 8, 20, 49.

[108] Report from the Select Committee on Education, 1844, quoted in A.G. Austin, ed. 1963. *Select Documents in Australian Education, 1788–1900.* Melbourne: Sir Isaac Pitman & Sons Ltd., p. 84.

[109] P.W. Musgrave. 1979. *Society and the Curriculum in Australia.* Sydney: George Allen & Unwin, p. 109.

read school books laden with religious and scriptural references.[110] When national schools were eventually founded, a similarly religious curriculum carried over. In fact, an 1854 report found that children attending state schools were more knowledgeable about Scripture than children attending denominational schools.[111] Religious and moral training thus formed a central part of the Australian curriculum in the mid-nineteenth century.

The Emergence of the Government School, 1848–1880

By 1880, control of education had shifted decisively, with the state replacing the church as the dominant player in the educational domain. State schooling initially arose in response to mounting concerns that the denominational system was failing to address rural education. Already by 1839, Governor George Gipps had raised the alarm, arguing that the inherent logic of the denominational system meant that "even in our capital, a large proportion of the Population shall remain uneducated; and out of Sydney there shall ... be scarcely any education at all," because the various denominations would "stand one in the way of the other, and by competing where they ought to combine, defeat the common object of them all."[112] The cost of the system was also growing unwieldy; the decision, under the 1836 Church Act, to provide funding to the schools of all major denominations quickly proved incredibly expensive, and by 1841 Gipps was forced to cut back on the funding the state was providing to each individual school.[113] The 1844 Select Committee on Education, referenced above, excoriated the denominations for their inefficiency, echoed Gipps' concerns that the denominational system produced unnecessary expenditures through overschooling, and recommended that a uniform system of public schools be established on an interdenominational basis.[114] Finally, in 1848, the New South Wales government established a pioneering system of National Schools to go alongside the denominational schools, under a "dual system" of National and Denominational Boards.[115]

Over the next twenty-five to thirty years, as I discuss in detail below, state schooling expanded dramatically through the systematization and rationalization of this dual system. The boards were initially consolidated, and ultimately

---

[110] Jan Kociumbas. 1997. *Australian Childhood: A History*. St. Leonards, NSW: Allen & Unwin, p. 51; Barcan, *Short History*, pp. 108–09.

[111] Wendy J. Relton. 1962. "The Failure of the Dual System of Control of Education in N.S.W." *Australian Journal of Education* 6: 133–42, p. 139.

[112] Quoted in Austin, *Select Documents*, p. 61.

[113] Patricia Curthoys. 2002. "State Support for Churches, 1836–1860." Pp. 31–51 in *Anglicans in Australia: A History*, edited by Bruce Kaye. Melbourne: Melbourne University Press, pp. 34–35.

[114] Report from the Select Committee on Education, 1844, quoted in Austin, *Select Documents*, pp. 83–85.

[115] This system was passed on to Victoria and Queensland upon their separation from New South Wales in 1851 and 1860 respectively, while a parallel system developed independently in Van Diemen's Land (Tasmania). See Hogan, *Sectarian Strand*, p. 83.

abolished in favor of a centralized state system of education that left the denominational schools outside the ambit of government control or support. Between 1872 and 1893, each colony passed an act that created a ministry of education, abolished the appointed boards that had governed education theretofore, eliminated state subsidies for denominational schools, and made education both free and compulsory.[116] As a result of these acts, Protestant denominational schooling collapsed. By 1900, only two percent of all children in New South Wales were attending Protestant schools.[117] The one exception, as in the United States, was Catholic denominational schools, which instead expanded, as I discuss in greater detail below.

Religious education remained an important part of education in most Australian schools even after the passage of these "free, compulsory, and secular" acts, although its form and strength varied from state to state. Australian religious education, as it developed in the state schools, was modeled on the Irish National Board (INB) system initially developed in Ireland and imported to New South Wales in 1848. The INB system featured two types of religious instruction: (1) selected Scripture readings given by the teacher from a set of readers compiled and approved by a panel of Irish Protestant and Catholic leaders; and (2) denominational instruction given by visiting clergymen to students of their denomination on a weekly basis.[118] The "free, compulsory, and secular" acts drew selectively upon these two types of religious education; in Queensland, only visiting instruction was offered, and only outside of school hours; in South Australia, Bible reading was maintained as an optional program at the beginning of the school day; New South Wales, Tasmania, and Western Australia retained both Bible reading and clerical instruction; while Victoria eliminated religious instruction altogether.[119] Thanks to the interfaith collaboration that had gone into the INB readers, these books tended to be somewhat less overtly anti-Catholic than many American texts, but they (and the new "Australian" readers introduced in the late nineteenth century) continued to promote the virtues of faith, God, and the Bible.[120]

---

[116] These acts were passed in Victoria (1872), Queensland (1875), South Australia (1875), New South Wales (1880), Tasmania (1885), and Western Australia (1893). See Austin, *Australian Education*, p. 174.

[117] Richard Broome. 1980. *Treasure in Earthen Vessels: Protestant Christianity in New South Wales Society, 1900–1914*. St. Lucia: University of Queensland Press, p. 50.

[118] A.A. Langdon. 1986. *The Anatomy of Religious Education in Schools*. Sydney: Christian Education Publications.

[119] Alan Barcan. 1980. *A History of Australian Education*. Melbourne: Oxford University Press, pp. 134–37, 148; Peter Wellock. 1977. "The Search for Educational Respectability: Religious Education in Australian Government Schools in the Twentieth Century." *Journal of Christian Education* 58: 30–47, p. 44.

[120] S.G. Firth. 1970. "Social Values in the New South Wales Primary School 1880–1914: An Analysis of School Texts." Pp. 123–59 in *Melbourne Studies in Education, 1970*, edited by R.J.W. Selleck. Melbourne: Melbourne University Press, pp. 128, 138, 143.

Ecclesiastical Displacement and State-Building from the Top Down

Church versus State: Catholics, Anglicans, and Liberals in the Educational Domain

In contrast to the United States, where the state-building process was primarily advanced by a grassroots movement commanding substantial support from religious leaders, the Australian state-building process occurred largely from the top down, orchestrated by government officials often over substantial clerical opposition. The new state schools faced particularly fierce opposition from the two largest and most established denominations, the Church of England and the Roman Catholic Church. Although, as I discuss below, these two churches increasingly found themselves at odds over state schooling, they typically shared a hostile attitude toward the emerging state system that threatened to marginalize their educational efforts.

Like their American counterparts, Australian Catholics staunchly opposed the creation of state schools. According to Australian Catholics, the only acceptable kind of education was one in which Catholic doctrine permeated the entirety of the curriculum, such that "the authority of the Church will be fully recognized, and that method of instruction observed which shall have for its first object the eternal welfare of souls."[121] In practice, this meant Catholic parochial schools alone. The various proposed forms of religious instruction in state schools also met familiar objections. Bible reading was unacceptable because the Bible could not be used authoritatively if it were not accompanied by the doctrines and interpretations of the Church. It was also unacceptably Protestant; as Archbishop Thomas Carr explained, "The reading of the Bible without note or comment" meant "introducing the Protestant principle of private judgment."[122] Nor was nondenominational religious instruction acceptable, since the Church held that there was no common ground between Catholics and Protestants, and insisted that the premise of nondenominationalism led inexorably to "the deadliest of errors, indifferentism – the frightful notion that all religious tenets are mere matters of opinion, that men have neither treasure nor responsibility in the one revealed Divine Truth."[123]

The Church of England, too, opposed the state's entry into education. Though its period of *de facto* establishment had been brief and legally dubious, the Church continued to think of itself as an established church worthy of special prerogatives.[124] Accordingly, it viewed efforts to build up state schooling as a challenge to its ascendancy, and opposed them throughout the first half of the nineteenth

---

[121] Provincial Council of 1869, quoted in Austin, *Australian Education*, p. 200.
[122] Quoted in Fogarty, *Catholic Education in Australia*, Vol. 2, *Catholic Education under the Religious Orders*. Melbourne: Melbourne University Press p. 460.
[123] Provincial Council of 1869, quoted in Austin, *Australian Education*, p. 199.
[124] Austin, *Australian Education*, p. 7.

century.[125] In the years before the Dual Board system was established in 1848, Anglican leaders successfully blocked efforts to introduce government schools. In 1836, Anglican Archbishop William Broughton rallied a broad Protestant coalition against a proposal to implement an experimental set of national schools under the INB model.[126] Because the INB system used selected Scripture readings instead of the entire Bible, Broughton argued that the plan would "require the Protestant to surrender the very groundwork of his faith, and [prepare] the way for the ultimate reestablishment of Popery."[127] Six years later, Broughton blocked an alternative proposal, this time arguing that because it did not include specifically Anglican religious instruction, it therefore constituted "a Bill of Attainder and Exclusion against the Church of England."[128] Only mounting financial pressures upon the church and its schools convinced Broughton to relent to the introduction of National Schools in 1848.[129]

The opposition of the two largest churches to state education meant that there was less of a fusion between religious and nationalist sentiments in Australian education. Far from possessing a "Native Protestant" ideology, then, as did their American counterparts, Australian advocates of state schooling were more strongly motivated by straightforward liberal ideals. The key tenets of liberalism – that society could and should be improved through concerted action, that societal harmony would emerge by downplaying social divisions, that progress belonged to all members of society, and that the state had the ability and consequently the duty to act in the service of those goals – were the driving ideology of those in favor of state schooling. As historian J.S. Gregory observes, the rise of the Australian government school above all reflected "a determination to make the State, in action and law, the symbol of a common citizenship."[130]

Yet if the impulse behind state-building was largely liberal, it was not anti-religious; indeed, many of the most prominent advocates of state schooling were "people of deep religious conviction themselves [who] respected the deeply held beliefs of others."[131] For them, a robust state education system

[125] Wendy Relton. 1959. "The Relations of the Church and State in Education in New South Wales, 1788–1880." Unpublished M.Ed. Thesis, University of Sydney, pp. 96–97.

[126] Ross Border. 1962. *Church and State in Australia 1788–1872: A Constitutional Study of the Church of England in Australia*. London: S.P.C.K., pp. 99–102.

[127] Quoted in Kelvin Grose. 1966. "William Grant Broughton and National Education in New South Wales, 1829–1836." Pp. 137–58 in E.L. French, ed., *Melbourne Studies in Education, 1965*. Melbourne: Melbourne University Press, p. 151.

[128] Quoted in Relton, "Relations of the Church and State," p. 109.

[129] Kelvin Grose. 1961. "1847: The Educational Compromise of the Lord Bishop of Australia." *Journal of Religious History* 1: 233–48, p. 245.

[130] J.S. Gregory. 1973. *Church and State: Changing Government Policies toward Religion in Australia, with Particular Reference to Victoria since Separation*. North Melbourne, Vic.: Cassell Australia, pp. 117–18.

[131] Marion Maddox. 2014. *Taking God to School: The End of Australia's Egalitarian Education?* Sydney: Allen & Unwin, p. 54.

was the best means of diminishing religious divisions and securing religion's place in society.[132] Many of these supporters hailed from the smaller Protestant denominations. In particular, Baptists and Congregationalists often spearheaded campaigns for both secular education and the elimination of state aid.[133] These denominations, alongside Methodists and Presbyterians, formed the core of a Protestant coalition that was increasingly supportive of state schooling, and which eventually grew to encompass the Church of England by 1880, as I discuss below. Thus, although state-building did not express itself in overtly religious terms, "religious secularists" were essential to the Australian state-building process.

From Dual Boards to Combined Boards: Rationalization and Systematization

The state-building process in Australian education required the active displacement of the existing denominational school sector. This occurred through successive waves of rationalization and systematization, coordinated by legislators and other government agents, which centralized administrative control in a single governing body. The Dual Board system established in New South Wales in 1848 created two appointed boards – Denominational and National – to manage the two types of schools. Originally, the National Board was conceived of as "essentially supplementary" in character.[134] Its key goal was to inaugurate state schooling in areas where the denominational system was failing to provide it. To do this, the Board hired two men to ride around the country districts as Board agents, advertising and organizing national schools.[135] The agents assiduously avoided establishing schools in areas where denominational schools already existed, both in deference to the denominational schools and because many rural ministers were hostile to the new effort.[136] Within three years, forty-two National schools were in operation in New South Wales and Victoria.[137]

Although control of the new state schools was centralized in the National Board, the Board initially envisioned an active role for the local community.

---

[132] See, e.g., Stephen Chavura. 2014. "'… But in Its Proper Place …': Religion, Enlightenment, and Australia's Secular Heritage: The Case of Robert Lowe in Colonial NSW, 1842–1850." *Journal of Religious History* 38(3): 356–76, p. 376; David Stoneman. 2014. "Richard Bourke: For the Honour of God and the Good of Man." *Journal of Religious History* 38(3): 341–55, p. 352.

[133] K.J. Cable. 1963. "Religious Controversies in New South Wales in the Mid-Nineteenth Century. II: The Dissenting Sects and Education." *Journal of the Royal Australian Historical Society* 49(2): 136–48, pp. 145–46; Fogarty, *Catholic Education*, Vol. 1, pp. 120–23.

[134] Gregory, *Church and State*, p. 34.

[135] A.G. Austin. 1958. *George William Rusden and National Education in Australia, 1849–1862.* Melbourne: Melbourne University Press, pp. 26–29.

[136] Austin, *George William Rusden*, p. 54; Austin, *Australian Education*, pp. 51–52; Keith Moore. 2005. "Bestowing 'Light' upon 'the Moral, Physical, and Intellectual Culture of Youth': Promoting Education in the New Colonial Society of Brisbane between 1846 and 1859." *Journal of Educational Administration and History* 37(2): 203–17, p. 210.

[137] Austin, *Australian Education*, p. 54.

Despite the traditional weakness of local government in Australia,[138] the National Board required localities to pay one-third of the initial building and ongoing maintenance costs of a school; in return, the state paid for the remaining construction costs, schoolbooks, and the teacher's salary.[139] The board also required that every new National school be sponsored by a board of Local Patrons, who would take charge of school management, inspect schools and teachers, fix tuition rates, and issue yearly reports.[140] Once a school was opened and its teachers appointed, the Board entrusted the Local Patrons with the management of the school except in extreme circumstances.[141] To further encourage contact between the school and its community, the Board invited "known clergymen or other gentlemen of the neighborhood" to conduct supplementary inspections of the schools.[142]

EFFICIENCY AND THE SUPPRESSION OF DENOMINATIONAL SCHOOLS. Despite its early promise, the Dual Board system proved both unwieldy and ineffective. Beginning in the 1860s, therefore, legislators in most states took steps to combine the two boards into a single authority. In New South Wales, both boards ran out of money in 1864 and initiated plans to withdraw support from some schools.[143] This crisis moved the New South Wales legislature to pass a new education act in 1866 that combined administrative control of national and denominational schools under a new, unitary Council of Education. Introducing the bill to Parliament, Henry Parkes insisted that the bill was necessary by pointing to the persistence of the very problems that had led to the creation of the Dual Board system: the existing system continued to be "unnecessarily expensive" and "in an alarming degree limited in its supply."[144] New South Wales thus joined Victoria (1862), Queensland (1860), and Tasmania (1854) in creating a unitary board to manage education.[145]

---

[138] Kelvin Grose. 1965. "Sir George Gipps and Municipal Institutions in New South Wales." *Journal of the Royal Australian Historical Society* 51: 148–53.

[139] Ray Bass. 1980. *Education in Lismore: A Century and a Quarter of Progress.* Lismore, NSW: Northern Rivers College of Advanced Education, p. 7.

[140] S.H. Smith and G.T. Spaull. 1925. *History of Education in New South Wales (1788–1925).* Sydney: George B. Philip and Son, p. 184. For a similar scheme in South Australia, see Malcolm Vick. 1992. "Community, State, and the Provision of Schools in Mid-Nineteenth Century South Australia." *Australian Historical Studies* 25(98): 53–71.

[141] John Mumford. 1994. "Encouragement of Local Control in National Education, New South Wales, 1848–1866." *Journal of Educational Administration* 32(4): 53–62, p. 56.

[142] C. Turney. 1970. "The Rise and Decline of an Australian Inspectorate." Pp. 160–213 in *Melbourne Studies in Education, 1970,* edited by R.J.W. Selleck. Melbourne: Melbourne University Press, p. 161.

[143] A.W. Martin. 1962. "Faction Politics and the Education Question in New South Wales." Pp. 25–47 in *Melbourne Studies in Education, 1960–1961,* edited by E.L. French. Melbourne: Melbourne University Press, p. 34.

[144] Quoted in Barcan, *Short History,* p. 128.

[145] Fogarty, *Catholic Education,* Vol. 1, pp. 63–67.

The legislation creating the combined boards decisively favored the national schools. The combined boards placed a welter of new restrictions on denominational schools, tightened up the conditions under which they could receive aid, and eliminated state aid for construction and maintenance costs – although support for teachers' salaries continued to be provided.[146] In New South Wales, the 1866 legislation further stipulated that denominational schools had to open their doors to children of other denominations to remain eligible to receive aid, and placed stringent restrictions on when and where new denominational schools could be established.[147] These restrictions both made the expansion of the denominational sector extremely difficult, and reduced the incentives for many Protestant denominations to continue operating their schools. In effect, as political scientist Michael Hogan has observed, "denominational schools were being invited to retire gracefully from the field."[148]

These restrictions on denominational school expansion were accompanied by efforts to suppress and amalgamate many existing denominational schools, which were seen as the root of the inefficiencies in the system. In its first five years, the New South Wales Council of Education "energetically engaged in closing down" denominational schools and "assimilating those that survived into the public school system."[149] These efforts were matched in Victoria, where its new Common Schools Board (CSB) began to aggressively withdraw support from "unnecessary" denominational schools in 1868. CSB officials expressed hope that its "system of amalgamation, and where necessary of suppression," would "have the effect of encouraging large and efficient schools, and doing away with small and inefficient ones."[150] In rural areas, the CSB formally declared its intent to give preference to national schools, reasoning that the national schools' nondenominational education would better permit them to serve students from all religious backgrounds in sparsely populated areas.[151]

The net effect of these policies, which gave preference to state schools while increasingly disadvantaging denominational schools, was to dramatically reduce the strength of the denominational sector in the educational sphere. In New South Wales, the number of denominational schools dropped by almost half between 1866 and 1880, a decline that was particularly pronounced

---

[146] Fogarty, *Catholic Education*, Vol. 1, pp. 60, 68–71.

[147] Austin, *Australian Education*, p. 118; Barcan, *Short History*, pp. 129–30.

[148] Hogan, *Sectarian Strand*, p. 88.

[149] Barcan, *Short History*, pp. 142–43.

[150] Quoted in Ken Elford. 1971. "Church, State, Education, and Society: An Analysis of Aspects of Eastern Australian Society circa 1856–1872." Unpublished Ph.D. Dissertation, University of Sydney, p. 301.

[151] P.J. Pledger. 1961. "The Common Schools Board, 1862–1872." Pp. 95–114 in *Melbourne Studies in Education, 1959–1960*, edited by A.G. Austin. Melbourne: Melbourne University Press, pp. 109–10.

among Protestant schools.[152] In Victoria, too, the proportion of denominational schools nosedived. Whereas in 1862 there were two and a half times as many church schools as national schools, by 1870 the number of national schools had surpassed the number of denominational schools.[153]

THE ECLIPSE OF LOCAL CONTROL. In addition to fostering the state schools at the expense of the denominational schools, the combined boards also took steps to curtail the limited powers that had been assigned to local boards. Criticism of the local boards began almost as soon as they were created. Local boards often failed to adequately manage their schools, especially in country districts where conditions were hardest.[154] Even in more densely settled areas, however, where local boards were more effective, only one in four local boards provided "considerable service" in accordance with their envisioned role.[155] In 1854, William Wilkins, an agent of the National Board, conducted a tour of the colony's national schools, and reported that "the majority are in a most unsatisfactory condition" because the local patrons were neglecting the schools. Wilkins recommended that the state take "the power of the local patrons and ... place it in the hands of an inspector."[156]

When the colony consolidated the boards, therefore, it also assumed many of the functions previously allocated to the local patrons, such as inspections. In the early years of the Dual Board system, inspections were left to local patrons. Officials on the National Board concluded, however, that "means of adequate supervision, through local patrons, do not in general exist," and that without "an efficient inspection, emanating from a central authority, no permanent good can be effected."[157] Thus, under the 1866 law, inspection methods were rigorously prescribed through the Council of Education. Additionally, the combined boards took greater control over curriculum and staffing than had their predecessors. In 1867 in New South Wales, for instance, new regulations established standards of proficiency and salaries for teachers, introduced a new curriculum, specified textbooks, elaborated disciplinary measures, and created new classification rules for students.[158] Thus, under the combined boards, those functions of school management and supervision that had previously been left

---

[152] Fogarty, *Catholic Education*, Vol. 1, p. 241.

[153] L.J. Blake. 1973. "The Common Schools Period." Pp. 79–163 in *Vision and Realisation: A Centenary History of State Education in Victoria*, edited by L.J. Blake. Vol I. Melbourne: Education Department of Victoria, p. 105.

[154] Jean Ely. 1973. "The Institutionalization of an Ideal: Centralization in Educational Administration, New South Wales, 1848–1880." Pp. 225–50 in *Melbourne Studies in Education, 1973*, edited by S. Murray Smith. Melbourne: Melbourne University Press, pp. 241–42.

[155] Mumford, "Encouragement of Local Control," p. 61.

[156] Quoted in Bruce Smith. 1990. "William Wilkins's Saddle-Bags: State Education and Local Control." Pp. 66–90 in *Family, School, and State in Australian History*, edited by Marjorie R. Theobald and R.J.W. Selleck. Sydney: Allen & Unwin, p. 66.

[157] Quoted in E.J. Payne. 1968. "The Management of Schools in New South Wales (1848–1866): Local Initiative Suppressed." *Journal of Educational Administration* 6(1): 69–86, p. 76.

[158] Barcan, *Short History*, pp. 130–31.

to local committees were increasingly brought under the central control of the combined boards and standardized.

The Final Break: From Boards to Ministries, and the End of State Aid

Although the combined boards raised national schools to a dominant position and substantially weakened local control, these trends were fully realized through the creation of ministries of education and the abolition of state aid between 1872 and 1893. Ongoing calls for operational efficiency lay behind the abolition of state aid. Faced with continued uneven and inefficient schooling,[159] educational officials laid the blame at the feet of the denominational school system. In testimony before a Royal Commission on Education in Victoria in 1866, the secretary of the CSB argued that the denominational system "acts in two ways prejudicially; first it creates a number of unnecessary schools, and then it prevents their diminution in number by amalgamation."[160] Colonial officials responded by excluding denominational schools from the state-run educational system altogether, erecting statutory prohibitions against state aid which remained in place until the 1960s.[161]

Meanwhile, the rapid expansion of state schooling led to calls for a stronger and more accountable administrative apparatus. In New South Wales, the Council of Education pleaded for the establishment of a full-time ministry in 1876, warning that the demands of managing the schools had outstripped their administrative capacity.[162] Likewise, the increasing cost of the burgeoning educational system raised concerns about the propriety of unelected boards being given charge of disbursing such large sums. In Victoria, James Wilberforce Stephen, the sponsor of the 1872 Education Act, declared that a ministry was required because schooling had been "placed in the hands of an irresponsible Board, altogether away from the control of this House, and country." In New South Wales, too, Henry Parkes, sponsor of the 1880 Public Instruction Act, expressed a desire to replace the "irresponsible" council, whose form was "not in harmony with the other institutions of the colony," with a "responsible" board that could more legitimately manage the growing educational budget.[163]

---

159 This unevenness could be stark; in Victoria, the 1866 Royal Commission found that nearly 85,000 children were receiving no formal education even as some towns were providing up to six schools for just 537 students. See Gregory, *Church and State*, p. 98.

160 Quoted in L.J. Blake. 1973, "Free, Compulsory, and Secular." Pp. 167–238 in *Vision and Realisation: A Centenary History of State Education in Victoria*, edited by L.J. Blake. Vol. 1. Melbourne: Education Department of Victoria, p. 172.

161 Hogan, *Sectarian Strand*, pp. 93–94.

162 Martin, "Faction Politics and the Education Question," p. 45.

163 Quoted in J.R. Lawry. 1972. "The Free, Compulsory, and Secular Education Acts Reassessed." Pp. 211–27 in *Melbourne Studies in Education, 1972*, edited by R.J.W. Selleck. Melbourne: Melbourne University Press, pp. 215, 226.

The creation of ministries of education "accomplished the ruin of local school government."[164] Whatever residual powers the local boards controlled, such as appointment of teachers, were centralized in the new ministries. In Victoria, the Education Act removed power over staffing and curriculum from local committees, and created new "Boards of Advice" with sharply delimited powers. Any hope that the Boards of Advice might use these powers to affect educational change was dashed in a series of power struggles with the Victorian Ministry in the 1870s.[165] Thereafter, the boards "became mere ciphers – when they functioned at all."[166] In New South Wales, meanwhile, the Public Instruction Act reduced local boards to an optional and honorary ornament.[167] Unsurprisingly, the local boards rapidly fell into desuetude.[168] The top-down state-building process had reached fruition, with the state firmly in charge of education through a set of centralized state ministries.

Religious Conflict and Australian Education

As in the United States, religious conflict interacted with the state-building process, helping to shape the ultimate form of the nineteenth-century settlement. First, conflict among religious groups acted as a spur that encouraged educational reformers to centralize administration and weaken local control. In Victoria, the denominations competed to gain control over local boards – and the decisions about religious instruction that were entrusted to them. In some locales, Anglicans and non-Anglican Protestants nominated rival slates, both of which would apply to the CSB for recognition as the official local board for a school. Unsurprisingly, this led to administrative chaos.[169] Even when a mixed denominational board was successfully created for a school, board members from different denominations often could not agree on how to provide religious instruction, or even which teachers to hire.[170] Indeed, teachers actively lobbied for a centralized appointment process in hopes that it would eliminate the local prejudices that threatened the security of their appointments.[171]

One result of these local battles, and the broader opposition by Anglican and Catholic leaders to state education in general, was a growing consensus that the churches were an obstacle to effective education. As a result, religious

---

[164] Denis Grundy. 1972. *"Secular, Compulsory, and Free": The Education Act of 1872.* Melbourne: Melbourne University Press, p. 5.

[165] Grundy, *Secular, Compulsory, and Free*, pp. 71, 75, 93.

[166] John W. Collins-Jennings. 1971. "Non-Professional and Non-Governmental Organisations and the Provision of Public Education, 1850–1969." Unpublished M.Ed. Thesis, University of Melbourne, p. 149.

[167] Bass, *Education in Lismore*, p. 59.

[168] Smith and Spaull, *History of Education in New South Wales*, pp. 185–87.

[169] Elford, "Church, State, Education, and Society," pp. 261, 270–72.

[170] Grundy, *Secular, Compulsory, and Free*, pp. 18–19, 75.

[171] Lawry, "Free, Compulsory, and Secular Acts Reassessed," p. 217.

conflict was regularly invoked in debates surrounding each successive act to centralize control and reduce the power of the denominational system. In New South Wales, Parkes used religious conflict to justify creating the Council of Education in 1866; he blamed the inferior quality of education in that colony on "the unseemly contention amongst ... the clergy of the various churches," and averred that, as a result of sectarian conflict, there were a multitude of "children who, whilst ministers of religion are caviling over a division of the spoils, are left destitute of all instruction."[172] In Victoria, the ongoing battles over religious education and teaching appointments made centralized control seem particularly appealing. Stephen declared that only "the central authority – the State" had the power to counter the influence of denominationalism in Victorian education, and expressed his belief that placing teachers under centralized supervision would effectively eliminate any meddling in the appointment process.[173]

Thus, religious conflict contributed to the decision to reduce local control and centralize decision-making. Beyond this, however, it also influenced decisions regarding the content of religious education in the government schools. The dynamics of religious conflict were cross-cutting and varied from colony to colony. Variations in these dynamics help explain why different colonies adopted different policies toward religious education in the government schools, with some embracing a nondenominational (Protestant) curriculum, and others rejecting religious instruction altogether. Because Catholics and non-Anglican Protestants represented two equal and opposing blocs, the position taken by the Church of England often proved paramount. The complex effects of religious conflict can be seen by comparing New South Wales, where a nondenominational approach prevailed, and Victoria, where strict secularism triumphed.

Religious Conflict and the Government School Curriculum in New South Wales and Victoria

In New South Wales, the Church of England slowly came to support government schooling between 1860 and 1880. In 1866, the Public Schools Act initially proposed to include a variant of the dual INB system of religious instruction. Catholics flatly opposed the measure, but Anglicans hedged. Although the legislation provided for SRI by visiting clergy, Anglicans were disconcerted by its provisions for "secular instruction" only in the public schools. However, Anglicans suggested that they could support the bill if it were altered to permit Scripture reading. The act was quickly amended to specify that "the words 'secular instruction' shall be held to include general religious teaching as distinct from dogmatic or polemical theology." This "rather extraordinary definition" secured Anglican support for the measure, and New South Wales

---

[172] Quoted in Austin, *Australian Education*, p. 119.
[173] Quoted in Lawry, "Free, Compulsory, and Secular Acts Reassessed," p. 215.

formally embraced both "general religious teaching" (GRT, in the form of Scripture reading) and SRI.[174] With these dual provisions in place, Anglicans quickly proved strong supporters of the public schools. Within three years, leading Anglican journals were openly advocating converting the Church of England's country schools into public schools, and refocusing their energies on providing SRI.[175] By 1880, Anglicans had joined the other Protestant denominations in supporting the public schools and the dual GRT–SRI provisions for religious instruction.

This growing accord between Anglicans and other Protestants meant that educational debates in New South Wales increasingly turned on a straightforward Protestant–Catholic divide. Anti-Catholicism had been a part of Australian life from its founding, but it intensified substantially after 1865.[176] With Anglicans supporting public education and Protestant denominational schools in decline, the question of state aid was reduced to a question of state aid for Catholic schools in the public mind. Thus, when New South Wales finally moved to eliminate state aid in 1880, the debate was quickly engulfed in ferocious Protestant–Catholic conflict. Liberal proponents of state schools stoked anti-Catholic sentiment to try to build Protestant support for their program.[177] Events came to a climax in 1879, when the Catholic bishops of New South Wales issued a Joint Pastoral Letter reiterating their demand that the state should continue to subsidize a separate system of Catholic schools, and excoriating the public schools as "seed-plots of future immorality, infidelity, and lawlessness."[178] The letter inflamed public opinion, and the 1880 Public Instruction Act, which directly transferred the 1866 language regarding religious instruction, passed by an overwhelming margin. In short, a Protestant accord on GRT and united opposition to Catholic demands yielded a strongly Protestant-inflected dual system of religious education, where both Scripture reading and denominational instruction were incorporated into the public school curriculum.

In Victoria, by contrast, religious conflicts and alliances were far more fragmented, leading to a significantly different result. Baptists, Congregationalists, and skeptics – all ardent supporters of state schooling – were proportionally stronger in Victoria than in New South Wales, while the Anglican and

---

[174] P.D. Davis. 1964. "The 1866 Controversy: Religious Teaching in Public Schools." *Journal of Christian Education* 7(2/3): 83–95, pp. 91–95.

[175] P.D. Davis. 1973. "New Wine in Old Bottles: Another Look at the Case for Denominational Religious Instruction in Public Schools and Some Reflections on the Work of the Council of Education, 1867–1879." *Journal of Christian Education* 16(1): 51–61, pp. 57–58.

[176] Malcolm Campbell. 2005. "A 'Successful Experiment' No More: The Intensification of Religious Bigotry in Eastern Australia, 1865–1885." *Humanities Research* 12(1): 67–78; Hogan, *Sectarian Strand*, pp. 34, 65–67.

[177] Hogan, *Sectarian Strand*, pp. 90–91.

[178] Quoted in Patrick O'Farrell. 1969. *Documents in Australian Catholic History.* Vol. 1. *1788–1883*. London: Geoffrey Chapman, p. 393.

Catholic churches were relatively weaker.[179] Further complicating matters, the Anglican Church, which opposed the Catholic Church on the school question in New South Wales, found itself allied with Catholics against advocates of government schooling in Victoria. Like his Catholic counterpart, the Anglican Bishop of Melbourne opposed the "ungodly" state schools, the idea of mixed denominational instruction, and the very idea of a system of education that systematically separated religious and secular instruction.[180] Both churches thus resisted efforts to reduce the role of denominational schools in Victoria. Crucially, Anglican–Catholic opposition helped to sink several efforts to end state aid without ending religious instruction in the Victorian public schools. In 1867, Anglican and Catholic leaders organized a vigorous campaign to scuttle legislation known as the Higinbotham Bill, which contained provisions for nondenominational religious instruction.[181] Three years later, the two churches helped defeat a similar bill, Catholics because they did not want to lose state aid, and Anglicans because they thought the legislation's visiting instruction provisions were too weak.[182]

The churches' unstinting resistance to state education led to the rise of "anti-denominationalist" sentiment in Victoria.[183] Because the Church of England was also opposed, it was the churches as a whole who took the blame for the failure of educational legislation, rather than the Catholic Church alone. The key catalyst for this development was the failure of the Higinbotham Bill, which soured both Victorian politicians and the Melbourne press on the idea that compromise with the churches would ever be possible on educational matters.[184] The failure of the Higinbotham Bill encouraged politicians to enact drastic legislation that they hoped would definitively end the ongoing conflict with the churches over education.[185] Frustration with denominationalism was evident in the debate around the 1872 Education Act, which Stephen introduced by declaring that he would not allow children "to grow up in ignorance during the long years that might elapse before the various sects agreed as to

---

[179] W.W. Phillips. 1986. "Religion." Pp. 418–35 in *Australian Historical Statistics*, edited by Wray Vamplew. Sydney: Fairfax, Syme, and Weldon, pp. 421–22; Pledger, "Common Schools Board," p. 98. While the "atmosphere of doubt and questioning" promoted by Victorian skeptics undoubtedly contributed to the starkly secular outcome in that state, J.S. Gregory argues that the movement for secular schools was "not an anti-religious movement," and in fact was led by "prominent churchmen of deep religious convictions." See Gregory, *Church and State*, pp. 115, 74.

[180] Kenneth E. Dear. 1966. "Bishop Perry and the Rise of National Education in Victoria, 1848–1873." Pp. 159–86 in *Melbourne Studies in Education, 1965*, edited by E.L. French. Melbourne: Melbourne University Press, pp. 177–79.

[181] Gregory, *Church and State*, p. 101.

[182] Grundy, *Secular, Compulsory, and Free*, pp. 21–23, 27.

[183] While anti-Catholicism was evident in Victoria, it was only part of a broader expression of disgust with the intransigence of the churches in general. See Gregory, *Church and State*, p. 141.

[184] Austin, *Australian Education*, pp. 184–89.

[185] Grundy, *Secular, Compulsory, and Free*, p. 11.

the quality and quantity of religious instruction to be imparted in the common schools."[186]

The ultimate result of this anti-denominationalist agitation was a strictly secular education act. Not only did the 1872 Education Act end state aid to denominational schools, it also eliminated all religious instruction in the public schools. In contrast with New South Wales, where "secular" instruction was legally held to encompass "general religious teaching" through nondenominational Scripture reading, there was no such protective caveat in the Victorian Education Act. Instead, the law declared that, "In every State school secular instruction only shall be given, and no teacher shall give other than secular instruction in any State school building." Department officials under the new education ministry fully enforced this provision. In 1876, the Victorian school readers were systematically purged not merely of their Scripture sections, but of any and all literary references of a religious character as well.[187] In the end, therefore, the combined opposition of the Catholic and Anglican Churches generated an "anti-denominational" spirit among liberals and nonconformist Protestants that ultimately yielded what was, at the time, in all likelihood the most secular educational system in the world.[188]

The Catholic Response

Catholics responded to the elimination of state aid by reinforcing their own denominational system. Catholic schools declined at a much slower rate than Protestant schools under the combined boards, largely because Catholics had already begun to transition to an organizational model less dependent on state support. By the late 1860s, a Catholic association had been created to organize fundraising for the independent Catholic system. Similarly, nuns had begun to take over most of the teaching responsibilities, thus providing an inexpensive teaching staff.[189] By the 1870s, Catholic schooling had essentially shifted into the independently supported system that it would remain through the 1960s.

Catholic bishops used their hortatory and ecclesiastical powers to build support for these schools among the laity. At its Provincial Council in 1869, the Catholic bishops admonished Catholics that they were "bound to use every exertion to erect ... Catholic schools in which the authority of the Church [would] be fully recognized."[190] The bishops' 1879 Joint Pastoral letter denouncing the public schools – which caused such consternation in New South Wales – also instructed Catholics that they were required to send their

---

[186] Quoted in Blake, "Free, Compulsory, and Secular," p. 197.

[187] Gregory, *Church and State*, pp. 136, 144, 172–73.

[188] Victoria was an extreme case; as discussed above, every other colony made some provision for religious instruction, either through denominational instruction by visiting clergy or by nonsectarian Scripture reading.

[189] Fogarty, *Catholic Education*, pp. 222–33; Hogan, *Sectarian Strand*, p. 94.

[190] Decrees on Education, Provincial Council of 1869, quoted in Austin, *Select Documents*, p. 216.

children to Catholic schools unless expressly exempted by their parish priest.[191] Some Catholic bishops began denying the sacraments to parents who did not send their children to Catholic schools.[192] These directives had their desired effect, and from the 1880s through to the mid-twentieth century, the Catholic school system enrolled around one in six school-aged children in Australia.[193] By the end of the century, therefore, the Catholic system had survived the abolition of state aid, and persisted as the primary exception to the state-dominated educational sector.

By 1880, the nineteenth-century settlement in Australian education had solidified. Education was primarily in the hands of free, publicly controlled, highly centralized systems of government schools, organized at the state level, that laid claim to a monopoly on public funds and – Victoria aside – featured a curriculum with an established place for religious instruction. Denominational schools, by contrast, including Catholic denominational schools, were expressly excluded from public funding in order to secure the efficiency and dominance of the single, rationalized, government system.

CONCLUSION

By the 1880s, the state-building process in both Australia and the United States had produced remarkably similar secular settlements. Each country possessed a robust system of state-run education, strong barriers against public financing of religious schools, and religious instruction in the public schools – although the kind of and extent to which religious instruction was given in any state or municipality did vary. Moreover, in both countries the residual denominational sector in education was dominated by Catholic schools. Generally speaking, Catholics in both countries demanded state aid, and rejected the "nondenominational" exercises held in the public schools, whereas Protestants of all stripes supported both the restrictions on state aid and the pan-Protestant religion in the public schools. This established, in each country, a strong Protestant–Catholic divide on matters pertaining to religion and education that persisted throughout the duration of the settlement.

Although their settlements were similar, the way the state-building process had interacted with the existing institutional terrain and with religious actors led the two nations to develop significantly different administrative structures. The grassroots movement for common schools in the United States embraced and coopted the existing network of denominational schools, bequeathing a decentralized system where local districts controlled most features of education,

---

[191] Thomas A. O'Donoghue. 2001. *Upholding the Faith: The Process of Education in Catholic Schools in Australia, 1922–1965.* New York: Peter Lang, p. 21.
[192] Barcan, *Short History*, pp. 215–16.
[193] O'Donoghue, *Upholding the Faith*, p. 21.

including power over curriculum and appointments. By contrast, the top-down creation of national schools in Australia required the restriction and displacement of existing denominational schools, culminating in highly centralized state ministries of education which created uniform rules within each colony on all administrative matters, including staffing and curriculum. These divergent administrative forms would have an important impact on the role of religion over the duration of the nineteenth-century settlement. As we shall see in the next part of the book, the decentralized American system proved far more permeable to religious and professional actors who sought to secularize the public schools than did the insulated, centralized Australian system.

THE NINETEENTH-CENTURY SETTLEMENT IN TRANSITION

Administrative Centralization and Secularization, 1880–1945

With state schooling established as the dominant partner in education by 1880, a durable secular settlement had been established in each country with strongly similar characteristics: religion was permitted in public schools, and financial support was barred from flowing to religious schools. Yet, in the United States, the nineteenth-century settlement began to erode almost immediately, particularly in the public schools, where the prevalence of religious devotionals began a slow but steady decline. In Australia, by contrast, the nineteenth-century settlement proved remarkably immune to political or professional challenge until its precipitous reformulation in the 1960s.

Part II of this book examines the divergent fates of the nineteenth-century settlements, and it focuses on how systems of educational administration affected the politics of religion – and hence the trajectory of secularization – between the late nineteenth century and the end of World War II. In so doing, it uncovers important distal trends that set the stage for the transformation of the 1960s. While the events of the 1960s were dramatic, they cannot be understood simply in terms of their immediate historical context. Political processes are often big and slow-moving, with effects that only unfold over extended historical periods.[1] The rise of the twentieth-century settlement likewise depended upon dynamics generated by the unfolding of religious conflict and professionalization over the long term.

These chapters argue that variations in administrative institutions are central to explaining why public school devotionals declined in the United States, but not in Australia. In the United States, the decentralized system of local board control made American education *permeable* to challenges by Catholics, Jews, and other religious minorities dissatisfied with the pan-Protestant,

---

[1] Paul Pierson. 2004. *Politics in Time: History, Institutions, and Social Analysis.* Princeton: Princeton University Press, pp. 79–102.

"non-sectarian" devotionals so central to the nineteenth-century curriculum. These challenges eroded religion's position in the public schools from the bottom up. At the same time, the decentralized development of education also unleashed strong professionalizing dynamics among American educators, ultimately leading to the development and diffusion of new, professional pedagogical ideas that rapidly marginalized religion from the top down. In Australia, by contrast, centralized control over education *insulated* educational policy from minority challenges, and attenuated professional development among teachers. This contributed to conservatism and stasis in Australian education throughout the early twentieth century, both in general and more specifically in regards to religious policies.

Taken together, Chapters 3 and 4 illustrate how differences in the organization of administration can shape the development of secularization both by mediating political contests and by helping to constitute actors with particular motives and interests. By the end of World War II, thanks to robust secularizing processes that were facilitated by American administrative institutions, the United States would already have moved substantially in the direction of the strict separationist settlement it would formally adopt in the mid-twentieth century. In Australia, by contrast, the nineteenth-century settlement persisted until administrative decentralization in the 1960s finally altered the institutional dynamics of religious politics.

3

Slow Secularization in the Permeable American State

INTRODUCTION

In December 1872, the Ohio Supreme Court ruled that the Ohio state constitution did not "enjoin or require religious instruction, or the reading of religious books, in the public schools of the state."[1] Its decision, which brought to a close four years of wrangling in response to the Cincinnati school board's decision to prohibit the reading of the Bible in that city's schools, represented the first time in American history that a court had upheld the removal of religious instruction from the public schools. For good reason, therefore, scholars have hailed the decision as "a watershed" that "forever changed the way people looked at nonsectarian Bible reading."[2] Yet the substantive and symbolic importance of the decision has often overshadowed its key holding: the importance of respecting the prerogative of the Cincinnati school board to make its own decisions regarding religious instruction. "The legislature having placed the management of the public schools under the exclusive control of directors, trustees, and boards of education," the Court reasoned, "the courts have no rightful authority to interfere by directing what instruction shall be given, or what books shall be read therein."[3] This great symbolic blow against public school devotionals, in other words, rested upon a legal defense of local control.

During the late nineteenth and early twentieth centuries, local control was crucial to determining the course of secularization in the United States. The decentralization of educational policy authority meant that religious practices varied widely around the country. This fragmentation in turn facilitated the

---

[1] *Board of Education of the City of Cincinnati* v. *John D. Minor et al.*, 23 Ohio St. 211 (1872), p. 211.
[2] Steven K. Green. 2012. *The Bible, the School, and the Constitution: The Clash that Shaped Modern Church-State Doctrine*. New York: Oxford University Press, pp. 134–35.
[3] *Board of Education* v. *Minor*, p. 211.

advance of two key secularizing processes, religious conflict and professionalization, leading to a slow decline in the prevalence of religious instruction in the public schools. Local control meant that religious practices had to be responsive to local, not statewide, political dynamics. In religiously heterogeneous areas, religious minorities – especially Catholics and Jews – were able to challenge the pan-Protestant devotional exercises by lobbying local boards to change their policies. Where they commanded significant political power, religious minorities could leverage their local strength to effect compromises or outright eliminate the offending practices. Further, over time, these ongoing conflicts over Bible reading and other religious practices created a climate in which school boards came to perceive religion as being dangerously controversial, generating a new conventional wisdom among administrators that eschewed religion in the interest of political harmony.

Decentralized control also facilitated early professionalization in the United States. The decentralized system encouraged the development of professional associations and educational periodicals, which provided a platform for the exchange and development of educational ideas that challenged the traditional religious underpinnings of American education. The development of privately controlled research universities in the late nineteenth century gave impetus to the development of these theories. Perhaps most importantly, the position of city superintendent (a local management position with no analogue in Australia) provided a rich supply of educational leaders who were motivated to advance progressive educational reforms, and who had sufficient local control to enact reforms in their own, autonomous school districts.

Squeezed from below by religious conflict, and from above by professionalization, Protestant devotionals declined over the century before 1960. This chapter examines how America's decentralized education system facilitated the secularization of American education during this period, destabilizing the nineteenth-century settlement and creating the conditions for the Supreme Court's dramatic rulings of the 1960s. As we will see, by the time the Supreme Court ruled in *Engel* and *Schempp*, religion's prevalence in the public school curriculum had already decreased markedly. And these trends owed much to the political dynamics made possible by the local control and dispersion of authority characteristic of the American educational system.

THE DECLINE OF RELIGION IN AMERICAN SCHOOLS FROM 1840 TO 1962: AN OVERVIEW

The late nineteenth and early twentieth centuries saw a slow – but far from uniform – erosion of religion's place in the American curriculum. The decline of religious instruction is clearly visible in the practice of Bible reading. Bible reading was perhaps the most widespread devotional practice in the nineteenth-century public schools, not just because of the central role it played in the "nonsectarian" religious education scheme advanced by Horace Mann and others, but also because it was seen as less controversial than prayer.[4] Over the second half of the nineteenth century, the Bible ceased to be used as a textbook and instead was increasingly read devotionally as a standalone segment of the school day. The Bible's use became more exclusively devotional just as controversy over its use became more widespread (see below); accordingly, devotional Bible reading became a rallying cry for many Protestants and educators, who encouraged its more consistent use in the schools.[5]

Survey statistics prior to 1890 are fairly unreliable,[6] but it can be said that in the late nineteenth century, Bible reading was commonplace, though not universal. In New England, where it had been a central part of Puritan education since colonial days, Bible reading came closest to being a universal practice.[7] Yet elsewhere, its usage was far less uniform. The use of the Bible was most common in cities and other established areas, and less common on the frontier; in many Western states, Bible reading never caught on as a common practice.[8] Still, Bible reading was a dominant practice: memoirs from the period are replete with memories of regular Bible reading,[9] and most major cities in the Northeast and Midwest experienced serious controversies over Bible reading during the late nineteenth century.

The early twentieth century evinces a much clearer pattern. As Figure 3.1 demonstrates, Bible reading declined over the first half of the twentieth century, before collapsing precipitously after the Supreme Court rulings of the 1960s.[10]

---

[4] R. Laurence Moore. 2000. "Bible Reading and Nonsectarian Schooling: The Failure of Religious Instruction in Nineteenth-Century Public Education." *Journal of American History* 86(4): 1581–99, p. 1583.

[5] Lloyd P. Jorgenson. 1987. *The State and the Non-Public School, 1825–1925.* Columbia: University of Missouri Press, pp. 132–35; Moore, "Bible Reading and Nonsectarian Schooling," p. 1597.

[6] Unsourced claims about the prevalence of Bible reading from the late nineteenth century state that eighty percent of American schools were conducting Bible reading, a figure which is probably somewhat high. See, e.g., Philip Schaff. 1888. *Church and State in the United States.* New York: G.P. Putnam's Sons, p. 75. The eighty percent figure was still being given as late as 1916, however. See Sara Whedon. 1916. "The Essential Place of Religion in Education: Synopsis of Essays Presented in Contest." Pp. 93–134 in National Education Association, *The Essential Place of Religion in Education.* Ann Arbor, MI: National Education Association, p. 111.

[7] United States Office of Education. 1896. *Report of the Commissioner of Education, made to the Secretary of the Interior for the Year 1894–1895.* Washington, DC: Government Printer, Vol. 2, p. 1656.

[8] United States Office of Education. 1904. *Report of the Commissioner of Education, made to the Secretary of the Interior for the Year 1903.* Washington, DC: Government Printer, Vol. 2, p. 2448.

[9] See, e.g., the selections in Barbara Finkelstein. 1989. *Governing the Young: Teacher Behavior in Popular Primary Schools in Nineteenth Century United States.* New York: The Falmer Press, pp. 214–27, 258–64, 270–88.

[10] Data in Figure 3.1 are drawn from United States Office of Education, *Report … for the Year 1894–5,* p. 1656; United States Office of Education, *Report … for the Year 1903,* p. 2445; Richard B. Dierenfield. 1962. *Religion in American Public Schools.* Washington, DC: Public Affairs Press, p. 51; H. Frank Way. 1968. "Survey Research on Judicial Decisions: The Prayer and Bible Reading Cases." *Western Political Quarterly* 21: 189–205, p. 199; Richard B.

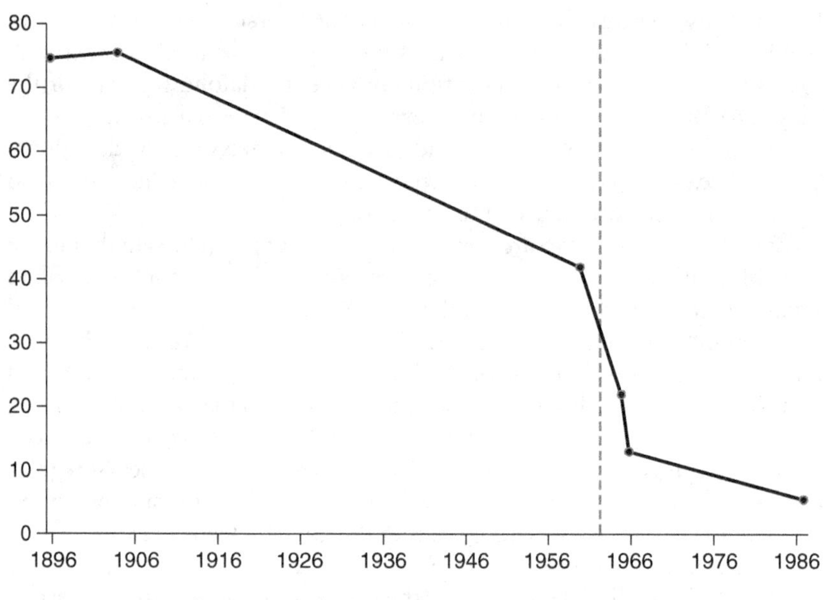

FIGURE 3.1. Bible reading in American public schools, 1896–1987
Note: The vertical dashed line indicates the date (1963) of the *Abington* v. *Schempp* decision banning Bible reading.

The United States Commissioner of Education surveyed school districts in 1896 and again in 1903 regarding their use of the Bible, and found that approximately three-quarters of school districts incorporated Bible reading.[11] Some sixty years later, political scientist Richard Dierenfield surveyed school districts and found that only forty-two percent of schools read the Bible, a sharp decline from the turn of the century.[12] This decline occurred despite a concerted effort by Protestants to pass mandatory Bible reading laws in many states, especially in the South and Northeast. The decline in devotional use of the Bible occurred in conjunction with the secularization of the broader curriculum, as religiously tinged readers and providential histories were slowly replaced with a more secular and naturalistic set of textbooks.[13] Although a number of alternative

Dierenfield. 1967. "The Impact of the Supreme Court Decisions on Religion in Public Schools." *Religious Education* 62: 445–51, pp. 447–48; Richard B. Dierenfield. 1986. "Religious Influence in American Public Schools." *The Clearing House* 59: 390–92. This figure originally appeared in Damon Mayrl. 2015. "How Does the State Structure Secularization?" *European Journal of Sociology* 56(2): 207–39, p. 214.

[11] U.S. Office of Education, *Report ... for the Year 1903*, Vol. 2, p. 2445.

[12] Dierenfield, *Religion in American Public Schools*, p. 51.

[13] See, e.g., Warren A. Nord. 1995. *Religion and American Education: Rethinking a National Dilemma*. Chapel Hill: University of North Carolina Press, pp. 68–70; and James W. Fraser.

religious practices, such as released time, dismissed time, and extramural Bible study for credit, were introduced in some cities, they were never extremely widespread and their use was often fiercely contested.[14]

While the overall trend is clear, Bible reading's actual standing varied considerably across states and districts. This variation reflects the impact of local control. Because Bible usage was determined locally, a crazy quilt of Bible-reading practice developed in the early twentieth century. In larger and more religiously heterogeneous cities and states, Bible reading declined in the face of persistent attacks by religious minorities and indifference by progressive educators. In relatively homogeneous areas, however, especially in the South, Protestant majorities maintained religious devotionals, even buttressing them in some states by securing the passage of mandatory Bible-reading legislation.[15] Such actions were relatively rare, however, and only twelve states (and the District of Columbia) had mandatory Bible legislation on the books by 1963. Elsewhere, great variety in actual practice was the rule.

Significantly, funding for parochial schools did *not* evince such wide diversity, precisely because the issue was successfully nationalized in the late nineteenth century. As discussed in Chapter 2, state-level constitutional restrictions on funding "sectarian" schools became nearly universal in the late nineteenth century as the issue became a central rallying cry in national politics.[16] The near-passage of the Blaine amendment, which would have amended the Constitution to prevent such expenditures, and the ensuing Congressional requirement that new states adopt parallel provisions as a condition of statehood, gave a federal push to this trend.[17] By 1962, every state but Vermont had incorporated some provision restricting funds for religious schools into its constitution.[18] Unlike Bible reading, where opposition was to an extent an ecumenical affair (see below), Catholics were unable to recruit allies in their campaign for public aid for their schools – Jews, Unitarians, and liberal Protestants all opposed diverting funds to religious schools. The issue of public funding for

1999. *Between Church and State: Religion and Public Education in a Multicultural America.* New York: St. Martin's Griffin, pp. 120–21.

[14] Robert Michaelsen. 1970. *Piety in the Public School: Trends and Issues in the Relationship between Religion and the Public School in the United States.* New York: Macmillan, pp. 170–85.

[15] This tendency can be seen in state surveys from the early twentieth century, which reveal that Bible reading was far more common in counties with smaller Catholic populations. See, e.g., Daniel Richard Unger. 1969. "The Use of the Bible in Pennsylvania Public Schools: 1834–1963." Unpublished Ph.D. dissertation, University of Pittsburgh, pp. 114–15. See below for more on state Bible-reading laws.

[16] Ursula Hackett. 2014. "Republicans, Catholics, and the West: Explaining the Strength of Religious School Aid Prohibitions." *Politics and Religion* 7: 499–520, p. 507.

[17] Joseph P. Viteritti. 1998. "Blaine's Wake: School Choice, the First Amendment, and State Constitutional Law." *Harvard Journal of Law and Public Policy* 21: 657–718, pp. 672–73.

[18] Donald E. Boles. 1963. *The Bible, Religion, and the Public Schools.* Ames: Iowa State University Press, p. 43.

religious schools was thus easier to leapfrog to the state level, sharply curtailing local influence.

THE PERMEABLE STATE: DECENTRALIZED CONTROL AND RELIGIOUS CONFLICT

Education in the United States is highly decentralized by any standard, and especially so in comparison with Australian schools. Today, authority over American education is divided among nearly 14,000 local school districts. Remarkably, this represents a *consolidation* of educational authority from the historic norm; at the outbreak of World War II, more than 117,000 school districts managed American education.[19] As discussed in Chapter 2, local control has been a central feature of American education since the nineteenth century. Local school districts are responsible for the development of curriculum, the employment and oversight of teachers, and the maintenance of school buildings.[20] Although state and federal governments have taken on an increased role in funding – and imposing curriculum and teaching standards upon – local schools since the 1960s, America still has "the most decentralized school governance in the Western world."[21]

Local control gave rise, in the nineteenth century, to an important feature of the American educational system not found in Australia: the city superintendent. Beginning in the late 1830s, and with increasing frequency after 1870, urban school boards began to hire superintendents to supervise and coordinate the development of their rapidly growing systems. Between 1870 and 1920, the number of superintendents skyrocketed from 70 to 2,798.[22] As agents of the local boards who employed them, superintendents were fundamentally local officials. The actual powers of any given superintendent varied widely from city to city, but typically included the supervision of teachers and preparation

[19] National Center for Education Statistics. 2015. *Digest of Education Statistics*. Washington, DC: NCES, Table 98. Available online at http://nces.ed.gov/programs/digest/d12/tables/dt12_098. asp (accessed 28 March 2016).

[20] Thomas Corcoran and Margaret Goertz. 2005. "The Governance of Public Education." Pp. 25–56 in *The Public Schools*, edited by Susan Fuhrman and Marvn Lazerson. New York: Oxford University Press, pp. 31–32.

[21] William J. Reese. 2005. *America's Public Schools: From the Common School to "No Child Left Behind."* Baltimore: Johns Hopkins University Press, p. 329. On the rise of federal and state mandates, see Jeffrey Henig. 2013. *The End of Exceptionalism in American Education: The Changing Politics of School Reform.* Cambridge: Harvard Education Press; and Diane Ravitch. 2014. *Reign of Error: The Hoax of the Privatization Movement and the Danger to America's Public Schools.* New York: Vintage, pp. 278–89.

[22] Ellwood P. Cubberley. 1922. *Public School Administration: A Statement of the Fundamental Principles Underlying the Organization and Administration of Public Education.* Boston: Houghton Mifflin, pp. 58 n.1, 59 n.1.

of the course of study.[23] By the turn of the twentieth century, city superintendents would become more uniformly powerful, coming to have "probably … more impact on the everyday management of education than any other set of individuals."[24] This power was obtained, in many instances, by arguing from the professional authority of educational expertise, as I discuss in detail below.

By contrast, state departments of education have historically been quite weak. Although technically the chief educational officer in each state, the state superintendent was a largely powerless position during the nineteenth century. In Wisconsin, for instance, the state superintendent was given the general power to supervise schools, but not the power to enforce his decisions. Local officials accordingly acted essentially as they pleased, frequently ignoring the orders of the state superintendent.[25] Efforts in the nineteenth century to systematize the schools and transfer greater power to state officials failed; although many of the trappings of a centralized system were instituted, these provisions were more formal than real in most states.[26] State bureaucracies remained "small and mostly clerical in function"; even in 1890, the median size of state education departments was two – the superintendent and one assistant.[27]

In short, American education was governed locally, with effective authority over personnel, examinations, finance, and curriculum residing with local school boards. State officials' roles were largely ceremonial and hortatory, with more formal than real power until well into the twentieth century. And in the cities, authority was often transferred to superintendents, who were given varied powers to coordinate and manage education. These features would have an important impact on the fate of religion in America's public schools in the 1850–1950 period.

The Politics of Religion in a Decentralized System

Local boards were the central sites for conflict over religion from the early nineteenth century onwards. By decentralizing curricular authority and situating it close to local communities, the structure of American education empowered local actors to attempt to influence educational policy, including on matters of religious instruction. Accordingly, controversy over religious exercises began

---

[23] David Tyack. 1974. *The One Best System: A History of American Urban Education*. Cambridge: Harvard University Press, pp. 88–91.

[24] David Tyack and Elizabeth Hansot. 1982. *Managers of Virtue: Public School Leadership in America, 1820–1980*. New York: Basic Books, p. 96.

[25] Lloyd P. Jorgenson. 1956. *The Founding of Public Education in Wisconsin*. Madison: State Historical Society of Wisconsin, pp. 97–103.

[26] Thomas B. Timar. 1997. "The Institutional Role of State Education Departments: A Historical Perspective." *American Journal of Education* 105(3): 231–60.

[27] David Tyack, Thomas James, and Aaron Benavot. 1987. *Law and the Shaping of Public Education, 1785–1954*. Madison: University of Wisconsin Press, pp. 50, 61–62.

almost immediately after the creation of common schools. While Catholics were the earliest and most sustained critics of pan-Protestant devotionals, they were not the only ones; as the nineteenth century progressed, other religious outsiders, such as Jews, Unitarians, and freethinkers, also raised their voices against such practices.[28] They were often joined by Baptists (who had their own long tradition of opposition to state-supported religion) and a growing number of liberal Protestants, who increasingly objected to making religious minorities participate in majority religious exercises, viewing it as a violation of religious freedom and the golden rule.[29]

The broadly dispersed control over curriculum through thousands of local boards created myriad opportunities for these religious minorities and their Protestant sympathizers to influence policy in areas where they commanded political strength. Local control did not always lead to the elimination of religious instruction; defenders of Bible reading frequently won, while at other times compromises were struck. But in all cases, decentralized control facilitated ongoing controversy over religious instruction in the public schools.

Local Political Clout and the Elimination of Bible Reading

In large cities and other areas where religious diversity was great, local educational control provided opportunities for religious minorities to challenge and outright eliminate majoritarian religious exercises. Nineteenth-century school board members were quite responsive to constituent pressure, and frequently adjusted the curriculum in response to local political forces.[30] This dynamic carried over to debates about Bible reading. As discussed in Chapter 2, Catholics protested religious exercises in several eastern cities as early as the 1840s, but these challenges typically failed because they lacked sufficient clout.[31] As religious diversity grew in the cities, however, Catholics and other minorities began to achieve successes. Because religious minorities tended to cluster in larger cities,[32] they could amass sufficient political influence to capture or control local boards of education. At the same time, urban school boards themselves

<hr>

[28] James Hennesey. 1981. *American Catholics: A History of the Roman Catholic Community in the United States.* New York: Oxford University Press, p. 185.

[29] On the diverse array of Protestant objections in the 1870s, see David B. Tyack. 1970. "Onward Christian Soldiers: Religion in the American Common School." Pp. 212–55 in *History and Education: The Educational Uses of the Past,* edited by Paul Nash. New York: Random House, p. 232.

[30] David L. Angus and Jeffrey E. Mirel. 2001. "Presidents, Professors, and Lay Boards of Education: The Struggle for Influence over the American High School, 1860–1910." Pp. 3–42 in *A Faithful Mirror: Reflections on the College Board and Education in America,* edited by Michael C. Johanek. New York: The College Board, pp. 5–7.

[31] Joan DelFattore. 2004. *The Fourth R: Conflicts over Religion in America's Public Schools.* New Haven: Yale University Press, pp. 15–43.

[32] Roger Finke and Rodney Stark. 1988. "Religious Economies and Sacred Canopies: Religious Mobilization in American Cities, 1906." *American Sociological Review* 53(1): 41–49, p. 44.

diversified, making them increasingly open to the arguments of those constituents who claimed that Bible reading was an essentially Protestant activity with no place in the supposedly "common" school.

Perhaps the most consequential incident of this type was the "Bible War" that took place in Cincinnati between 1869 and 1873, and produced the court case with which this chapter begins.[33] In 1869, Cincinnati was one of the largest cities in the American West and also one of the country's most religiously diverse cities. Catholics, Jews, Unitarians, Universalists, and freethinkers all made the city home in sizable numbers. The Cincinnati Board of Education was similarly diverse, numbering at least ten Catholics and two Jews among its forty members.

In the summer of 1869, acting on the initiative of a Catholic board member's proposal, the Board of Education entered into negotiations with Catholic officials to bring Catholic parochial schools under the control of the Cincinnati public school district. In conjunction with this proposal, a board member "without an obvious institutional commitment"[34] proposed a resolution repealing the regulation requiring opening devotionals, and declaring that "religious instruction and the reading of religious books, including the Holy Bible, are prohibited in the common schools of Cincinnati, it being the true object and intent of this rule to allow the children of the parents of all sects and opinions, in matter of faith and worship, to enjoy alike the benefit of the common-school fund." The proposal was intended as "an olive branch signifying the good faith of the board and the intention to make the common schools religiously neutral."[35] Nevertheless, it touched off an uproar among the press and the public, and the city divided sharply, with the Protestant establishment arguing that the Bible was central to the moral and civic task of the public schools, and a coalition of religious and political liberals, Catholics, and Jews arguing that the instruments of the state should be secular. On 1 November 1869, the Board passed the resolution by a vote of 22–15, with all of the Catholic Board members voting in favor, and the majority of the Protestants voting against. Furious Protestants took the Board to court, but the Ohio Supreme Court upheld the Board and stated that its decision was an appropriate exercise of local authority.[36]

The Cincinnati Bible War had several important consequences. Most immediately, it encouraged several other cities in Ohio to follow Cincinnati's example

---

[33] Except where noted, the next three paragraphs are based upon Robert Michaelsen. 1969. "Common School, Common Religion? A Case Study in Church–State Relations, Cincinnati, 1869–70." *Church History* 38(2): 201–17.

[34] Michaelsen states that the member "appears to have been either a nominal Protestant or a man with no religious affiliation." See Michaelsen, "Common School," p. 204 n.12.

[35] Stephan F. Brumberg. 2003. "The Cincinnati Bible War (1869–1873) and Its Impact on the Education of the City's Protestants, Catholics, and Jews." *The American Jewish Archives Journal* 54(2): 11–46, p. 23.

[36] *Board of Education v. Minor.*

and eliminate Bible reading.[37] More significantly, it represented an occasion for opponents of pan-Protestant devotionals to articulate strong civic arguments against the practices.[38] In the wake of the events in Cincinnati, many liberal Protestants would come to rethink their position and become advocates for the elimination of devotional exercises, giving weight to the ongoing campaign against them.[39]

Perhaps most importantly, however, the Cincinnati Bible War inspired a welter of additional campaigns against Bible reading, forcing school boards in multiple cities to address the issue in the ensuing decades. In 1875, the school board in Buffalo, New York, elected to exclude the Bible from its classrooms.[40] That same year, in neighboring Rochester, a proposal from a Jewish school board member to forbid religious exercises drew support from Baptists, and passed on a 14–2 vote despite evangelical objections. Acknowledging the conscience claims of Jews, Unitarians, and Catholics, the board passed a set of supplementary resolutions declaring that "the spirit of true religion requires that we should show regard for the conscientious scruples of others which we would have them, in similar circumstances, show us."[41] In Chicago, a two-decade campaign by Catholics to ban the Bible – in which they were joined by a coalition of Jews, Unitarians, liberal Protestants, and nonbelievers – finally succeeded, also in 1875.[42] And in Atlanta, that city's fledgling public schools excluded Bible reading in 1873 after the President of the Board of Education – a respected former Governor and staunch disestablishmentarian Baptist – declared his opposition to the practice.[43]

Concerted political campaigns were not the only route to curricular change, however. Where Catholics held an outright majority in a school district, devotional exercises were sometimes dropped unceremoniously. The unwieldy ward system in large Northeastern cities made this particularly feasible. In 1871, for instance, a muckraking reporter for the *New York Times* conducted an exposé

[37] Bernard Mandel. 1949. "Religion and the Public Schools of Ohio." *Ohio Archaeological and Historical Quarterly* 58: 185–206, p. 195.

[38] Michaelsen, "Common Schools," p. 212.

[39] See, e.g., Henry Ward Beecher. 1869. "Henry Ward Beecher on the School Question." *New York Tribune*, 3 December, p. 5; E.P. Hurlbut. 1870. *A Secular View of Religion in the State, and the Bible in the Public Schools.* Albany, NY: Joel Munsell; and Samuel Thayer Spear. 1876. *Religion and the State, or, The Bible and the Public Schools.* New York: Dodd, Mead.

[40] Steven K. Green. 1992. "The Blaine Amendment Reconsidered." *Journal of Legal History* 36: 38–69, p. 47.

[41] Quoted in Benjamin Justice. 2005. *The War that Wasn't: Religious Conflict and Compromise in the Common Schools of New York State, 1865–1900.* Albany: State University of New York Press, p. 178.

[42] James W. Sanders. 1977. *The Education of an Urban Minority: Catholics in Chicago, 1833–1965.* New York: Oxford University Press, pp. 24–25.

[43] Philip N. Racine. 1990. "Public Education in the New South: A School System for Atlanta, 1868–1879." Pp. 37–57 in *Southern Cities, Southern Schools: Public Education in the Urban South,* ed. David N. Plank and Rick Ginsberg. Westport, CT: Greenwood Press, pp. 50–51.

on Bible reading in that city's schools. He found that in heavily Catholic wards, the Bible had been summarily abandoned at the behest of the Catholic ward trustees. In the Fourth Ward, he reported, the city's Board of Education had found out about the trustees' action, and had ordered the clerk not to pay the teachers' salaries in order to compel them to read the Bible. The situation was resolved when one of the Catholic trustees "carried off the Sacred Book from School No. 1 under his arm one morning" in order to definitively prevent the practice.[44]

During the late nineteenth century, and continuing well into the twentieth, local challenges to Bible reading became commonplace. Although Catholics were at the leading edge of the charge, Jews also became increasingly outspoken in their opposition. In 1905, the Central Conference of American Rabbis launched a broad public campaign against religious devotionals with a widely distributed tract entitled "Why the Bible Should Not Be Read in the Public Schools," and successfully argued against Bible reading in the Washington, DC schools.[45] By the outbreak of World War I, local protests were increasingly displacing Bible reading even in relatively smaller cities such as Indianapolis and Greenville, Mississippi.[46] In each case, local control created pressure points that religious outsiders could use to leverage local political strength into policy change regarding religious education.

Local Control and Church–State Compromises

While religious minorities were able to outright eliminate Bible reading in some cities, in others they leveraged local control over educational policy into compromise measures that contributed to considerable variation in local practice – what historian Benjamin Justice has termed "peaceable adjustments."[47] Peaceable adjustments were most frequently realized in financial compromises between public school systems and Catholic parochial schools. In small country towns with few resources and overwhelmingly Catholic populations, public schools would sometimes be entirely dissolved, with the school board simply "renting" space in the Catholic school for local children, or recognizing an existing parochial school as a "public" institution.[48] In somewhat larger cities as diverse

---

[44] *New York Times.* 1871. "The Bible and the Schools." 16 July, p. 8. See also a follow-up report with similar observations in other parts of the city: *New York Times.* 1871. "The Bible and the Schools." 29 November, p. 1.

[45] Naomi W. Cohen. 1992. *Jews in Christian America: The Pursuit of Religious Equality.* New York: Oxford University Press, pp. 105–06.

[46] Cyrus Adler, ed. 1917. *The American Jewish Year Book, 5677.* Philadelphia: The Jewish Publication Society of America, pp. 84–85

[47] Justice, *The War that Wasn't*, p. 15.

[48] For an excellent analysis of the social and political dynamics of Catholic public schools in New Mexico, see Kathleen Holscher. 2012. *Religious Lessons: Catholic Sisters and the Captured Schools Crisis in New Mexico.* New York: Oxford University Press, especially pp. 8, 46–48. See also *Knowlton* v. *Baumhover*, 182 Iowa 691 (1918).

as Savannah, Georgia, Poughkeepsie, New York, and Stillwater, Minnesota, Catholic leaders convinced local boards to create "Catholic public schools." Under these plans, parochial school buildings were typically ceded or leased to public officials, with the understanding that various "Catholic" aspects of the school – such as staffing and/or holiday observances – would be retained. Catholic religious instruction was typically moved so as to occur immediately after the end of the official school day, so that the daily instruction in public and Catholic schools would be equivalent.[49] In practice, Catholic public schools were often indistinguishable from regular Catholic parochial schools.[50] These arrangements typically lasted so long as no one complained, and were quickly shut down when objections were raised.[51] Still, even well into the twentieth century, especially in the Midwest, Catholic public schools persisted, and became a frequent source of litigation in the state courts.[52]

Peaceable adjustments also occurred on the question of devotionals in the public schools. In the first half of the nineteenth century, a typical compromise was to allow parents to specify which version of the Bible (Protestant King James or Catholic Douay) they wanted their children to read.[53] Later in the century, a similar compromise occurred informally in cities with no formal policy on Bible reading. There, as in many wards of New York City, "teachers could conduct whatever exercises that they deemed appropriate for the pupils and that would preserve their jobs." In largely Catholic districts, therefore, the Douay Bible would be regularly read instead of the King James Bible.[54] In other cities, Catholic and Protestant students were divided up by denomination and sent to study religion with teachers of the same faith.[55] Interestingly, some Protestant communities also favored, or took advantage of, local control in order to retain a more sectarian curriculum. In the Upper Midwest, for example, with its large concentration of Swedish and Norwegian immigrants, public schools frequently shaded seamlessly into Lutheran ones.[56]

[49] For Savannah, see Michael Gannon. 1997 [1964]. *Rebel Bishop: Augustin Verot, Florida's Civil War Prelate*. Gainesville: University Press of Florida, pp. 171–91. For Poughkeepsie and Stillwater, see Jay P. Dolan. 1985. *The American Catholic Experience: A History from Colonial Times to the Present*. Garden City, NY: Doubleday, pp. 271–75.

[50] For vivid descriptions of such schools, see Alvin W. Johnson and Frank H. Yost. 1948. *Separation of Church and State in the United States*. Minneapolis: University of Minnesota Press, pp. 105–12.

[51] See, e.g., J. A. Burns. 1912. *The Growth and Development of the Catholic School System in the United States*. New York: Benziger Brothers, pp. 262–67.

[52] See generally Holscher, *Religious Lessons*; and below, Chapter 5.

[53] William Kailer Dunn. 1958. *What Happened to Religious Education? The Decline of Religious Teaching in the Public Elementary Schools, 1776–1861*. Baltimore: The Johns Hopkins Press, pp. 223–24.

[54] Justice, *The War That Wasn't*, p. 170.

[55] JoEllen McNergney Vinyard. 1998. *For Faith and Fortune: The Education of Catholic Immigrants in Detroit, 1805–1925*. Urbana: University of Illinois Press, p. 42.

[56] Virginia Lieson Brereton. 1998. "Education and Minority Religions." Pp. 279–304 in *Minority Faiths and the American Protestant Mainstream*, edited by Jonathan D. Sarna. Urbana: University of Illinois Press, p. 283.

Perhaps the most creative local compromise, however, occurred when local officials simply redrew district boundaries to create religiously homogeneous districts. In rural New York State, as Justice notes, "the issue of religion found resolution in the broader pattern of ethnically based school districts."[57] As demographic patterns changed, Catholics and Protestants appealed to officials to alter district boundaries to create ethnically and religiously homogeneous new districts. In one case, eighteen Protestant families attempted to create a new district separate from a mixed Protestant–Catholic district. A lawyer for the family declared that a new school district was necessary because "the children of the eighteen families of 'Raceville' and vicinity are all Protestant, while a large majority of the pupils attending the district school are Catholic. There are a large number of families in district ten who refuse to send their children to the district school under the above-mentioned circumstances."[58]

Local Control as Two-Way Street: Protestants' Defensive Maneuvers
If local control sometimes allowed for compromises that kept a place for religion in the public schools, it also afforded Protestants similar opportunities to ensure that majoritarian practices continued to be taught to local children. Protestants' local defense of Bible reading began in the wake of dramatic national controversies over Bible reading, such as those in New York City (1840) and Cincinnati (1869) discussed above. In Detroit, despite near parity between Catholics and Protestants in the general population, "militant" Protestants leveraged superior numbers on the Board of Education in 1845 to overturn that city's decision of two years earlier to exclude Bible reading from the city's schools.[59] In Albany, New York, the school board dismissed a local rabbi's petition to discontinue religious exercises in 1875 by taking a laissez-faire approach to the question and passing the buck to local teachers and principals.[60] During the 1910s and 1920s, the campaign to reassert Bible reading often found its greatest success at the local level, as hundreds of local communities nationwide introduced or strengthened Bible-reading requirements.[61]

However, as non-Protestants gained strength, Protestants increasingly took steps to shield curricular decisions on religious instruction from local influence. In Northeastern cities where ward-based systems facilitated minorities' attempts to exclude pan-Protestant practices or substitute them with Catholic practices, Protestants saw centralizing administrative reforms (discussed in greater detail below) as a means of reducing minorities' influence on religious policies. Administrative reform campaigns at times took on an explicitly

---

[57] Justice, *The War That Wasn't*, p. 68.
[58] Quoted in Justice, *The War That Wasn't*, p. 77.
[59] David L. Angus. 1980. "Detroit's Great School Wars: Religion and Politics in a Frontier City, 1842–1853." *Michigan Academician* 12(3): 261–80, pp. 263–65.
[60] Justice, *The War That Wasn't*, pp. 174–75.
[61] Adam Laats. 2010. *Fundamentalism and Education in the Scopes Era: God, Darwin, and the Roots of America's Culture Wars*. New York: Palgrave Macmillan, pp. 3, 147.

sectarian dimension in the late nineteenth century. In New York, for example, reformers railed against the ethnic politics that they claimed infested the city's schools. The coalition in favor of abolishing ward boards included moral reformers "determined to uphold Protestant values in polyglot New York City." They urged the Mayor to sign the 1896 legislation reorganizing the New York City schools by arguing that it would weaken the Catholic Church.[62] By contrast, teachers, many of them Catholics, unsuccessfully opposed the reforms, arguing that the city's diversity required community control in order to ensure that religious and cultural differences would be respected.[63]

Eventually, Protestants also tried to take curricular decisions out of the hands of local authorities altogether. Beginning in the 1910s, a broad-based Protestant and frequently anti-Catholic campaign worked to pass laws mandating Bible reading at the state level. The National Reform Association, an interdenominational and "unapologetically Protestant" group, avidly sponsored mandatory Bible reading laws in the early twentieth century, including Pennsylvania's pioneering 1913 legislation.[64] Elsewhere, the Ku Klux Klan was a major sponsor of such efforts. Anti-Catholicism and the militant defense of Protestantism were central to the Klan's identity during the 1910s and 1920s, and protecting Bible reading and Protestant religion in the public schools became a particular focus of the Klan's energies.[65] The Klan lent its strong support to compulsory Bible-reading legislation laws in Alabama, New Jersey, Kentucky, and Florida; and tried to pass similar laws in Indiana, Michigan, and Ohio.[66] Between 1913 and 1930, eleven states and the District of Columbia passed mandatory Bible-reading legislation, thereby taking the issue away from local authorities and enshrining the practice in state law.[67]

---

[62] Tyack, *One Best System*, pp. 148–50.

[63] Kate Rousmaniere. 1997. *City Teachers: Teaching and School Reform in Historical Perspective*. New York: Teachers College Press, p. 14.

[64] John William Lowe, Jr. 1987. "The Holy Experiment and Education: The Public School Bible Reading Legislation of 1913 in Pennsylvania." Unpublished Ed.D. Thesis, Teachers College, Columbia University, pp. 154–74.

[65] Kelly J. Baker. 2011. *Gospel According to the Klan: The KKK's Appeal to Protestant America, 1915–1930*. Lawrence: University Press of Kansas.

[66] John Higham. 1981 [1955]. *Strangers in the Land: Patterns of American Nativism, 1860–1925*. 2nd edn. Westport, CT: Greenwood Press, pp. 293–94; Laats, *Fundamentalism and Education in the Scopes Era*, pp. 139–58; Glenn Michael Zuber. 2004. "Onward Christian Klansmen! War, Religious Conflict, and the Rise of the Second Ku Klux Klan, 1912–1928." Unpublished Ph.D. Thesis, Department of Religious Studies, Indiana University, pp. 324–25. Whether these campaigns succeeded or failed often depended on how unified each side could keep its members. Bible-reading legislation in Virginia, for instance, failed because Baptists and Methodists split on the merits of the bill, while the Pennsylvania bill appears to have succeeded largely because of an internal split within the Catholic Church at the time. On Virginia, see Sadie Bell. 1969 [1930]. *The Church, the State, and Education in Virginia*. New York: Arno Press and the New York Times, pp. 513–21; on Pennsylvania, see Lowe, "Holy Experiment and Education," p. 107.

[67] Tyack et al., *Law and the Shaping of Public Education*, p. 165.

Local control thus facilitated religious conflict over public school devotionals, but in ways that yielded divergent outcomes. Protestants leveraged local control to maintain religious instruction in relatively homogeneous, often rural, communities where there were few if any religious minorities. In communities that were more religiously mixed, however, religious minorities had greater success in forging compromises or eliminating Bible reading altogether. Bible reading appears to have been most likely to decline in those locales where Catholics had enough strength to make Bible reading a serious political issue, but where they were not so strong that they could simply swap out the KJV for the Douay wherever they liked. Secularization was thus most likely to occur in districts – many of them urban – where the population was substantially mixed and religious conflict the most likely to prove intractable.

Though the result of any particular local conflict depended on local factors, the aggregate trend was to facilitate a diverse array of arrangements for religious instruction, enable the slow erosion of devotionals in the rapidly diversifying cities and counties of the Northeast and Midwest, and make religious conflict over public school devotionals a regular feature of American educational politics. Indeed, the very fact of conflict eventually became consequential in its own right, influencing how administrators thought about the role of religion in public education.

The Effect of Local Control: Religion as a Controversial Administrative Problem

While local control in many instances enabled religious minorities to eliminate devotional exercises, it also contributed to the development of a climate of administrative wariness toward religion. Religious instruction was an enormous administrative headache for many school districts during the late nineteenth and early twentieth centuries. By the late nineteenth century, the idea that religion would be likely to do more harm than good, from an administrative perspective, had consolidated into received wisdom among educational officials and school board members. This wariness of controversy, even in places where political dynamics might have favored Protestant successes, often convinced administrators, concerned above all with minimizing conflict and ensuring the smooth operation of their school systems, to exclude religious exercises.

Excluding controversial (or potentially controversial) religious material from the classroom has a long history in American education – Protestant denominational catechisms, for example, were early casualties in the name of non-controversiality.[68] But while particular Protestant doctrines had been excluded in the past, the arrival of large numbers of Catholics caused many officials to begin to understand the Bible *itself* as something belonging to the part rather than to the whole. Following past practice, they excluded it. This tendency

---

[68] Leo Pfeffer. 1953. *Church, State, and Freedom.* Boston: Beacon Press, p. 282.

was already visible by the 1850s, when the visiting Swedish educationist Per Siljeström observed that, in "many places" in New England, Bible reading "has been discontinued, and justly so, in accordance with the established principles, as there is one Christian sect, the Roman Catholics, who object to it."[69] Young teachers assigned to religiously mixed towns on the Indiana frontier were similarly advised to avoid using the Bible so as not to exclude Catholic children.[70] Elsewhere in the Midwest, some local boards, anticipating controversy, excluded the Bible from the very outset of their school systems. In St. Louis, the school board prohibited religious instruction in order to prevent any "collision or jealousy among our fellow citizens upon the subject of sectarian influence," while in Detroit, the Bible was excluded on the ground that it constituted "the source of all the bitterness of sectarian animosity" and therefore threatened the "fixed purpose of establishing a system of free schools."[71]

After the Cincinnati Bible War, this view of the Bible as inherently controversial gained currency, and preemptive exclusion began to be advocated as a means of avoiding controversy. In New Haven, Connecticut, the Board of Education voted to discontinue religious exercises in 1877. Noting the rising Catholic population, they expressed concern that "there was no valid reason why a change in the preponderance of influence in the community should not change the exercises [from Protestant] to Roman Catholic, or Jewish, or Rationalistic form, as the case may be." Fearing that such a prospect would lead to political and sectarian controversy in the school system, they declared they could only avoid such a fate by effecting "its entire secularization, and in no other way."[72] Even in Cincinnati, where voters irate about the "Bible War" threw out the old school board in 1870, the newly elected, pro-Bible board chose not to bring the Bible back, instead deciding that "a greater effort should be made to make the Public Schools less objectionable to Catholics if we desire to avoid an irrepressible conflict."[73]

[69] Per Adam Siljeström. 1969 [1853]. *The Educational Institutions of the United States: Their Character and Organization*, trans. Frederica Rowan. New York: Arno Press & The New York Times, p. 230.

[70] Letter, Cynthia Bishop to Nancy Swift, 16 May 1854. Reproduced in Polly Welts Kaufman. 1984. *Women Teachers on the Frontier*. New Haven: Yale University Press, pp. 174–75.

[71] St. Louis board quoted in Selwyn K. Troen. 1975. *The Public and the Schools: Shaping the St. Louis System, 1838–1920*. Columbia: University of Missouri Press, p. 40; Detroit board quoted in Vinyard, *For Faith and Fortune*, p. 19.

[72] Quoted in Sister Mary Paul Mason. 1953. *Church–State Relationships in Education in Connecticut, 1633–1953*. Washington, DC: Catholic University of America Press, p. 162. The Board was turned out of office the following year by a "Bible ticket" supported by all of the clergy in New Haven. The Catholic leadership, who had entered into a gentleman's agreement with Protestant clergy to create a new system of instruction permitting multiple forms of worship in religiously diverse schools, wound up being betrayed by the new slate of Board members. The new Board declared that the carefully wrought compromise was impracticable, and simply reinstated the old system of Protestant Bible reading. Disappointed Catholics withdrew their children from the public schools.

[73] Quoted in Michaelsen, "Common School," p. 211.

State superintendents, too, in their nonbinding advice to local boards, also put forward noncontroversiality as a guiding principle after the Cincinnati Bible War. In Illinois, Superintendent John Brooks suggested to local districts that when no one objected to religious exercises, the Bible should be read and daily prayers offered, but that when objections were raised, such exercises should not be held.[74] Similarly, in Virginia, that state's first State Superintendent was asked to clarify state policy on Bible reading after a conflict had arisen in Alexandria in 1871. "The subject of religious worship in the public schools is one which has occasioned great trouble in other States, and I thought it best for the school law to be silent on the subject," he confessed. But noncontroversiality again was to be a guiding principle: "Where it is agreeable to those concerned, and conducive to order and morals to have such exercises, I can see no objection to its being allowed ... But if serious complaint, disorder, or trouble of any kind would be likely to result from their introduction, they ought not to be allowed."[75]

As the nineteenth century came to a close, concerns about controversy and divisiveness melded with rhetoric about the "common" school to cement an understanding of religion as divisive. School leaders' rhetoric was shot through with concern about group conflict of all kinds,[76] including religious conflict, and the argument that the common school should combat divisiveness lent itself to policies that excluded potentially divisive religious exercises. As the Bible increasingly came to be understood, not as a common text, but as a sectarian text in and of itself, educators sought to expand the nonsectarian ideal by downplaying religious devotionals.[77] "It is impossible to have any such unsectarian religion that is not regarded as sectarian by the more earnest religious denominations," declared U.S. Commissioner of Education William T. Harris in 1903, by way of discouraging use of Bible, prayers, and catechism in the public schools.[78] A few years later, a member of the New York City Board of Examiners reflected that excising religion to avoid controversy was a widespread practice: "No one seems to want in this country any system whereby school children shall be divided, for any purpose, along sectarian lines. If any form of exercise is found to give offense to any, our procedure is rather to cut out that exercise, not to try to adapt it to differentiated groups."[79]

---

[74] Daniel W. Kucera. 1955. *Church–State Relationships in Education in Illinois*. Washington, DC: Catholic University of America Press, p. 85.

[75] Quoted in Bell, *Church, State, and Education in Virginia*, pp. 425–26.

[76] Tyack, *One Best System*, p. 73.

[77] Steven K. Green. 2008. "The Insignificance of the Blaine Amendment." *Brigham Young University Law Review* 2008: 295–333, p. 307.

[78] William T. Harris. 1903. "The Separation of the Church from the School Supported by Public Taxes." *Journal of Addresses and Proceedings of the National Educational Association* 1903: 351–60, p. 354.

[79] Walter L. Hervey. 1907. "Moral Education in the Public Elementary Schools." *Religious Education* 2(3): 81–85, p. 82.

Throughout the first quarter of the twentieth century, many school boards justified their decisions to eliminate Bible reading on the grounds that requiring it would likely generate controversy.[80] In the context of an American educational system where professional educators were assuming much greater control over policy-making, the congealing of a received wisdom that devotional exercises were divisive and potentially controversial did little to encourage educators to embrace devotions. By contrast, it likely contributed to their willingness to let religion drop by the wayside as new, progressive educational reforms began to be instituted in the early twentieth century, as I discuss in the next section.[81]

Local control of educational policy thus contributed to the slow erosion of religion's place in the public schools by enabling it to become a perennial source of political controversy. Directly, political action by religious minorities eliminated devotionals in those cities where they could muster sufficient political muscle to influence local school boards. Indirectly, the climate of controversy that enveloped religious exercises encouraged administrators to abandon or downplay religious exercises in the name of comity. With administrative control over education dispersed widely, American policy toward religious education fragmented in the late nineteenth and early twentieth centuries, subject to local political conditions and the campaigns of those groups invested in religious education (or its elimination).

DECENTRALIZATION AS SPUR TO EDUCATIONAL PROFESSIONALIZATION

While religious conflict began to erode religion from below through thousands of local challenges, religion was simultaneously being marginalized from above by novel professional ideas about the form and content of education. Flourishing under the banner of "progressive education," this new approach to schooling had little place for traditional religious instruction. The rise of progressive education was part of a broader process of professionalization that reshaped American education in the late nineteenth and twentieth centuries. During this time, education became a self-conscious and increasingly

---

[80] See, e.g., Charles A. Israel. 2001. *Before Scopes: Evangelicalism, Education, and Evolution in Tennessee, 1870–1925*. Athens: University of Georgia Press, p. 120; Zuber, "Onward, Christian Klansmen!," p. 344.

[81] Even here, however, innovations were sometimes read through the lens of controversy. In 1916, a prize-winning essay in an NEA-sponsored competition on how to improve religious education extolled the promise of teaching the Bible as history and literature rather than devotionally. But still, the author cautioned, "It would not be wise, of course, to push the matter in any locality to the point of open antagonism." See Laura H. Wild. 1916. "The Essential Place of Religion in Education, with an Outline of a Plan for Introducing Religious Training into the Public Schools." Pp. 30–47 in National Education Association, *The Essential Place of Religion in Education*. Ann Arbor, MI: National Education Association, p. 45.

self-assertive profession whose claims to expertise rested on an emerging specialized body of knowledge in educational psychology. The new educational knowledge, standards, and leaders that this professionalization engendered posed a strong challenge to religion's traditional place at the center of the curriculum.

America's decentralized educational system facilitated this professionalization in both direct and indirect ways. Indirectly, decentralized control encouraged the development of a vibrant, autonomous professional infrastructure of journals, institutes, and associations in which progressive ideas could be debated and refined. Existing outside the control of any educational authority, these professional platforms proved receptive to progressive critiques of existing pedagogical practices. Directly, the lack of centralized planning meant that progressive initiatives and ideas could be applied experimentally in single school districts by local progressive leaders; these experimental initiatives often proved successful, spurring other districts to implement them.

The Professionalization of American Education

American education professionalized slowly but steadily throughout the latter half of the nineteenth and the early twentieth centuries. This professionalization had many aspects, including the rise of organizations – such as the National Education Association (NEA) – which could make claims to speak on behalf of educators; the development of longer educational careers among teachers; and the creation of instruments of professional closure such as increased training and teacher certification requirements. Most importantly, however, educators developed a new form of specialized knowledge, which an emerging cadre of educational experts could draw upon to speak authoritatively on educational matters.

This new professional knowledge, rooted mainly in psychology, displaced traditional approaches that had dominated American education since colonial times. For most of the nineteenth century, the practice of education was quite austere in both form and content. Education was typically "teacher-centered" – teachers stood at the front of the room and led the entire class through regimented call-and-response drills of facts to be learned.[82] Pupils accordingly spent most of their time in school memorizing facts and reciting them back to the teacher. These didactic practices complemented a relatively small and basic curriculum, consisting of Christian morality, personal discipline, and a few basic academic subjects, such as spelling, geography, and mathematics.[83]

---

[82] Larry Cuban. 1993. *How Teachers Taught: Constancy and Change in American Classrooms, 1890–1990*. 2nd edn. New York: Teachers' College Press, p. 26.
[83] Reese, *America's Public Schools*, p. 29.

Beginning in the mid-nineteenth century, however, and accelerating dramatically toward the turn of the twentieth, these traditional educational practices and curriculum were rapidly transformed by a new set of approaches that shifted the focus away from such didactic instruction and displaced religion from its traditional position at the center of the curriculum. Three shifts in particular were important. First, the "teacher-centered" pedagogy of the early nineteenth century was challenged by a "child-centered" pedagogy that accorded a central position to the child's learning process.[84] "Child-centered" education drew on the work of late-eighteenth-century European reformers such as Johann Pestalozzi and Johann Froebel, who argued that education should be tailored to meet the child's needs and interests. By the 1880s, educational journals were beginning to state that "the nature of the child" "lies at the basis of modern primary education ... [and is] the master-key to the whole mystery of education,"[85] and to encourage teachers to reform their teaching to harmonize it with this new understanding of the learning process. "The child should be the center of all educational work," pleaded one educator before the NEA in 1888. "The child's nature is sacred, and its harmonious culture according to its nature and destiny should be our highest aim."[86]

Second, and perhaps more consequentially, the rise of educational psychology provided an alternative, scientific knowledge base that rapidly replaced religion as the epistemic foundation of educational practice.[87] Whereas Pestalozzi and Froebel had argued the case for child-centered education from traditional philosophical (even religious) grounds,[88] the emergence of psychology created a scientific rationale for a child-centered approach to education. By applying insights from psychology to their research, pioneering educational psychologists such as G. Stanley Hall aimed to "place education for the first time on a scientific basis," and to make scientific inquiry into the learning process "the center around which the education of the future will be organized."[89] Indeed, as educational psychology began to be more widely known and admired, it inspired a wide array of pedagogical innovations, including the "individualization" of schooling to adjust it to the abilities of different types of children; the breakdown of traditional subject barriers in an attempt to make knowledge more relevant and readily understandable to children; and

---

[84] Reese, *America's Public Schools*, pp. 79–117.

[85] Quoted in George M. Thomas, Lisa R. Peck, and Channin G. De Haan. 2003. "Reforming Education, Transforming Religion, 1876–1931." Pp. 355–94 in *The Secular Revolution: Power, Interests, and Conflict in the Secularization of American Public Life*, edited by Christian Smith. Berkeley: University of California Press, p. 372.

[86] C.H. McGrew. 1888. "An Ideal Professional Training School for Kindergartners and Teachers." *Journal of Proceedings and Addresses of the National Educational Association* 1888: 339–53, p. 339.

[87] Ellen Condliffe Lagemann. 2000. *An Elusive Science: The Troubling History of Education Research*. Chicago: University of Chicago Press.

[88] Reese, *America's Public Schools*, pp. 86–89.

[89] G. Stanley Hall. 1894. "Editorial." *Pedagogical Seminary* 3(October): 3–7.

the promotion of children's autonomy, particularly efforts to encourage children to have a greater say in what they learned.[90] By 1920, psychology was the acknowledged "master science" of education, its theories influencing nearly every aspect of educational thought and practice.[91]

Third, a group of educators loosely united under the general banner of "progressive education"[92] began to develop new ideas about the purpose of education that posed a fundamental challenge to the entire educational enterprise. Educational progressives embraced a broad-ranging set of educational reforms, including administrative reforms that would increase the power of educational experts to direct public schools (see below). More importantly, however, progressives advanced a dynamic conception of education that saw it not simply as a means of transmitting culture and knowledge from one generation to the next by instructing children in established bodies of knowledge, but instead as "the fundamental method of social progress and reform."[93] Progressives saw education as a potential solution to the social dislocations associated with rapid industrialization, urbanization, and immigration, and argued that traditional aspects of the curriculum with less relevance to modern conditions should be phased out in favor of newer and more relevant offerings in the sciences, vocational and industrial education, physical education, and so forth.[94] By the 1920s, the progressive view that the curriculum "should not be based on traditions of the past or the customs of a community," but rather should constantly be altered and reevaluated "to keep abreast of the progress made in social and economic organization," had become official wisdom among educators.[95]

---

[90] Cuban, *How Teachers Taught*, pp. 40, 50; G. Stanley Hall. 1901. "The Ideal School as Based on Child Study." *Journal of Addresses and Proceedings of the National Educational Association* 1901: 474–88; Arthur Zilversmit. 1993. *Changing Schools: Progressive Education, Theory and Practice, 1930–1960.* Chicago: University of Chicago Press, p. 18.

[91] Ellwood P. Cubberley. 1920. *The History of Education.* Boston: Houghton Mifflin.

[92] Historians of education typically identify a wide array of reform movements with the "progressive" label. Lawrence Cremin identifies four major reform movements with the term: "the effort to render schools more individually and socially useful by introducing vocational instruction into the curriculum; the effort to turn schools into social centers; the effort to remove the schools from politics; and the effort to make schooling scientific." Together, these four reform movements are usually credited with expanding the scope of American education, enlarging and reorganizing the curriculum, altering the materials used in instruction, varying the grouping of students, and promoting systematization and bureaucratization. See Lawrence A. Cremin. 1988. *American Education: The Metropolitan Experience, 1876–1980.* New York: Harper & Row, pp. 223, 230–31.

[93] John Dewey. 1966 [1897]. "My Pedagogic Creed." Pp. 44–59 in *John Dewey: Selected Educational Writings*, edited by F.W. Garforth. London: Heinemann, p. 47.

[94] See generally Lawrence A. Cremin. 1961. *The Transformation of the School: Progressivism in American Education, 1876–1957.* New York: Vintage Books.

[95] NEA Department of Superintendence. 1925. *Third Yearbook: Research in Constructing the Elementary School Curriculum.* Washington, DC: Department of Superintendence of the National Education Association of the United States, p. 24.

More radical still, an increasing number of educators argued that the schools' goal should be to raise children capable of making these adjustments and contributing to social reform on their own. "If we train our children to take orders … and fail to give them confidence to act and think for themselves," declared John Dewey and his daughter Evelyn, "we are putting an almost insurmountable obstacle in the way of overcoming the present defects of our system."[96] Progressive educators like Dewey thus emphasized critical thinking skills to encourage children to question authority, abandon atavistic institutions, and devise novel solutions to social challenges. Children were no longer to be instructed in received truths, but instead to be encouraged to question and challenge social conventions. As the Massachusetts Education Commissioner summarized it succinctly in 1931, "It is not the function of the public school to teach children what to think, it is the function of the public school to teach them how to think."[97]

Educational Professionalization and the Marginalization of Religion

The shift to a child-centered pedagogy and the rise of new progressive understandings of education undercut religion's traditional place at the center of the curriculum in multiple ways. Most basically, the expansion of the curriculum to include multiple new subjects forced religion to compete for limited time and space during the school day.[98] One churchman lamented, in 1912, that "the pressure upon the teacher to get a certain definite and rather large amount of work accomplished within the semester is so great" that "pointing out the religious implications and spiritual lessons of the subjects at hand" had become nearly impossible.[99]

More fundamentally, however, the transformation of education from a teacher-centered, didactic, and static enterprise to a child-centered, experiential, and dynamic one disrupted the educational context that sustained religious instruction. Religious education fit easily in a pedagogical approach that emphasized the transmission of culture through direct instruction from authority. It fit much less easily in a pedagogy of experience-based learning in the service of social reform. Progressive educators were inclined to be skeptical of attempts to teach specific religious or moral beliefs, and they pressed their case in the early twentieth century. By the 1930s, this approach was formulated into explicit policy within the NEA:

The development of a philosophy of life, or a religion, is based on the learning process … No imposition of the thinking of another, however well fortified with threats and promises,

[96] John Dewey and Evelyn Dewey. 1915. *Schools of To-Morrow*. London: J.M. Dent & Sons, pp. 303–04.
[97] Quoted in Thomas et al., "Reforming Education," p. 373.
[98] B. Edward McClellan. 1999. *Moral Education in America: Schools and the Shaping of Character from Colonial Times to the Present*. New York: Teachers College Press, p. 46.
[99] Richard C. Hughes. 1912. "The Limitations of Public Schools, the Opportunity of the Churches." *Religious Education* 6: 578–86, p. 584.

can give the individual a ready-made philosophy, or a set of superior values. Any other mode than following the processes of education through their natural course of questioning, testing, and forming judgments, is poorly suited to self-realization through democratic processes.[100]

In line with their emphasis on critical thinking, therefore, progressive educators argued that children should be taught how to make sound moral judgments *in general*, rather than instructed in specific religious tenets.[101]

Further, new scientific approaches to learning seemed to some educators to be fundamentally incompatible with religious instruction. "The principle of religious instruction is authority; that of secular instruction is demonstration and verification," declared William Torrey Harris to the NEA in 1903. "It is obvious that these two principles should not be brought into the same school, but separated as widely as possible."[102] Dewey similarly observed that, while "the spirit of our schooling is permeated with the feeling that ... every professed truth must submit to a certain publicity and impartiality," religious believers saw religion as "peculiarly revealed, not generally known; authoritatively declared, not communicated and tested in ordinary ways." For Dewey, the rise of educational science set up an "increasing antinomy between the standard for coming to know in other subjects of the school, and coming to know in religious matters."[103]

In this atmosphere, the supernatural elements of religious education, in particular, were marginalized and treated with suspicion. Even the president of the Religious Education Association (REA) – a group founded in 1903 to *promote* religious education – argued in 1919 that education should not "encourage the delusive belief in supernatural agencies and dependence upon them, but it should be such as to convince everybody that things can be controlled and moulded by the power of man; that existing situations need not be accepted with resignation but may be transformed by human effort."[104] Similarly, in 1937, the NEA's Educational Policies Commission rejected the very idea of using revealed religion in the classroom, calling instead for "the utmost possible emancipation from the dictates of a priori or dogmatic notions, whether of theological revelation, Colbertian mercantilism, Ricardian individualism, or Marxian communism."[105]

---

[100] Educational Policies Commission. 1938. *The Purposes of Education in American Democracy*. Washington, DC: National Education Association of the United States, p. 71.

[101] McClellan, *Moral Education*, p. 57.

[102] Harris, "Separation of the Church from the School," p. 353.

[103] John Dewey. 1966 [1908]. "Religion and Our Schools." Pp. 212–28 in *John Dewey: Selected Educational Writings*, edited by F.W. Garforth. London: Heinemann, p. 223.

[104] Arthur Cushman McGiffert. 1919. "Democracy and Religion." *Religious Education* 14: 156–61, p. 157.

[105] Educational Policies Commission. 1937. *The Unique Function of Education in American Democracy*. Washington, DC: National Education Association, p. 61.

These new scientific understandings spelled particular trouble for the devotional reading of the Bible. Precisely because "the contemplative, individualistic, and supernaturalistic type of religious thought and life is being superseded by the active, social, and scientific way of considering and accomplishing things," said one educator in 1909, the Bible itself would have to be put to the ends of professional education, and not vice versa: "There may be found a way to use the Bible for instruction and training ... [But it] would be necessary to select biblical material that would be suitable for childhood and youth, and to use it in accordance with pedagogical principles."[106] Accordingly, the REA encouraged its members to shift their focus away from Bible reading, and to focus instead on character and moral education, Sunday school, and released-time programs.[107] At the same time, they also tried to retool religious education by reimagining and redefining religion in ever-woollier terms that obviated its more problematic aspects, that did not require the reading of the Bible, and that could be less problematically incorporated into the public school curriculum. In this vein, religious education advocates variously reimagined religion as "an all pervading, infinite and eternal energy," as "an attitude, a spiritual relationship," or even as the simple appreciation of truth.[108] In 1916, a prize-winning essay in a competition sponsored by the NEA flatly declared that "religious education is something other and something more than instruction in the Bible," and that true religious education would emerge organically from the "inner religious vitality" of the school.[109]

The Infrastructure of Educational Professionalization

The professionalization of American education was abetted by a vibrant and autonomous infrastructure. This infrastructure consisted of an array of mechanisms of knowledge exchange, including journals and other educational periodicals; teachers' associations; and institutes of teacher training and (later) universities and research centers, which together permitted educators to develop an identity as a profession, and enabled them to exchange ideas about

[106] Clyde Weber Votaw. 1909. "Method of School and Church in Moral and Religious Education." *Religious Education* 4(5): 410–17, pp. 411–12, 416.

[107] George Albert Coe. 1909. "Annual Survey of Progress in Religious and Moral Development." *Religious Education* 4(1): 7–22, p. 11; Steven A. Schmidt. 1983. *A History of the Religious Education Association*. Birmingham: Religious Education Press, pp. 42–44.

[108] Joseph Swain. 1909. "Religious Education and the Public Schools." *Religious Education* 4(4): 348–52, p. 351; Benjamin S. Winchester. 1911. "The Religious Element in Current Public Education." *Religious Education* 6: 261–67, p. 265; Thomas A. Mott. 1906. "The Means Afforded by the Public Schools for Moral and Religious Training." *Journal of Addresses and Proceedings of the National Education Association* 1906: 35–42, p. 41.

[109] Charles E. Rugh. 1916. "The Essential Place of Religion in Education and an Outline of a Plan to Introduce Religious Teaching into the Public Schools." Pp. 5–30 in National Education Association, *The Essential Place of Religion in Education*. Ann Arbor, MI: National Education Association, pp. 12, 23.

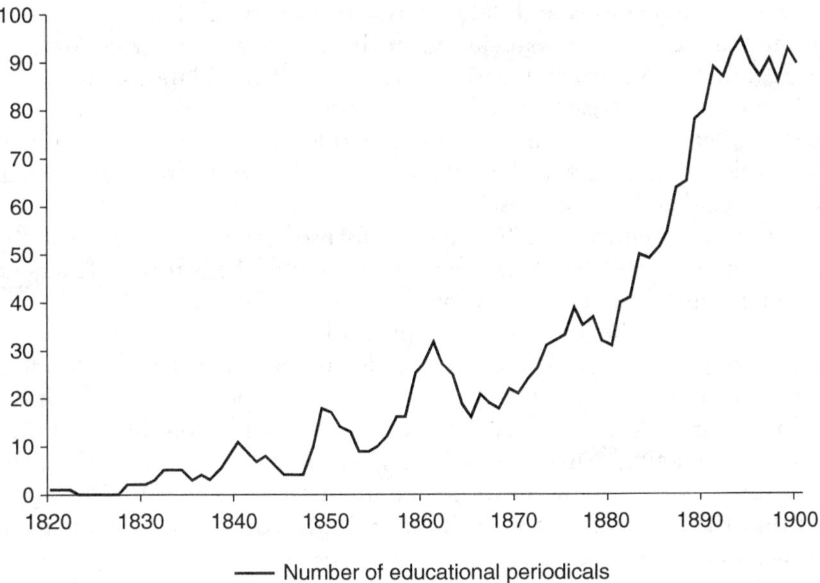

FIGURE 3.2. The rise of nineteenth-century American educational periodicals

the character of their shared enterprise. It provided a space in which traditional educational practices could be criticized and analyzed, and in which new educational ideas could be raised, discussed, debated, elaborated, and disseminated.

America's Autonomous Professional Infrastructure

American education was built upon an impressive infrastructure of professional and professionalizing institutions. First among them were educational periodicals – journals, magazines, and reviews devoted to educational issues or aimed at educational audiences. As Figure 3.2 demonstrates, educational periodicals began to appear in the United States in the late 1810s. Their total number grew by fits and starts until 1870, before multiplying dramatically in the last quarter of the nineteenth century. By 1900, over ninety such publications were in existence in the United States.[110]

In addition to periodicals, the American professional infrastructure also included a large number of educational associations. The earliest teaching associations were local, typically beginning as social ventures in the cities of the Northeast at the turn of the nineteenth century. They were soon supplemented

[110] Data in Figure 3.2 are drawn from Sheldon Emmor Davis. 1970 [1919]. *Educational Periodicals during the Nineteenth Century*. Metuchen, NJ: Scarecrow Reprint Corporation, pp. 92–117.

with state-level associations and, later, national ones. Several early efforts to build a national educational association in the 1830s were abortive or only attained regional influence. But with the creation of the National Teachers' Association (later the NEA) in 1857, educational associations obtained a permanent presence at local, state, and national levels.[111] In addition to their important role as forums for the development of professional educational knowledge (detailed below), these associations were important sites where educators built an identity as a "self-conscious profession with a philosophy and a program of its own."[112] At the opening session of the National Teachers' Association, for instance, the association declared that, among its several aims, it desired "to advance the interests of the profession of teaching."[113] Attendees heard an address by William Russell that called upon teachers to "make their work a profession – not just an ordinary vocation."[114] Indeed, throughout the nineteenth century and into the twentieth, the NEA had a resolutely professional focus, displaying a marked lack of interest in working conditions or other industrial issues. As one historian summarized it, "The [NEA's] leaders assumed that the building of a profession took precedence over problems of the personal welfare of teachers."[115]

Beyond journals and associations, America's professional infrastructure included a wide array of educational institutions with significant to total autonomy from those local school boards who made hiring decisions. Teachers' institutes were among the most common. Typically sponsored by state superintendents of education, teachers' institutes developed into a major force in teacher education, and often functioned as the primary means of educating teachers in rural areas. In 1887, the U.S. Office of Education reported that nearly half of all American teachers attended teachers' institutes, usually to receive ongoing in-service education in contemporary educational developments.[116] In addition to teachers' institutes, private universities and research centers thrived in nineteenth-century America. These private institutions of advanced education, crucially, were not dependent upon state or municipal financial support, and did not have to answer to state officials in terms of their curriculum. They therefore had sufficient autonomy to allow them to function as sites for the development of new ideas, and as platforms from which to criticize the existing system with relative impunity.

---

[111] Mildred Sandison Fenner. 1945. *NEA History: The National Education Association: Its Development and Program*. Washington, DC: National Education Association, pp. 11–13.

[112] R. Freeman Butts and Lawrence A. Cremin. 1953. *A History of Education in American Culture*. New York: Holt, Rinehart, and Winston, p. 456.

[113] Quoted in Butts and Cremin, *History of Education in American Culture*, p. 288.

[114] Quoted in Edgar B. Wesley. 1957. *NEA: The First Hundred Years: The Building of the Teaching Profession*. New York: Harper & Brothers, p. 23.

[115] Wesley, *NEA*, p. 280.

[116] James W. Fraser. 2007. *Preparing America's Teachers: A History*. New York: Teachers College Press, pp. 65–72.

The Autonomous Professional Infrastructure and the Rise of Professional Knowledge

This vibrant autonomous professional infrastructure facilitated professionalization by providing multiple sites where professionalizing ideas could be raised, debated, and disseminated relatively free from threat of official censure. Journals and other educational periodicals played a crucial role in this regard. Many of the first ideas challenging received pedagogical orthodoxy were initially imported to the United States through educational journals. The first issue of Russell's *American Journal of Education* (1826–1839), for instance, stated that "The conductors of the Journal will make it their constant endeavor to aid in diffusing *enlarged and liberal views of education.*"[117] The journal lived up to this charge, playing a key role in publicizing Pestalozzi's criticisms of rote, mechanical instructional methods. More important than Russell's *American Journal of Education*, however, was Henry Barnard's journal of the same name, begun in 1855. Aimed squarely at a sophisticated audience, the *American Journal of Education*'s articles on comparative education, educational history, and educational biography brought European ideas before American educational audiences and greatly influenced educational leaders in the late nineteenth century.[118]

As the nineteenth century progressed, professional associations became increasingly important sites for debates over new educational ideas, practices, and approaches. Educational associations often sponsored conventions where professionalizing educators could come together for the exchange of ideas and mutual support. Most important in this regard were the debates and publications of the NEA. The NEA's influence within the teaching profession was profound; thanks to its role as the central clearinghouse for educational discussion and debate, its "annual conventions became marts for the interchange of educational ideas."[119] By the late nineteenth century, the NEA had begun to act as an informal policy-making body for educators. In 1884, the NEA formed the National Council of Education, whose declared object was "the consideration and discussion of educational questions of general interest and public importance, and the presentation, through printed reports, of the substance of the discussions and the conclusions formulated. It shall be its object to reach and disseminate correct thinking on educational questions."[120] In this pursuit, it proved largely successful, sponsoring reports on controversial issues and promoting investigation, research, and debate within the NEA and among educators more generally.

---

[117] "Prospectus." 1826. *American Journal of Education* 1(1): 1–4, p. 2. Emphasis in original.

[118] Davis, *Educational Periodicals*, pp. 54–55.

[119] Wesley, *NEA*, p. 24.

[120] National Education Association. 1885. *The National Council of Education: Proceedings of Fourth Annual Meeting.* Boston: New England Publishing Co., p. 64.

The NEA's various committee reports were extremely important in disseminating novel educational ideas and practices. The 1893 Committee of Fifteen on elementary education promoted a scientific approach to education, advocating that teachers be trained in the latest scientific practices, including child study and psychology, and for the curriculum to be "realistically related to the child's social and natural environment."[121] Between 1894 and 1906, the papers and reports of the NEA's Department of Child Study helped to promote educational research, and in the years leading up to World War I, committee reports favorable to community study, group cooperation, and an integrated curriculum helped to promote those progressive educational practices.[122] These reports, alongside the more self-consciously promotional publications of the independent Progressive Education Association, were written "in highly palatable forms ... [with] wide circulation," and proved to have considerable influence on curriculum and pedagogy.[123] Already by 1892, the NEA's reports had begun to garner a wide national audience, and by 1910, the NEA was a dominant player in educational debates.[124]

The NEA's influence extended to religious instruction. As sociologist Kraig Beyerlein has demonstrated, the NEA was a crucial forum in which nineteenth-century educators debated the appropriate role for religion in the public schools.[125] In the mid-nineteenth century, NEA leaders favored religion in the public schools, going so far as to pass a resolution commending devotional Bible reading in 1869. Yet over the last quarter of the nineteenth century, religion's place in the public school became a central topic of debate within the organization. Some members voiced concern that religious exercises could provoke conflict and controversy in an increasingly pluralistic society. Thus, James Pyle Wickersham argued before the NEA in 1881, "[Public schools] have changed because the times have forced changes upon them – changed to suit the complex demands of modern society, with its multiplied sects and varied religious opinions. In circumstances like the present, public education must either be in good degree secular, or it must be abandoned."[126] By the turn of the twentieth century, the argument that religion was unscientific and unsuited for modern society was also being voiced in the association's debates.[127] These

---

[121] National Education Association. 1895. *Report of the Committee of Fifteen on Elementary Education, with the Reports of the Sub-Committees.* New York: National Education Association.

[122] Wesley, *NEA*, pp. 199–200.

[123] William Edward Eaton. 1975. *The American Federation of Teachers, 1916–1961.* Carbondale: Southern Illinois University Press, p. 182.

[124] Angus and Mirel, "Presidents, Professors, and Lay Boards," pp. 25, 35.

[125] Kraig Beyerlein. 2003. "Educational Elites and the Movement to Secularize Public Education: The Case of the National Education Association." Pp. 160–96 in *The Secular Revolution: Power, Interests, and Conflict in the Secularization of American Public Life,* edited by Christian Smith. Berkeley: University of California Press.

[126] Quoted in Beyerlein, "Educational Elites," p. 178.

[127] Thomas et al., "Reforming Education," pp. 384–85.

arguments proved persuasive, and in 1902 the NEA passed a new resolution, calling for the Bible to be read as literature rather than as a "theological book."[128] Some twenty years later, the NEA's Department of Superintendence would go still further, declaring that "religious teaching belongs to the church. The purpose of the school is to give morale and encouragement to such teaching but not to undertake it."[129] In this way, professional associations became sites where a professional consensus in favor of a more secular curriculum was developed.

Further, the wide array of teacher-training institutions, from normal schools to teachers' institutes, served as vehicles for the dissemination of progressive ideas. Child-centered, scientific, and progressive educational ideas rapidly permeated the curriculum of the normal schools in the late nineteenth century. Educational psychology began to filter into the state normal schools as early as the 1870s, and was a regular feature in many by the 1890s. In Michigan, for example, prospective teachers were required to undertake observation and analysis in required psychology classes, and the normal school's catalog of classes declared that "instruction in Psychology must precede any ... instruction in methods of teaching" because "the art of teaching must be based upon the science of education, and ... the science of education has its ultimate basis in the science of mind."[130] An NEA survey of normal schools in 1886 found that psychology and science of education were among the courses most frequently provided in normal schools.[131]

Finally, toward the end of the nineteenth century, and with increasing force in the twentieth century, research universities grew into sites for the development, testing, and promulgation of novel educational ideas and practices.[132] These ideas, developed by professors in fledgling departments and schools of education, were often subsequently published and debated in educational journals and associations. Research universities provided institutional resources for the development of scientific and progressive educational ideas. They also provided strong motivation for the development and elaboration of such ideas. In order to justify its position as a discipline, educational academics needed to provide a compelling rationale that education – theretofore seen as a relatively straightforward and banal occupation – was worthy of study in a university

---

128 "Report of the Committee on Resolutions." 1902. *Journal of Proceedings and Addresses of the National Education Association* 1902: 26–28, p. 27.

129 NEA Department of Superintendence. 1924. *Second Yearbook: The Elementary School Curriculum*. Washington, DC: Department of Superintendence of the National Education Association of the United States, p. 93.

130 Quoted in Christine A. Ogren. 2005. *The American State Normal School: "An Instrument of Great Good."* New York: Palgrave Macmillan, pp. 129–30.

131 Quoted in Wesley, *NEA*, p. 83.

132 Thomas S. Popkewitz. 1991. *A Political Sociology of Educational Reform: Power/ Knowledge in Teaching, Teacher Education, and Research*. New York: Teachers College Press, pp. 81–84.

setting.[133] This dynamic helped to drive the move toward more scientific approaches to education in the late nineteenth century. Perhaps unsurprisingly, therefore, many of the most prominent educational theorists, such as Hall and Dewey, held positions in these new departments and schools of education.[134]

In short, the highly elaborated autonomous professional infrastructure in the United States in the late nineteenth century provided a series of platforms in which professionalizing ideas could be developed, debated, and disseminated, thereby promoting the professionalization of education. The increasing interconnections between journals, professional associations, and institutions of higher education allowed new scientific and progressive approaches to the theory and practice of education to insinuate themselves deeply into the educational community.

Decentralized Governance and America's Vibrant Professional Infrastructure

This vibrant, autonomous professional infrastructure was closely linked to the development of schools in a context of decentralized control. The grassroots development of common schools encouraged educational boosterism, which in turn encouraged the development of journals and associations promoting education. More importantly, the juxtaposition of strong local district control with weak state supervision created a variety of incentives that encouraged educational administrators to promote professionalization. Weak state superintendents viewed professionalization as a tool they could use to enhance their own influence. Meanwhile, local educational administrators – the city and county superintendents – saw in professionalization the means of expanding their own autonomy relative to their employers, the strong local boards. Finally, America's laissez-faire approach to higher education provided ample room for private universities to pioneer the research university model, with its corresponding departments of education and educational research programs, largely free from any state controls or restrictions. In sum, the structure of and distribution of authority in American education did little to restrict, and a great deal to encourage, the rise of professional journals, associations, and leaders.

Local Initiative and the Origins of America's Professional Infrastructure

As discussed in Chapter 2, the creation of public education in the United States was largely left to local initiative, achieved through a nationwide grassroots campaign to create common schools. This campaign required common school advocates to engage in considerable boosterism to encourage local communities to buy into the common school. Two of their most effective weapons in this strategy

---

[133] Tyack, *One Best System*, pp. 135–36.
[134] Cremin, *American Education: The Metropolitan Experience*, p. 168; Fraser, *Preparing America's Teachers*, p. 142.

were educational associations and educational periodicals. Many associations were founded to function simultaneously as forums for discussion and as agents of educational promotion. The American Institute of Instruction (AII), for example, was founded in Boston in 1830 as a learned debating society for educational issues, and in this capacity it published and distributed a series of lectures and essays on educational innovations. However, members of the AII also saw themselves as fundamentally concerned with promoting the public understanding of education in New England and the Midwest. In addition to its lectures and publications, therefore, it also sponsored a series of "lyceums," in which a series of speakers traveled around New England from town to town to challenge public apathy toward education and recruit teachers for the common schools.[135]

Educational periodicals were even more closely tied to educational boosterism in the early nineteenth century. Especially in the 1840s, state-level education journals proliferated, and many of these were explicitly devoted to the promotion of public education.[136] A review of early educational publications shows that "the great aim was promotion and direction of a public school system in the process of becoming." The *Ohio School Journal*, for instance, declared its aim in 1846 to "awaken the whole community to a lively sense of the importance of education to a free people, and of the common school as the means by which all the youth of the State are to be educated."[137] The fundamentally hortatory purpose of many of these journals can be seen in their titles: eighteen of the earliest educational periodicals had the word "Advocate" in their title, while others titled themselves the "Pioneer," "Clarion," or "Disseminator." These journals were a key tool for common school proponents in their overall campaign for public education in the mid-nineteenth century.

State Superintendents: the Professionalizing Incentive of Weakness

Weak state-level education departments further encouraged the development of the professional infrastructure. As discussed above, state superintendents typically possessed highly circumscribed formal powers. State superintendents therefore encouraged professional institutions not only to promote education, but also informally to extend their influence over teachers. In California, for example, State Superintendent John Swett encouraged the professionalization of teachers as a means of counteracting arbitrary decisions by local school boards. From his position, he pushed for enhanced training and certification of teachers, and increased support for teachers' institutes and normal schools.[138]

---

[135] Paul H. Mattingly. 1975. *The Classless Profession: American Schoolmen in the Nineteenth Century*. New York: New York University Press, pp. 34–38, 90–92. As self-styled "missionaries" in the cause of education, it is perhaps unsurprising that the lyceum organizers deliberately appropriated the Methodists' "circuit rider" model as they designed their lyceum series.

[136] Davis, *Educational Periodicals*, pp. 15–18.

[137] Quoted in Davis, *Educational Periodicals*, p. 17.

[138] Tyack et al., *Law and the Shaping of Public Education*, p. 93.

In this regard, he followed in the footsteps of Henry Barnard, Connecticut's first Superintendent, who created the first teachers' institute and who (alongside Horace Mann) subsequently convinced several state legislatures to back the creation and financing of teachers' institutes.[139]

Like many other state superintendents, Swett also distributed a state-funded educational journal to teachers and school trustees around the state. Journals were a common tool used by state superintendents to pursue their goals. In some states, state superintendents actually initiated the first school journals. In other states, they offered to subsidize school journals that were already being produced by state teachers' associations. State officials saw these journals as an important means of communicating with local and district officials.[140] In some cases, in fact, they were accused of exercising undue influence over the content of the journals. A column in the *Wisconsin Journal of Education* in 1881, for instance, accused the editors of that journal of publishing "only what is right and becoming to emanate from this department of public service, and a multitude of things that ought to be said through the columns of an educational journal are never uttered."[141]

In addition to journals, state superintendents used educational associations as means of extending their influence. In fact, something of a symbiotic relationship between the associations and the state superintendents emerged in the nineteenth century, as each used the other to advance its goals and interests. A particularly intimate example of this dynamic took place in Illinois. On the day after Christmas, 1853, the Secretary of State, who also served as *ex officio* Superintendent of Common Schools, met with several school principals in a Methodist church to form the Illinois State Teachers' Association so that they might better agitate on behalf of public education. Two years later, the State Teachers' Association successfully lobbied the legislature for the formal creation of an independent Office of State Superintendent.[142] If associations sometimes helped to create state superintendencies, state superintendents also helped to create and to direct educational associations. In California, the State Superintendent convinced the legislature to pass a law in 1852 that authorized the state superintendent to sponsor yearly meetings for all school teachers.[143] By the mid-nineteenth century, state educational associations "tended to be dominated by the state superintendents, who used them to extend their own influence in standardizing educational practice."[144]

139 Butts and Cremin, *History of Education*, p. 287.
140 Davis, *Educational Periodicals*, pp. 23–25, 37.
141 Quoted in Davis, *Educational Periodicals*, pp. 45–46.
142 Robert G. Bone. 1957. "Education in Illinois before 1857." *Journal of the Illinois State Historical Society* 50: 119–40, pp. 133–35.
143 Tyack et al., *Law and the Shaping of Public Education*, p. 89.
144 Tyack and Hansot, *Managers of Virtue*, p. 49.

City Superintendents: Motivated Professional Leadership

A third way that decentralized education encouraged the professionalization of American education was through the local office of city superintendent. As administrative employees of local school districts, superintendents were torn between the requirement that they effectively and efficiently administer education, and the petty politics, capricious demands, and micromanaging tendencies of their local school boards.[145] City superintendents thus had clear structural incentives to promote the development of professional knowledge and standards, since they could use these claims to expertise to expand their power and autonomy relative to the local boards of education who employed them.

Consequently, superintendents were often at the forefront of the professionalizing campaign during the late nineteenth and early twentieth centuries. City superintendents provided a seemingly bottomless fount of leadership for educational associations like the NEA. Prominent superintendents such as James Greenwood of Kansas City and Jesse Newlon of Denver served as presidents of the NEA, and superintendents saturated the smaller committees and subsections of the NEA most closely concerned with setting professional standards.[146] The Department of Superintendence, the superintendents' subsection of the NEA, was an "annual clearinghouse of evolving theories and practices" where curricular policies and educational standards were hammered out.[147] Superintendents also dominated the influential Council of Education, the "inner sanctum within the NEA" where disputed educational issues were resolved, and "heresies and false notions of education" were rooted out.[148] Superintendents also served as editors of prestigious educational journals, university professors and presidents, and as important advisors and conduits to the United States Commissioner of Education in the late nineteenth and early twentieth centuries. One of the most famous, William Torrey Harris, onetime superintendent of schools in St. Louis, actually rose to become United States Commissioner of Education following an extended stint in leadership in the NEA.[149]

The new expertise that superintendents helped to generate in these capacities quickly accrued to their benefit. As the twentieth century dawned, superintendents "increasingly argued that only experts, not laypeople on school boards, could keep apprised of the latest pedagogical ideas through wide reading, professional correspondence, and association with other urban leaders."[150]

---

[145] David Tyack. 1976. "Pilgrim's Progress: Toward a Social History of the School Superintendency, 1860–1960." *History of Education Quarterly* 16(3): 257–300, p. 278.

[146] Raymond E. Callahan. 1964. *Changing Conceptions of the Superintendency in Public Education, 1865–1964.* Cambridge: New England School Development Council, p. 16; Wesley, *NEA*, pp. 284–85, 296–97.

[147] Wesley, *NEA*, p. 284.

[148] Tyack and Hansot, *Managers of Virtue*, pp. 99–100.

[149] Callahan, *Changing Conceptions*, p. 5; Tyack and Hansot, *Managers of Virtue*, p. 137.

[150] Reese, *America's Public Schools*, p. 60.

In Pittsburgh, the local teachers' association successfully argued in 1911 that educational decisions should be put in the hands of the superintendent because of the superintendent's perceived expertise in educational matters:

Teaching is a profession that renders an expert service; consequently only experts can decide with uniform wisdom and success regarding the qualifications of members or would-be members of the profession ... Arrangement of courses of study, daily programs, plans for grading, examinations, and promotions are matters within the function of an expert superintendent, which no school board member need interfere with, except for final approval or rejection. So, too, the appointment, promotion and dismissal of teachers requires prolonged special training and observation. Similarly, the provisions for supervision, the selection of textbooks and other forms of school apparatus and equipment, presupposes expert knowledge and service.[151]

The superintendents' promotion and deployment of a new, professional educational discourse had concrete benefits: the expansion of their powers in urban school districts. Though the consolidation of power was slow, uneven, and contested, control over the daily affairs of urban districts – including authority over curriculum, hiring, and supervision – shifted inexorably toward superintendents.[152] In this way, the superintendents who provided the leadership that helped to professionalize education ultimately benefited from the authority it bestowed upon them as educational experts. And, as discussed below, they used these increased powers to implement professionalizing reforms in their local school systems that worked to marginalize religious practices.

Private Higher Education, Tertiary Innovation, and the Rise of Educational Research

A final way that decentralized education contributed to the professionalizing of American education was through its largely independent system of higher education. Unlike in Australia, where, as I will show in the next chapter, centralized educational systems were deeply entangled with institutions of higher education, local control over education meant that there were few if any centralized controls over hiring, association, or criticism in American universities. During the nineteenth century, teacher training was widely dispersed among a diverse array of private academies, teachers' institutes, and normal schools, all of which were independent of those local school boards with hiring authority.[153] Institutions of higher education, especially those devoted to education and teacher training, faced few state-imposed constraints on their curriculum or practices, enabling them to pursue more aggressive professionalizing agendas.

---

[151] Quoted in William H. Issel. 1967. "Teachers and Educational Reform during the Progressive Era: A Case Study of the Pittsburgh Teachers Association." *History of Education Quarterly* 7(2): 220–33, p. 230. Emphasis in original.

[152] Tracy L. Steffes. 2012. *School, Society, and State: A New Education to Govern Modern America, 1890–1940.* Chicago: University of Chicago Press, pp. 28–29.

[153] See generally Fraser, *Preparing America's Teachers.*

America's dynamic private educational sector, with its still greater autonomy, played a particularly key role as the incubator for the research university model from the 1870s onward. Unlike traditional colleges, which had a limited curriculum and focused on transmitting existing knowledge, the research university focused on producing new knowledge in a novel structure organized around research, graduate education, disciplinary specialization, academic freedom, and student independence.[154] Importantly, the first universities that adopted this model were private institutions. Many of these, such as Johns Hopkins, Clark, Cornell, and the University of Chicago, were created *de novo* through the newfound largesse of charitable American industrialists.[155] The model quickly spread to several established private colleges such as Harvard, Yale, and Stanford, and a few public universities, such as the Universities of Michigan and Wisconsin. By moving professorial research to the fore, the research university encouraged the development of disciplines, departments, and their concomitant specialized knowledge.[156]

Thanks to the decentralized, diverse, and autonomous nature of American higher education, the research university model – and, ultimately, the development of education as a scholarly discipline – flourished. Since teacher training was not monopolized by state colleges, research universities were able to develop new departments of education in the late nineteenth and early twentieth centuries. Universities saw, in education, an opportunity to strengthen their institutions and attract students. But at the same time, as discussed above, this required education to justify itself as a distinct field of scholarship in order to secure its place within the research university model. Emerging departments of education in America's research universities thus rapidly became centers for the development of professional knowledge and the training of educational administrators. And the ongoing interaction of educational researchers and administrators in the universities and the professional associations helped spread new educational ideas and practices throughout America's decentralized educational system.[157]

Decentralization and the Spread of Progressive Practices

Local control also contributed more directly to the ultimate spread of new professional knowledge and practices in the early twentieth century. Thanks to

---

[154] See, e.g., Laurence R. Veysey. 1965. *The Emergence of the American University*. Chicago: University of Chicago Press.

[155] Christian Smith. 2003. "Introduction: The Secularization of American Public Life." Pp. 1–96 in *The Secular Revolution: Power, Interests, and Conflict in American Public Life*. Berkeley: University of California Press, p. 75.

[156] Roger L. Geiger. 2000. "Introduction: New Themes in the History of Nineteenth-Century Colleges." Pp. 1–36 in *The American College in the Nineteenth Century*, edited by Roger Geiger. Nashville, TN: Vanderbilt University Press, p. 33.

[157] Steffes, *School, Society, and State*, pp. 31–33; Tyack, *One Best System*, pp. 133–36.

fragmented control over educational policy, progressively inclined city superintendents could use their local schools as sites for the introduction of educational experiments which, in turn, could then be copied by other districts.
Generally speaking, the implementation of educational reforms was a slow
and piecemeal process, decoupled considerably from their acceptance in professional forums.[158] In matters of religious education, this decoupling of theory
and practice provided plenty of room for the negotiation of local compromises
that perpetuated religious instruction.[159] However, the net effect was more typically to reduce the role of religious instruction – especially Bible reading – in
the public schools. Local control, in short, allowed secularizing reforms to
spread effectively, even if entire states did not adopt them as official policy.

The city superintendency, again, proved pivotal to the spread of these
reforms. Because superintendents were situated at a unique crossroads – as
administrative leaders at the local level, and as members of an emergent educational elite developing policy ideas at the national level – they were strategically positioned to simultaneously develop and enact professional reforms.
Urban superintendents were "carriers of an adapted cosmopolitanism,"
acquired through their professional training and participation in professional
associations.[160] Superintendents thus acted as the conduits through which professional standards and norms came to influence local policies. Progressive
superintendents made urban districts "the most important arena for school
reform in the first half of the twentieth century."[161] Among others, William
Torrey Harris pioneered science education in the St. Louis schools in the 1870s,
Ella Flagg Young used the Chicago schools to experiment with giving teachers a greater say in the development of the elementary curriculum, and Jesse
Newlon used the Denver schools in the 1920s as a platform to build "flexible,
activity-centered schools that linked daily life to what students learned."[162] As
these experiments were publicized as successes, other districts used them as
models for their own reform programs.[163] Reforms thus typically spread slowly
and unevenly, but also widely, through a pattern of experimentation, publicity,
and imitation. Even if entire states did not adopt a given reform, it could still
become relatively widespread thanks to local initiative and imitation.

As with other features of the traditional curriculum, the slow spread, district
by district, of progressive and other pedagogical reforms helped to marginalize

---

[158] McClellan, *Moral Education*, pp. 60–61.
[159] Thomas et al., "Reforming Education," p. 357.
[160] Tyack, "Pilgrim's Progress," p. 274.
[161] Reese, *America's Public Schools*, pp. 122–23.
[162] On St. Louis, see William J. Reese. 2007. *History, Education, and the Schools.* New York: Palgrave
Macmillan, p. 67; on Chicago, see George S. Counts. 1928. *School and Society in Chicago.*
New York: Harcourt, Brace and Company, pp. 66–67; on Denver, see Cuban, *How Teachers
Taught*, pp. 78–80.
[163] Thomas et al., "Reforming Education," p. 373.

religion's position in the early twentieth century. In a pattern that mirrored the broader fortunes of Bible reading, progressive reforms had their greatest impact in urban districts where superintendents were strongest and most professionalized, but relatively less impact in rural and Southern districts where professionalization was weaker.[164] At times, this reflected superintendents' overt opposition to religious instruction,[165] but more often it reflected the fact that educational reforms often displaced the traditional materials, methods, and organization in which those exercises were embedded, without providing the same – or any – role for religion in the new, reformed system.

The case of Muncie, Indiana, helps to illustrate. In the mid-1920s, conducting research for their classic study *Middletown*, Robert and Helen Lynd observed a public school system rich with religious elements. During basketball season, students attended chapel services led by local clergy, and teachers were seen to pressure students to attend optional Bible classes run by the YMCA.[166] Even more strikingly, the city's "Course of Study of the Elementary Schools" was studded with religious ideas and practices:

The first paragraph in the "Course of Study of the Elementary Schools" enjoins upon the teachers that "all your children should join in opening the day with some exercise which will prepare them with thankful hearts and open minds for the work of the day … The Bible should be heard and some sacred song sung." The School Board further instructs its teachers that geography should teach "the spirit of reverence and appreciation for the works of God – that these things have been created for [man's] joy and elevation … that the earth in its shape and movements, its mountains and valleys, its drought and flood, and in all things that grow upon it, is well planned for man in working out his destiny"; that history should teach "the earth as the field of man's spiritual existence"; that hygiene create interest in the care of the body "as a fit temple for the spirit"; finally that "the schools should lead the children, through their insight into the things of nature that they study, to appreciate the power, wisdom, and goodness of the Author of these things. They should see in the good things that have come out of man's struggle for a better life a guiding hand stronger than his own … The pupils should learn to appreciate the Bible as a fountain of truth and beauty through the lessons to be gotten from it…"[167]

Although the Lynds concluded that religion was less central to Muncie's schools than it had been thirty-five years before, it still clearly held a central position in the mid-1920s.

---

[164] Cuban, *How Teachers Taught*, p. 144; Steffes, *School, Society, and State*, p. 12. As Tyack notes, this partly reflects the fact that rural superintendents tended to be more embedded in their local communities and thus more apt to "internalize the values of the communities they served" rather than the cosmopolitan and professional ethos of their urban counterparts. See Tyack, "Pilgrim's Progress," p. 274.

[165] As occurred, e.g., in Indianapolis; see Zuber, "Onward, Christian Klansmen!," p. 355.

[166] Robert S. Lynd and Helen Merrell Lynd. 1957 [1929]. *Middletown: A Study in Modern American Culture*. San Diego: Harcourt and Brace, pp. 219, 395–96.

[167] Lynd and Lynd, *Middletown*, p. 204.

When the Lynds returned to Muncie in 1937, however, the picture had changed dramatically. Gone are the references to chapel services. Nor do the Lynds note the religious tone of the Course of Study. The only reference to religion in the public schools is a brief note indicating that the optional YMCA Bible classes continued to draw students.[168] Instead, their description of the schools is given over to a discussion of the impact of a "ten-year program of school planning and reorganization" that had been implemented in 1928. This reorganization entailed nothing less than "the redefinition of the philosophy of education in Middletown" into a child-centered program with "emphasis upon small classes and individual differences as over against mass education and conformity."[169] The Lynds illustrated this transformation by quoting from a 1933 district planning report:

From the beginning of time until recent years, world change has developed slowly. As a result, knowledge was traditionally handed down. Such a process became authoritative and the accepted basis of knowledge. Many held to such a traditional philosophy and advocated that to learn is basically acquisition and acceptance on authority. Ours is a different philosophy. It *advocates that the aim of education should be to enable every child to become a useful citizen, to develop his individual powers to the fullest extent of which he is capable, while at the same time engaged in useful and lifelike activities ... We believe in the doctrine of equal educational opportunity for every child to develop according to his abilities, interests, and aptitudes.*[170]

It is hardly surprising that, under this new regime, the Lynds found so little religion in the schools' formal program.

CONCLUSION

Religion's position in American public schools declined between 1860 and 1960 as a result of challenges by religious minorities to the prevailing system of pan-Protestant devotionals, and the displacement of traditional curriculum and pedagogy by new, professional educational ideas and practices. Both minority challenges and professional development were facilitated by the permeable, decentralized character of American educational administration. Because educational policies and practices were decided locally, they could be challenged locally in areas where religious minorities attained sufficient strength, and they could be altered locally by superintendents strategically positioned at the intersection of local control and an emerging national profession. Moreover, the local development of common schools encouraged the development of the very professional infrastructure that nurtured and helped

---

[168] Robert S. Lynd and Helen Merrell Lynd. 1937. *Middletown in Transition: A Study in Cultural Conflicts*. New York: Harcourt, Brace and Company, pp. 84 n.17, 305.
[169] Lynd and Lynd, *Middletown in Transition*, pp. 219–20.
[170] Quoted in Lynd and Lynd, *Middletown in Transition*, pp. 220–21. Emphasis in original.

disseminate those professional reforming ideas that would eventually contribute to religion's marginalization in the first half of the twentieth century. In each of these aspects, American education contrasted sharply with the highly centralized, tightly controlled system of administration prevalent in Australia, to which we turn in the next chapter.

4

Settlement Stability in the Insulated Australian State

In 1938, the eminent comparative educationist Isaac Kandel surveyed the structure and operation of Australian education. He was struck by its "high degree of centralization," which had commendably "brought facilities for education within the reach of all children of school age." Nevertheless, Kandel sounded an alarm. "The efficiency attained by centralized control may be purchased at too great a price. A central authority tends to grow by the power which it wields and when such an authority exercises at once the rights to legislate, ... to execute, and to judge, the result is inevitably rule by a bureaucracy which imposes its will and ultimately secures uniformity in aspects of the educational process where uniformity is least desirable."[1]

Kandel was not the first observer – nor would he be the last – to remark upon the highly centralized administration of Australian education, nor to raise concerns about its sclerotic effects on educational practice. Just a year before Kandel published his study, an education conference held in Sydney featured a virtual parade of speakers urging Australians to break the shackles of bureaucratic rule. The *Sydney Mail* reported, "Behind all the discussions and lectures at the conference was an evident urge to condemn educational methods that are based on rigid centralization."[2] Australian education at midcentury was, in fact, highly centralized. Under the Australian system, the state education departments coordinated and controlled all aspects of schooling, from staffing and curriculum to teacher training. Despite moves in the last decades of the

---

[1] I.L. Kandel. 1938. *Types of Administration, with Particular Reference to the Educational Systems of New Zealand & Australia*. Auckland: New Zealand Council for Educational Research, pp. 47, 50–51.

[2] Quoted in John P. Hughes. 2002. "Harold Wyndham and Educational Reform in Australia, 1925–1968." *Education Research and Perspectives* 29(1): 1–268, p. 69.

twentieth century to decentralize administration, to this day Australian education remains remarkably centralized, with power concentrated in state departments and very few real powers delegated to the local level.

This chapter examines how Australia's centralized education system affected the pace and timing of secularization in Australian schools. In contrast to the United States, where devotional Bible reading declined over the first half of the twentieth century, religious instruction persisted, and even became more widespread, in Australian schools. In many states, students in 1960 encountered religion in the curriculum in much the same way that their great-grandparents might have encountered it in 1880; in others, they encountered a more robust religious presence. After 1960, however, religion's place in the public school was called into question, and ultimately transformed. Yet while much had changed by 2000, most students still found "scripture" to be a regular component of their public education. Secularization occurred, but it was only partial; while some religious aspects of the curriculum were eliminated, others were retained, and even strengthened.

Why was religious education so secure for so long in Australian schools? And when secularization occurred, why was it only partial? The answer can be found in Australia's highly centralized system of educational administration. The centralized administrative pattern had a generally conservative influence upon Australian education, and this was true of Australian schools' relationship to religious education as well. Centralization inhibited two key secularizing processes, religious conflict and professionalization, before 1960. The strong central administrative apparatus insulated departmental policies, including policies regarding religious education, from challenges by religious minorities. There were few opportunities for those opposed to religious instruction to "capture" or otherwise influence the administrative apparatus. Even more consequentially, the strong centralized system suppressed professionalization among educators. Centralized control over teacher training, public service regulations prohibiting criticism of government policy, and a strong inspectorate retarded the influence of progressive education and promoted conservatism among teachers. Accordingly, the nineteenth-century settlement continued to function undisturbed for nearly a century. Only when this tight control was relaxed after 1960 did religious instruction come in for consequential criticism. Attempts to decentralize curricular decision-making, give teachers more professional freedom, and emphasize local involvement in the schools both created new problems for the old system and provided a framework for reworking official policy on religious instruction.

RELIGIOUS EDUCATION IN AUSTRALIAN SCHOOLS
FROM 1880 TO 2000

As discussed in Chapter 2, the struggle to establish common schools in Australia yielded state educational systems with varied policies regarding religious education. Victoria took the hardest line against religious education, forbidding teachers and clergy from providing anything other than "secular instruction," and expunging all religious material from school readers.[3] By contrast, New South Wales embraced religious education. Under the Public Instruction Act of 1880, teachers were required by law to provide "general religious teaching" (GRT), including Scripture reading, from official, state-sanctioned Scripture readers. Additionally, clergy were given the "right of entry" to visit the state schools once a week in order to provide supplementary SRI to the children of their denomination.[4] This dual system of GRT and SRI proved popular; it was also adopted in Western Australia and Tasmania. Other colonies allowed religious instruction subject to restrictions. Queensland forbade Bible reading but allowed SRI by visiting clergy outside of school hours; and South Australia forbade SRI but permitted teacher-led Bible reading, though only as an optional exercise at the beginning of the school day.[5]

Over the course of the twentieth century, these various arrangements would begin to converge. Queensland would join New South Wales, Western Australia, and Tasmania in providing both GRT and SRI during school hours. Meanwhile, South Australia and Victoria would pass legislation permitting SRI. In those states that had adopted the dual GRT/SRI system from the start, there was little to no change. By 1950, SRI by visiting clergy was essentially a universal practice throughout the country, and most Australian states also required mandatory, teacher-led Bible reading.[6]

This period of consensus lasted slightly less than two decades. Beginning in the late 1960s, Australian schools grew more secular – but only partially so. Facing a crisis in religious education, the states responded by establishing formal commissions to reconsider their religious education policies. Most reached similar conclusions: SRI was to be retained, while GRT was to be transformed from Christian Scripture reading to a broader and more objective "studies of religion" course, or phased out altogether. The only exceptions were South Australia, where SRI was abolished and replaced with studies of religion course; and Queensland, where schools retain the option of including Scripture reading as part of their regular course of instruction.[7] The general

---

[3] J.S. Gregory. 1973. *Church and State: Changing Government Policies towards Religion in Australia, with Particular Reference to Victoria since Separation.* North Melbourne, Vic.: Cassell Australia, pp. 144–45, 172–73.

[4] Walter Phillips. 1981. *Defending "A Christian Country": Churchmen and Society in New South Wales in the 1880s and after.* St. Lucia: University of Queensland Press, pp. 208–09.

[5] Alan Barcan. 1980. *A History of Australian Education.* Melbourne: Oxford University Press, pp. 134–37, 148; Peter Wellock. 1977. "The Search for Educational Respectability: Religious Education in Australian Government Schools in the Twentieth Century." *Journal of Christian Education* 58: 30–47, p. 44.

[6] L. Wigney. 1958. "Provisions for Religious Education in the State School Systems of Australia and in the Territory of Papua New Guinea." *Journal of Christian Education* 1(2): 69–80.

[7] Cathy Byrne. 2014. *Religion in Secular Education: What, in Heaven's Name, Are We Teaching Our Children?* Leiden: Brill, pp. 168–73.

trend, however, was clear: didactic, Christian Scripture reading by teachers would go, while denominational instruction by visiting clergy would be retained. The position of religious education in each state over time is summarized in Table 4.1.

In this chapter, I draw heavily (though not exclusively) upon evidence from New South Wales. I do so in part because, as the oldest and most populous state in the federation, its policies influenced developments in other states and affected more people than those of any other state. More importantly, however, its trajectory allows us to examine the political dynamics surrounding *both* SRI *and* GRT – the most controversial and dynamic element of religious education – in particular detail. Battles over Scripture reading were not the only flashpoint, but they did tend to throw into high relief the politics of symbolic representation and professional expertise. A close examination of the politics of religious education in New South Wales, then, provides particular insight into the dynamics of secularization in Australia more generally.

THE INSULATED STATE: CENTRALIZATION AND THE ECLIPSE OF LOCAL INPUT

Since the late nineteenth century, Australian educational policy has rested in the hands of the state education departments. Although departmental administrators were ultimately responsible to elected officials in the state legislature, they had nearly unfettered control over all educational matters, including budgeting, staffing, and curriculum. To ensure uniformity, course syllabi and teaching techniques were prescribed by the central offices in great detail. These policies were monitored and enforced through an efficient and exacting cadre of inspectors who visited each school on a regular basis to evaluate staff, disseminate regulations, and maintain discipline. Teacher training, too, was monopolized by the departments, with nearly all teachers being trained by the department in official state-run training colleges.[8]

Under this centralized system, there was effectively no local governance. With policies and curriculum determined by the department, local schools and the headmasters who managed them had little leeway to alter the scope or content of the formal curriculum. Accordingly, unlike in the United States, where responsible officials on local school boards found themselves in nearly

---

[8] As I discuss below, this uniformity and centralization weakened somewhat after 1960, though the overall system remains quite centralized to this day, especially in comparison with American schooling. On administrative aspects of the Australian system in the early- to mid-twentieth century, see generally W.G. Walker. 1970. "The Governance of Education in Australia: Centralization and Politics." *Journal of Educational Administration* 8(1): 17–40. On inspection and teacher training, see especially John Cleverley. 1972. "The State Primary School Teacher between the Wars." Pp. 77–98 in *Australian Education in the Twentieth Century: Studies in the Development of State Education*, edited by J. Cleverley and J. Lawry. Camberwell, Vic.: Longman Australia, pp. 78, 85–86.

TABLE 4.1. *Religious education provisions in the Australian states, 1880–2000*

State	Religious education provisions in 1880		Religious education provisions in 1950		Religious education provisions in 2000	
	General religious teaching (GRT)	Visiting clerical instruction (SRI)	General religious teaching (GRT)	Visiting clerical instruction (SRI)	General religious teaching (GRT)	Visiting clerical instruction (SRI)
New South Wales	Mandatory Bible reading	Yes	Mandatory Bible reading	Yes	Studies of religion course	Yes
Tasmania	Mandatory Bible reading	Yes	Mandatory Bible reading	Yes	None	Yes
Western Australia	Mandatory Bible reading	Yes	Mandatory Bible reading	Yes	Studies of religion course	Yes
Queensland	None	Optional before or after school	Mandatory Bible reading	Yes	Bible reading permitted as local option	Yes
South Australia	Optional before school	No	Optional before school	Yes	Studies of religion course	No
Victoria	None	No	None	Yes	None	Yes

constant contact with parents and other interested local citizens, the Australian system insulated decision-makers in the capital cities from community pressures. "If there is one thing which marks [Australian education] off from the formal systems of other western societies," concluded Australian educationist W.G. Walker in 1970, "it is its comparative isolation from citizen opinion and control."[9]

With educational decision-making removed to the state capitals, there was little to stimulate local interest in education. Foreign visitors and local educators alike regularly lamented the "almost impregnable wall of indifference or apathy" toward education among the Australian public.[10] "Local interest is dead," complained the visiting New Zealand school inspector Henry Hill in the 1890s, "for the people have already become the true Lotus-eaters of education."[11] Nearly a half-century later, Kandel observed that "the long tradition of centralization has resulted in apathy or misdirected interest on the part of the public."[12] Department officials, by contrast, viewed local participation with suspicion, and did little to encourage it. Although most schools established local Parents and Citizens Associations in the early twentieth century, these "P&Cs" were chartered and tightly regulated by the Department. The associations were "not [to] exercise any authority over the teaching staff ... or management of the school," and any "political or religious discussions" were strictly forbidden.[13] Department officials were quick to smother any potential challenges welling up within the P&Cs. For example, when several P&Cs attempted to organize against the reintroduction of state aid in the mid-1960s, Department officials invoked the regulation against "political or religious discussions" to shut down their activities.[14] Far from being independent bodies where local political disagreements could find effective expression, therefore, P&Cs were essentially little more than tightly controlled booster clubs for formal departmental goals.

Subject to the demands of the Minister and Parliament, but otherwise insulated from political pressures, educational bureaucrats were free to pursue a conservative administrative approach that preserved existing practice. In New South Wales, officials hewed to a strongly legalistic approach that placed great

---

[9] Walker, "Governance of Education in Australia," p. 32.

[10] *Teachers' Journal*, 20 May 1938, quoted in B.K. Hyams and B. Bessant. 1972. *Schools for the People? An Introduction to the History of State Education in Australia*. Camberwell, Vic.: Longman Australia, p. 164.

[11] Henry Hill. 1896. *Education: The School Systems of Australia*. Napier: Daily Telegraph, p. 11.

[12] Kandel, *Types of Administration*, p. 52.

[13] I.S. Henry, Memorandum, "Review of Status of Parents and Citizens' Associations," 6 December 1965. State Records New South Wales, Kingswood, NSW [hereafter SRNSW] 5/8312.2.

[14] Memorandum, "Parents and Citizens' Associations: Deputation to the Minister," 26 May 1967. SRNSW 5/8312.2, p. 2; Letter, Nan O'Brien to J.B. Renshaw, 11 March 1965. SRNSW 13/7159–67/41667; Letter, Dora Elizabeth French to A.W. Stephens, 9 March 1965. SRNSW 13/7159–67/41667; Letter, A.G. Bond to C.B. Cutler, 29 June 1967. SRNSW 5/8312.2; Letter, Joan Edwards to E. Willis, 20 July 1972. SRNSW 13/7159–67/41667; Letter, E.A. Willis to J. Edwards, 29 August 1972. SRNSW 13/7159–67/41667.

emphasis on enforcing departmental regulations in a uniform manner, and used their cadre of inspectors to ensure that teachers strictly adhered to regulations. Any proposed variation or experimentation in practice required explicit approval from the central office, which was rarely given. Instead, even the most minor rules were strictly enforced. For example, in 1922, an Anglican minister in Sydney wrote to the Department to request an exemption to the rule that SRI classes could only be held on school premises. He asked for permission to hold his burgeoning classes on the grounds of a local church whose meeting hall the school was already renting and using as a classroom. The minister pointed out that the children were already regularly "marched several times daily from the school *past the Church in question*," and suggested that the local Head Mistress was in favor of making an alteration. The Department, however, refused the request, stating simply that "the Minister has found it necessary and desirable that the provisions of the Act in this regard be fully observed."[15]

With no responsible local officials to petition, the only path available to those who sought to influence policy was to petition departmental officials directly. Yet the central administration was remarkably impervious to external pressure. More powerful groups could send deputations, but officials could summarily refuse to meet with any deputation without giving any reason. More often, however, deputations were given a "polite hearing" that amounted to little more than "procrastination." Most written complaints were typically ignored by departmental officials, as petitioners were routinely brushed away with vague assurances that matters were under consideration.[16] Even those groups with considerable political power and in the good graces of the department often found it difficult to move the bureaucratic machine. Between 1880 and 1940, Protestants in Victoria regularly but unsuccessfully petitioned the Department of Education to increase the amount of religious content in the public schools.[17] Similarly, in New South Wales, the Protestant churches, through their agent, the Council of Religious Education,[18] tried and failed to convince officials to institute a formal program of morning prayers in the public schools in the 1930s.[19]

---

[15] Letter, Paul Dryland to Peter Board, 7 February 1922. SRNSW 20/13031/"Religious Instruction 1913–21" (emphasis in original); Letter, Peter Board to Paul Dryland, 28 February 1922. SRNSW 20/13031/"Religious Instruction 1913–21."

[16] John W. Collins-Jennings. 1971. "Non-Professional and Non-Governmental Organizations and the Provision of Public Education, 1850–1969." Unpublished M.Ed. Thesis, University of Melbourne, pp. 106–07.

[17] L.J. Blake. 1973. "Free, Compulsory, and Secular." Pp. 165–238 in *Vision and Realisation: A Centenary History of State Education in Victoria*, edited by L.J. Blake. Vol. 1. Melbourne: Education Department of Victoria, pp. 223–25; Edward Sweetman, Charles R. Long, and John Smyth. 1922. *A History of State Education in Victoria*. Melbourne: The Education Department of Victoria, p. 147.

[18] After 1948, this group became the Council for Christian Education in Schools (CCES), discussed below.

[19] NSW Council of Religious Education Executive Minutes, 6 April 1933. Uniting Church Archives, North Parramatta, NSW [hereafter UCA] 70327; NSW Council of Religious Education Minutes,

The Politics of Religion in an Insulated System

Religious conflict played a very limited role in this insulated system. Protestants constituted a numerical majority in each Australian state, and their collective size worked to their advantage. Because department officials were ultimately responsible to the legislature, they could not risk offending dominant, well-organized groups like the Protestant churches who could credibly claim to speak for sizable constituencies. Protestants, therefore, were not only more likely to find a sympathetic ear among administrators, but they could also circumvent intractable administrators if need be by directly lobbying legislators. Yet they rarely needed to, because Department officials' conservative, legalistic approach usually favored Protestant interests. Since the education laws themselves embodied the Protestant-friendly nineteenth-century settlement, simply allowing the law to be applied as written worked in Protestants' favor. By contrast, there were few consequences for ignoring minority complaints. Catholics and other religious minorities typically found themselves excluded and ignored, with few avenues available to them to protest policies they found offensive or discriminatory.

Administrators in New South Wales regularly expressed their strong support for, and took steps to bolster, the existing system of religious instruction.[20] This support went hand in hand with the Department's cozy relationship with the Protestant churches. Under the aegis of the Council for Christian Education in Schools (CCES), representatives from the various Protestant denominations worked assiduously from the 1920s to build relationships with department officials. By the early 1950s, CCES could boast that it had "established itself [to the Department] as the responsible organization in matters affecting Religion in Schools."[21] Department officials regularly expressed their support for the Council's aims and even colluded with them to expand religious education in the absence of legal or regulatory change. The Director-General assured CCES representatives in 1951 that the Department was informally encouraging schools to perform worship services at the start of the school day, and the CCES representatives came away with the impression that "the Department was prepared to ... do anything possible to encourage religion in schools."[22]

1 May 1933. UCA 70327; NSW Council of Religious Education Minutes, 7 August 1933. UCA 70327; NSW Council of Religious Education Executive Minutes, 17 July 1935. UCA 70327.

[20] These steps included making arrangements to facilitate the scheduling of SRI, urging teachers to emphasize the spiritual and religious aspects of their work, and sponsoring in-service courses designed to improve teachers' skills in teaching Scripture. See, e.g., Memorandum, "Special Religious Instruction in High Schools," 14 June 1915. SRNSW 20/13031/"Religious Instruction, 1913–21"; S.H. Smith. 1929. "The Director's Address." *Education Gazette* 23 (June), pp. 81–82; "A Call to the People of Australia," *Education Gazette*, 1 September 1952, p. 295; "Post-College Courses for Western Area Teachers, 1954," *Education Gazette*, 1 July 1954, p. 161.

[21] Council for Christian Education in Schools, "Annual Report," March 1952, p. 2. UCA 70322.

[22] Council for Christian Education in Schools, "Report on Interviews with Director-General of Education," unattributed report, no date [1952]. UCA 70322.

Departmental representatives even attended the Council's planning conference in 1952, to provide suggestions for how to improve a revised syllabus of
Protestant SRI.[23] The representative "strongly emphasized the warm sympathy
for the Council's efforts that is felt by [the Director of Secondary Education]
and [his] inspectors."[24]

Where Protestants enjoyed a less favorable relationship with administrators,
they were still able to advance their interests through appeals to politicians
and the public. Using this strategy, Protestants made headway in those states
which had adopted more starkly secular education acts in the late nineteenth
century. In Queensland, a campaign led by the Anglican Church and the "Bible
in Schools League" won a referendum in 1910 that made Bible reading mandatory in public schools.[25] In South Australia, where religious instruction had
been limited to Bible reading before the beginning of the school day, Protestant
leaders finally succeeded in 1941 in convincing legislators to pass legislation
to provide for SRI by visiting clergy.[26] Even in Victoria, religious leaders eventually succeeded in reintroducing religious education. In 1950, with the support of Catholic leaders concerned about the dangers of secularism, Protestants
finally triumphed in their lengthy campaign to reintroduce SRI to Victorian
schools.[27] Four years later, the state went still further by opening the school
doors to Protestant chaplains.[28]

While Protestants enjoyed positive relations with the Department and
the Ministers, Catholics encountered a frosty reception. Although Catholics
repeatedly approached Department officials in pursuit of subsidies for their
denominational schools, Department officials took a hard line against anything
that hinted at a return of state aid. In 1930, as the Depression gripped New
South Wales, the Department halted a program in operation in Sydney that
brought starving schoolchildren to local churches for charitable meals during
school hours. "Once we permit one Church or one private organization to
encroach on school time, others will come along with a like request and the
result will be chaos," declared the Director-General of Education.[29] Catholics

---

[23] Letter, Dudley Hyde to John McKenzie, 18 August 1952. SRNSW SZ72; Letter, Director of
Secondary Education to Dudley Hyde, 28 August 1952. SRNSW SZ72.

[24] A.H. Pelham to Director of Secondary Education, Report, "Syllabus Conference of the Council
for Christian Education in Schools," 21 September 1952. SRNSW SZ72.

[25] E.R. Wyeth. [1955]. *Education in Queensland: A History of Education in Queensland and in
the Moreton Bay District of New South Wales*. Melbourne: Australian Council for Educational
Research, pp. 163–70.

[26] D.M. Waddington, W.C. Radford, and J.A. Keats. 1950. *Australian Council of Educational
Research Review of Education in Australia, 1940–1948*. Melbourne: Melbourne University
Press, p. 80.

[27] Phillip K. Newell. 1968. "The Enactment and Operation of the 1950 Amendment to the
Victorian Education Act." Unpublished M.Ed. thesis, University of Melbourne.

[28] Ray Bass. 1976. "Chaplaincy in Victorian State Secondary Schools." *Journal of Christian
Education* 57(2): 7–19.

[29] S.H. Smith, Memorandum, "Auburn and Newtown: Distribution of Soup to Children," 18 July
1930. SRNSW 19/8239.4.

could do little but rail in anger. In 1935, the Bishop of Goulburn told members of the Holyname Society: "An appeal to reason, to justice, and fair play is useless where prejudice prevails, and it is therefore necessary for you, the Catholic men of N.S.W., to appeal in the only way that has any telling effect – that is, the appeal of the ballot box."[30]

But if Catholics had little success persuading department administrators, they faced similarly little sympathy from parliamentarians. Unlike in the United States, where local control created some incentives for Catholic claims to be considered, state legislators had few incentives to entertain Australian Catholics' requests to change educational law and policy. The larger politics of the state legislature worked against their interests. After strong Catholic support helped the Labor Party win control of the New South Wales Parliament in 1912, many Catholics expected the resumption of state aid, but their hopes were dashed as Labor refused to move beyond extending bursaries to students at Catholic high schools.[31] The Catholic Federation bitterly complained that they "could not induce [the Labor Party] even to listen to us. Indeed, we found a strong undercurrent amongst nominally Catholic Labourites against introducing the education question at all, lest it might 'injure the movement' ... Indeed, one day last week, a selected Labour candidate said to Mr. Cleary 'personally I believe in your claims, officially I must oppose them.' "[32]

Not only did Catholics oppose the ban against state aid, but also the Department's "officially Protestant" religious education curriculum.[33] For at least the first thirty-five years of its operation, Catholics protested by refusing to participate in SRI classes in the state schools.[34] They also lodged protests over other "sectarian" matters that made their way into the system, but these protests were typically dismissed out of hand. In December 1920, for instance, the Catholic Federation complained unsuccessfully about the use of the Protestant Lord's Prayer in some schools, and asked for the Catholic

---

[30] "Subsidy for Schools: Urged by Bishop of Goulburn." *Labour Daily*, 23 January 1935. Copy in SRNSW SZ74.

[31] Jeff Kildea. 2002. *Tearing the Fabric: Sectarianism in Australia, 1910–1925*. Sydney: Citadel Books, p. 3.

[32] P.S. Cleary, quoted in Patrick O'Farrell, ed. 1969. *Documents in Australian Catholic History*. Vol. 2, *1884–1968*. London: Geoffrey Chapman, pp. 313–15. These negative encounters discouraged Catholic activism around state aid in the second quarter of the twentieth century; see below, Chapter 6.

[33] P.S. Cleary, quoted in O'Farrell, *Documents in Australian Catholic History*, p. 315.

[34] "Scripture-Reading in Schools: Mr. Hartley on the New South Wales System," *South Australian Register*, 27 February 1893. Copy available in SRNSW 20/13030; Peter Board to William Holman, Memorandum, "New Zealand: Religious Instruction in State Schools," 16 July 1914. SRNSW 20/13031/"Religious Instruction 1913–21"; *Catholic Education Conference of New South Wales, 17–20 January 1911: Statement, Resolutions, Proceedings*, quoted in O'Farrell, *Documents in Australian Catholic History*, p. 88. Even into the 1930s, Catholics provided less than five percent of all SRE lessons. See unattributed note appended to Frank Bell, "Religious Instruction in State Schools: A Plea for Co-operation," 7 June 1937, SRNSW 20/13031/"Religious Instruction 1926–1938."

version to be used in addition to the "Authorized" Protestant version. The Department acknowledged that its policy did not condone the use of the Lord's Prayer, but added that as the difference between the two versions appeared to be of "little consequence," it was not prepared to act on the Federation's request.[35] Another Catholic complaint in 1931 was disposed of by asserting that the Lord's Prayer was allowed so long as it was said in the context of "general religious teaching."[36] Catholic complaints about anti-Catholic bias in schoolbooks were likewise dismissed. The Catholic Federation also petitioned the Department in 1920 to remove several offensive statements from the history textbooks.[37] Department officials held an audience with Federation representatives the following February, where they rebuffed nearly every claim, rejected Catholic authorities, and dismissed the complaints as "ridiculous" or "too trivial to deserve a moment's consideration." Magnanimously, officials did agree that future printings could be altered "without any sacrifice of honor" to remove a "conjecture" that "Had [King] John been slain, the murderer would probably have been accounted a saint."[38]

As for other religious minorities, they faced significant obstacles just to be able to provide the SRI lessons that the Act allegedly guaranteed them. Smaller denominations required departmental approval to provide SRI, but this approval was not always granted. Jehovah's Witnesses, in particular, were denied permission to provide SRI by Department officials who determined that their lack of appointed clergy meant they did not constitute a "religion." Indeed, until 1987 departmental regulations specifically instructed teachers not to permit Jehovah's Witnesses to give SRI.[39] However, even those religious groups who received departmental approval to give instruction sometimes faced obstacles. Religions with only one student in a school were prevented from giving instruction on the grounds that "to isolate a single pupil ... would be most unfortunate."[40] If a principal suspected that a religious group was not on the list of approved denominations, that group would have to wait until the principal received formal confirmation of approval from the Department before they could begin providing SRI.[41]

[35] Peter Board, Memorandum, "Use of Lord's Prayer in Schools: Letter from Catholic Federation," 28 February 1921. SRNSW 19/8239.5.

[36] Memorandum, "Repetition of the Lord's Prayer and Use of Hymns in Schools," unattributed, 26 June 1931. SRNSW 19/8239.5, p. 5.

[37] Letter, C. Lawlor to Thomas Mutch, 28 April 1920. SRNSW 20/13220.

[38] Memorandum, K.R. Cramp and J.H. Smairl to P. Board, 1 March 1921. SRNSW 20/13220, p. 5.

[39] New South Wales. Department of Education. 1975. *Handbook: Instructions and Information for the Guidance of Teachers.* Book 3. 3rd edn. Sydney: Author, p. 65; *Education Gazette,* 9 June 1987, p. 104.

[40] Harold Wyndham, Memorandum, "Special Religious Instruction in Schools (Section 18): The case of the Nazarene Bible College," 3 August 1961. SRNSW 8/2268.

[41] This occurred to both Christian Scientists and Mormons. See Letter, V.E. Armstrong to Director of Primary Education, 18 February 1967. SRNSW 12/5971–67/40846; Letter, Frederick J. Walker to H.M. Morgan, 12 November 1975. SRNSW 12/11011.2–68/42885.

In sum, the lack of local control over any aspect of educational administration, and the concentration of authority in strong centralized bureaucracies, created a political climate favorable to majority sensibilities, and decidedly hostile to religious minorities. Insulated to a considerable extent from political pressure, parliamentarians and administrators were able to adopt a legalistic, conservative, and fundamentally majoritarian approach to religious education and state aid that protected the privileges of the Protestant majority and easily neutralized religious minorities' complaints. In this kind of system, it is not surprising that religious instruction survived – and even grew stronger – in the years before 1960.

CENTRALIZATION AND THE SUPPRESSION OF PROFESSIONALIZATION

If centralized educational systems insulated administrators from religious conflict, they also inhibited educational professionalization. The progressive educational ideas that defined education as a self-conscious discipline in the United States and Europe were slow to take root in Australia. Australian teachers, constrained by civil service regulations and subject to detailed scrutiny by a vigilant inspectorate, found it difficult to build a professional infrastructure or experiment with new ideas. Meanwhile, close ties between education departments and tertiary institutions constrained the influence of progressive thought and retarded the development of educational research. Consequently, teachers organized on a primarily industrial rather than professional basis, and professional educational knowledge had a very limited impact on Australian education – and on religious instruction – until the 1960s.

The New Education and the Australian Professional Infrastructure

As in the United States, a movement for educational reform swept Australia in the early 1900s. Like the progressive movement in the United States, the "New Education" called for a child-centered approach to education, the embrace of insights from psychology, and new classroom methods that emphasized critical thinking.[42] Inspired by these principles, educational administrators had early success reforming some of the most egregious shortcomings of the nineteenth-century system. The pupil–teacher system was eliminated in favor of formal training in teachers' colleges; new practical subjects such as music, home economics, and the manual arts entered the curriculum; and kindergartens, technical and vocational schools, and secondary schools were introduced.[43] Yet the New Education ultimately had little impact on either

---

[42] Peter Meadmore. 2003. "The Introduction of the 'New Education' in Queensland, Australia." *History of Education Quarterly* 43(3): 372–92, pp. 373–77.

[43] Barcan, *History of Australian Education*, pp. 204–19, 225–29.

the austere pedagogy of the Australian classroom, or the overall organization of and approach to the primary curriculum.[44] Despite the New Education's calls for a more child-centered, engaging, and flexible pedagogy, rigid discipline and formal teaching methods continued to characterize Australian classrooms. Australian scholars who visited the United States in the early 1930s were struck by the stark differences in teaching methods. "In Australia, the traditional subject-matter divisions and the formal method of approach still predominate. In some States they hold almost undisputed sway," wrote the Australian educationist Kenneth Cunningham upon his return from a sojourn in the United States.[45] His colleague, C.R. McRae, was blunter in his assessment: "I come from a country rather reactionary in matters educational."[46]

Part of the reason that the New Education had such a limited impact on Australian education is that Australia's professional infrastructure in education was remarkably anemic. Simply put, there were few forums for the expression or dissemination of professional educational ideas. Before 1930, when the Australian Council for Educational Research (ACER) was founded through a grant from the Carnegie Corporation, there were no independent educational research centers in Australia. Nor, apart from the teachers' unions, did any professional organizations exist; no system of in-service training kept teachers abreast of educational developments; and few journals devoted to professional debates were published. This aspect of Australian education shocked Kandel when he visited in 1937:

The [Australian Council for Educational Research is] all the more important because there are no other centers for educational research in [Australia] … As contrasted with England and the United States with literally hundreds of organizations there is an almost complete absence of associations and societies for the study of education and allied subjects. The directors and the inspectors of the Australian States have annual meetings of their respective groups, but their proceedings are not published … The absence of professional organizations is paralleled by an absence of professional journals except those published by the teachers' associations and unions; articles of general educational interest appear in these journals but their pages are in the main devoted to a consideration of matters affecting the status of teachers, fresh regulations, news, and occasionally notes of lessons on the courses of study as they are.[47]

The weakness of Australia's professional infrastructure meant that there were very few places for a robust professional discussion about pedagogy and educational theory to take place. Would-be reformers in the 1950s complained

---

[44] Craig Campbell and Helen Proctor. 2014. *A History of Australian Schooling*. Crows Nest, NSW: Allen & Unwin, pp. 108, 135; Hyams and Bessant, *Schools for the People?*, p. 168.

[45] Kenneth S. Cunningham. 1934. *Educational Observations and Reflections, Being Some Comments on Present Day Education in the United States, England, and Australia*. Melbourne: ACER, p. 37.

[46] C.R. McRae. 1933. *An Australian Looks at American Schools*. Melbourne: Melbourne University Press, p. 17.

[47] Kandel, *Types of Administration*, pp. 80–81.

that "literally thousands of good books on education have been published in England and America, but ... few of them become widely known among Australian teachers."[48] To be sure, educational journals featured occasional articles addressing advances in educational theory, and teachers' conferences and union meetings acted as platforms for disseminating New Education ideas throughout the early twentieth century.[49] But these progressive moments were overshadowed by discussions of established practice, salary, and tenure.

Consequently, the spread of new professional knowledge was slow among Australian teachers, and old approaches and pedagogical techniques persisted into the mid-twentieth century. Teachers remained "isolated in their own little kingdoms," recalled R.A. Reed of his time as a teacher in Victoria in the 1940s. "If they did meet with teachers from other schools they were more concerned to discuss salaries, conditions, and promotion than educational philosophy."[50] As late as 1955, when prominent American educational historian R. Freeman Butts visited Australia, the lack of interest in novel educational ideas was still palpable: "I do not sense that strong professional organizations are constantly at work promoting discussion and exchange of ideas, criticizing practices and theories, and stimulating new procedures and new probings."[51]

The Department as Panopticon: Administrative Controls and Teacher Conservatism

The weakness of Australia's professional infrastructure in education was in many respects the product of Australia's centralized educational system. An extensive system of centralized administrative controls restricted how teachers could teach and what they could say. A system of inspectors and restrictive public service regulations combined to limit teachers' ability to organize, criticize, or innovate. Over time, these controls shaped teachers' interests, reducing their incentives to challenge existing educational practice. Consequently, teachers remained largely silent about pedagogical matters and fundamentally conservative in their approach to education. To the extent that they did mobilize to improve their lot, they did so as unions concerned with salaries and working conditions, rather than as a profession concerned with teaching standards or educational methods.

[48] Donald McLean. 1955. "Reading for Teachers." *Education* (NSW), 6 July, p. 4.

[49] Campbell and Proctor, *History of Australian Schooling*, pp. 117, 134, 137; Hughes, "Harold Wyndham," p. 23; David McCallum. 1990. *The Social Production of Merit: Education, Psychology, and Politics in Australia, 1900–1950*. London: Falmer Press, pp. 28, 32.

[50] R.A. Reed. 1975. "Curriculum Reform in Victorian Secondary Schools in the Late Sixties." Pp. 214–24 in *Melbourne Studies of Education, 1975*, edited by S. Murray-Smith. Melbourne: Melbourne University Press, p. 216.

[51] R. Freeman Butts. 1955. *Assumptions Underlying Australian Education*. New York: Teachers College, Columbia University, p. 79.

The Inspectorate and the Production of Conformity

One of the most important controls on teachers was a system of departmental inspectors. Inspectors visited each school at least once a year to assess teachers and ensure that departmental regulations and syllabi were being carried out faithfully and successfully. Though inspectors in the early twentieth century were encouraged to advise and mentor teachers, in reality their duty was "to inspect the schools and report on them."[52] The inspectors' reports were essential to teachers' career prospects. During the late nineteenth century, under the "payment by results" system, teachers' pay and promotions were dependent upon positive reports by the inspectors. After the reforms of the early twentieth century, pay was no longer tied to formal evaluation, but promotion still depended upon positive reports from the inspectors.[53] These inspectorial reports were supplemented, and often influenced, by an extensive system of public examinations, including examinations to enter and matriculate from Australian high schools.[54] Inspectors took note of examination results, and used them in their annual assessments of teachers. In this way, the examination became a test of both "a boy's ability and of a teacher's thoroughness."[55]

The inspectorate was a powerful and conservative force in Australian education throughout the first half of the twentieth century. Many inspectors resisted efforts in the early twentieth century to implement New Education reforms that would have given teachers greater freedom to teach creatively.[56] Although they declared themselves to be champions of progressive education, in reality, "they adopted the names, slogans, and messages of 'the new education' but then identified them with their own practices which were conservative."[57] Thus one Victorian inspector declared, regarding educational reform, "There must be activity ... but it should be freedom and activity to do what ought to be done."[58] In New South Wales, the Director of Education (himself a former inspector) told teachers in 1926 that the freedoms they had experienced under the first years of the reforms were to be replaced by "reasonable

---

[52] Testimony of Peter Board, in South Australia. 1912. *Royal Commission on Education.* Adelaide: Government Printer, p. 189.

[53] P.W. Musgrave. 1979. *Society and the Curriculum in Australia.* Sydney: George Allen & Unwin, p. 67.

[54] S.H. Smith. 1928. "Secondary and Super-Primary Education in Australia." *School Review* 36(2): 121–27, pp. 121–22.

[55] R.W.G. Mackay. 1929. "The Examination System in the Primary and Secondary Schools." *Australian Quarterly* 1(3): 121–31, p. 124.

[56] On this dynamic in New South Wales, see A.R. Crane and W.G. Walker. 1957. *Peter Board: His Contribution to the Development of Education in New South Wales.* Melbourne: Australian Council for Educational Research, p. 87. For Queensland, see John Lawry. 1972. "Understanding Australian Education, 1901–14." Pp. 1–31 in *Australian Education in the Twentieth Century: Studies in the Development of State Education,* edited by J. Cleverley and J. Lawry. Camberwell, Vic.: Longman Australia, pp. 13–14.

[57] Cleverley, "The State Primary School Teacher," p. 88.

[58] Quoted in Cleverley, "The State Primary School Teacher," p. 88.

freedom" within the confines of the syllabus, and under the watchful eye of the inspector.[59]

Under this system, teachers had strong incentives to tailor their lessons to the demands of the inspectors. John Cramer, an Oregon superintendent who visited Australia in 1935 on a grant from the Carnegie Corporation, reported that inspection and examination decisively shaped how teachers approached their job. In the Australian system, he wrote, "a teacher's salary and position depend upon his classification and efficiency rating ... A good teacher, who is anxious to advance, is always very much interested in these two factors, and two questions are frequently in his mind. 'What will the examination expect my pupils to know?' and 'What will the inspector expect of me this year?' "[60] What Australian inspectors expected was typically meticulous adherence to the official syllabus. Inspectors objected to the smallest deviations, including the use of materials or teaching techniques that were not specifically mentioned in the syllabus.[61] As late as 1970, a teacher complained that an inspector had threatened to "rubbish" him for using an unauthorized textbook in his English classes.[62] In those states where Scripture reading was part of the official syllabus, inspection ensured that teachers would not fail to teach it. In New South Wales, GRT was "placed on exactly the same footing as other subjects, and at the annual inspection of schools Scripture teaching is examined the usual way."[63] Well into the 1960s, the District Inspectors ensured that Scripture was being taught according to the approved syllabus.[64]

The inspection system thus discouraged any sort of innovation or experimentation among teachers. That the inspectorate looked with disapproval upon teachers displaying pedagogical initiative was not lost on outside observers. In 1938, Kandel observed that "Originality and initiative are discouraged, and a teacher or headmaster who introduces some experiment or innovation may even be written off by an inspector for 'showmanship.' "[65] Two decades later, Butts similarly reported that "Teachers are reluctant to try new methods or to experiment when such ventures might appear simply to be equated with inefficiency by the inspector."[66] Far from experimenting with new practices, Australian teachers actually regularly requested more detailed

[59] R.J.W. Selleck, B.K. Hyams, and E.M. Campbell. 1983. "The Directors: F. Tate, W.T. McCoy, and S.H. Smith." Pp. 12–80 in *Pioneers of Australian Education*. Vol. 3, *Studies of the Development of Education in Australia, 1900–1950*, edited by C. Turney. Sydney: Sydney University Press, p. 71.

[60] J.F. Cramer. 1936. *Australian Schools through American Eyes*. Melbourne: Australian Council for Educational Research, p. 28.

[61] See, e.g., Crane and Walker, *Peter Board*, p. 83.

[62] Letter, I.G. Lancaster to Secretary, Primary Education Committee, 19 March 1970. Noel Butlin Labour Archives, Australian National University, Canberra [hereafter NBLA], N111/433.

[63] Letter, G.R. Thomas to K.S. Cunningham, 18 February 1932. SRNSW 19/8239.5, p. 2.

[64] K.J. Burns. 1963. "Education in Religion and Morals in the Primary Schools of New South Wales." Unpublished M.Ed. Thesis, University of Sydney, pp. 260–61.

[65] Kandel, *Types of Administration*, p. 62.

[66] Butts, *Assumptions Underlying Australian Education*, p. 65.

(and restrictive) syllabi from departmental officers. Inspectors in Victoria reported that teachers complained that a new course of study introduced in the early 1930s was insufficiently specific and "did not indicate clearly enough what was 'required.' "[67] In Queensland, the Teachers' Union requested in 1937 that the syllabus be redesigned to show the expected progress on a month-to-month basis.[68] In the end, the inspectors' power over the teachers bred conservatism and conformity.

Departmental Regulations and the Quieting of Criticism

Departmental regulations provided a further constraint on teachers' ability to professionalize. Australian teachers, as state employees, were considered part of the civil service, subject to the same regulations as other civil servants. Although civil servant status created job security, it also restricted what teachers could do and say. In New South Wales, where teachers were most fully integrated into the civil service, teachers were enjoined from "publicly comment[ing] upon the administration of any Department of the State."[69] In South Australia, teachers were told to "carefully refrain from the expression of opinions calculated to offend the religious or political views of either the pupils or their parents," while in Victoria, a constitutional amendment prohibited teachers from criticizing the administration of any government department.[70] These regulations extended to the inspectorate as well. In Queensland, inspectors were "given to understand that they are not to indulge in any outspoken expression of opinion" about the workings of the department.[71] And in Western Australia, the Inspector-General confessed to feeling "gagged" and constrained from criticizing the educational system.[72]

Public service regulations were wielded by Department officials on an as-needed basis to keep teachers in line. When teachers tried to raise concerns about educational practices, Department officials were often quick to silence them. In the 1870s, teachers in New South Wales published an article in a fledgling teachers' journal calling for the legislature to heed teachers' concerns. Department officials responded dramatically to this mild criticism by shutting down the journal, suspending the editors from the teaching service, and exiling

[67] Cunningham, *Educational Observations and Reflections*, p. 59.

[68] Musgrave, *Society and the Curriculum in Australia*, p. 67.

[69] New South Wales. Department of Education. 1962. *Handbook: Instructions and Information for the Guidance of Teachers*. Sydney: Government Printer, p. 174

[70] R.D. Goodman. 1955. "Teachers' Status in Australia." Unpublished Ph.D. Thesis, Australian National University, p. 213.

[71] Quoted in C. Turney. 1975. *Sources in the History of Australian Education, 1788–1970*. Sydney: Angus and Robertson, p. 71.

[72] B.K. Hyams. 1972. "Cyril Jackson and the Introduction of the New Education in Western Australia." Pp. 240–70 in *Pioneers of Australian Education*. Vol. 2, *Studies of the Development of Education in the Australian Colonies, 1850–1900*, edited by C. Turney. Sydney: Sydney University Press, p. 249.

the journal's editor to a remote Outback school.[73] In 1898, a teacher who encouraged parents to petition the Department for improved accommodation was officially censured for "disloyal and insubordinate conduct,"[74] and during the 1920s officials invoked the regulations to stifle criticism of educational policy on multiple occasions.[75] The regulations were periodically reasserted throughout the early- to mid-twentieth century. "From time to time there are press reports of a teacher being reprimanded or disciplined by a public service board for speaking out publicly in criticism of something he considers to be deserving of criticism," commented one Australian observer in 1968. "Like the British Navy, [teachers] are destined to be a silent service."[76]

Not surprisingly, outsiders early on denounced the educational systems for perpetuating a "conspiracy of adulation with regard to its undoubted merits, [and a] conspiracy of silence with regard to its equally undoubted defects."[77] "Criticism of the educational methods and traditions of the Department was often regarded as insolent and was met with hostility," observed educational reformer George Knibbs, "and admissions by departmental officers or teachers that the criticism was just was regarded as personal disloyalty."[78] Even though enforcement of such regulations waned over time, their mere presence had a chilling effect both on teachers' willingness to criticize the system, and on their ability to organize. As educational historian Bruce Mitchell notes, the regulations were "an excuse for the timid to remain silent. Most teachers had neither the desire nor the courage to voice their grievances publicly."[79]

The Effect of Administrative Controls: Industrialism Over Professionalization

The combination of close inspectorial supervision and strict departmental regulations affected how teachers organized. Unlike their American counterparts, who organized primarily on a professional basis, Australian teachers organized instead on an industrial basis, as unions.[80] Although their rights to

---

[73] Robert Marden Pike. 1965. "'The Cinderella Profession': The State School Teachers of New South Wales, 1880–1963: A Sociological Profile." Unpublished Ph.D. Thesis, Department of Sociology, Australian National University, p. 15.

[74] Lesley Dunt. 1993. *Speaking Worlds: The Australian Educator and John Dewey, 1890–1940.* Melbourne: University of Melbourne History Department, p. 18.

[75] Bruce Mitchell. 1975. *Teachers, Education, and Politics: A History of Organizations of Public School Teachers in New South Wales.* St. Lucia: University of Queensland Press, pp. 89, 149–50.

[76] P.H. Partridge. 1968. *Society, Schools, and Progress in Australia.* New York: Pergamon Press, pp. 192–93.

[77] Francis Anderson. 1901. *The Public School System of New South Wales.* Sydney: Angus and Robertson, p. 1.

[78] G.H. Knibbs. 1905. "Educational Liberty." *Australian Journal of Education* 3(1): 9.

[79] Mitchell, *Teachers, Education, and Politics*, p. 89.

[80] Although many of the earliest Australian educational associations initially featured a mix of professional and industrial activities, they were frequently founded in response to threats to employment conditions, and increasingly turned their attention to industrial issues as they transformed

criticize department policies may have been curtailed by departmental regulations, their rights under trade union laws provided a sound legal basis for
organizing and criticizing.[81] Yet organizing on this basis meant that Australian
teachers' groups focused heavily on industrial issues and wages, rather than on
professionalizing reforms to pedagogy or curriculum. The constitution of the
New South Wales Teachers' Federation (NSWTF), for instance, discouraged
consideration of curricular issues; and the Federation's meetings throughout
the 1920s focused on federation finances, arbitration, service conditions, and
salaries to the near-total exclusion of educational matters.[82]

Australian teachers' focus on industrial issues, and their inattention to
professional education questions, was frequently criticized. In 1955, Butts
lamented that "Australian teachers, imbued with the trade union tradition, are
over-organized on matters of salary, security, and tenure, but under-organized
with respect to professional stimulation, exchange of ideas, and mutual
criticism."[83] In 1975, A.G. Maclaine similarly observed that:

teachers' unions have been criticized for directing their activities mainly towards
improving salaries and conditions of service and public recognition of professional
status of teachers without making any notable corresponding efforts towards professionalizing the service, particularly by helping to improve educational practices and to
upgrade professional expertise among teachers ... In fact, teachers' unions have so far
taken no major responsibility for the professional growth of teachers as expressed, for
example, in the active initiation of in-service courses for teacher improvement or significant research ... Even the journals published by teachers' unions in Australia generally
give more space to material concerned with working conditions than to articles and
information designed to stimulate professional thought and practice.[84]

The industrial focus of the teachers' unions dovetailed neatly with the conservative approach to educational matters fostered by departmental inspections
and regulations to protect, for all intents and purposes, the Australian curriculum from teacher criticism. This was as true of religious education as it was
of other subjects. When a radical communist faction developed in the NSWTF
in the late 1920s, it initially called for the abolition of scripture and religious
teaching from the schools. However, as its leaders gained power within the
Federation in the 1940s, it dropped these radical demands in the face of

---

into trade unions. See B.K. Hyams. 1972. "Teacher Organization in South Australia, 1875–95."
  Pp. 180–86 in *Australian Teachers: From Colonial Schoolmasters to Militant Professionals*,
  edited by A.D. Spaull. South Melbourne, Vic.: Macmillan Australia, p. 180; Hyams and Bessant,
  Schools for the People?, pp. 81–82.
[81] Mitchell, *Teachers, Education, and Politics*, pp. 32–39; Partridge, *Society, Schools, and Progress*,
  p. 193; Andrew Spaull. 1986. "The State and the Formation and Growth of Australian Teachers'
  Unions, 1915–1925." *History of Education Review* 15(1): 34–48, p. 43.
[82] Mitchell, *Teachers, Education, and Politics*, p. 80.
[83] Butts, *Assumptions Underlying Australian Education*, p. 79.
[84] A.G. Maclaine. 1975. *Australian Education: Progress, Problems, and Prospects*. Sydney: Ian
  Novak, p. 127.

widespread disagreement on the part of teachers, who evinced "indifference or conservatism about the quality of education, and anxiety about salaries."[85] Indeed, a 1963 analysis of NSWTF policy toward religion concluded that:

nothing has been added to thought on education in religion and morals by the Teachers' Federation as a body representative of the opinions of over twenty thousand teachers. The inability of the Federation to offer any one policy as its own in this matter is not surprising, having regard to the variation in opinion of its members. However it is significant that very little discussion has been reported. The Federation has been too busy with economic and political problems and issues upon which teachers are agreed to spend valuable time on a topic so open to subjective judgments and widespread disagreement.[86]

When it came to professional reforms, regarding religion or any other matter, Australian teachers were simply not major advocates in the years before 1960.

A Profession Without Apostles: Centralization and the Taming of Progressive Education

While centralized controls shaped teachers' interests in ways that led them away from curricular and pedagogical matters, the centralized education system also contributed to the slow development of progressive educational thought in Australian colleges and universities. Tight central control over teacher training provided disincentives both to the development of novel professional ideas in Australia's teaching colleges and to the creation of separate education departments or research programs in the universities. Consequently, Australia did not develop robust centers for educational research until the second half of the twentieth century, meaning that progressive ideas had to be imported from Europe and the United States. These imported ideas, in turn, often arrived in an attenuated form that posed little challenge to the existing system of religious education.

Higher Education, Teacher Training, and the Inhibition of Educational Research

Until the 1970s, Australian teachers' colleges were integral components of state departments of education, specifically charged with training and providing teachers for the state educational system. Departments provided aspiring teachers with scholarships to the training colleges, and in return the trainees agreed to serve as teachers within the state system for a set period. As departmental organs subject to complete central control and operating to serve the needs of the department, the training in the colleges focused squarely on the content and approved teaching methods specified in the state curriculum.

---

[85] Mitchell, *Teachers, Education, and Politics*, pp. 173–74.
[86] Burns, "Education in Religion and Morals," pp. 136–37.

Although the principals of the teachers' colleges were often enthusiastic supporters of the New Education, and took steps to include progressive educational ideas in the college curriculum,[87] these efforts had to take a back seat to the more prosaic demands of the education departments. Following his visit to Australia in 1935, Cramer reported that the colleges' primary goal appeared to be "producing a competent school-room technician whose training has been largely restricted to the syllabus he will be expected to teach ... In one teacher's college, when I asked what the trainees are taught, I was told that they had psychology, principles and history of education, but that most of all they re-learned everything that was in the primary syllabus that they would later be expected to teach."[88]

The fact that the employing agency and the training authority were one and the same created additional problems for intellectual life in the teachers' colleges. Because teachers' colleges operated as part of the public service, they were required to hire staff from within the state teaching service, leading to "a form of professional inbreeding" that supported and perpetuated existing methods.[89] Departments also meddled mightily in the internal affairs of the teachers' colleges, deciding their curricula and even the content of their syllabi, in accordance with the perceived needs of the departments; hiring and firing faculty over the heads of the college principals; and even suspending college principals for insubordination.[90] For all these reasons, concluded B.K. Hyams, "even though ... a spirit of enquiry and innovation [might] flourish in them, the colleges were frequently reminded of their role in serving the ultimate objectives and even specific purposes of the state provider of their clients."[91]

Universities had greater autonomy, but in contrast with the United States, where educational research flourished in dozens of university departments of education, Australian universities were slow to develop programs in education or to encourage educational research. In part this was because most Australian universities were small, undergraduate institutions throughout the first half of the twentieth century.[92] Yet the tightly centralized system of teacher training did little to encourage the development of educational research in Australian

---

[87] Campbell and Proctor, *History of Australian Schooling*, pp. 137, 149; Bill Green and Jo-Anne Reid. 2012. "A New Teacher for a New Nation? Teacher Education, 'English,' and Schooling in Early Twentieth-Century Australia." *Journal of Educational Administration and History* 44(4): 361–79, p. 369.

[88] Cramer, *Australian Schools through American Eyes*, p. 25.

[89] Maclaine, *Australian Education*, p. 36.

[90] Hughes, "Harold Wyndham," p. 200; B.K. Hyams. 1979. *Teacher Preparation in Australia: A History of Its Development from 1850 to 1950*. Hawthorne, Vic.: Australian Council for Educational Research, p. 94; A.D. Spaull and L.A. Mandelson. 1983. "The College Principals: J. Smyth and A. Mackie." Pp. 81–117 in *Pioneers of Australian Education*. Vol. 3, *Studies of the Development of Education in Australia, 1900–1950*, edited by C. Turney. Sydney: Sydney University Press, pp. 110–11.

[91] Hyams, *Teacher Preparation in Australia*, p. 95.

[92] Partridge, *Society, Schools, and Progress*, p. 122.

universities. In the years before World War II, university programs in education typically relied upon part-time staff from the teachers' colleges, who, as Department employees, were subject to civil service regulations constraining criticism.[93] Universities considering establishing separate Faculties of Education in the interwar years often hesitated to do so out of fear that departmental regulations would constrain faculty from speaking freely about educational matters.[94] Similarly, the supply of potential students for university education departments was unpredictable, since most potential students were teacher trainees who were subject to recall and assignment by state education directors at any time. For example, the Director of Education in New South Wales twice in the 1920s prevented teachers' college students from pursuing university coursework, diverting them directly into the teaching service instead.[95] This naturally presented something of a disincentive for universities to invest in their education programs, and universities remained largely dissociated from teacher training into the 1960s.[96] Accordingly, university education programs stagnated, and educational research in the universities was extremely limited before World War II.[97]

Attenuated Progressivism and the Persistence of Religious Instruction

With few indigenous educational and research centers, Australia was not a center of original progressive educational thought. Accordingly, the departmental administrators at the forefront of the educational reform movement typically encountered progressive ideas third-hand, in books written by British interpreters. Australian administrators thus read about progressive ideas as interpreted in light of the British situation, and tried to apply them to the Australian context.[98] The results were often unrecognizable. The reception of John Dewey's ideas is a case in point. As historian Lesley Dunt convincingly argues, whereas Dewey envisioned his educational reforms as part of a broader strategy of social change, Australians tended to see them as practical reform measures that could be implemented while maintaining the social status quo. Indeed, Australians tended to draw most heavily on those ideas of Dewey's that viewed educational reform as a means of preserving and stabilizing social order, such as his focus on moral education.[99]

---

93 Alan Barcan. 2000. "The Andersonians and Progressive Education, 1930–1968." *Melbourne Studies in Education* 41(1): 91–114, p. 100.

94 Hyams, *Teacher Preparation in Australia*, pp. 98–100.

95 Hyams, *Teacher Preparation in Australia*, p. 82.

96 G.W. Bassett. 1964. "The Training of Teachers." Pp. 142–61 in *Education for Australians: A Symposium*, edited by R.W.T. Cowan. Melbourne: F.W. Cheshire, p. 151.

97 Julia Horne and Geoffrey Sherington. 2013. "'Dominion' Legacies: The Australian Experience." Pp. 284–307 in *Universities for a New World: Making a Global Network in International Higher Education, 1913–2013*, edited by Deryck M. Schreuder. New Delhi: Sage Publications India, p. 302.

98 W.F. Connell. 1980. "British Influence on Australian Education in the Twentieth Century." Pp. 162–79 in *Australia and Britain: Studies in a Changing Relationship*, edited by A.F. Madden and W.H. Morris-Jones. London: Frank Cass, p. 178.

99 Dunt, *Speaking Worlds*, pp. 14, 33, 36, 52–53, 58–60, 66, 90, 104.

Within the context of preserving the status quo, an emphasis on "moral education" left plenty of room for traditional Christian virtues and practices to persist in the schools. In New South Wales, in fact, the religious education curriculum changed scarcely at all over the first two-thirds of the twentieth century. In 1904, a formal commission issued a damning report on the New South Wales educational system that is usually regarded as one of the seminal documents of the New Education. Yet the report found little to criticize in the system of religious instruction,[100] and, despite the many curricular reforms introduced in the name of the New Education in the ensuing years, few if any changes were made to religious education.[101] If anything, religious education grew stronger and more entrenched as the twentieth century progressed. Although the "progressive" 1905 syllabus merely instructed teachers that "the systematic reading of the authorized Scripture Lessons ... should be regularly followed," by 1952, teachers were being instructed to make their GRT lessons "reverent and vivid" since "the most precious privilege of the individual teacher is the opportunity of imbuing his pupils with a deep sense of their responsibility towards their God and their fellows."[102]

In short, centralized control suppressed professionalization in Australia. Tight departmental controls hindered the development of an autonomous professional infrastructure and discouraged educational research. They also shaped teachers' interests, encouraging them to organize as unions who focused on industrial matters rather than professional ones. Progressive, professionalizing reforms thus had very little secularizing impact on the Australian curriculum during the first half of the twentieth century, allowing religious instruction to persist undisturbed.

DECENTRALIZATION AND SECULARIZATION:
THE CASE OF NEW SOUTH WALES, 1960–2000

The impact that centralization had on generating continuity in religious education policy can be seen by examining what happened when that stark centralization was relaxed. Beginning in the 1960s, state education departments,

---

[100] New South Wales. Commission on Primary, Secondary, Technical, and Other Branches of Education. 1904. *Interim Report of the Commissioners on Certain Parts of Primary Education.* Sydney: Government Printer [hereafter *Knibbs–Turner Report*], pp. 148–50, 157. In fact, the Report actually called for *strengthening* the SRI provisions and implementing an additional ethics component to the curriculum.

[101] See nearly identical descriptions of the religious education curriculum in *Knibbs–Turner Report*, p. 149; Letter, Assistant Under-Secretary to G.A. Judkins, 22 June 1921. SRNSW SZ74, p. 1; and Memorandum, "New South Wales: Religious Instruction in Public Schools," unattributed, 20 January 1926. SRNSW 19/8239.4. Echoes of the Report were still visible into the 1930s; see, e.g., Letter, G.R. Thomas to W.J. Adey, 15 July 1932. SRNSW 19/8239.5, p. 1.

[102] Cf. NSW Department of Public Instruction. 1905. *Course of Instruction for Primary Schools.* Sydney: Government Printer, p. 40; New South Wales. Department of Education. 1952. *Curriculum for Primary Schools.* Sydney: Government Printer, pp. 160, viii.

responding to external criticisms and new political incentives, began to loosen their grip on educational administration.[103] By decentralizing administrative and curricular authority to regions and, ultimately, individual schools, local voices gained greater influence over the content of the curriculum. By also relaxing restrictive regulations over teachers and teachers' colleges, new educational ideas and innovative practices permeated Australian education with remarkable speed. Not surprisingly, religious education was transformed in these years in ways that made it somewhat more secular. Unlike the United States, however, religious instruction retained a place in the school curriculum, but its position, content, and meaning were transformed. Decentralization thus contributed to secularization by altering the administrative patterns that had sustained traditional religious education for nearly a century.

The Emergence of an Independent Educational Infrastructure, 1930–1970

Progressive educational theories became a dominant force in Australian education beginning in the late 1960s. In part, this was due to the development of an expanded professional educational infrastructure in which progressive ideas could be developed, expounded, and transmitted. Between 1945 and 1970, the number of professional forums for intellectuals, educationists, and other educational specialists expanded; the university system more than doubled in size and began to devote more attention to educational research; and the teacher training process was extended from two to three years, creating more room for educational theory to permeate what had been an extraordinarily practical curriculum. These changes allowed progressive educational ideas to gain traction and a position from which they would ultimately transform Australian education.

Education research and discussion began to grow in Australia with the creation of ACER in 1930. The New Education Fellowship conferences, organized by ACER in 1937, brought a coterie of progressive educationists to Australia and stimulated extensive professional discussion and new organizations.[104] ACER was the first of several new independent organizations devoted to promoting educational research and progressive educational ideas. These research institutes were soon complemented by a series of prestigious

[103] New South Wales, the focus of this section, was actually a laggard in this regard; other states, especially Victoria and South Australia, took earlier and much more aggressive steps to give schools greater control over administrative and curricular matters. The dynamics in New South Wales highlighted here thus lie on the conservative end of the reform spectrum, but they are not unrepresentative of the changes shaping either Australian education generally, or religious education specifically. For an overview of developments in the other states, see Barcan, *History of Australian Education*, pp. 348–64.

[104] K.S. Cunningham, G.A. McIntyre, and W.C. Radford. 1939. *Review of Education in Australia, 1938*. Melbourne: Melbourne University Press, pp. 111–12; Hyams and Bessant, *Schools for the People?*, pp. 162–65.

academies established to promote knowledge, advise government officials, and create forums for intellectual discussion; new subject associations, such as the Australian Association of Mathematics Teachers; and new periodicals devoted to "the development of a soundly informed profession and ... the lively yet solid discussion of educational ideas and practices."[105] The growth in the number of venues where educational ideas could be discussed and the status quo criticized relatively free from restrictions encouraged the spread of progressive and even radical educational ideas.[106]

Even more important, however, was the growth and transformation of Australian higher education. The foundation of the Australian National University in 1946 marked a turn to university research, backed by Commonwealth dollars, that Australia's other universities soon began to emulate.[107] In the decade after World War II, most Australian universities introduced the Ph.D. degree and expanded their Master's degree offerings in education.[108] The growth of university education departments both encouraged the development of educational research and prompted the creation of new courses in educational theory and curriculum that brought progressive ideas to the attention of teachers and administrators. In the teachers' colleges, too, progressive ideas spread as teacher-training courses expanded from two to three years, providing additional time for courses in educational theory. By the mid-1960s, most teachers' colleges were teaching "foundations of education" courses that encouraged teachers to see their work in a broader social and developmental context, to evaluate it critically, and to be open to experimentation and change. These courses were supplemented by new and expanded in-service education programs designed to keep teachers abreast of contemporary educational developments, which encouraged teachers to pay attention to developments in educational theory and methods.[109]

As a result of this renewed attention to research and educational theory, progressive educational ideas favoring organizational self-government, democratic and community involvement, and a downplaying of absolutes gained currency in Australian education.[110] These ideas influenced both the pattern of administration and the content of the curriculum. In Victoria, where progressive ideas

[105] W.F. Connell. 1993. *Reshaping Australian Education, 1960–1985*. Melbourne: ACER, pp. 23–24, 154, 255; "The Function of the Australian Journal of Education." 1969. *Australian Journal of Education* 13(1): 1–2, p. 2.

[106] For an illuminating discussion of this dynamic in the context of mathematics, see N.F. Ellerton and M.A. Clements. 1988. "Reshaping School Mathematics in Australia, 1788–1988." *Australian Journal of Education* 32(3): 387–405, esp. pp. 393ff.

[107] Horne and Sherington, "'Dominion' Legacies," pp. 294–95, 302–03.

[108] W.C. Radford. 1957. "Educational Research in Australia, 1950–1956." *Australian Journal of Education* 1(1): 45–54, pp. 45–46.

[109] Connell, *Reshaping Australian Education*, pp. 172–73, 195, 388–90.

[110] Alan Barcan. 1965. *A Short History of Education in New South Wales*. Sydney: Martindale Press, p. 259; Connell, *Reshaping Australian Education*, pp. 142–44.

had their strongest impact, curricular control began to be devolved to local schools as early as 1966.[111] In New South Wales, the Department of Education published a new statement of the *Aims of Primary Education in N.S.W.* in 1974 that represented a radical departure from previous syllabi. It emphasized diversity; explicitly declared its reliance upon "the evidence which has accumulated, particularly over the last decade, on child growth and development"; told teachers that syllabi were to be understood as "guides rather than detailed prescriptions"; and encouraged them to focus more on "fundamental aims and objectives than on detailed content."[112] For the next decade, progressive education, reduced structure, and child-centered education dominated education in New South Wales – a marked turnaround from the hyper-traditional curriculum of the early 1960s.[113]

Administrative Decentralization and the Triumph of Progressive Education, 1960–1980

This dramatic turnaround coincided with – and helped to advance – the loosening of the tight central control characteristic of Australian education since the late nineteenth century. By the mid-1970s, both the restrictive public service regulations and detailed supervision by the inspectorate were on the way out, and teachers' colleges were formally emancipated from the state departments of education. Moreover, state education departments began a conscious policy of devolving administrative and curricular control that accelerated rapidly after 1960. As decision-making powers were devolved, first to principals and then to teachers, experimentation ensued, allowing the new ideas which had been percolating in the expanding universities and research centers to transform the curriculum from within.

From Head Office to Local Principal: the Devolution of Administrative Authority

In the wake of World War II, the New South Wales government encouraged a policy of decentralization. To stem the drift of population to the major cities, as well as to redistribute an increasingly unmanageable volume of work at the head office, the Department of Education opened a regional office in the southwestern country town of Wagga in 1948, quickly followed by six more within a decade. By the end of the 1960s, these administrative regions were

---

[111] Musgrave, *Society and the Curriculum in Australia*, p. 84.

[112] New South Wales. Department of Education. 1974. *Aims of Primary Education in N.S.W.: An Interim Statement*. Sydney: Government Printer, pp. ii, 6.

[113] Alan Barcan. 1988. *Two Centuries of Education in New South Wales*. Kensington, NSW: New South Wales University Press, pp. 287–88. This heyday of progressive experimentation was curtailed in the 1980s by a "back-to-basics" movement and a turn to neoliberalism in education. See Campbell and Proctor, *History of Australian Schooling*, pp. 224–27.

responsible for a number of important functions, including coordinating consultant services and in-service training for primary and secondary teachers.[114]

The devolution of administrative matters to regional offices was complemented by moves to devolve curricular control to local schools and teachers. School principals were increasingly given greater responsibility for the program and character of their individual schools. In 1962, the New South Wales Director of Primary Education declared the beginning of "a new era for the principalship" that would feature "the lifting of direction and the encouragement of individuality."[115] Concomitantly, teachers were being asked to take a larger role in programming through new and less prescriptive syllabi. A series of syllabus revisions during the 1950s and 1960s gave teachers increased leeway to allocate time and select content within the context of the course syllabus.[116] By 1970, academics were noting that "many principals are taking the initiative in developing highly distinctive features in their school programmes," and that in so doing they were aided by administrative officials who were "encouraging the present generation of teachers to try out new ideas."[117]

In the 1970s, the devolution of authority over curricular and administrative matters to schools accelerated dramatically as it was taken up as formal government policy. In 1973, the Commonwealth government, following a report on Australian education that recommended that "responsibility should be devolved as far as possible upon the people involved in the actual task of schooling," made consultation between local stakeholders and school administrators a requirement for some new federal grants.[118] The New South Wales government similarly began to take steps to promote local control, proposing the creation of new "school councils" and organizing conferences on "school-based decision making."[119] These moves led to a rapid diversification in school programming; by 1978, the New South Wales Department of Education celebrated the fact that "the apparent uniformity of previous generations of schools is disappearing as schools develop a more visible individuality."[120]

[114] Hughes, "Harold Wyndham," pp. 88–92.

[115] O.R. Jones. 1962. "The Complete Principal." Pp. 288–98 in *The School Principal: A Symposium*, edited by O.R. Jones. Melbourne: F.W. Cheshire, p. 293.

[116] Barcan, *Short History*, p. 254; Connell, *Reshaping Australian Education*, p. 144.

[117] David Dufty. 1970. "Changing the Social Studies Curriculum." *Education Gazette*, 1 June, pp. 212–21, p. 218.

[118] Australia. Interim Committee for the Australian Schools Commission. 1973. *Schools in Australia*. Canberra: Australian Government Publishing Service, p. 10; Peter Meadmore. 2001. "Free, Compulsory, and Secular? The Re-Invention of Australian Public Education." *Journal of Education Policy* 16(2): 113–25, p. 117.

[119] New South Wales. Department of Education. 1973. *The Community and Its Schools: A Consultative Paper on Regionalization and Community Involvement in Schools*. Sydney: Government Printer; New South Wales. Department of Education. 1978. *School Based Decision Making: Report of the N.S.W. State Conference, Sydney, November 3–5, 1978*. Sydney: NSW School Based Decision Sharing Project.

[120] New South Wales. Department of Education. 1978. *The Executive Structure in N.S.W. Primary Schools: A Discussion Paper*. Sydney: Author, p. 4. See also Malcolm Skilbeck and Glen Evans.

While administrative devolution did not always lead to greater community participation, it did encourage schools to pay closer attention to their communities, and to be more sensitive to local diversity. As early as 1962, principals were being advised to "give very real consideration to the community's characteristics" and to "use their initiative in adapting the course of studies to local needs and conditions."[121] As the department embraced multicultural education in the mid-1970s, it began to actively encourage schools to adapt their curriculum in light of local diversity. By 1976, the Minister for Education reported that the schools were already accommodating this diversity: "In communities with high migrant density, schools have developed policies and procedures which reflect the many cultures and backgrounds of those communities."[122] In support of this goal, regional offices provided multiculturalism consultants and in-service programs to help principals and teachers learn how to "analyze a school and its community" and devise culturally sensitive programs,[123] and by 1983, the Department had devised a formal Multicultural Education Policy, as well as an "intercultural" policy statement that advised teachers that "The identification of specific cultural values, attitudes, and beliefs is a skill essential to the *management* of cultural difference."[124] As control was decentralized in this context, the curriculum was increasingly tailored to the cultural particularities of local settings.

Administrative Decentralization and the Atrophy of Central Controls

The devolution of authority over the curriculum to local schools was accompanied by the weakening of the administrative constraints that had encouraged teachers to conform to the official syllabi in previous years – namely, public service regulations, examinations, and the inspection system. Public service regulations gave way under a relentless onslaught by the Teachers' Federation. In 1970, an education advisory commission was created that removed teachers from control of the Public Service Act but retained their legal status as civil servants, answering to the Director-General.[125] In a context where department officials were increasingly transferring responsibility to teachers and principals, this move greatly reduced restrictions on the teachers. An independent

---

1976. *Innovation in In-Service Education and Training of Teachers*. Paris: OECD Centre for Educational Research and Innovation, p. 6.

[121] L.M.J. Gordon. 1962. "The Principal and the Community." Pp. 254–87 in *The School Principal: A Symposium*, edited by O.R. Jones. Melbourne: F.W. Cheshire, p. 259.

[122] Letter, Eric Willis to W. Jegorow, 13 January 1976. SRNSW 12/11020.1–74/27481.

[123] L.A. Findlay, Memorandum, "Minister's Annual Report, 1977," 29 December 1977, p. 3; and P.W. Matthews, Memorandum, "Annual Report 1977," 22 February 1978, pp. 7–8. SRNSW 12/11034.1–77/29395.

[124] New South Wales. Department of Education. 1983. *Intercultural Education: A Support Document to the Multicultural Education Policy, 1983*. Sydney: Government Printer, p. 3. Emphasis in original.

[125] Mitchell, *Teachers, Education, and Politics*, pp. 176–78, 192.

education commission was ultimately established in 1980, removing the last vestiges of Public Service control.

The inspectorate, too, was effectively neutered as a force constraining educational innovation. Over the course of the 1960s and 1970s, the inspectorate's power over teachers waned as the inspectors' functions were progressively reduced or redistributed to other agents. Their role as formal assessors and examiners was increasingly transferred to principals by the early 1960s, and in some states formal inspection of teachers had ceased altogether by the early 1970s.[126] The inspectors' advisory role – always more theoretical than real – was increasingly supplanted by the provision of in-service education and new consultants. Finally, the growth of the educational system increased inspectors' administrative responsibilities, thereby greatly reducing inspectors' direct contact with the schools. In 1971, a departmental working party on inspection and advisory services recommended reducing the frequency of inspections, devolving greater responsibility for evaluation to school principals and staff, and decentralizing the inspectorate.[127] By the early 1980s, the inspectorate had effectively ceased to have an inhibiting influence on teachers.

Finally, centralized departmental control over the teachers' colleges also gave way in the 1960s and 1970s. In part, this occurred in response to pressure from the federal government, which vigorously entered the field of tertiary education in the postwar years.[128] Faced with Commonwealth objections to the close integration of teachers' colleges and the departments, most states took steps to grant their colleges greater autonomy in the late 1960s and early 1970s.[129] From 1974 onward, the federal government assumed responsibility for the state teachers' colleges, and the administration of teacher education was transferred from the state education departments to a new, independent higher education authority. With this new autonomy, the teachers' colleges (now "Colleges of Advanced Education") expanded their course offerings in the humanities and social sciences and devoted additional attention to courses in educational theory and curriculum.[130] In the process, it provided a more supportive environment for "politically and socially radical interpretations of the nature of teaching and the curriculum."[131]

---

126 Barcan, *History of Australian Education*, p. 645; W.G. Walker. 1964. "Educational Administration." Pp. 193–217 in *Education for Australians: A Symposium*, edited by R.W.T. Cowan. Melbourne: F.W. Cheshire, p. 204.

127 Connell, *Reshaping Australian Education*, pp. 643–51.

128 See, e.g., Australia. 1964. *Tertiary Education in Australia*, Vol. 1. *Report of the Committee on the Future of Tertiary Education in Australia*. Melbourne: Government Printer.

129 Allan Pitman. 1993. "Centralized Control and Teacher Education in Australia." Pp. 343–68 in *Changing Patterns of Power: Social Regulation and Teacher Education Reform*, edited by Thomas S. Popkewitz. Albany: State University of New York Press, p. 346.

130 Connell, *Reshaping Australian Education*, pp. 390–92.

131 Alan Barcan. 2001. "The Nineteen Eightees: Prelude to Curricular Reform." *Melbourne Studies in Education* 42(1): 45–78, p. 61.

Decentralization and the Transformation of Religious Education

The relaxation of central controls and the spread of progressive ideas had a profound effect on religious education policy.[132] Under the nineteenth-century settlement, religious instruction in New South Wales featured both teacher-led lessons from official Scripture readers (GRT) and denominational instruction by visiting clergy (SRI); many schools also held regular assemblies featuring the Lord's Prayer or the singing of Christian hymns.[133] The system worked without much controversy until the 1960s. In 1962, however, a humanist group complained that the GRT provisions in the social studies syllabus were intolerably Christian, and violated the requirement that only "secular instruction" be given in the public schools.[134] The NSWTF backed the complaint, expressing concern that teachers were being forced to teach beliefs they did not hold.

The Department agreed to revise the syllabus, but the new syllabus set off another uproar. It eschewed any prescriptive detail, redefined GRT as "the teaching of ethical principles," called for the protection of "the private right to religious belief," and encouraged teachers to "think of the Bible as a rich source of teaching material" to be used alongside the "writings of other religions."[135] In short, it made the study of religion objective. This time, the churches erupted in protest. The Premier of New South Wales, chastened by the Archbishop of Sydney, ordered a new "General Religious and Moral Education" (GRME) syllabus to be drafted that largely restored the original syllabus. It instructed teachers that "Stories are to be presented objectively," but it continued to rely exclusively upon the official Scripture readers as its sole text.[136] Although the humanists took the Department to court, the New South Wales Supreme Court ultimately upheld the legality of Christian religious instruction in the public schools.[137]

Yet while the dual system weathered the humanist challenge, it nevertheless slowly collapsed over the following decade. First, for a variety of reasons that I discuss below, many teachers quietly stopped providing GRT. A survey of teachers in 1977 found that only nineteen percent of infants (kindergarten) and ten percent of primary teachers were providing GRT on a weekly basis as

[132] For a fuller discussion of these developments, with greater focus on administrators' motives, see Damon Mayrl. 2011. "Administering Secularization: Religious Education in New South Wales since 1960." *European Journal of Sociology* 52(1): 111–42.

[133] A.A. Langdon. 1986. *The Anatomy of Religious Education in Schools.* Sydney: Christian Education Publications.

[134] For an excellent overview of the controversy, see Grant S. Harman. 1975. "Pressure Group Politics in Education: A Case Study." Pp. 84–100 in *Sociology of Australian Education: A Book of Readings,* edited by Donald E. Edgar. Sydney: McGraw-Hill.

[135] Ernest Wetherell. 1964. "Full Text of Syllabus." *Sunday Telegraph,* 16 August, p. 4.

[136] New South Wales. Department of Education. 1964. *Curriculum for Primary Schools: General Religious and Moral Education.* Sydney: Government Printer, p. 5.

[137] *Benjamin* v. *Downs and Another* [1976] 2 NSWLR 199. For further discussion, see Chapter 5.

required by the Department, while forty-three percent of infants and sixty-one percent of primary teachers never taught it at all.[138] Second, a severe crisis emerged in the provision of SRI, brought about by expanding enrollments and a trend toward ecumenism.[139] By the late 1960s, most churches found themselves unable to provide ministers or representatives for their scheduled lessons, and in many schools SRI became irregular and unpredictable – when it happened at all. With GRT in apparent decline, and SRI becoming a burgeoning administrative headache, pressure grew on the Department to reconsider its entire policy regarding religious education. A committee was appointed in 1974 to consider the matter.

In 1980, the committee issued a report (the Rawlinson Report) calling for a series of changes designed to strengthen SRI, including greater flexibility in its format and timetabling. It also called for GRT to be retained in a modified form that emphasized objectivity and multiplicity of viewpoints; and for the continuation of religious observances in those schools where they were "appropriate to the local situation."[140] Officials accepted and implemented its recommendations regarding SRI, but did nothing regarding GRT, which continued to fall further into abeyance during the 1980s.[141] However, a further set of reforms in 1990 accorded religion a prominent place in the new "Human Society and Its Environment" section of the primary curriculum, and supported the development of a "Studies of Religion" course in the secondary schools.[142] By 2000, the Rawlinson reforms had effectively been adopted as government policy, and religious education was transformed: GRT was changed from prescriptive Bible reading to objective studies of religion, religious exercises were approved to the extent that they were "appropriate" to local circumstances, and the rights of visiting clergy were preserved under new, streamlined SRI provisions.[143] A similar pattern took place in other states, where teacher-led Scripture reading was dropped while SRI was retained and reinforced.

---

[138] New South Wales. Department of Education. 1980. *Religion in Education in N.S.W. Government Schools* [hereafter *Rawlinson Report*]. Report of the Committee Appointed by the Minister for Education to Consider Religious Education in N.S.W. Government Schools. Sydney: Government Printer, p. 43.

[139] A.W. Black. 1975. *Religious Studies in Australian Public Schools*. Melbourne: Australian Council for Educational Research.

[140] *Rawlinson Report*, pp. 107–15.

[141] A.A. Langdon. 1991. "Religious Education in the Public (Government) Schools of New South Wales: Part I: General Religious Education." *Journal of Christian Education* 101: 29–46, p. 44.

[142] Terry Metherell. 1989. *Excellence and Equity: New South Wales Curriculum Reform: A White Paper on Curriculum Reform in New South Wales Schools*. Sydney: NSW Ministry of Education and Youth Affairs, pp. 16, 39.

[143] These characteristics (objective GRT, protected SRI, and religious exercises on an "appropriate" basis) continue to inform the state's current religious education policy. See New South Wales. Department of Education and Communities. 2015. "Religious Education Implementation Procedures." Available online at https://www.det.nsw.edu.au/policies/curriculum/schools/spec_religious/REimplementproced.pdf (accessed 28 March 2016).

Decentralization and Secularization

The decentralization of administrative and curricular authority to local schools had an important impact on these changes. The collapse of GRT in the late 1960s and early 1970s occurred thanks to the confluence of a number of factors – a strategy of benign neglect by wary administrators, the devolution of authority over GRT to teachers and principals, the rise of progressive understandings of the curriculum, and growing sensitivity to the needs of local communities. Yet beneath all these disparate factors were the relaxation of centralized control and the devolution of administrative and curricular authority to local schools. As the centralized administrative structure relaxed, secularizing processes of religious conflict and professionalization were unleashed that rapidly undermined the old settlement.

Devolution was an integral part of a pragmatic attempt by Department administrators to avoid a repeat of the syllabus controversy of the early 1960s. While they recognized that the syllabus was problematic, they also realized that "There are certain elements in the long-established provision of Scripture stories and reading which cannot be abandoned … without great public outcry."[144] Their solution was twofold: first, to scale back on any efforts to promote GRT, even as they allowed it to remain on the books; and second, to give greater authority over GRT to teachers and principals. In the immediate wake of the controversy, a number of active supports to GRT were quietly abandoned. In-service courses on religious education were dropped, the production of new Scripture readers was halted, and GRT essentially disappeared from departmental correspondence and planning documents.[145] As the Department essentially stopped promoting its own syllabus, older teachers were left wondering whether the GRME syllabus was still in effect, while younger teachers were often not aware of it at all.[146]

The quiet abandonment of departmental support was complemented by moves to devolve authority over religious instruction to principals and teachers. In many respects, religious education was one of the first curricular areas to experience greater teacher and school autonomy. The 1964 GRME syllabus told teachers that they were "free to select topics in these [Scripture] books for presentation when and where they are considered appropriate to the needs of [their] pupils."[147] Within three years, the Minister for Education reported that GRT was being provided "under quite elastic conditions" in order to accommodate teachers' varied religious beliefs.[148] While hard data on teacher practices

---

[144] H.S. Wyndham, Memorandum, "Primary Curriculum Scripture," 21 June 1963. SRNSW 8/2268.

[145] For a more detailed discussion of these developments, see Mayrl, "Administering Secularization," pp. 125–26.

[146] Indeed, the Rawlinson Report found that almost one-third of primary school teachers, including majorities of recent trainees, were not even *acquainted* with the GRME syllabus. See *Rawlinson Report*, p. 201, Table F.37.

[147] New South Wales. Department of Education, *General Religious and Moral Education*, p. 5.

[148] Letter, Charles Cutler to B.G. Judd, 5 July 1967. SRNSW 19/8249.

is unavailable, it seems undeniable that this elasticity contributed to teachers' quiet extralegal abandonment of GRT in the late 1960s and early 1970s. While some teachers continued to teach the Scripture Readers as they had before, those who were hostile to GRT, or who taught large numbers of non-Christian students, stopped providing GRT altogether when it became clear that they would face no consequences for doing so.[149] Others, in the absence of clear departmental directives, appear to have begun to avoid "an aspect of the curriculum about which they were unsure."[150] By 1976, an NSWTF ad hoc committee on religious instruction concluded that "in the primary schools even the present provision is being ignored [as the result of] less prescriptive curricula requirements."[151]

The collapse of GRT was further hastened by the advance of progressive ideas and methods in the 1960s and 1970s. The breakdown of subject barriers that progressive education entailed both complicated the provision of GRT and called into question the utility of keeping "Scripture" as a separate course of study.[152] More importantly, progressive education, which emphasized social values and a focus on education rather than instruction, seemed at odds with the certainties of religion in important ways. The official departmental publication, the *Education Gazette*, published an article in 1969 advising teachers that education's purpose was to help students "accept, tolerate, and live with doubt." The article noted that, while "this does not mean that faith should be destroyed," it did mean that "education should prepare and equip children" for "continuous examination of principle."[153] This vision, clearly incompatible with traditional religious instruction, was explicitly adopted in the Department's 1974 *Aims of Primary Education* statement, which declared that "the central aim of education" was, in part, "to guide individual development ... [toward] moral autonomy."[154] Some teachers saw these new guidelines as superseding the GRME syllabus, contributing to the decline of GRT.[155]

[149] New South Wales Jewish Board of Deputies, Memorandum, "Department of Education Curriculum for Primary Schools on General Religious and Moral Education," September 1965, pp. 3–4. Archive of Australian Judaica, Sydney, New South Wales, NSWJBD Box 39.

[150] Alan Langdon. 1976. "New South Wales." Pp. 3–6 in *Religious Education in the State Schools of the Australian States, the A.C.T., and New Zealand*. Mount Martha, Vic.: Australian Council of Churches Division of Education, p. 4.

[151] Bronwyn Marks, Memorandum, "Recommendations to Executive/Council on Religion in Government Schools Ad Hoc Committee," 4 June 1976, p. 1. NBLA N111/440.

[152] H.J. Neil. 1971. "Policy Proposals of the Council for Christian Education in Schools." Paper presented at the National Conference on Christian Education in Government Schools, Southport, Qld., November.

[153] R.D. Wall. 1969. "New Tasks for Education." *Education Gazette*, 1 October, pp. 490–97, p. 496.

[154] New South Wales. Department of Education, *Aims of Primary Education*, p. 1.

[155] A.J. Craig, Memorandum, "Submissions to Committee: Summary of Main Points," May 1977. SRNSW 12/11024.2–75/47882, p. 15.

Finally, the Department's decision to pursue school-based curriculum management and a multicultural policy encouraged schools to become more sensitive to the varied religious needs of their students. As religious diversity increased among both teachers and students,[156] the idea of allowing schools to adjust their religious education policies to suit local conditions was increasingly offered as the solution to the problem of religious pluralism. The Minister for Education observed in 1967 that one reason why no "formal decision" had been made to implement a "corporate act of worship" at the beginning of the school day was that "the establishment of such a practice in any school, to be of value, must be on the initiative of the school principal and with the support of staff and parents."[157] As principals were given increased responsibility over the curriculum more generally, they were called upon to answer the question of how much religion, and of what variety, to provide. The department's policy encouraged the matching of religious education policy to community context, primarily by departicularizing GRT and by making sure that religious observances had local support.

Indeed, this focus on local communities ultimately governed the new policy toward religious education that emerged after 1980, starkly influencing which aspects of the old system were retained or transformed. The Rawlinson Report's recommendations emphasized local control as an administrative solution to the problems posed by the old religious education system. In deliberating over the position of GRT, it quickly became clear that there would be no return to the days of a relatively didactic Christian syllabus. In light of growing religious diversity, the Committee acknowledged the impossibility of coming up with "certain common data" for GRT: "how can you demand teaching about Christianity in predominantly Jewish or Muslim communities?"[158] Instead, the Committee advocated a shift from "General Religious Teaching" to "General Religious Education," a "broader concept ... which aims to provide understanding of the major forms of religious thought and expression characteristic of our society and also of other societies in the world."[159] The move paved the way for a new course that embraced the idea of teaching *about* religion in an objective sense, thereby aligning religious education with reforms in other areas of the curriculum that emphasized diversity and less prescriptive curricular statements.

---

[156] Between 1947 and 1976, the proportion of non-Christians in Australia doubled (from 0.5% to 1.0%), while the number of those claiming no religion skyrocketed from 0.3% to 8.3%. See Gary D. Bouma. 1995. "The Emergence of Religious Plurality in Australia: A Multicultural Society." *Sociology of Religion* 56(3): 285–302, p. 288.

[157] Cutler to Judd, 5 July 1967.

[158] A.J. Craig, Memorandum, "Progress Report by Subcommittee on Place of Religion in Education," February 1977, p. 2. SRNSW 12/11024.2–75/47882.

[159] *Rawlinson Report*, p. 73.

However, the Committee was unwilling to completely exclude religion from the schools. The Committee feared that eliminating all religious observances would "be in conflict with the [larger] community's cultural norms" and would create "a gulf between the school and the community."[160] Instead, they turned to local control as a means of insulating religious exercises from potential controversy. The Report advocated putting decisions about religious observances in the hands of local schools, such that "religious observances as are appropriate to the local situation should continue to be permissible." Any observances that occurred should "reflect the general view of parents and teachers," and should "employ forms of observance which maximize corporateness and minimize divisiveness." Although the Committee recognized that "in certain closely-knit communities with religious homogeneity, corporate acts of worship ... might be an appropriate expression of the life of the community," in other schools, such as those "serving a multi-religious local community ... the proper place for religious worship would be in the context of Special Religious Education or in voluntary meetings." In this way, not only did the Report argue that "different practices [should] occur in different communities," it also reconceived SRI as a firewall that could contain particularism within the multifaith school.[161]

Thus, the decentralization of educational administration that took place in New South Wales after 1960 facilitated the curricular transformations that undermined traditional religious instruction in the government schools after that time. The devolution of curricular control and the lifting of departmental monitoring mechanisms, coupled with an administrative policy of benign neglect, cleared the way for the decline of GRT, while a concerted effort to make schools more responsive to their communities facilitated the reorganization of SRI and corporate worship policies.

CONCLUSION

Religious education in Australia was sustained throughout the late nineteenth and early twentieth centuries by the centralized character of its administration. A near-total lack of local control meant that religious minorities had a very difficult time challenging policies regarding religious education. Tight centralized control of teacher training, public service regulations, and a watchful inspectorate inhibited professionalization in the late nineteenth and early twentieth centuries. As a consequence, the secular settlement reached in the last quarter of the nineteenth century persisted nearly unchanged until the 1960s. Only when Australian education departments began to loosen their control over

---

[160] "Religious Observances in Government Schools: A Paper Prepared by the R.E. Subcommittee," July 1978. SRNSW K283992–75/47957.
[161] *Rawlinson Report*, pp. 66–67, 75.

schools and teachers in the postwar era did significant change occur. Given the freedom to innovate and implement progressive educational ideas, and encouraged to pay greater heed to their increasingly religiously diverse local settings, teachers and principals increasingly eschewed the more didactic elements of the traditional religious curriculum. Even still, Australian education managed to preserve a position for religious instruction to the present day.

PART III

FORGING THE TWENTIETH-CENTURY SETTLEMENT

Political Mobilization and (De)secularization since 1945

The previous part of the book dealt with the dynamics of religion and education under the aegis of the nineteenth-century settlement, focusing on how administrative institutions helped to advance or retard two key secularizing processes, professionalization and religious conflict. As we have seen, the period between 1870 and 1945 saw the slow decline of devotionals in American public schools as religious outsiders and educational professionals took advantage of decentralized administration to implement more secular policies. And it also saw the persistence of religious instruction in Australian schools, as centralized administrative structures stymied efforts either to challenge from without, or to transform from within, the educational policies established in the late nineteenth century.

Part III takes up the story from 1945 onwards, to explain why American and Australian secular settlements diverged in the mid-twentieth century. To do so, it focuses on the process of religious conflict, and how it interacted with the institutional terrain in each country. The dynamics of religious conflict changed significantly at midcentury, as the longstanding Protestant–Catholic divide began to break down in both countries. As it did, new alliances began to form around religious education, generating new political pressures that contributed to the emergence of new settlements in each country. In the United States, the new twentieth-century settlement featured the "strict separation" of church and state, which rejected both public aid to religious schools and public school devotionals. In Australia, by contrast, the new twentieth-century settlement embraced a version of "neutrality" that permitted both public aid ("state aid") to religious schools and devotional religious exercises in the public schools.

While religious conflict was central to the emergence of both of these settlements, the institutional settings in which religious education policy was renegotiated varied. In the United States, strict separation was promulgated through the courts, which effectively nationalized what had been a fragmented and fundamentally local policy toward religion. Meanwhile, the new Australian settlement was worked out through traditional parliamentary processes, thanks to peculiar features of Australia's electoral institutions.

Part of the reason that settlement change was determined by the courts in the United States, but the legislature in Australia, was that these institutions were differently available to those political forces who were most active in defining the terms of the new settlements. A key feature of the postwar debates about religion and education was their increased organization and coordination. Parallel efforts to exclude devotionals from the public schools, and to reinstate state aid to religious schools, developed in both countries. Thus, the new twentieth-century settlements to a large extent represent the outcome of *active campaigns* – by Jews, Protestants, and civil libertarians in the United States, and by Catholics in Australia – that brought the new dynamics of religious conflict to bear on religious education policy in an unusually forceful and consequential manner. Each group succeeded in redefining the appropriate relationship between religion and education by identifying favorable institutional terrain, and taking advantage of rules and procedures that accorded them maximum leverage in obtaining their aims. The settlements that resulted were therefore largely dependent on the strategic choices made by those campaigns.

Accordingly, the two chapters that follow focus on the secularizing (United States) and desecularizing (Australia) campaigns that dominated the renegotiation of policies toward religion and education in the postwar era. While showing how those campaigns expressed the changing dynamics of religious conflict in the postwar era, they also reveal how particular political institutions provided opportunities for political action that were not available in the other country. In so doing, these two chapters both explain the emergence of the new settlements in each country, and also demonstrate how those settlements reflected both concerted political action and particular features of each country's political institutions.

5

Secularization and the Courts in Postwar America

Congress shall make no law respecting an establishment of religion, or prohibiting the free exercise thereof…[1]

The Commonwealth shall not make any law for establishing any religion, or for imposing any religious observance, or for prohibiting the free exercise of any religion, and no religious test shall be required as a qualification for any office or public trust under the Commonwealth.[2]

INTRODUCTION

On 2 March 1898, delegates to Australia's constitutional convention voted to include a section in their new Constitution guaranteeing religious freedom and prohibiting religious establishment.[3] Australia's Section 116 was deliberately modeled on the religion clauses of America's First Amendment in what one Australian legal scholar has termed "a fairly blatant piece of transcription."[4] Yet despite its nearly identical language, Section 116 has been interpreted vastly differently from its American counterpart. While American courts have read the First Amendment broadly, as creating a "wall of separation" between church and state, the Australian High Court has interpreted Section 116 narrowly, as prohibiting only the "statutory recognition" of a single church. These divergent interpretations have led the courts to play decidedly different roles in defining how secular education would be in each country: while American

---

[1] United States Constitution, Amendment I.

[2] Australian Constitution, Section 116. The "religious test" portion of this section is derived from Article V of the United States Constitution.

[3] Richard Ely. 1976. *Unto God and Caesar: Religious Issues in the Emerging Commonwealth, 1891–1906.* Melbourne: Melbourne University Press, p. 86.

[4] Clifford L. Pannam. 1963. "Travelling Section 116 with a U.S. Road Map." *Melbourne University Law Review* 4: 41–90, p. 43.

courts have, since the late 1940s, taken the lead in forging a new secular settlement in education, Australian courts have been only minor players.

Why did the courts play such a central role in the negotiation of America's new secular settlement? In this chapter, I argue that it is because they constituted an accessible institutional target for a concerted, strategic campaign to redefine and nationalize America's religious education policy. In the face of theological division and new ecumenical trends, the divide between Protestants and Catholics that had long structured the politics of religious education began to break down in the mid-twentieth century. At the same time, new players – Jews and civil libertarians – forcefully entered the debate over religion and education in the postwar years. These developments altered the dynamics of religious conflict, destabilizing the established politics of the nineteenth-century settlement and creating room for an assertive campaign for "strict separation" of church and state largely organized by the new players. Motivated by a pastiche of concerns ranging from fear of Catholic power, to opposition to religious dogmatism, to communal self-defense, these separationist groups shepherded the Supreme Court to an embrace of strict separation. Targeting the Court was a risky, but ultimately successful, tactical gamble by those who sought to overturn the nineteenth-century settlement and nationalize religious education policy. The triumph of strict separation was thus an *achieved phenomenon*, advanced by organized interests in the service of ultimately political ends.

These organized interests targeted the courts as favorable institutional terrain for their campaign. American courts were institutionally available, both procedurally and hermeneutically, in the postwar era in ways that mattered for the separationists' campaign. Relaxed standing rules and multiple constitutional points of entry provided separationists with relatively smooth procedural access to the courts. More importantly, the Supreme Court's embrace of legal realism around midcentury encouraged it to reach decisions in light of broader social and political factors – factors which were strategically highlighted by the separationists. The importance of this institutional availability becomes clear when contrasted with the Australian courts, where restrictive standing procedures and a highly text-driven legalist hermeneutic combined to thwart separationist litigation in that country.

Accordingly, this chapter examines how changes in the dynamics of religious conflict intersected with favorable institutional terrain to facilitate the emergence of a new settlement in education. I begin with an overview of the role of the courts in defining the legality of religious education, first in the state courts before 1947, and then in the Supreme Court after World War II. I then situate the analysis in the context of the changing dynamics of religious conflict at midcentury. Although old divisions persisted, new divisions and new actors were emerging, complicating alliances and positions on religious education policy and giving rise to a new campaign to renegotiate the secular settlement in education. From there, I focus on the separationist legal campaign, highlighting the organizational, strategic, and tactical efforts that contributed to its success. Finally, I contrast the American experience with the Australian, and show how American courts were more institutionally available than their Australian counterparts, making the courts an attractive institutional target for the strict separationists.

RELIGION AND EDUCATION IN THE AMERICAN
COURTS: AN OVERVIEW

Intimations of Separation: Litigation in the State Courts, 1854–1947

While battles over the relationship between religion and education exploded into the Supreme Court in the postwar era, the American legal system had already been intimately involved in crafting the acceptable parameters of that relationship for nearly one hundred years. Prior to 1947, legal challenges to public school devotionals and public aid for religious schools were waged almost entirely at the state level, relying on state constitutional provisions governing religion. While the number of cases touching on religion and education in any given year was typically small, their cumulative effect was quite substantial: By the end of World War II, state courts had decided 78 cases on these topics. These cases were essentially an extension of the ongoing battles between Catholics and Protestants that had preoccupied many local school boards since the 1830s. Catholics were the dominant force behind challenges to religion in the public schools. Of the twenty-one cases challenging public school devotionals before 1947, at least sixteen (seventy-six percent) were brought by Catholics or their allies; of the six cases where a state supreme court ruled against religion in the public schools, all but one case was initiated by a Catholic plaintiff.[5] Protestants, for their part, challenged municipal and state efforts to provide aid to Catholic schools, though they had less success in these efforts. Nevertheless, by 1946, Protestants and their allies had filed more than fifty suits in the state courts, challenging everything from direct payments to the provision of public water to parochial schools.[6]

Between the Civil War and World War II, state courts generally upheld the Protestant-friendly settlement reached in the mid-to-late nineteenth century. State courts were typically unsympathetic to Catholic arguments that the

---

[5] Information on the religious backgrounds of the plaintiffs was culled from Joan DelFattore. 2004. *The Fourth R: Conflicts over Religion in America's Public Schools.* New Haven: Yale University Press, pp. 47–49, 58–60; Otto Templar Hamilton. 1927. *The Courts and the Curriculum.* New York: Bureau of Publications, Teachers College, Columbia University, pp. 112–13; Leo Pfeffer. 1953. *Church, State, and Freedom.* Boston: Beacon Press, p. 165; and a review of the court decisions.

[6] For a detailed listing of state court cases before 1947, see Damon Mayrl. 2011. "Secular Conversions: Politics, Institutions, and Religious Education in the United States and Australia, 1800–2000." Ph.D. Dissertation, Department of Sociology, University of California, Berkeley, pp. 138–39 nn.5–8.

Bible was a sectarian text (and therefore in violation of state constitutional prohibitions on "sectarian instruction" in public schools) or that Bible reading constituted a form of forced worship (thereby running afoul of constitutional guarantees of freedom of conscience). By a greater than two-to-one margin, courts rejected challenges to religious devotionals, often reasoning that America was a Christian nation, and that public school religion unproblematically reflected majority opinion.[7] At the same time, courts generally struck down public aid arrangements. Protestants' challenges to such practices were not uniformly successful, but by 1940, eight of nine state courts that had considered the legality of "Catholic public schools" had ruled against them.[8]

Nevertheless, cracks in the settlement began to show during this period, as a few courts began the slow process of working out an alternative understanding of how church and state ought to relate to one another in education. In particular, in those cases where a court struck down religion in the public schools, some state courts began to move away from a "Christian nation" view toward a more expansive understanding of pluralism. The Illinois Supreme Court, for example, in striking down Bible reading in 1910, declared that "All stand equal before the law – the Protestant, the Catholic, the Mohammedan, the Jew, the Mormon, the free-thinker, the atheist." Even while conceding that "this is a Christian State ... [even] a Protestant state," the court emphatically declared that "the law knows no difference between the Christian and the Pagan, the Protestant and the Catholic. All are citizens. Their civil rights are precisely equal ... There can be no distinction based on religion."[9] Moreover, the decline of the "Christian nation" assumption increasingly led some courts to view devotional exercises not as a source of unity, but instead as a potential source of conflict. The Wisconsin Supreme Court, in striking down Bible reading in 1890, insisted that the state must be "Godless, in the same sense that the executive, legislative, and administrative departments are Godless" because "There is no such source and cause of strife, quarrel, fights, malignant opposition, persecution, and war, and all evil in the state, as religion ... Let it once enter our common schools, they would be destroyed."[10]

Although few in number, these state court decisions nevertheless provided the germ of an alternative jurisprudential approach, one skeptical of religion in the schools, which helped prepare the ground for the rise of strict separationism after World War II. Indeed, the Supreme Court – though not bound by

---

[7] H. Frank Way. 1987. "The Death of the Christian Nation: The Judiciary and Church–State Relations." *Journal of Church and State* 29: 509–29, p. 519. For a representative example, see *Church* v. *Bullock*, 104 Tex. 1 (1908).

[8] "Catholic Schools and Public Money." 1941. *Yale Law Journal* 50: 917–27, p. 924. The number of courts that had ruled against Catholics in no-aid cases more generally was eight out of twelve by 1920. See Way, "Death of the Christian Nation," p. 522.

[9] *People ex rel. Ring* v. *Board of Education*, 245 Ill. 334, 92 N.E. 251 (1910), pp. 346, 349.

[10] *State ex rel. Weiss* v. *District Board*, 76 Wis. 177, 44 N.W. 967 (1890), p. 219 (Orton J., concurring).

any state court decision – drew upon these state court decisions as it defined its own position on the questions in the 1960s.[11]

Nationalization through Separation: the Supreme Court, Religion, and Schools since 1947

Despite its frequent appearance in the state courts, religious education went unlitigated in the federal courts before World War II. Beginning with the 1947 case *Everson* v. *Board of Education*, however, the Supreme Court moved to clarify and nationalize policy regarding religion and education. In *Everson*, the Court "incorporated" the Establishment Clause (i.e., declared that it applied to the states as well as the federal government), and equated disestablishment with a "wall of separation between church and state" that was to be "kept high and impregnable." Writing for the Court, Justice Hugo Black declared that this meant that:

neither a state nor the Federal Government can set up a church. Neither can pass laws which aid one religion, aid all religions, or prefer one religion over another. Neither can force nor influence a person to go to or to remain away from church against his will or force him to profess a belief or disbelief in any religion. No person can be punished for entertaining or professing religious beliefs or disbeliefs, for church attendance or non-attendance. No tax in any amount, large or small, can be levied to support any religious activities or institutions, whatever they may be called, or whatever form they may adopt to teach or practice religion. Neither a state nor the Federal Government can, openly or secretly, participate in the affairs of any religious organizations or groups, and vice versa.[12]

The Establishment Clause, therefore, "comprehensively forb[ade] every form of public aid or support for religion."[13] The following year, in *McCollum* v. *Board of Education*, the court applied this interpretation to a released-time education program in Champaign, Illinois.[14] Rejecting the idea that "the First Amendment was intended to forbid only government preference of one religion over another," the court struck down on-premises released-time education, declaring that "in the relation between Church and State, 'good fences make good neighbors.'"[15]

---

[11] See especially *School District of Abington Township* v. *Schempp*, 374 U.S. 203 (1963), pp. 215 (Clark J., majority opinion), 278 (Brennan J., concurring), in which the Court explicitly referred to state court decisions on devotional exercises.

[12] *Everson* v. *Board of Education*, 330 U.S. 1 (1947), pp. 15–18.

[13] *Everson* v. *Board of Education*, p. 32 (Rutledge J., dissenting).

[14] In released-time education, children were excused from their regular school-day schedule for an hour a week to meet with church representatives for denominational instruction. For a good overview of released-time and the political dynamics surrounding it at midcentury, see Jonathan Zimmerman. 2002. *Whose America? Culture Wars in the Public Schools*. Cambridge: Harvard University Press, pp. 135–50.

[15] *McCollum* v. *Board of Education*, 333 U.S. 203 (1948), pp. 211, 232.

In *Everson* and *McCollum*, the Supreme Court established a jurisprudence of "strict separation," which raised the longstanding American ideal of "separation of church and state" into formal judicial doctrine.[16] While the court did permit off-premises released-time instruction in *Zorach* v. *Clauson* in 1952,[17] this strict separationist doctrine otherwise led the court to reject a series of state and local programs providing for public school devotionals. In *Engel* v. *Vitale*, decided in 1962, the Supreme Court outlawed school prayer.[18] The following year, the Court struck down Pennsylvania's Bible-reading statute in *Abington Township* v. *Schempp*.[19] Subsequent decisions extended the prohibition on public school devotionals to encompass officially sponsored student prayer, prayer at graduation ceremonies, silent meditation, the display of the Ten Commandments, and the teaching of creationism.[20] In these decisions, the Court has consistently rejected the possibility of devotionals in the public schools as a violation of the Establishment Clause, declaring that "the Constitution guarantees that government may not coerce anyone to support or participate in religion or its exercise, or otherwise act in a way which 'establishes a [state] religion or religious faith, or tends to do so.' "[21]

In the course of these decisions, the Supreme Court drew upon the arguments previously laid out in state court decisions, focusing on religious diversity and the potential for conflict that inhered in devotional exercises. In *McCollum*, Justice Frankfurter noted that released time education "actively furthers inculcation in the religious tenets of some faiths [only], and, in the process, sharpens the consciousness of religious differences."[22] In *Engel*, similarly, Justice Douglas averred that "once government finances a religious exercise, it inserts a divisive influence into our communities," noting in particular that "nondenominational" prayer "does not conform to all of the tenets of the Jewish, Unitarian, and Ethical Culture groups."[23] And in his concurrence to *Schempp*, Justice Brennan pointed out that:

our religious composition makes us a vastly more diverse people than were our forefathers ... including as it does substantial minorities not only of Catholics and Jews but as well of those who worship according to no version of the Bible and those who worship no God at all. In the face of such profound changes, practices which may have

---

[16] Philip Hamburger. 2002. *Separation of Church and State*. Cambridge: Harvard University Press, p. 479.

[17] *Zorach* v. *Clauson*, 343 U.S. 306 (1952).

[18] *Engel* v. *Vitale*, 370 US 421 (1962).

[19] *Abington Township* v. *Schempp*.

[20] *Epperson* v. *Arkansas*, 393 U.S. 97 (1968); *Stone* v. *Graham*, 449 U.S. 39 (1980); *Wallace* v. *Jaffree*, 472 US 38 (1985); *Lee* v. *Weisman*, 505 US 577 (1992); *Santa Fe Independent School District* v. *Doe*, 530 US 290 (2000).

[21] *Lee* v. *Weisman*, p. 587.

[22] *McCollum* v. *Board of Education*, pp. 227–28 (Frankfurter J., concurring).

[23] *Engel v. Vitale*, p. 442 (Douglas J., concurring)

been objectionable to no one in the time of Jefferson and Madison may today be highly offensive to many persons, the deeply devout and the nonbelievers alike.[24]

Thus, an awareness of religious diversity and concern about the potential for religious conflict suffused the Court's opinions on devotionals, and buttressed their call for strict separation in the public schools.

Yet even as the Court moved to strike devotionals from the public schools, it also acted to uphold the prohibition on public aid. Although *Everson* permitted indirect public aid (in the form of bus transportation) to parochial schools, the Supreme Court moved in 1971 to firmly close the door on any direct public aid. In *Lemon* v. *Kurtzman*, the Court rejected plans in Pennsylvania and Rhode Island that would have provided state subsidies for parochial schoolteachers' salaries. The Court declared that the Establishment Clause required that laws must (1) "have a secular legislative purpose," (2) have an effect that "neither advances nor inhibits religion," and (3) not lead to "excessive government entanglement with religion."[25] This so-called *Lemon* test was used through the 1970s and 1980s to strike down multiple laws providing direct and indirect assistance to religious schools,[26] and reached its apogee in a 1985 decision which struck down portions of the Elementary and Secondary Education Act (ESEA) that provided auxiliary services to religious schools.[27] Since that time, however, the Court has relaxed its understanding of "separation" somewhat, allowing some indirect forms of aid that are provided in a "nondiscriminatory" manner, including voucher and scholarship tax credit programs that support religious schools.[28] However, direct grants to religious schools continue to be forbidden under the Supreme Court's definition of "establishment."[29] I discuss these more recent developments in greater detail in the Epilogue.

In short, the Supreme Court since 1947 has nationalized American policy regarding religion and education, adopting a "strict separationist" reading of the First Amendment that prohibits devotionals in the public schools. At the same time, it has generally rejected efforts to provide public aid to religious schools, although some recent decisions have opened the door to more substantial indirect aid. Yet while the Court has been a major force for policy change, it did not act alone. Rather, "strict separation" was brought before the Court through the concerted and sustained advocacy of a wide-ranging coalition of separationist groups. These groups reflected the altered dynamics of religious conflict that dominated mid-twentieth-century America, and

---

[24] *Abington Township* v. *Schempp*, pp. 239–40 (Brennan J., concurring).

[25] *Lemon* v. *Kurtzman*, 403 US 602 (1971), pp. 612–13.

[26] E.g., *Committee for Public Education and Religious Liberty (PEARL)* v. *Nyquist*, 413 US 756 (1973); *Meek* v. *Pittinger*, 421 US 349 (1975); *Wolman* v. *Walter*, 433 US 229 (1977).

[27] *Aguilar* v. *Felton*, 473 US 402 (1985).

[28] *Mitchell* v. *Helms*, 530 US 793 (2000); *Zelman* v. *Simmons-Harris*, 536 US 639 (2002); *Arizona Christian School Tuition Organization* v. *Winn et al.*, 131 S.Ct. 146 (2011).

[29] Douglas Laycock. 2006. "Church and State in the United States: Competing Conceptions and Historic Changes." *Indiana Journal of Global Legal Studies* 13: 503–41, p. 523.

their campaign took advantage of institutional features that enhanced the Court's receptiveness to their arguments.

THE NEW DYNAMICS OF RELIGIOUS CONFLICT AT MIDCENTURY

The postwar legal campaign to redefine and nationalize America's religious education policy took place in the context of – and partly as the result of – growing instability in the dynamics of religious conflict. The longstanding divide between Catholics and Protestants, while still fundamental to American religious life, began to weaken at midcentury as new theological divisions emerged among Protestants, and as Catholics grew increasingly integrated into the American mainstream. As the old divide began to weaken, both Protestants and Catholics found themselves adopting unfamiliar positions, especially on public school devotionals. Meanwhile, new players – most importantly, Jews and civil libertarians – aggressively entered into the old debates over religious education, inserting powerful new voices for strict separation into the conversation. As the political dynamics of religious conflict began to shift, it opened the door to a renegotiation of the nineteenth-century settlement and the emergence of strict separation.

Protestant–Catholic Divisions in Flux

In the period from 1920 to 1960, the Protestant–Catholic divide began to weaken. Although it continued to play a preeminent structuring role in debates over religion and education until the 1960s,[30] there were signs as early as the 1930s that Protestant–Catholic antagonism was beginning to fade. On the Protestant side, the unity of the Protestant Establishment had been permanently fractured in the 1920s by theological conflict between modernists and fundamentalists.[31] While modernists (or liberals) emphasized the place of reason alongside faith and sought to adapt religious understandings to align them with modern science, fundamentalists rejected this approach in favor of a reassertion of the truth of Scripture.[32] This theological split ultimately resulted in serious organizational division: by the 1940s, the new National Association of Evangelicals (NAE) was coordinating conservative evangelicals, while the National Council of Churches served as an umbrella group for the increasingly liberal mainline churches.[33]

---

[30] On ongoing Protestant–Catholic tensions during this period, see generally James T. McGreevy. 2003. *Catholicism and American Freedom: A History*. New York: W.W. Norton, pp. 138–88.

[31] Robert T. Handy. 1984 [1971]. *A Christian America: Protestant Hopes and Historical Realities*. Rev. 2nd edn. New York: Oxford University Press, pp. 159–84.

[32] On the rise of modernism, see William Hutchison. 1976. *The Modernist Impulse in American Protestantism*. Cambridge: Harvard University Press; and Ferenc Morton Szasz. 1982. *The Divided Mind of Protestant America, 1880–1930*. Alabama: University of Alabama Press.

[33] Christian Smith. 1998. *American Evangelicalism: Embattled and Thriving*. Chicago: University of Chicago Press, pp. 11–12. The National Council of Churches was known as the Federal Council of Churches until 1950.

The rise of liberal Protestantism and the fragmenting of the Protestant Establishment introduced a new impulse into interfaith relations: positive engagement with other religious faiths. Beginning in the 1920s, liberal Protestants began to embrace interfaith work, ecumenism, and goodwill movements in an attempt to build bridges and trust between people of different faiths.[34] In contrast, fundamentalists and other conservative Protestants decisively rejected this approach, preferring to evangelize and reemphasize their core religious truths. By the 1940s, these two approaches to religious pluralism had become so central to the Protestant divide that they had begun to produce feedback effects. Conservative Protestants began to demand increased orthodoxy and doctrinal purity to prove they were not tainted with modernism, while liberal Protestants began to adopt ever more inclusive and tolerant public stances to avoid being cast as fundamentalists.[35] Thus, by midcentury, Protestants no longer spoke with a united voice, and a substantial number of them had self-consciously adopted a more open stance toward other religions.

While Protestants grew increasingly divided, Catholics moved inexorably toward the mainstream of American society, entering the managerial and professional classes in large numbers, and rising to prominent positions in national politics.[36] After World War II, Catholics' integration into American society accelerated. John F. Kennedy was elected as the nation's first Catholic president in 1960. The G.I. Bill brought higher education to massive numbers of Catholics, who thrived in the universities and parlayed their educational gains into increased participation in law, business, and medicine.[37] By 1970, Catholics had attained occupational, educational, and economic parity with Protestants.[38] Catholic intellectuals, such as John Courtney Murray, articulated a new stance on social and political questions that "Americanized" Catholicism in a more liberal, Protestant-friendly direction.[39] These stances were ultimately endorsed in the early 1960s by the Second Vatican Council, which broke down theological, liturgical, and devotional barriers between Protestants and Catholics.[40] While Protestants maintained their suspicions of Catholics at

[34] Kevin Schultz. 2011. *Tri-Faith America: How Catholics and Jews Held Postwar America to Its Protestant Promise.* New York: Oxford University Press, pp. 29–41.

[35] David A. Hollinger. 2013. *After Cloven Tongues of Fire: Protestant Liberalism in Modern American History.* Princeton: Princeton University Press, p. 21.

[36] Andrew M. Greeley. 1989. *Religious Change in America.* Cambridge: Harvard University Press, pp. 78–79; Liston Pope. 1948. "Religion and the Class Structure." *Annals of the American Academy of Political and Social Science* 256: 84–91, pp. 85–86.

[37] James Hennesey. 1981. *American Catholics: A History of the Roman Catholic Community in the United States.* New York: Oxford University Press, pp. 283, 288.

[38] Charles R. Morris. 1997. *American Catholic: The Saints and Sinners Who Built America's Most Powerful Church.* New York: Times Books, p. 256.

[39] Jay P. Dolan. 1985. *The American Catholic Experience: A History from Colonial Times to the Present.* Garden City, NY: Doubleday, p. 407; McGreevy, *Catholicism and American Freedom,* pp. 189–215.

[40] Robert Wuthnow. 1988. *The Restructuring of American Religion: Society and Faith since World War II.* Princeton: Princeton University Press, p. 94. On Vatican II, see generally Melissa J.

midcentury, Catholics no longer seemed as socially, politically, or theologically foreign as they had before.[41]

The slow breakdown of the Protestant–Catholic divide destabilized the long-standing positions each group held regarding religious education, and allowed new configurations to emerge. Protestants remained united in opposition to public aid, but they increasingly parted ways over the issue of public school devotionals. Perhaps influenced by their interfaith interactions, liberal Protestants grew ambivalent about public school religion. The transition was heralded by the prominent mainline publication *Christian Century*, which went from championing the constitutionality of school prayer in 1947, to tepidly defending prayer while acknowledging it was spiritually and pedagogically unsound in 1952, to openly endorsing the *Engel* decision outlawing it in 1962 as "faithful to the First amendment."[42] Similarly, the liberal-Protestant-dominated National Council of Churches moved, in less than a decade, from endorsing "the reverent reading of selections from the Bible"[43] to completely opposing it. In 1963, the organization embraced the *Schempp* decision banning Bible reading with the resounding admonishment that "Neither the church nor the state should use the public school to compel acceptance of any creed or conformity to any specific religious practice."[44] The following year, it further affirmed that "pluralism ... requires that Protestant churches redefine their position," and rejected any "attempt to turn the clock backward by an effort to give constitutional sanction to Theism, or to the Christian religion or practice as the official religion or practice of the nation."[45]

Yet even as the mainline churches shifted against religion in the schools, conservative Protestants redoubled their support. Conservative Protestants held fast to the belief that America was a Protestant nation, and viewed the secularization of the public schools as an attack on their place in society.[46] Many, like evangelist Billy Graham, decried the *Engel* decision for perverting "freedom of religion" into "freedom from religion."[47] Many more raised their voices

Wilde. 2007. *Vatican II: A Sociological Analysis of Religious Change*. Princeton: Princeton University Press.

[41] Martin E. Marty. 1996. *Modern American Religion*. Vol. 3. *Under God, Indivisible, 1941–1960*. Chicago: University of Chicago Press, pp. 253, 417, 432, 438.

[42] *Christian Century*. 1947. "Getting Down to Cases." 10 December, pp. 1512–14; *Christian Century*. 1952. "Prayers in Public Schools Opposed." 9 January, p. 35; *Christian Century*. 1962. "Prayers, Bibles, and Schools." 24 October, pp. 1279–80.

[43] Quoted in Vincent J. Flynn. 1954. "Strategies for Making Adequate Provision of Religious Education for All Our Young." *Religious Education* 49: 93–103, p. 103.

[44] National Council of Churches. 1963. "The Churches and the Public Schools: A Policy Statement of the National Council of Churches." *Journal of Church and State* 5: 176–80, p. 177.

[45] National Council of Churches. 1964. "Separation and Interaction of Church and State." *Journal of Church and State* 6: 147–53, p. 150.

[46] Adam Laats. 2012. "Our Schools, Our Country: American Evangelicals, Public Schools, and the Supreme Court Decisions of 1962 and 1963." *Journal of Religious History* 36(3): 319–34.

[47] Quoted in Leo Pfeffer. 1984. *Religion, State, and the Burger Court*. Buffalo, NY: Prometheus Books, p. 86.

in outrage the following year after the *Schempp* decision. Harold Ockenga, the evangelical president of Fuller Theological Seminary, lamented that the decision "leaves America in the same position as Communist Russia."[48] The NAE, for its part, warned that *Schempp* threatened to "create a moral and religious vacuum in our educational system ... thus threatening the very foundations of our society." It called for "the active resistance to any hostility toward a religiously based view of life as it may appear in the public schools."[49]

Catholics, too, switched their position on devotionals in the 1940s. While maintaining their demands for public aid, they began to call formally for more religious content in public education. This changing position reflected Catholics' growing confidence in their place in American society. So long as the devotionals were not overtly Protestant, Catholics were willing to sign off.[50] As the Court began to issue its separationist decisions, Catholics responded by becoming ever more vocal in their support for public school devotionals. Responding to the *McCollum* decision prohibiting released-time education in the late 1940s, the American bishops issued a statement condemning the ruling as a "judicial 'establishment of secularism' that would ban God from public life."[51] Four years later, they further argued that "if religion is important to good citizenship ... then the state must give recognition to its importance in public education."[52] Over the next two decades, Catholic publications launched a series of attacks on "secular humanist" and Jewish organizations, accusing them of attempting to drive religion out of the schools.[53] By the end of the 1960s, Catholics had become "the most vigorous defenders of religious practices in the public schools."[54]

Beyond the Protestant–Catholic Divide: Jews and Civil Libertarians

As Protestant and Catholic positions entered into flux in the postwar years, new groups emerged as influential voices within the religious field. Most consequential among these were civil libertarians and Jews. Civil libertarians provided a strong, nonreligious voice on behalf of a purely secular state. Devoted

[48] Quoted in Daniel K. Williams. 2010. *God's Own Party: The Making of the Christian Right.* New York: Oxford University Press, p. 65.

[49] National Association of Evangelicals. 1964. "Church and State Separation." Available online at http://nae.net/church-state-separation-1964/ (accessed 28 March 2016).

[50] Schultz, *Tri-Faith America*, p. 127.

[51] National Catholic Welfare Conference. 1984 [1948]. "The Christian in Action." Pp. 82–89 in *Pastoral Letters of the United States Catholic Bishops.* Vol. 2, *1941–1961*, edited by Hugh J. Nolan. Washington, DC: United States Catholic Conference, p. 89.

[52] National Catholic Welfare Conference. 1984 [1952]. "Religion: Our Most Vital National Asset." Pp. 148–57 in *Pastoral Letters of the United States Catholic Bishops.* Vol. 2, *1941–1961*, edited by Hugh J. Nolan. Washington, DC: United States Catholic Conference, p. 154.

[53] Gregg Ivers. 1995. *To Build a Wall: American Jews and the Separation of Church and State.* Charlottesville: University Press of Virginia, pp. 83, 102–03, 138–41.

[54] Leo Pfeffer, quoted in Zimmerman, *Whose America*, p. 175.

to the protection and advancement of "civil liberties" – those individual rights that citizens may assert against the government – and of the Bill of Rights in particular, civil libertarians understood the Establishment Clause to mean absolute "separation of church and state," in education and elsewhere. Civil libertarians' general orientation was liberal and broadly humanist, and in this regard, they followed in the footsteps of earlier freethinking proponents of a strongly secular state.[55] Civil libertarians, however, did not so much continue this tradition as attract members of that tradition to a cause that was considerably more broad-based, topically and demographically. By dint of their focus on constitutional issues and personal freedoms, civil libertarians also drew the support of many liberal Protestants, Unitarians, and Jews.[56] Civil libertarians worked closely with religious groups and counted many religious leaders among their ranks, especially in more conservative corners of the country.[57] These religious connections gave civil libertarians a much broader, and stronger, base of support than their more anticlerical predecessors, while their dogged defense of the Bill of Rights – not just religious freedom alone – gained them widespread support in American society.

More consequential, in the long run, was the emergence of a strong and overtly *religious* voice on behalf of strict separation – the American Jewish community. The immediate postwar years saw the rapid integration of Jews into American civic life. In the wake of the Holocaust, anti-Semitism declined dramatically, and the formal and informal barriers that had excluded Jews from social and civic life came tumbling down.[58] In the process, Jews became coequal participants with Protestants and Catholics in American public life. References to America's "Judeo-Christian heritage" became commonplace after World War II, and American culture increasingly oriented itself to the idea that it had become a "tri-faith" society.[59] The affirmation of Judaism as a thoroughly American religion was authoritatively announced in 1955 with the

---

[55] E.g., the National Liberal League, discussed in Hamburger, *Separation of Church and State*, pp. 287–334.

[56] Indeed, liberal Protestant ministers and Reform Jewish rabbis featured prominently in the early organizing committees of the American Civil Liberties Union (ACLU). See William Sloane Coffin. 2006. "Roger Baldwin and the Separation of Church and State." Pp. 216–18 in *Liberties Lost: The Endangered Legacy of the ACLU*, edited by Woody Klein. Westport, CT: Praeger, p. 216; and Lucille Milner. 1954. *Education of an American Liberal*. New York: Horizon Press, pp. 68–69, 123. While liberal Protestants and Jews continued to play prominent roles within the organization throughout the mid-twentieth century, Catholics were notably absent from ACLU leadership during that period. See Samuel Walker. 1999 [1990]. *In Defense of American Liberties: A History of the ACLU*. 2nd edn. Carbondale: Southern Illinois University Press, pp. 98, 222.

[57] Judy Kutulas. 2006. *The American Civil Liberties Union and the Making of Modern Liberalism, 1930–1960*. Chapel Hill: University of North Carolina Press, pp. 46, 61.

[58] Edward S. Shapiro. 1992. *A Time for Healing: American Jewry since World War II*. Baltimore: Johns Hopkins University Press, pp. 28–59.

[59] Schultz, *Tri-Faith America*, pp. 57–96.

publication of Will Herberg's *Protestant–Catholic–Jew*. In surveying the "three great branches or divisions of 'American religion,'" Herberg concluded that Judaism had joined Protestantism and Catholicism "as one of the three 'religions of democracy.'"[60]

The new prominence and acceptance of Jews in American society both coincided with and encouraged greater Jewish activity on church–state matters. In the century leading up to World War II, a quiet but staunch commitment to strict separation had been developing in the Jewish community. Jews generally believed that "public religion in the United States could never be truly neutral, for it always connoted an advantage to Christianity."[61] In the ideal of "separation of church and state," however, they saw an all-American principle that they could use to defend their interests. Beginning in the early twentieth century, therefore, Jews began to publicly advocate against public school devotionals at the local level.[62] After World War II, Jews adopted a more vocal, aggressive stance, ultimately becoming "the key player in the campaign to deny religion a privileged position in the public sphere."[63] Nowhere was this attitude more evident than in education, where strict separation was seen as an essential defense against Christian hegemony: in the words of the American Jewish Congress (AJC), "Experience has shown that whenever religion intrudes into the public school, sooner or later Jewish children will be hurt."[64] As they had done since the nineteenth century, Jews opposed Bible reading and prayer in the schools. They also opposed any attempts at public aid. Jews had a longstanding "passionate love affair with public schooling," in no small part because they saw it as a means of breaking down religious prejudice and integrating Jewish children further into American society.[65] Their opposition to public aid, therefore, derived both from concerns that public aid would weaken

---

[60] Will Herberg. 1983 [1955]. *Protestant–Catholic–Jew: An Essay in American Religious Sociology.* Chicago: University of Chicago Press, pp. 38, 198.

[61] Naomi W. Cohen. 1992. *Jews in Christian America: The Pursuit of Religious Equality.* New York: Oxford University Press, p. 5.

[62] See, e.g., Leonard Bloom. 1980. "A Successful Jewish Boycott of the New York City Public Schools – Christmas 1906." *American Jewish History* 70(2): 180–88; Cohen, *Jews in Christian America*, p. 105; and Robert T. Handy. 1998. "Minority–Majority Confrontations, Church–State Patterns, and the U.S. Supreme Court." Pp. 305–334 in *Minority Faiths and the American Protestant Mainstream*, edited by Jonathan D. Sarna. Urbana: University of Illinois Press, p. 323.

[63] Kenneth D. Wald. 2005. "American Jews and the Public Role of Religion." Pp. 27–43 in *Taking Religious Pluralism Seriously: Spiritual Politics on America's Sacred Ground*, edited by Barbara A. McGraw and Jo Renee Formicola. Waco, TX: Baylor University Press, p. 37.

[64] American Jewish Congress pamphlet (1957), quoted in Schultz, *Tri-Faith America*, p. 127.

[65] Naomi W. Cohen. 1984. *Encounter with Emancipation: The German Jews in the United States, 1830–1914.* Philadelphia: Jewish Publication Society of America, p. 91. See also Virginia Lieson Brereton. 1998. "Education and Minority Religions." Pp. 279–304 in *Minority Faiths and the American Protestant Mainstream*, edited by Jonathan D. Sarna. Urbana: University of Illinois Press, pp. 290–94.

support for public schools, and that parochial schools would help to sustain religious prejudice.[66]

The emergence of the Jewish community as a strong and active advocate for strict separation in the postwar years was a fateful development for a number of reasons, but none more so than that they were more capable of successfully pressing the case for strict separation in public education than any other group. Jewish protests exposed the sectarian aspects of "nonsectarian" devotionals in a way that Catholic protests could not; as historian David Hollinger has noted, Jewish complaints threw the "Protestant matrix" of American public life into "bold relief."[67] And unlike civil libertarians, whose large humanist constituency threw them open to the charge of "godlessness," Jews were an undeniably *religious* voice on behalf of secularism. As Reform leader Simon Wolf put it in 1905, while protesting religious exercises in the Washington, D.C. schools: "If there be any contributions which the Jews have made to the world, it is the Bible and the religions which are derived therefrom. They, of all people, cannot be suspected of hostility either to the Bible or to religion."[68]

CRAFTING STRICT SEPARATION: STRATEGIC LITIGATION AND THE SUPREME COURT, 1947–1980

Thus, by the mid-twentieth century, the dynamics of religious conflict in the United States had changed considerably in some ways, and were in a great deal of flux in others. While Protestants remained united in opposition to public aid, they were increasingly divided over the propriety of public school devotionals, even as Catholics increasingly warmed to them. These changes opened the door for a renegotiation of the nineteenth-century settlement, largely through the work of two new entrants: civil libertarians and Jews. As the dynamics of religious conflict grew more complex and fragmented, these new actors – alongside some Protestants – took to the courts in an effort to forge a new, strict separationist settlement.

The Organized Interests Behind Strict Separation

Despite academic and popular characterizations to the contrary, America's system of strict separation is properly understood neither as the inevitable result of modernization or religious pluralism, nor solely as the product of the whimsical dictates of an "activist" Supreme Court. Rather, it is best understood as a political accomplishment, actively advanced through a well-organized strategic

---

[66] Diana Selig. 2008. *Americans All: The Cultural Gifts Movement*. Cambridge: Harvard University Press, p. 142.

[67] David A. Hollinger. 1996. *Science, Jews, and Secular Culture: Studies in Mid-Twentieth-Century American Intellectual History*. Princeton: Princeton University Press, p. 19.

[68] Quoted in Cohen, *Jews in Christian America*, p. 105.

litigation campaign. As political scientist Gregg Ivers has noted, "the major cases responsible for landmark decisions did not arrive on the Supreme Court's doorstep like orphans in the night. They were instead the result of concerted and calculated efforts often supported by organized interests."[69]

During the two decades following World War II, three major organizations advanced strict separation: Protestants and Other Americans United for the Separation of Church and State (POAU), the American Civil Liberties Union (ACLU), and the American Jewish Congress (AJC). These groups represented, respectively, the three major groups advocating strict separation: Protestants, civil libertarians, and Jews. Each group had a specific niche in the organizational ecology of strict separation: POAU defended the "no-aid" leg of the nineteenth-century settlement, the ACLU took the lead on sponsoring cases, and the AJC served as the intellectual center of the effort, particularly the effort to expunge devotionals from the public schools. Together, these groups targeted the courts to nationalize policy on religious education.

Protestants and Other Americans United

Protestants and Other Americans United for Separation of Church and State (POAU) was the most traditional of the three groups. It represented the voice of Protestant separationism, and was largely motivated by the desire to preserve Protestant dominance against a perceived Catholic threat. Founded in 1947 in response to the *Everson* decision, the group had close ties to the Protestant establishment. Its first officers were seminary presidents, and its board included many prominent Protestant clergy, including the former president of the Federal Council of Churches and the President of the Southern Baptist Convention.[70] Although POAU's founders spanned the Protestant theological spectrum, its strong opposition to public aid ultimately proved most appealing to those Protestants whose vision of separation was motivated by suspicion of, if not outright antagonism toward, Catholics. Consequently, charges of anti-Catholicism dogged the group well into the 1960s, making it something of an "organizational pariah" among more ecumenically oriented Protestant groups such as the Federal Council of Churches and the National Council of Christians and Jews.[71] Still, it commanded enormous popular support, especially in the South and Midwest, and had substantial financial resources.[72]

During the postwar period, POAU's major contribution to the development of strict separation was its campaign to prevent the funding of "Catholic public

---

[69] Ivers, *To Build a Wall*, p. 13.

[70] Kathleen Holscher. 2012. *Religious Lessons: Catholic Sisters and the Captured Schools Crisis in New Mexico*. New York: Oxford University Press, pp. 113–18.

[71] Sarah Barringer Gordon. 2010. *The Spirit of the Law: Religious Voices and the Constitution in Modern America*. Cambridge: Belknap Press, pp. 72–77.

[72] Luke Eugene Ebersole. 1951. *Church Lobbying in the Nation's Capital*. New York: Macmillan, p. 71.

schools."[73] In New Mexico, Missouri, Kentucky, Ohio, and other states, POAU sued to shut down local funding arrangements for Catholic schools during the 1950s. These suits were designed as much to capture attention and sway public opinion in favor of separation as they were to end the violations; nevertheless, POAU's legal advocacy blocked public aid arrangements in dozens of localities in the 1950s and 1960s.[74] While POAU was eager to defend against the possibility of public aid for parochial schools, it was, following traditional Protestant practice, much less interested in challenging devotionals in the public schools. POAU attorneys often saw no problem with devotionals; in one Catholic public school challenge, in fact, the local attorney alleged as part of his initial complaint that the nuns at the school were failing to conduct daily Bible readings as the law required.[75] As the Supreme Court interpreted the Establishment Clause in stricter terms, however, POAU modified its positions to include opposition to devotionals, even though doing so created serious divisions within the organization. Conservative Protestants, long the lifeblood of the organization, began to abandon it, so that by the 1970s the group would change its name to the simpler "Americans United," and reinvent itself as the liberal, secular, special-purpose organization familiar to most Americans today.[76]

Of the three major separationist organizations, POAU was the most traditional. Until the 1960s, its understanding of "separation" was the classic Protestant version which opposed public aid but permitted devotionals. But it was also traditional in terms of its legal campaigns, which it waged through state courts on a case-by-case basis while giving little thought to the larger jurisprudential implications of its cases. In this regard, it was unlike the ACLU and AJC, which (as I discuss below) advocated a far stricter version of separation, focused on the federal courts, and actively attempted to shape jurisprudence through targeted legislation.[77] Nevertheless, POAU's dogged, systematic challenges to Catholic public schools were an important part of the strict separationist campaign in the postwar era.

The American Civil Liberties Union
The ACLU represented a liberal ideal of separation, motivated in large part by opposition to dogmatic political restrictions on expression. Its activities on

[73] For more on Catholic public schools, see above, Chapter 3.

[74] C. Stanley Lowell. 1966. *Embattled Wall: Americans United: An Idea and a Man.* Washington, DC: Americans United, p. 114. For a detailed account of one such case in New Mexico, see Holscher, *Religious Lessons.*

[75] Frank J. Sorauf. 1976. *The Wall of Separation: The Constitutional Politics of Church and State.* Princeton: Princeton University Press, p. 35.

[76] Gordon, *Spirit of the Law,* pp. 85–86, 89–94.

[77] POAU's challenges could at times be rash and indelicately stated. Accordingly, it had a lower success rate in the courts than the more deliberate ACLU and AJC, who tended to regard POAU as something of a "loose cannon" and avoided working with them when possible, especially before the 1960s. See Gordon, *Spirit of the Law,* p. 82.

behalf of strict separation grew out of its preliminary focus on free speech rights. Though it rose in fame in part thanks to its involvement in the *Scopes* trial challenging Tennessee's ban on the teaching of evolution,[78] the ACLU was not particularly interested in religious issues in its early years.[79] In fact, during the 1920s, ACLU directors were quite divided on the wisdom of opposing religion in the schools.[80] Its first formal statement on devotionals, written in 1932, was relatively moderate, opposing compulsory Bible-reading but lending qualified support to released-time education.[81]

But support for a stricter reading of separation grew throughout the 1930s. By the early 1940s, the ACLU was expressing opposition to Bible reading, released-time, and public aid, and also beginning to get involved in court cases challenging those practices – most notably, in the *Everson* case challenging transportation subsidies.[82] In the 1950s, the push toward an even stricter interpretation of separation was driven by local ACLU affiliates. Although the national ACLU tried to back away from strict separation somewhat in the early 1950s – hedging on the permissibility of prayer, for instance, and stocking its church–state committee with prominent accommodationist clergymen – independent-minded local ACLU affiliates drove strict separation forward by sponsoring the high-profile devotionals cases of the 1960s. The New York Civil Liberties Union, much to the chagrin of national officers, sponsored the *Engel* case outlawing school prayer, while it was the Philadelphia Civil Liberties Union that sponsored Ellery Schempp's challenge to Bible reading in Pennsylvania.[83]

In the campaign for strict separation, the ACLU was the great sponsor and innovator. The ACLU sponsored more religion cases than any other group between *Everson* and *Lemon*, acting as the driving force bringing these cases to the courts.[84] Moreover, alongside the Jehovah's Witnesses, the ACLU pioneered the strategy of repeated litigation as a means to social change on religious

---

[78] Though famous today as a battle between science and religion, the ACLU was primarily interested in *Scopes* as a defense of academic freedom. See Edward J. Larson. 1997. *Summer for the Gods: The Scopes Trial and America's Continuing Debate over Science and Religion.* New York: Basic Books, pp. 73–81.

[79] William A. Donohue. 1985. *The Politics of the American Civil Liberties Union.* New Brunswick, NJ: Transaction Books, p. 301; Walker, *In Defense of American Liberties*, p. 68.

[80] Walker, *In Defense of American Liberties*, pp. 76–77.

[81] David Edison Bunting. 1942. *Liberty and Learning: The Activities of the American Civil Liberties Union in Behalf of Freedom of Education.* Washington, DC: American Council on Public Affairs, p. 29.

[82] Bunting, *Liberty and Learning*, pp. 29, 66; Daryl R. Fair. 1997. "The *Everson* Case in the Context of New Jersey Politics." Pp. 1–21 in *Everson Revisited: Religion, Education, and Law at the Crossroads*, edited by Jo Renée Formicola and Hubert Morken. Lanham, MD: Rowman & Littlefield, pp. 8–11.

[83] Stephen D. Solomon. 2007. *Ellery's Protest: How One Young Man Defied Tradition & Sparked the Battle over School Prayer.* Ann Arbor: University of Michigan Press, pp. 31–40; Walker, *In Defense of American Liberties*, pp. 223–24.

[84] Sorauf, *Wall of Separation*, p. 69.

matters.[85] And the ACLU's work on free speech and other civil liberties played a key role in reorienting the court toward individual rights more generally. The ACLU was instrumental in developing the doctrine of incorporation, which extended the protections of the Bill of Rights to the states, and not just the federal government, and it helped forge the judicial doctrine that religious liberty held a "preferred position" requiring broad legal protection.[86]

The American Jewish Congress

The AJC provided the dominant Jewish voice on behalf of strict separation. The AJC was one of the three major Jewish defense agencies, alongside the American Jewish Committee (AJCommittee) and the Anti-Defamation League of B'Nai B'rith (ADL).[87] Like its fellow defense agencies, the AJC was motivated by traditional Jewish concerns to protect the rights of American Jews and other religious minorities. However, the AJC was less afraid than the other groups to rock the boat, less wedded to social norms and assimilationism, and more receptive to agnostic or secular Jews.[88] These characteristics made it a leader within the Jewish community in its advocacy of a de-Christianized public sphere, and "the most vocal Jewish organization in America" on church–state matters at midcentury.[89]

Although the AJC was at the forefront of the Jewish campaign for strict separation, it often collaborated with the other major Jewish defense organizations. Indeed, the AJC, AJCommittee, and ADL participated as *amicus curiae*[90] in more church–state cases between 1947 and 1969 than even POAU, making

[85] Ivers, *To Build a Wall*, pp. 15–17, 51. The Jehovah's Witnesses litigated thirty-nine free speech and free exercise cases between 1938 and 1946; see Shawn Francis Peters. 2000. *Judging Jehovah's Witnesses: Religious Persecution and the Dawn of the Rights Revolution*. Lawrence: University Press of Kansas.

[86] Walker, *In Defense of American Liberties*, pp. 79–81, 106–07. Justice Harlan Stone articulated the "preferred position" rationale (see further discussion below) in dissent in *Jones* v. *Opelika*, a case involving the free speech rights of the Jehovah's Witnesses. See 316 U.S. 584 (1942), p. 608. The ACLU was heavily involved in the case, filing briefs and working on legal strategy with the Witnesses' lawyers. See Merlin Owen Newton. 1995. *Armed with the Constitution: Jehovah's Witnesses in Alabama and the U.S. Supreme Court, 1939–1946*. Tuscaloosa: University of Alabama Press, pp. 89–90, 98–101.

[87] Steven Windmueller. 2002. "'Defenders': National Jewish Community Relations Agencies." Pp. 13–66 in *Jewish Polity and American Civil Society: Communal Agencies and Religious Movements in the American Public Sphere*, edited by Alan Mittleman, Jonathan D. Sarna, and Robert Licht. Lanham, MD: Rowman and Littlefield, pp. 29–30.

[88] Ivers, *To Build a Wall*, pp. 46–50.

[89] Kevin M. Schultz. 2007. "'Favoritism Cannot Be Tolerated': Challenging Protestantism in America's Public Schools and Promoting the Neutral State." *American Quarterly* 59(3): 565–90, p. 576.

[90] An *amicus curiae* ("friend of the court") is an actor who is not party to a suit, but who provides a brief or other information to the Court that presents legal arguments or a discussion of a case's broader implications, so as to help the Court reach a more reasoned decision. See further discussion below.

the Jewish defense agencies three of the top four petitioners (along with the ACLU) before the Supreme Court during that period. And from 1968 to 1980, no organization other than the ACLU participated in more church–state litigation than the three Jewish defense organizations. Together, these Jewish groups devised a legal strategy that focused initially on driving Christian devotionals from the public schools, and then – beginning in the late 1960s – on defending the principle of separation by challenging public aid to parochial schools.[91]

If the ACLU was the great sponsor of separationist litigation, the AJC was its intellectual center. Although the entire legal department at the AJC had a very high reputation, the AJC's nationwide recognition as the central intellectual node in the legal campaign for strict separation was primarily due to the prominence of its main counsel, Leo Pfeffer.[92] Pfeffer was an Orthodox Jew who educated his children in Jewish day schools.[93] He was also a prolific author and scholar of church–state relations, whose "books, articles, and briefs constitute[d] the most polished expression of the strict separationist constitutional position,"[94] and who was "by general consensus ... the dominant, driving force among separationist attorneys."[95] Pfeffer was an adroit legal strategist, articulating the arguments for strict separation not only through the AJC's *amicus* briefs, but also through briefs that he ghost-wrote for other organizations (such as the ACLU) in cases where the AJC was not a formal participant.[96] Indeed, until the very end of the twentieth century, the Supreme Court essentially adopted Pfeffer's analysis on church–state matters in education wholesale. Pfeffer and the AJC "became household words among supporters and opponents alike" during the postwar decades.[97] As a result, critics of strict separation regularly directed their anger at Jews in general – and Pfeffer specifically – after controversial cases restricting public school devotionals, even where the AJC was not the formal sponsor of the case.[98]

[91] Ivers, *To Build a Wall*, pp. 101–88.

[92] Sorauf, *Wall of Separation*, pp. 75–76.

[93] Lawrence Grossman. 2002. "Mainstream Orthodoxy and the American Public Square." Pp. 283–310 in *Jewish Polity and American Civil Society: Communal Agencies and Religious Movements in the American Public Sphere*, edited by Alan Mittleman, Jonathan D. Sarna, and Robert Licht. Lanham, MD: Rowman and Littlefield, pp. 293–95.

[94] Richard E. Morgan. 1980 [1968]. *The Politics of Religious Conflict: Church and State in America*. 2nd edn. Washington, DC: University Press of America, p. 55.

[95] Sorauf, *Wall of Separation*, p. 159. This recognition is widespread; according to political scientist Gregg Ivers, it is "impossible to overestimate the impact that Leo Pfeffer, as an individual and as a public-interest lawyer, had on the development of church–state law during the latter half of this century." See Ivers, *To Build a Wall*, p. 222.

[96] Jonathan D. Sarna. 2002. "Church–State Dilemmas of American Jews." Pp. 47–68 in *Jews and the American Public Square: Debating Religion and Republic*, edited by Alan Mittleman, Jonathan D. Sarna, and Robert Licht. Lanham, MD: Rowman and Littlefield, pp. 59–60.

[97] Cohen, *Jews in Christian America*, p. 125.

[98] For a particularly stark example from the wake of the *Engel* decision, see *America*. 1962. "Editorial: To Our Jewish Friends." 1 September, p. 665.

The Strategic Campaign for Strict Separation

Separationist organizations thus drew from a wide array of positions in the changing field of religious conflict: Protestant, liberal, humanist, and Jewish. This broad-based coalition was highly organized, enabling them to successfully execute a long-term campaign to develop and nurture a favorable jurisprudence through strategic case management. In contrast to nineteenth- and early-twentieth-century litigation, which tended to be sporadic and oriented to the particulars of a single case, postwar separationist litigation was far more systematic and sustained, employing "test case tactics" such as the careful selection of favorable cases, the recruitment of sympathetic plaintiffs, and meticulous attempts to control the timing and sequence of litigation.[99] Nor was their goal simply to rectify perceived local injustices through judicial means. Instead, strict separationist litigators during the mid-twentieth century sought to create precedents, shape legal opinion, and craft an entirely new body of federal jurisprudence that would effectively nationalize policy regarding religion in public life, including its role in education.

Cultivating the Law

While the strategy of targeting the Supreme Court had the potential for unmatchable rewards, it was also extremely risky: an unfavorable decision would set the cause back just as much as a favorable decision would advance it. Accordingly, separationist leaders carefully selected the cases they chose to bring up for review, as well as the content of those cases. Separationist organizations examined each potential case to determine whether it was a good vehicle to bring the arguments they wished to advance before the Court. They carefully managed the trial record during the earliest stages of litigation, to make sure that the facts presented to the court would allow them to strategically compose their arguments in the most favorable light.[100] In the *Schempp* case, for instance, the ACLU carefully structured its lines of questioning and the evidence it introduced during the trial phase in order to dramatize the specifics of the offending practices so that they could clearly make their case that the practices were both devotional and sectarian.[101]

Separationist leaders chose their battles, pursuing only those cases they believed would allow for the creation of lasting precedents and favorable jurisprudence. At times, the ACLU and AJC explicitly weighed the relative merits of different cases. For instance, the AJC's Leo Pfeffer urged the ACLU to back off from its *Engel* challenge to school prayer because he believed the

---

[99] Richard C. Cortner. 1981. *The Supreme Court and the Second Bill of Rights: The Fourteenth Amendment and the Nationalization of Civil Liberties*. Madison: University of Wisconsin Press, p. 283.
[100] Morgan, *Politics of Religious Conflict*, p. 80.
[101] Solomon, *Ellery's Protest*, pp. 144–52, 156–71.

prayer involved was insufficiently sectarian. He argued instead that *Schempp*, which involved Bible reading, was more promising; and he preferred still more strongly a third case, *Chamberlin*, because it featured a multitude of questionable practices that could be amply documented in the trial record.[102] As part of this strategic evaluation, separationist organizations sometimes backed off on cases that threatened to set a bad precedent. During the 1950s, the AJC grew concerned that Cold War anticommunist fervor and McCarthyism might incline judges to look unfavorably on challenges to devotionals.[103] Thus, although the AJC expressed preliminary interest in a 1955 challenge to Tennessee's Bible-reading law, they withdrew their support after the Tennessee Supreme Court upheld the constitutionality of the practice.[104] In fact, they discouraged the plaintiff from appealing the case to the Supreme Court, judging that the case was insufficiently strong to win an appeal.[105] These kinds of strategic decisions over the merits and prospects of cases reflected the deep concerns separationist attorneys had with selecting the best vehicles for presenting their views.

Separationist organizations also used *amicus curiae* ("friend of the court") briefs to raise issues for the court's consideration – and thereby potentially influence its decision – in those cases where they either could not or would not directly sponsor litigation. *Amicus* briefs were an especially important tactic for the Jewish organizations, who were typically cautious about being the public face of potentially explosive challenges to public school devotionals. Thus in *McCollum*, *Engel*, and *Schempp*, the ACLU or another entity formally sponsored the cases, but Pfeffer and the AJC presented many of the separationists' most persuasive arguments to the court through their clearly articulated *amicus* briefs.[106] These briefs proved highly influential. In *McCollum*, the first case touching on religion in the public schools, the *amicus* brief Pfeffer authored on behalf of the Jewish community clearly shaped the justices' understanding of the issues in the case. Pfeffer argued in that brief that "divisiveness … inevitably results whenever sectarianism enters the public school."[107] Justice Frankfurter kept a copy of Pfeffer's brief before him during the oral argument in *McCollum*, and was clearly influenced by its arguments as he crafted his

---

[102] *Chamberlin* v. *Dade County Board of Public Instruction*, 17 Fla. Supp. 183 (1961). These practices included not only prayers and Bible reading but also the singing of hymns, display of religious symbols, religious holiday observances, religious oaths, and a religious census of students. The case was ultimately decided by the Supreme Court the year after *Schempp* in a perfunctory opinion striking down the practices. For a discussion, see Ivers, *To Build a Wall*, pp. 124–26, 133.

[103] Solomon, *Ellery's Protest*, pp. 47–48.

[104] *Carden* v. *Bland*, 288 S.W.2d (Tenn., 1956).

[105] Ivers, *To Build a Wall*, pp. 127–29.

[106] Ivers, *To Build a Wall*, pp. 77–78, 102, 127, 131.

[107] Quoted in Leo Pfeffer. 1981. "Amici in Church–State Litigation." *Law and Contemporary Problems* 44: 83–110, p. 106.

concurring opinion.[108] Noting the "divergent views expressed in the [*amicus*] briefs submitted ... on behalf of various religious organizations," Frankfurter concluded that the released-time movement "has been a divisive and not an irenic influence in the community."[109] In this and other cases, separationists' (and particularly Pfeffer's) *amicus* briefs helped to frame the questions that the court ultimately decided in a strict separationist direction.[110]

Bringing Faith to the Fore: Negotiating the Religious Politics of Separation

Even as they worked to frame their arguments for the courts, separationist groups also had to negotiate the tricky religious politics of church–state separation. First and foremost, they had to defend themselves against the charge that strict separation was tantamount to atheism. Those opposed to strict separation were not afraid to accuse separationists of promoting godlessness and skepticism. Pfeffer observed this dynamic with concern, writing to lawyers at the ACLU that they had to work against those who would "make it appear that the fight against released time is a fight of atheism against religion."[111] In the context of the Cold War, the frequently heard charge that strict separationists were really atheists or communists required a vigilant defense. Defending itself in the *Engel* school prayer case, for example, the school board alleged that separationist plaintiffs had confused the "wall of separation between church and state" with an "iron curtain." In response, the ACLU's lawyer specifically defended his clients against this veiled accusation of atheism: "My adversaries are attempting to place me and my clients as the leaders of godlessness in our society. They point to us as atheists ... Nothing could be further from the truth. We come before this Court, representing four individuals with deep religious convictions" who believed "fervently in the right to prayer and belief in God."[112]

In fact, separationist groups often steered clear of opportunities to work with atheist plaintiffs. Both the AJC and POAU regarded atheists as a "kiss of death" because they inflamed both judges and their constituencies, who were heavily religious and disapproved of "alliances with the aggressively godless."[113] In

---

[108] Fowler V. Harper and Edwin D. Etherington. 1953. "Lobbyists before the Court." *University of Pennsylvania Law Review* 101: 1172–77, p. 1174.

[109] *McCollum* v. *Board of Education*, p. 228 n.19 (Frankfurter J., concurring).

[110] For other instances where Pfeffer's *amicus* briefs had a clear impact, see Stephen M. Feldman. 2003. "Religious Minorities and the First Amendment: The History, the Doctrine, and the Future." *University of Pennsylvania Journal of Constitutional Law* 6: 222–77, p. 250 (cf. *Abington Township* v. *Schempp*, p. 300); Pfeffer, "Amici in Church–State Litigation," p. 107 (cf. *Epperson* v. *Arkansas*).

[111] Quoted in James E. Zucker. 2007. "Better a Catholic than a Communist: Reexamining *McCollum* v. *Board of Education* and *Zorach* v. *Clauson*." *Virginia Law Review* 93: 2069–118, p. 2109.

[112] Quoted in Bruce J. Dierenfield. 2007. *The Battle over School Prayer: How Engel* v. *Vitale Changed America*. Lawrence: University Press of Kansas, pp. 113, 121.

[113] Sorauf, *Wall of Separation*, p. 49.

writing his brief in *McCollum*, for instance, Pfeffer took pains to consciously distance the Jewish community from the plaintiff, Vashti McCollum, an avowed atheist who had charged in her original complaint that religion was an opiate of the masses and a virus injected into the minds of children. In his *amicus* brief, Pfeffer wrote:

We wish to make clear our regret that the appellant chose to use the case as a medium for the dissemination of her atheistic beliefs and injected into the record the irreligious statements it contains. We wish not only to disassociate ourselves completely from the anti-religious views of the appellant, but wish to deplore the fact that the sponsors of the original petition chose the case as a means of inscribing such matter on the public record and confusing the basic issues in the case by dragging into it the unrelated issues of atheism vs. religion.[114]

Nor was avoiding atheism a feature of the religious separationists alone. The ACLU, too, demurred on proposed lawsuits led by atheists on several occasions out of fear of being tarred with the atheist label.[115] Most famously, perhaps, it refused to take on crusading atheist Madalyn Murray's challenge to Maryland's Bible-reading laws, preferring instead to work on *Schempp* and *Chamberlin*, which were similar but not burdened by an atheist plaintiff.[116]

To counter arguments that they only wanted to impose atheism in the schools, separationists focused on religious differences, typically arguing that diverse opinions among religious citizens required public institutions to be fully secularized. This theme was central to many of Pfeffer's *amicus* briefs. For instance, in his brief in *Tudor* v. *Board of Education*,[117] a case challenging the distribution of Gideon Bibles in New Jersey public schools, Pfeffer drew a sharp distinction between challenges to religion brought by "some atheists, some individual trouble makers," and challenges brought by religious citizens. The latter challenges were really about sectarianism, he argued, and required the courts to honor the scruples of all religious citizens by embracing strict separation as a means to neutrality.[118]

To further ensure that religious differences, and not the contrast between religion and atheism, would be central to the debate over the interpretation of the Establishment Clause, separationist organizations deliberately selected plaintiffs with religious objections. Tessim Zorach, the plaintiff in the second released-time case, was chosen as plaintiff by the ACLU and AJC because he was an Episcopalian who was "active in church affairs," and thus a more sympathetic figure than Vashti McCollum, the atheist plaintiff in the

---

[114] Quoted in Ivers, *To Build a Wall*, p. 79.
[115] Zucker, "Better a Catholic than a Communist," p. 2102.
[116] The flamboyant Murray responded, "The ACLU can go to hell, and take their opinions with them!" Quoted in Dierenfield, *Battle over School Prayer*, p. 172.
[117] *Tudor* v. *Board of Education*, 14 N.J. 31 (1953). The case, a victory for Pfeffer and the AJC, was appealed to the Supreme Court, but it refused to hear the case.
[118] Quoted in Schultz, *Tri-Faith Nation*, pp. 131–32.

first released-time case.[119] Although this foregrounding of religious plaintiffs was strategic, it was not simply cosmetic. There was an abundance of plaintiffs with religious objections to public school devotionals. Steven Engel, for instance, was an observant Jew who believed that prayer was intended to be meaningful, and objected to what he perceived as the trivializing of devotions that the Regents' Prayer represented.[120] Likewise, the Schempp family members were Unitarians who genuinely objected that the King James Bible conflicted with their beliefs through its representations of the divinity of Christ, the Immaculate Conception, the efficacy of petitional prayer, and the nature of God. As Ed Schempp testified, "A human father would not visit the sins upon the children of a fourth generation, in my opinion. That makes God less than man and I do not want my children believing that God is a lesser person than a human father. My concept of God is bigger than that."[121] Through the careful strategic foregrounding of plaintiffs such as these, strict separationist groups were able to steer the conversation away from atheism and toward the implications of religious difference.

Buttressing the Wall: From Policy to Practice Through Sustained Litigation

If the courts were central to separationist groups' strategy to strike devotionals from the public schools, they were equally essential to their follow-up campaign to turn those decisions into practical changes on the ground. Despite the Supreme Court's resounding decisions invalidating school prayer and Bible reading, the rulings were greeted with widespread noncompliance – even defiance – in the 1960s, especially in the South, where fully half of schools continued to feature Bible reading three years after *Schempp*.[122] In the face of this civil disobedience, separationist organizations leveraged the new law they had helped to create to compel compliance in recalcitrant districts. Whereas many local administrators were simply unresponsive to the Court's decisions, preferring to take no action rather than stir up controversy over practices that often enjoyed broad community support,[123] the courts readily enforced the Supreme Court's decisions when violations were brought to their attention.[124] In a new watchdog role, the separationist groups took noncompliant districts to court.

---

[119] Ivers, *To Build a Wall*, p. 86.

[120] Dierenfield, *Battle over School Prayer*, p. 96.

[121] Quoted in Solomon, *Ellery's Protest*, pp. 147–49.

[122] Richard B. Dierenfield. 1967. "The Impact of Supreme Court Decisions on Religion in Public Schools." *Religious Education* 62: 445–51, p. 451.

[123] Kenneth Dolbeare and Phillip Hammond. 1971. *The School Prayer Decisions: From Court Policy to Local Practice*. Chicago: University of Chicago Press, pp. 74, 113–15.

[124] Emma Long. 2012. *The Church–State Debate: Religion, Education, and the Establishment Clause in Post-War America*. New York: Continuum, pp. 109–12.

The great expense of these lawsuits "made disobedience on school devotions an unaffordable luxury" for most school districts, and in short order, the mere threat of a lawsuit was usually enough to spur administrative action.[125] By the 1970s, this sensitivity to legal costs encouraged most districts to become proactive about excluding devotionals.[126] Nevertheless, individual districts, often in rural or religiously homogeneous areas, continue to engage in forbidden devotionals to the present day, fostering occasional lawsuits.[127]

Ongoing legal action was similarly essential in sustaining the battle against public aid. After the *Lemon* decision decisively outlawing public aid to parochial schools was handed down in 1971, it did not prevent many states with large Catholic populations from trying to find ways to circumvent the ruling.[128] As Pfeffer observed, a pattern emerged among the states regarding public aid bills: "enact a law, appropriate monies to carry it out until the Supreme Court declares it unconstitutional, then enact a new one that hopefully avoids the provisions upon which the Court based its opinion, and continue paying under the new law ... [This is] a strategy that can be employed as long as the ingenuity of statutory-drafting lawyers lasts."[129] Thus, legal action became central to sustaining the *Lemon* precedent as well. Separationist groups brought multiple challenges against each new attempt to craft a constitutional bill providing public aid to Catholic schools, several of which reached the Supreme Court.

In short, the emergence of strict separation and the elimination of devotionals in American public schools was not an inevitable response to modernity or the product of zealous judges alone. Instead, it was largely an achieved outcome, advanced by organized interests through a deliberate and coordinated campaign that targeted and managed cases, actively worked to frame the issue in favorable terms, and followed up with additional litigation to entrench their victories. Yet this by itself is not an adequate explanation. American advocates were assisted in their campaign by a legal system that was institutionally accessible and hermeneutically available – a fact that becomes clear when compared against the Australian case. In the last section of this chapter, therefore, I place this campaign in its institutional context, to demonstrate that the emergence of strict separation in America was facilitated not only by its skilled advocates, but by favorable institutional terrain.

---

[125] Bruce J. Dierenfield. 1992. "Secular Schools? Religious Practices in New York and Virginia Public Schools since World War II." *Journal of Policy History* 4(4): 361–88, pp. 383, 377.

[126] John Witte, Jr. 2006. "Facts and Fictions about the History of Separation of Church and State." *Journal of Church and State* 48: 15–45, pp. 41–42.

[127] E.g., DelFattore, *Fourth R*, pp. 232–36, 275–78. For a recent example, see Eric Eckholm. 2011. "Battling Anew over the Place of Religion in Public Schools." *The New York Times*, 28 December, p. A10.

[128] *Lemon* v. *Kurtzman*.

[129] Pfeffer, *Religion, State, and the Burger Court*, p. 37.

COURTS AS INSTITUTIONAL CONTEXTS: STRICT SEPARATION
IN COMPARATIVE PERSPECTIVE

Strict Secularists in the Australian Courts, 1964–1981

Legal challenges on matters of religion and education have been quite rare in Australia. Between 1945 and 2000, only one challenge to public aid and one challenge to public devotionals were brought before the Australian courts.[130] The only High Court case was a 1981 challenge to state subsidies for religious schools.[131] Responding to the reintroduction of state aid (see Chapter 6), the Council for the Defence of Government Schools (DOGS), a coalition of educational groups, humanist associations, and Protestant defense agencies, launched a protracted legal challenge in 1971.[132] DOGS believed that Section 116's prohibition against "establishing any religion" should be interpreted in the same way as the American Establishment Clause, and argued that the provision of state aid to religious schools should consequently be held to violate the Australian Constitution.[133] However, the Australian High Court rejected the Supreme Court's broad reading of "establishment," instead ruling that Section 116 only forbade the "statutory recognition of a religion as a national institution"[134] or the "constitut[ing of] a particular religion or religious body as a state religion or state church."[135] Under this interpretation, Australia's constitutional prohibition on laws "for establishing any religion" was held not to preclude financial support made available to multiple churches; accordingly, the Court overwhelmingly upheld state aid in a 6–1 decision.

Meanwhile, neither the High Court nor any state court has yet had occasion to rule on the constitutionality of public school devotionals. In the postwar era, the only case dealing with public school devotionals to come before a court was a statutory challenge to New South Wales' Public Instruction Act in 1976.[136] That challenge originated in the controversy over "general religious teaching" in the New South Wales public schools between 1962 and 1964, discussed

---

[130] There has, however, been an uptick in church–state litigation since 2010. For details, see the Epilogue.

[131] *Attorney-General (Vic.) ex rel. Black* v. *Commonwealth* (1981) 146 CLR 559. As I discuss below, an earlier attempt by the Victorian Protestant Federation to challenge the federal government's decision in 1956 to subsidize interest payments of religious schools in Canberra did not make it to the courts.

[132] Benjamin Edwards. 2008. *WASPS, Tykes, and Ecumaniacs: Aspects of Australian Sectarianism, 1945–1981.* Brunswick East, Vic.: Acorn Press, p. 222.

[133] I.K.F. Birch. 1984. "State-Aid at the Bar: The *DOGS Case*." Pp. 31–54 in *Melbourne Studies in Education,* 1984, edited by Imelda Parker. Melbourne: Melbourne University Press, pp. 51–52.

[134] *Attorney-General (Vic.) ex rel. Black* v. *Commonwealth,* p. 653 (opinion of Wilson J).

[135] *Attorney-General (Vic.) ex rel. Black* v. *Commonwealth,* p. 598 (opinion of Gibbs J).

[136] *Benjamin* v. *Downs* (1976) 2 NSWLR 199. A more recent case in Victoria also unsuccessfully challenged devotionals on statutory grounds. See *Aitkin & Ors* v. *The State of Victoria's Department of Education and Early Childhood Development,* [2012] VCAT 1547.

above in Chapter 4. In the wake of that controversy, the Secular Education Society (SES), an offshoot of the New South Wales Humanist Society, decided to pursue legal action.[137] Following legal advice, SES decided not to bring a constitutional challenge under Section 116, but instead to argue that the Christian prayers, scripture readings, and hymn-singing included as part of the "general religious teaching" curriculum violated the Public Instruction Act's prohibition against the teaching of "dogmatic or polemical theology."[138] The New South Wales Supreme Court disagreed, ruling instead that "general religious teaching meant teaching in the Christian religion," and that the prohibition on "dogmatic and polemical theology" meant only "the doctrine authoritatively laid down by a *particular* Christian church."[139]

Between 1964 and 1981, therefore, Australian courts saw one challenge apiece to devotionals in the public schools, and to "state aid" for religious schools, that were roughly parallel to those that took place in the United States. Yet neither of these challenges succeeded. In light of the Australian experience, America's legal history becomes more puzzling. In comparative perspective, American courts both (1) played a larger role in the development of policies regarding religion and education, and (2) were far more open to interpretations of "establishment" that suggested or required "strict separation." In the remainder of this chapter, I explain both of these characteristics in terms of the institutional characteristics of the American courts, showing how they rendered them more available, structurally and hermeneutically, to strict separationist challenges.

Explaining the Prominence of Courts in the United States

Political Culture and Rights Consciousness

Courts have been central to American politics and culture from a very early date. As Alexis de Tocqueville famously observed in the 1830s, "a legalistic spirit ... extends far beyond" the courts in the United States, such that "judicial authority [is] invoked in almost every context," and "[t]here is hardly a political question in the United States which does not sooner or later turn into a judicial one."[140] The widespread popular awareness of the law derived at least in part from the American Constitution, whose Bill of Rights fostered the development of a strong "rights consciousness" among Americans.[141] Accordingly, "Americans were fascinated by rights, made extravagant claims in the name of

---

[137] "Religion in Primary Schools." 1967. *Viewpoints* 5(9): 38; "Religion in Schools." 1967. *Council for Civil Liberties Newsletter* 12: 6.

[138] *Benjamin* v. *Downs*, p. 199.

[139] *Benjamin* v. *Downs*, p. 209. Emphasis added.

[140] Alexis de Tocqueville. 1988 [1835–1840]. *Democracy in America*, edited by J.P. Mayer. New York: Harper Perennial, pp. 99, 269–70.

[141] Hendrik Hartog. 1987. "The Constitution of Aspiration and 'The Rights that Belong to Us All.'" *Journal of American History* 74(3): 1013–34, p. 1030.

rights, and developed social movements behind the banner of rights," drawing legal and constitutional considerations into the political sphere on a regular basis from at least the Civil War onwards.[142] Indeed, Americans' strong rights consciousness helps to explain both why civil libertarianism emerged and prospered in the United States, and why American Jews came to understand their interests as being tied to the principle of church–state separation. Both groups came to see their interests as being intimately tied to the celebrated rights guaranteed by the Constitution.

In Australia, by contrast, courts have been far less central to politics and culture. The Australian Constitution is not rights oriented. It contains no Bill of Rights, and the right to religious freedom in Section 116 is one of only four enumerated rights in the entire constitution.[143] The absence of a Bill of Rights has undoubtedly discouraged rights litigation generally by reducing the constitutional grounds on which such claims can be lodged.[144] But the lack of rights protections in the Australian Constitution also reflects a broader Australian belief that courts are and should be subordinate to Parliament. Australia's founders debated and deliberately rejected an American-style Bill of Rights during their constitutional convention. Instead, they placed their trust in the rule of law and the wisdom of Parliament, seeing parliamentary democracy and the common law as sufficient protectors of civil rights.[145]

Thus, to a certain extent, American courts played a larger role in determining the relationship between religion and education than Australian courts because courts have historically played a bigger role *in general* in the United States. At the same time, however, as multiple scholars have observed, the Supreme Court's role in protecting individual rights has expanded dramatically since World War II, and the courts have come to play a still larger role as a venue for resolving rights disputes – on religious matters and in education as in other areas.[146] As I discuss below, this shift partly reflects changes in the courts'

[142] Charles R. Epp. 1998. *The Rights Revolution: Lawyers, Activists, and Supreme Courts in Comparative Perspective*. Chicago: University of Chicago Press, p. 32.

[143] The other enumerated rights are the right to vote, the right to trial by jury, and the right to equal treatment by the various states. See Australian Constitution, Sections 41, 80, and 117.

[144] Henry Burmester. 2000. "Limitations on Federal Adjudication." Pp. 227–64 in *The Australian Federal Judicial System*, edited by Brian Opeskin and Fiona Wheeler. Melbourne: Melbourne University Press, p. 261.

[145] J.A. LaNauze. 1972. *The Making of the Australian Constitution*. Melbourne: Melbourne University Press, pp. 227–32.

[146] For instance, Robert Kagan refers to this development as the rise of "adversarial legalism," and declares contemporary litigation to be "both more extensive and more intense than that of the nineteenth century and the first half of the twentieth." See Robert A. Kagan. 2001. *Adversarial Legalism: The American Way of Law*. Cambridge: Harvard University Press, p. 36. Others observing the shift include Abram Chayes. 1976. "The Role of the Judge in Public Law Litigation." *Harvard Law Review* 89(7): 1281–316, p. 1284; William A. Fletcher. 1988. "The Structure of Standing." *Yale Law Journal* 98: 221–91, p. 227; and Mark Tushnet. 2008. "The Rights Revolution in the Twentieth Century." Pp. 377–402 in *The Cambridge History of*

identity and hermeneutic approach. But it also reflects certain constitutional and procedural features of the legal system – most importantly, state constitutional provisions and taxpayer standing – which provided American litigants with greater access to the courts. In Australia, these laws and procedures either did not exist or actively inhibited plaintiffs' attempts to gain a hearing before the courts. Accordingly, those plaintiffs who wanted to challenge the legality of religious education often found the legal system to be a hostile institutional pathway to their preferred political ends.

State Constitutional Provisions: Multiple Access Points for Legal Challenges

The plentiful state-level constitutional provisions protecting religious rights gave American separationists additional grounds for legal challenges, making state courts an early and regular venue for contesting the relationship between religion and education. Until the mid-twentieth century, state constitutions were the main resource for actors who sought to use the courts to influence religious education policy.[147] Nearly every American state constitution contains some language delimiting governmental action in religious affairs. At the end of World War II, forty-two states had constitutional provisions protecting freedom of conscience, twenty-nine states had constitutional provisions prohibiting compulsory attendance at worship ("compelled support" clauses), fifteen state constitutions had provisions prohibiting "sectarian instruction" in the public schools, and seven had an explicit disestablishment clause.[148] Just as important, many state constitutions contained explicit provisions banning the expenditure of state funds on religious schools. While some states had included "no-aid" provisions in their constitution as early as 1835, the number skyrocketed after the failed attempt in Congress to pass the Blaine Amendment in 1876 (see Chapter 2).[149] The number of states with "no-aid" provisions rose from fourteen in 1876, to twenty-nine by 1890, and to thirty-seven by 1920.[150] By 1963, nearly every state had some constitutional provision restricting public expenditures on religious schools.[151]

Law in America. Vol. 3, *The Twentieth Century and After (1920–),* edited by Michael Grossberg and Christopher Tomlins. New York: Cambridge University Press, pp. 377, 388.

[147] Robert K. Fitzpatrick. 2004. "Neither Icarus nor Ostrich: State Constitutions as an Independent Source of Individual Rights." *N.Y.U. Law Review* 79: 1833–72, p. 1836.

[148] John Witte, Jr. 2005 [2000]. *Religion and the American Constitutional Experiment.* 2nd edn. Boulder, CO: Westview Press, pp. 108–16.

[149] Steven K. Green. 2012. *The Bible, the School, and the Constitution: The Clash that Shaped Modern Church–State Doctrine.* New York: Oxford University Press, pp. 69–70, 230–33.

[150] Jill Goldenziel. 2006. "Blaine's Name in Vain? State Constitutions, School Choice, and Charitable Choice." *Denver University Law Review* 83: 57–99, p. 69. Goldenziel does not include Louisiana among these states, but its 1879 constitution enacted prohibitions against the diversion of public money to sectarian institutions. See Richard J. Gabel. 1937. *Public Funds for Church and Private Schools.* Washington, DC: Catholic University of America, p. 541.

[151] Donald E. Boles. 1963. *The Bible, Religion, and the Public Schools.* Ames: Iowa State University Press, pp. 43, 291 nn.19–23.

The presence of these state constitutional provisions, many of which were even stronger than the First Amendment, was made more salient in the last half of the nineteenth century as the various American states began to develop their own practice of judicial review.[152] In claiming the right to declare state laws unconstitutional, the state courts opened themselves up to litigation on issues of religion and education. As discussed above, religious plaintiffs leveraged these state constitutional provisions to cast their preferred policies as uniquely constitutional. Catholics drew on the "compelled support" provisions or those provisions prohibiting expenditures on "sectarian instruction" to challenge devotionals in the public schools. Protestants, meanwhile, used the various "no-aid" provisions to shut down Catholic public schools. Both before and after the incorporation of the Establishment Clause, therefore, state constitutions provided additional grounds on which to bring religious debates into the courts.

In Australia, by contrast, state constitutional provisions governing religion generally do not exist. Only Tasmania has a constitutional provision, enacted in 1934, protecting "freedom of conscience … and practice of religion."[153] It was therefore not possible in most states for potential litigants to challenge state actions on religion and education on state constitutional grounds. Nor was it possible to challenge state actions through the federal courts, because the religious freedom protections of Section 116 are held only to bind the action of the federal government, not the individual states.[154] Thus, as the South Australian Supreme Court explicitly declared in 1984, "there is no legal remedy available to any person who believes that his or her right to freedom of religious belief has been violated by that State's Parliament or Government."[155] Accordingly, challenges to devotionals could only be waged on statutory grounds. The New South Wales humanist challenge was waged as a challenge to the Education Act's provisions concerning "dogmatic religious teaching," because Section 116 was not thought to be legally applicable to the case.

Public Law and Taxpayer Standing: Enhanced Access to Courts

While state constitutional provisions made state courts an additional set of venues for American challengers, American rules governing public law – that

---

[152] Lawrence Friedman. 2005 [1973]. *A History of American Law*. 3rd edn. New York: Touchstone, pp. 256, 266–72.

[153] Tasmania, Constitution Act 1934, c.94, Section 46.

[154] Reid Mortensen. 2007. "The Unfinished Experiment: A Report on Religious Freedom in Australia." *Emory International Law Review* 21: 168–203, p. 170. During the 1960s, the Secular Education Society thought that other constitutional provisions, such as Covering Clause 5 in the British enabling statute and Section 109 of the Australian Constitution, might constrain action by the states, but these were never adjudicated. See Secular Education Society. 1967. *Honest to Children*. Sydney: Secular Education Society, p. 7.

[155] Quoted in Marion Maddox. 2011. "Are Religious Schools Socially Inclusive or Exclusive? An Australian Conundrum." *International Journal of Cultural Policy* 17(2): 170–86, p. 178.

is, law dealing not with personal injuries but with the public good – made those challenges procedurally possible. Understandings of public law governed whether plaintiffs had *standing* – i.e., whether they were legally recognized as an injured party authorized to file a suit before the court.[156] Standing rules were typically more salient for challenges to public aid, because, unlike school devotionals, plaintiffs could not claim standing on the grounds that they had been personally affected by public expenditures.[157] American and Australian observers alike recognized the obstacle standing requirements presented to constitutional challenges to public aid.[158] Yet despite these common concerns about standing, American challengers to public aid had an advantage in gaining standing that their Australian counterparts did not: a tradition of public law that allowed citizens to claim standing to challenge local expenditures through their status as taxpayers.

Under the Australian model of public law, the attorney-general was understood to be the unique "representative of the public interest," and had, for all intents and purposes, a monopoly on standing in public law cases, including constitutional challenges.[159] Individual citizens were not granted standing to bring a case before the court unless they could demonstrate a "special interest" in the matter that was greater than that of any other member of the public. Those who wished to challenge public expenditures thus had to convince the attorney-general to "grant fiat" – that is, file the suit on their behalf – through a "relator action."[160] The relator process presented an enormous procedural obstacle to those who wished to litigate. As sole formal representative of the public interest, the attorney-general had "absolute and unreviewable discretion to grant or refuse the fiat."[161] Yet a potential conflict of interest always existed between the attorney-general's role as guardian of the public interest, and his or her role as an elected official who is part of a ruling cabinet and possessed with administrative responsibilities.[162] Particularly for smaller or politically less important plaintiffs, attorneys-general had an incentive to refuse fiat

---

[156] Louis L. Jaffe. 1968. "The Citizen as Litigant in Public Actions: The Non-Hohfeldian or Ideological Plaintiff." *University of Pennsylvania Law Review* 116: 1033–47, p. 1033.

[157] Standing is regularly granted to parties who can demonstrate personal injury or specific interest in the outcome of a case. Thus, students being forced to read the King James Bible against their wishes would typically be able to claim standing on the grounds that they were personally affected by the policy.

[158] For the United States, see Morgan, *Politics of Religious Conflict*, p. 83. For Australia, see "Current Topics." 1964. *Australian Law Journal* 38: 145–46, p. 146.

[159] Australian Law Reform Commission. 1985. *Standing in Public Interest Litigation*. Report No. 27. Canberra: Australian Government Publishing Service, pp. 54–55. Standing rules were liberalized in the late 1990s, but the account of public law sketched here held through the early 1990s.

[160] Patrick Keyzer. 2010. *Open Constitutional Courts*. Sydney: Federation Press, pp. 4, 76–83.

[161] Australian Law Reform Commission, *Standing in Public Interest Litigation*, p. 60.

[162] See generally L.J. King. 2000. "The Attorney-General, Politics, and the Judiciary." *University of Western Australia Law Review* 29: 155–79.

in potentially politically explosive constitutional lawsuits.[163] Unsurprisingly, therefore, relator actions have been incredibly rare events, occurring only a dozen times since 1900.[164]

In short, the Australian model of public law placed tremendous obstacles in the path of would-be litigants interested in posing constitutional challenges to religious education. The refusal of attorneys-general to grant fiat hampered at least two proposed lawsuits to stop state aid. In 1957, a petition by the Victorian Protestant Federation to challenge interest subsidies to religious schools in Canberra was scuttled after Victoria's Catholic Attorney-General, a supporter of state aid, refused to grant fiat.[165] The DOGS lawsuit, as well, was repeatedly delayed by the need to obtain and then retain fiat. The suit took a decade to get to the High Court in large part because, first, it took a year to convince an attorney-general to file a relator action; and second, the suit was held up on several occasions when motions to amend the initial lawsuit (to address newly implemented legislation, for instance) required reapproval from the Victorian attorney-general in order to maintain the fiat.[166]

In the United States, by contrast, public law prerogatives were not monopolized by attorneys general, but were instead extended more broadly through "taxpayer standing." Taxpayer standing was a doctrine that allowed any taxpayer to challenge public expenditures. The doctrine initially developed in municipal courts in the United States in the 1840s, and spread to state courts by the 1880s. By 1960, taxpayers' suits were available in thirty-four states and in virtually every municipal jurisdiction.[167] However, taxpayers' suits were not permitted at the federal level, as the Supreme Court in 1923 had rejected a taxpayer challenge to federal expenditures.[168] At the same time, however, the Supreme Court accepted appeals from lower courts where standing was secured using taxpayers' suits, leading to the ironic situation where cases could rise to the Supreme Court via a state or local taxpayer challenge, but not from a federal challenge.[169]

The doctrine of taxpayer standing represented a democratic model of public law, where taxpayers were effectively commissioned as "an army of private

---

[163] This was harder to do when the plaintiff was powerful or had a large constituency. In the weeks after the initial passage of the Science Laboratories Bill in 1964, it was rumored that the Sydney Anglican Synod might support an application for fiat, in which event it was thought that the Commonwealth Attorney-General would "have no option but to grant authorization for legal procedures." (The rumored action never came to pass.) See P.N. Gill. 1965. "The Federal Science Grant: An Episode in Church–State Relations, 1963–1964." Pp. 271–354 in *Melbourne Studies in Education, 1964,* edited by E.L. French. Melbourne: Melbourne University Press, pp. 339–40.

[164] Keyzer, *Open Constitutional Courts,* p. 81.

[165] M.J. Ely. 1981. *Erosion of the Judicial Process: An Aspect of Church–State Entanglement in Australia, 1956–1980.* Melbourne: Defence of Government Schools, Victoria, p. 4.

[166] See generally Ely, *Erosion of the Judicial Process.*

[167] "Taxpayer Suits: A Survey and Summary." 1960. *Yale Law Journal* 69: 895–924, pp. 898–901.

[168] *Frothingham v. Mellon,* 262 U.S. 447 (1923).

[169] Louis L. Jaffe. 1960. "Standing to Secure Judicial Review in Public Actions." *Harvard Law Review* 74: 1265–314, p. 1281.

attorneys general" to defend the public interest.[170] Under this model, the procedural barriers to accessing the courts for constitutional challenges were significantly lowered. Taxpayers' suits were thus a common means of challenging state and local aid to religious schools, including textbook and transportation subsidies, from the nineteenth century onwards.[171] Notably, *Everson* v. *Board of Education*, the 1947 case that heralded the nationalization of educational policy on religious matters, began as a taxpayer's suit.[172] Taxpayer standing was so important to challenges on state aid that strict separationist groups included a challenge to the federal taxpayer standing prohibition as part of their legal campaign.[173] When the Supreme Court agreed to permit federal taxpayers' suits on Establishment Clause issues in its 1968 *Flast* v. *Cohen* decision,[174] it streamlined efforts in the 1970s and 1980s to challenge not just state and local, but federal appropriations to religious schools as well.[175] In short, taxpayer standing rendered American courts far more available to challengers than the Australian relator action, thereby facilitating challenges to public aid.

Explaining the Receptiveness of American Courts to Strict Separationist Arguments

While public culture, state constitutions, and standing rules help explain why religious education was litigated to a greater extent in the United States, the question still remains as to why American courts were so much more receptive to strict separationist arguments. The answer to that question lies in a confluence of factors present in the United States but not in Australia: beneficial timing, sympathetic plaintiffs, and – most crucially – a favorable legal hermeneutic.

Timing Differences
Political scientists have long observed that courts respond to their political environment.[176] The broader sociopolitical climate in which cases are

---

[170] *Associated Industries, Inc.* v. *Ickes*, 134 F.2d 694 (1943), p. 704.

[171] Kenneth Culp Davis. 1955. "Standing to Challenge Governmental Action." *Minnesota Law Review* 39: 353–430, pp. 388, 395 n.166.

[172] Arthur E. Sutherland. 1949. "Due Process and Disestablishment." *Harvard Law Review* 62: 1306–44, p. 1330 n.67.

[173] Ivers, *To Build a Wall*, pp. 150–64.

[174] *Flast* v. *Cohen*, 392 U.S. 83 (1968).

[175] Steven K. Green. 2011. "The Slow, Tragic Demise of Standing in Establishment Clause Challenges." *Advance: The Journal of the ACS Issue Groups* 5: 117–29, p. 120. Indeed, there was a huge spike in the number of cases that reached the Supreme Court on taxpayer standing grounds between 1965 and 1975, thanks largely to the Court's liberalization of standing law in *Flast*. See Nancy C. Staudt. 2003. "Taxpayers in Court: A Systematic Study of a (Misunderstood) Standing Doctrine." *Emory Law Journal* 52: 771–847, pp. 779–80.

[176] Robert A. Dahl. 1957. "Decision-Making in a Democracy: The Supreme Court as a National Policy-Maker." *Journal of Public Law* 6(2): 279–95; Howard Gillman and Cornell Clayton,

considered influences the courts by making certain considerations more salient and certain arguments more persuasive. The initial Supreme Court decisions on religion and education took place just after World War II and at the outset of the Cold War, at a moment when the Court was particularly attuned to the threat of totalitarianism. In this context, the hierarchical Catholic Church appeared threatening.[177] Likewise, the Holocaust sensitized the Court to the steep downside of intolerance toward religious minorities, especially Jews.[178] These dynamics helped predispose the court to be skeptical of Catholic claims and sympathetic to Jewish ones. Moreover, as discussed in Chapter 3, the Court's decisions on religion in the public schools took place in the context of declining devotionals. Its moves to exclude Bible reading and prayer from the schools were in line with preexisting trends.

In Australia, by contrast, the courts ruled on religion and education in the late 1970s and early 1980s. This placed it well into an ecumenical period, when Catholic–Protestant relations had improved dramatically and old sectarian hostilities among Christians had dwindled.[179] In such a context, critiques of Catholic schools were themselves subject to charges of sectarianism and anti-Catholicism. Moreover, the decision upholding state aid took place well after state aid had been reinstituted and become settled practice; even the school organizations, early opponents, had begun to work within the new system.[180] As with the Supreme Court, in many respects the High Court was simply affirming a policy development that had already come to fruition through the Australian Parliament.

Litigant Differences

If timing predisposed the courts to be sympathetic to certain claims and skeptical of others, the plaintiffs in the United States were uniquely positioned to take advantage of the zeitgeist. In the United States, the strict separationist coalition included a large number of explicitly *religious* actors. The leading role played by Jewish organizations, of course, was particularly important, both because their presence highlighted the partial character of pan-Protestant devotionals, and because their pleas for protection for religious minorities had special resonance in the post-Holocaust era. Yet Jews were not the only religious secularists to come before the courts. Liberal Protestants were a large

---

eds. 1999. *The Supreme Court in American Politics: New Institutionalist Perspectives.* Lawrence: University Press of Kansas; Gerald N. Rosenberg. 1991. *The Hollow Hope: Can Courts Bring About Social Change?* Chicago: University of Chicago Press.

[177] McGreevy, *Catholicism and American Freedom*, pp. 175–88.

[178] Michael Klarman. 1996. "Rethinking the Civil Rights and Civil Liberties Revolutions." *Virginia Law Review* 82: 1–67, p. 47.

[179] Edwards, *WASPS*.

[180] Michael Charles Hogan. 1978. *The Catholic Campaign for State Aid: A Study of a Pressure Group Campaign in New South Wales and the Australian Capital Territory, 1950–1972.* Sydney: Catholic Theological Faculty, pp. 237, 242.

constituency among civil libertarians and provided several plaintiffs before the court, while the mainline churches became staunch defenders of strict separation by the mid-1960s. And conservative Protestant groups, such as the Seventh-Day Adventists, Jehovah's Witnesses, and Southern Baptists, also contributed through their various campaigns for expansive free exercise protections or for restrictions on public aid. While atheists and humanists were also active participants in the strict separationist coalition, the sheer number and diversity of religious voices defending strict separation lent legitimacy and power to the movement. Religious leadership made it possible to cast the issue of religion and education as one of differences among religious groups, and not one of differences between atheists on the one hand and religious people on the other. It also legitimized the argument that separation was the antidote to sectarianism, not a contributor to it.

In Australia, by contrast, "strict separationist" litigants were drawn disproportionately from humanists and anti-Catholic Protestants. In contrast with the United States, Jews and civil libertarians were not major participants in Australian church–state debates of the 1960s. Australian Jews were internally divided and played only a minor role in the renegotiation of religious education policy.[181] Australian civil liberties organizations, for their part, have historically been weak, in large part because Australia lacks a Bill of Rights.[182] While the New South Wales Council for Civil Liberties did provide some initial support to the legal campaign against devotionals, it quickly disengaged and turned its attention to other matters. Accordingly, the fight against devotionals devolved to the Secular Education Society, a group with a largely humanist membership. Likewise, the campaign against state aid was led by DOGS, without the support of the mainstream churches or the Jewish community. DOGS, especially in its early years, had close ties with militant Protestant defense agencies, and its campaign literature was suffused with traditional anti-Catholic rhetoric.[183] DOGS' rash and militant style eventually alienated it from almost all allies, including the Protestant churches, who were increasingly warming to state aid as they saw its potential to assist their own elite private schools.[184]

Thus, while there were some "religious secularists" involved in the Australian campaign, they were, effectively, the *wrong kind* of religious secularists – that

[181] Damon Mayrl. 2015. "Minority Faiths and Religious Education Policy: The Case of Australian and American Jews, 1945–1980." Pp. 59–82 in *Issues in Religion and Education: Whose Religion?*, edited by Lori Beaman and Leo Van Arragon. Leiden: Brill.

[182] Brian Galligan and F.L. Morton. 2006. "Australian Exceptionalism: Rights Protection without a Bill of Rights." Pp. 17–39 in *Protecting Rights without a Bill of Rights: Institutional Performance and Reform in Australia*, edited by Tom Campbell, Jeffrey Goldsworthy, and Adrienne Stone. Burlington, VT: Ashgate, p. 36.

[183] Edwards, *WASPS*, pp. 223–25; see also Council for the Defence of Government Schools (N.S.W.), *D.O.G.S. Newsletter* 3(6), October 1972, p. 2. Copy available in Noel Butlin Labour Archives, Australian National University, Canberra [hereafter NBLA], N111/1119.

[184] See, e.g., DOGS (NSW) Press Release, 27 June 1972. NBLA N111/1119.

is, religious voices that raised fears of sectarianism in an ecumenical era. The militant Protestantism of DOGS cut an unsympathetic profile, and "limit[ed] its own effectiveness by reintroducing a discredited anti-Catholic sectarianism into the debate."[185] Its actions inevitably associated separation with sectarianism, rather than as its antidote.

Hermeneutic Differences: Realism Versus Legalism

LEGAL REALISM IN AMERICAN COURTS. While both timing and plaintiffs were important, these external factors were particularly important in the United States because of the legal hermeneutic, or interpretive approach, dominant in the Supreme Court at midcentury: *realism*. In contrast to traditional formalist approaches to the law, which argued that judges decided cases by "finding" the law through the mechanical and disinterested application of legal precedents, realism argued that judges necessarily responded to factors outside the law itself in reaching their decisions.[186] Because it understood judges to be active agents "making" the law, rather than dispassionate observers "discovering" the law, realism "cleared the way for judges and lawyers to talk openly about the political and economic considerations that in fact affect many decisions."[187] Further, it encouraged judges to look to sources outside the law, such as history and the social sciences, to inform their decision-making processes.[188] The influence of legal realism has been profound, becoming a distinguishing characteristic of American law. In the words of political scientist Robert Kagan, "Compared to most national judiciaries, American judges are less constrained by legal formalisms; they are more policy-oriented, more attentive to the equities (and inequities) of the particular situation."[189]

From its base in the law schools, legal realism gradually displaced formalism as the dominant approach to law over the first half of the twentieth century.[190] Its influence was amplified by its elective affinity with the effort to expand the powers of the federal government in the 1930s. In the wake of the Great Depression, President Franklin D. Roosevelt instituted a variety of new programs that

[185] Michael Hogan. 1987. *The Sectarian Strand: Religion in Australian History*. Ringwood, Vic.: Penguin Australia, p. 254.

[186] Edward A. Purcell, Jr. 1978 [1969]. "American Jurisprudence between the Wars: Legal Realism and the Crisis of Democratic Theory." Pp. 359–74 in *American Law and the Constitutional Order: Historical Perspectives*, edited by Lawrence M. Friedman and Harry N. Scheiber. Cambridge: Harvard University Press, p. 360.

[187] Brian Leiter. 2005. "American Legal Realism." Pp. 50–66 in *The Blackwell Guide to the Philosophy of Law and Legal Theory*, edited by Martin P. Golding and William A. Edmundson. Oxford: Blackwell Publishing, pp. 59–60.

[188] Michael Rustad and Thomas Koenig. 2000. "The Supreme Court and Junk Social Science: Selective Distortion in Amicus Briefs." *North Carolina Law Review* 72: 91–162, pp. 100–14.

[189] Kagan, *Adversarial Legalism*, p. 16.

[190] Purcell, "American Jurisprudence between the Wars," p. 360.

massively expanded the boundaries of the federal government.[191] However, the courts frequently struck these initiatives down as unconstitutional expansions of federal power.[192] Roosevelt responded by appointing a bevy of new justices who were devoted to the New Deal.[193] Not surprisingly, many of these justices had a realist understanding of the law, and were thus predisposed to take social and policy considerations into account in rendering decisions.[194] As a realist hermeneutic became entrenched on the bench after 1937, the Supreme Court reoriented its interpretation of the Constitution to allow for greater deference to Congressional power on economic matters and to executive power in general.[195]

Although its initial impact was to redefine the contours of state power in the economic sphere, the purposive, socially attuned approach that realism required also had implications for the court's position on religious matters. Religious freedom, for instance, would also come to be understood in its social and political context. Moreover, the Court's new willingness to approve broader executive and legislative powers also required the Court to begin to specify those fundamental rights that those powers could not abridge.[196] In 1938, the Court first suggested that "prejudice against discrete and insular minorities may be a special condition" requiring "correspondingly more searching judicial inquiry";[197] four years later, it further suggested that freedom of speech and

---

[191] William E. Leuchtenburg. 2009. *Franklin D. Roosevelt and the New Deal: 1932–1940.* New York: Harper.

[192] E.g., *Schechter Poultry Corp.* v. *United States,* 295 U.S. 495 (1935); *Carter* v. *Carter Coal,* 298 U.S. 238 (1936).

[193] William E. Leuchtenburg. 1995. *The Supreme Court Reborn: The Constitutional Revolution in the Age of Roosevelt.* New York: Oxford University Press, pp. 132–42; Barry Cushman. 2008. "The Great Depression and the New Deal." Pp. 268–318 in *The Cambridge History of Law in America.* Vol 3. *The Twentieth Century and After (1920–),* edited by Michael Grossberg and Christopher Tomlins. New York: Cambridge University Press, p. 270.

[194] Though Roosevelt's nominees were crucial to the triumph of realism on the Court, realist ideas had already begun to influence the Supreme Court well before Roosevelt's first appointment in 1937. See Barry Cushman. 1998. *Rethinking the New Deal Court: The Structure of a Constitutional Revolution.* New York: Oxford University Press, p. 155. This earlier, broader turn to realism was encouraged by the severe dislocations of the Great Depression, which were *prima facie* evidence for many that social and economic conditions required a place in legal analysis. See David Sikkink. 2003. "From Christian Civilization to Individual Civil Liberties: Framing Religion in the Legal Field, 1880–1949." Pp. 310–54 in *The Secular Revolution: Power, Interests, and Conflict in the Secularization of American Public Life,* edited by Christian Smith. Berkeley: University of California Press, p. 342.

[195] Edward A. Purcell, Jr. 2008. "The Courts, Federalism, and the Federal Constitution, 1920–2000." Pp. 127–74 in *The Cambridge History of Law in America.* Vol 3. *The Twentieth Century and After (1920–),* edited by Michael Grossberg and Christopher Tomlins. New York: Cambridge University Press, p. 145.

[196] Howard Gillman. 1994. "Preferred Freedoms: The Progressive Expansion of State Power and the Rise of Modern Civil Liberties Jurisprudence." *Political Research Quarterly* 47(3): 623–53, pp. 625, 642–48.

[197] *United States* v. *Carolene Products Co.,* 304 U.S. 144 (1938), p. 152 n.4.

freedom of religion held a "preferred position" that required aggressive Court protection.[198] Building on these two opinions, the Supreme Court increasingly began to focus on protecting individual rights and civil liberties, including religious rights; and began to develop an identity as an institution dedicated in large part to the protection of the rights of minorities, including religious minorities.[199] This shift in the Court's self-perception would further incline it toward the arguments of strict separationists after 1947.

LEGALISM IN AUSTRALIAN COURTS. In contrast to the American Supreme Court, the Australian High Court in the mid-to-late twentieth century was dominated by a highly formalistic hermeneutic known as *legalism*. Legalism requires courts to use the text as its touchstone, adhering closely to the particular words of the statute or constitutional provision; and insists that, in the absence of amendment, the meaning of the text remains constant from the moment of its initial enactment.[200] This narrow focus on the text necessarily downplays the role of principle, policy, context, and justice considerations in adjudication.[201] The High Court decisively embraced legalism and methodological formalism in its 1920 *Engineers' Case*, proclaiming that the "settled rules of construction" required reading constitutional language according to its "natural sense."[202]

As in the United States, the adoption of legalism in Australia was entwined with attempts to expand the powers of the federal government. In adopting legalism, the High Court found a means of permitting the progressive expansion of the powers of the federal government, allowing for the development of a muscular central state.[203] Thus, for example, the High Court used a formal, legalist reading of the Constitution to centralize revenue-raising authority in Canberra and permit the Commonwealth to impose binding conditions on the distribution of tax monies.[204] At the same time, legalism was a tool for building

---

[198] *Jones* v. *Opelika*, p. 608 (Stone J., dissenting).

[199] Indeed, the proportion of the Supreme Court's caseload devoted to rights issues rose from less than ten percent in the mid-1930s to almost seventy percent by the late 1960s. See Epp, *Rights Revolution*, p. 2.

[200] Jeffrey Goldsworthy. 2006. "Australia: Devotion to Legalism." Pp. 106–60 in *Interpreting Constitutions: A Comparative Study*, edited by Jeffrey Goldsworthy. New York: Oxford University Press, p. 121; Rachael Gray. 2008. *The Constitutional Jurisprudence and Judicial Method of the High Court of Australia: The Dixon, Mason, and Gleeson Eras.* Adelaide: Presidian Legal Publishers, pp. 19–20.

[201] Michael Taggart. 2008. "'Australian Exceptionalism' in Judicial Review." *Federal Law Review* 36: 1–30, p. 7.

[202] *Amalgamated Society of Engineers* v. *The Adelaide Steamship Co. Ltd.* (1920) 28 C.L.R. 129, pp. 148–49.

[203] Greg Craven. 1992. "The Crisis of Constitutional Literalism in Australia." Pp. 1–32 in *Australian Constitutional Perspectives*, edited by H.P. Lee and George Winterton. North Ryde, NSW: The Law Book Co., Ltd, p. 7.

[204] Bradley Selway and John M. Williams. 2005. "The High Court and Australian Federalism." *Publius: The Journal of Federalism* 35(3): 467–88, p. 485–86.

the power and legitimacy of the High Court itself. The adoption of legalism, with its claims to disinterestedness, allowed the High Court to legitimize judicial review against potential attacks while simultaneously acceding to demands for a stronger federal government.[205]

But the High Court's embrace of legalism was not solely driven by sympathies toward a stronger federal government or its own self-interest. It also reflected ongoing institutional links between Australia and Britain that oriented Australian jurists toward British law, which was dominated in the early twentieth century by formalist methods.[206] Until 1986, Australia retained formal legal ties with Britain, such that the High Court's decisions were subject to ultimate review at the Privy Council in London. The reality or threat of Privy Council review was a subtle but important influence on Australian courts.[207] The High Court alluded to Privy Council review as a partial justification for the turn to formalism in 1920. According to Justice Isaac Isaacs, writing for the Court, the "common sovereignty of all parts of the British Empire" pervaded the Constitution and had to be "taken into account in determining the meaning of its language":

The settled rules of construction which we have to apply have been very distinctly enunciated by the highest tribunals of the Empire. To those we must conform ourselves: for, whatever finality the law gives to our decisions on questions like the present, it is incumbent upon this Court in arriving at its conclusions to adhere to principles so established as it is admittedly incumbent upon the House of Lords or Privy Council in cases arising before those ultimately final tribunals.[208]

In subsequent years, in fact, the High Court reversed some of its own decisions to bring them into line with British law.[209] The fact that Privy Council decisions were binding on Australian courts meant that, as former Chief Justice Anthony Mason observed, there was "little disposition on the part of the High Court to develop a jurisprudence that was in any sense distinctively Australian or different from English law."[210] The result was an ongoing embrace of formal, legalistic interpretive methods in the Australian courts.

[205] Brian Galligan. 1987. *Politics of the High Court: A Study of the Judicial Branch of Government in Australia*. St. Lucia: University of Queensland Press, pp. 37, 96–97.

[206] Goldsworthy, "Australia," pp. 115, 155.

[207] Jason L. Pierce. 2006. *Inside the Mason Court Revolution: The High Court of Australia Transformed*. Durham: Carolina Academic Press, pp. 227–31.

[208] *Amalgamated Society of Engineers* v. *The Adelaide Steamship Co. Ltd.*, pp. 146, 148.

[209] F.C. Hutley. 1981. "The Legal Traditions of Australia as Contrasted with Those of the United States." *Australian Law Journal* 55: 63–70, p. 68.

[210] Anthony Mason. 2000. "The Evolving Role and Function of the High Court." Pp. 95–122 in *The Australian Federal Judicial System*, edited by Brian Opeskin and Fiona Wheeler. Melbourne: Melbourne University Press, p. 100. As Mason notes, the impact of these formal ties on the British orientation of the court can be seen in the "Australianisation" of the law that occurred after the formal abolition of Privy Court appeals in 1986 (p. 102).

THE IMPACT OF HERMENEUTICS. The different hermeneutic approaches of the two courts led them to analyze issues in the religion cases very differently. In the United States, according to the realist approach, cases were interpreted in light of the social and political realities of the postwar era. The Supreme Court's decisions reflected a much greater interest in history, for instance, and especially the history of religious conflict.[211] Justice Hugo Black's decision in *Everson* was centrally concerned with the problem of religious conflict in Europe as it pertained to the Founders' intent in framing the religion clause.[212] And in Justice Brennan's concurrence in *Schempp*, he undertook an extensive historical look at the history of Bible reading in the American public schools in order to justify his ultimate decision that "the panorama of history permits no other conclusion than that daily prayers and Bible readings in the public schools have always been designed to be, and have been regarded as, essentially religious."[213]

Additionally, American courts were far more interested in the social dynamics surrounding their decisions. These concerns are vividly illustrated in the private discussions the justices had after oral arguments in each case. During debate on the *Everson* case, for instance, the Protestant justices explicitly situated the New Jersey bus fares case in the context of ongoing Catholic demands for parochial school subsidies. Justice Wiley Rutledge expressed concern that, "Every religious institution in the country will be reaching into the hopper for help if you sustain this."[214] Likewise, in deliberations on *Schempp*, the justices considered the practicality of declaring who could and could not teach their religions in the public schools. "Schools can't be opened to every sect," claimed Justice Goldberg; "how about the Black Muslims? How about screwball groups? You can't draw a line that is a viable one."[215] And in conference discussions over the *Lemon* case outlawing direct public aid to religious schools, the justices expressed concern that publicly funded private schools could serve as an "escape valve" for parents fleeing desegregation in the South.[216] These external considerations, which were often highlighted in the oral arguments and *amicus* briefs of the strict separationists, encouraged the Supreme Court to read "establishment" in broad terms as a Jeffersonian "wall of separation" ultimately disallowing devotionals in the public schools.

---

[211] Damon Mayrl. 2007. "Courting History: Remembering Religious Pasts in Australian and American Court Decisions, 1945–1985." Paper presented at the First International Social Sciences Conference, Canberra, Australia, 13 December.

[212] *Everson v. Board of Education*, pp. 8–9.

[213] *Abington School Dist. v. Schempp*, p. 278 (Brennan J., concurring).

[214] Quoted in Del Dickson, ed. 2001. *The Supreme Court in Conference (1940–1985): The Private Discussions behind Nearly 300 Supreme Court Decisions*. New York: Oxford University Press, pp. 401–02.

[215] Quoted in Dickson, *Supreme Court in Conference*, p. 427.

[216] Thomas C. Berg. 2001. "Anti-Catholicism and Modern Church–State Relations." *Loyola University of Chicago Law Journal* 33: 121–72, p. 160.

In Australia, by contrast, the cases that came before the courts were interpreted solely in terms of the text and legal history of the constitutional provision or statute in the particular case posed to the court, leading to highly literalist opinions. In the *DOGS* case, the High Court decided how to interpret Section 116 with the aid of an early-twentieth-century dictionary,[217] while in *Benjamin* v. *Downs*, the New South Wales Supreme Court devoted nearly its entire opinion to determining what "general religious teaching" and "dogmatic instruction" meant to parliamentarians in 1880.[218] Neither court expressed any interest in history apart from the history of the statutory enactment. In a legalist world, slight textual differences were magnified into profound constitutional ones. This was especially so in the High Court, where the interpretation of Section 116 hinged not only on the meaning of "establishment" but also on minute distinctions between "*respecting* an establishment" and "*for* establishing," and "establishing *any* religion" versus "*an* establishment *of* religion."[219] Legalism thus contributed significantly to the extremely narrow interpretation given by the High Court to "establishment," and to the New South Wales Supreme Court's very partial reading of "general" religious teaching, which in the end upheld the legality of both devotionals and public aid.

CONCLUSION

By the mid-twentieth century, the nineteenth-century settlement in American education was in serious decay. Recurrent local challenges and professional reforms had undermined or eliminated religious education in many school districts. Changes in the dynamics of religious conflict further destabilized the settlement, as old oppositions weakened and new players with different ideas about how church and state ought to relate to one another in education entered the scene. In this context, the door was open to a new secular settlement in education.

The negotiation of this settlement took place through the courts because they were accessible to an organized and determined campaign for strict separation. Procedurally, taxpayer standing and state-level constitutional protections provided multiple points of entry to the courts. More importantly, the Supreme Court had embraced a new philosophy – legal realism – that made it more open to contextual factors, policy considerations, and rights claims than it had ever been. Strict separationists skillfully and strategically took advantage of this favorable terrain to articulate a new secular settlement that nationalized American religious education policy for the first time. Australian separationists, by contrast, found the courts to be unwelcoming territory. For this reason,

[217] *Attorney General (Vic.) ex rel. Black* v. *Commonwealth*, pp. 595, 606, 622.
[218] *Benjamin* v. *Downs*, pp. 207–08.
[219] Carolyn Evans. 2008. "Religion as Politics Not Law: The Religion Clauses in the Australian Constitution." *Religion, State, and Society* 36(3): 283–302, pp. 288–89.

while Australia also negotiated a new settlement in the postwar years, it was negotiated not through the courts, but through the federal parliament, as the next chapter shows.

While American courts remain an accessible institutional venue, the mere fact of their accessibility does not dictate strict separation. That strict separation triumphed at midcentury reflects the interests of the civil libertarians, Protestants, and Jews who argued on its behalf in the postwar years. As the dynamics of religious conflict have continued to churn in the United States since then, however, the same factors that made it accessible to the separationists at midcentury have more recently enabled new claimants to advance a different vision of religious education policy through the courts – a development that I take up in the Epilogue.

6

Desecularization and Electoral Institutions in Postwar Australia

INTRODUCTION

Between 1964 and 1973, the nineteenth-century settlement that banned "state aid"[1] to Australia's religious schools collapsed. A series of federal and state initiatives extended a trickle, then a torrent, of money to Catholic and other religious schools. By 1974, state aid was an accepted part of the Australian educational landscape, formally institutionalized in a new Schools Commission that doled out aid to religious schools on a recurrent per capita basis. The reintroduction of state aid represents the creation of a new settlement decidedly less "secular" than the one that preceded it. Whereas the former had refused any supportive relationship between the state and the churches in education, the new one treated church and state as collaborative partners in educational endeavors, under the banner of "religious neutrality."

Why was state aid reintroduced in Australia, but not the United States? As in the United States, Australia's new secular settlement emerged thanks to a shift in the dynamics of religious conflict, a coordinated campaign to realize a new secular settlement, and a set of political opportunities made possible by favorable institutional terrain. In Australia, Catholics led the campaign for the new settlement. The dynamics of religious conflict shifted in the 1960s as the long-standing conflict between Catholics and Protestants was replaced by an ecumenical spirit that greatly reduced Protestants' incentives to oppose state aid. At the same time, a split in the Australian Labor Party (ALP) led to the creation of a new, predominantly Catholic political party. This effectively transformed

---

[1] "State aid" is the common term for aid to religious schools in Australia. In the United States, a variety of terms were used, including "state aid," "parochaid," and "public aid." Of these, "public aid" appears to have been used most frequently, and I will use the dominant term for each country throughout the course of this chapter.

Catholics into political free agents whose votes were highly sought after, giving them powerful new leverage in federal and state politics.

This unprecedented political opportunity emerged in large part thanks to Australia's electoral institutions. Australia's preference-voting rules produced a relatively flexible party system with real political space for third parties. Catholics took advantage of this flexibility to create their own party in the mid-1950s, and manipulated the features of the preference-voting system to enhance their political influence during the 1960s. The institutional availability of the legislative pathway can be seen when the Australian experience is contrasted with a parallel campaign by Catholics for public aid in the United States. There, plurality voting encouraged a rigid two-party system. Within this system, Catholics were locked into an unfavorable party coalition with Southerners, who opposed their claims and compromised Catholics' efforts to obtain legislation that would have benefited Catholic schools.

I begin with an overview of the legislative return of state aid, focusing primarily on federal events but noting developments in the states. I then situate the analysis in the context of declining religious conflict, showing how the emergence of an ecumenical spirit reduced religious opposition to state aid in the postwar era. Next, I discuss the great split in the ALP that was the proximate cause of Catholics' political opportunity, and illustrate how Australia's electoral institutions – and Catholics' savvy manipulation of them – helped turn a political disaster for Catholics into a political advantage. I then delve into the Catholic campaign for state aid in the 1960s, showing how Catholics engaged with the Australian public and politicians intellectually, tactically, and politically, in order to maximize their opportunity. Finally, I contrast the Australian experience with the American one, showing how Australia's electoral institutions made a legislative pathway a realistic option that was not open to American Catholics.

FUNDING FOR AUSTRALIA'S RELIGIOUS SCHOOLS, 1945–1974: AN OVERVIEW

The nineteenth-century settlement prohibiting financial support for religious schools remained strong throughout the early twentieth century. Although persistent low-level agitation by Catholics yielded some indirect supports such as student scholarships, transportation concessions, and tax exemptions, political opposition by Protestants and widespread support for the nineteenth-century settlement kept direct state aid off the political agenda.[2] By the early 1950s, however, opposition to state aid showed signs of weakening. In 1951, under pressure from Catholic delegates (discussed in detail below),

---

[2] Ian R. Wilkinson, Brian J. Caldwell, R.J.W. Selleck, Jessica Harris, and Pam Dettman. 2006. *A History of State Aid to Non-Government Schools in Australia.* Canberra: Department of Education, Science, and Training, pp. 23–24.

the ALP passed a resolution calling for federal financing of "all forms of education." This marked the first time since the 1880s that a major political party had expressed openness to state aid.[3] The federal government under Liberal leadership also showed some openness to certain forms of state aid, expanding tax deductions for tuition fees and capital gifts to private schools, and agreeing to reimburse interest payments on loans for the construction of religious schools in the Australian Capital Territory.[4] Although many Protestant leaders raised howls of protest at these moves, Prime Minister Robert Menzies assured them that the program was not a precedent for future aid. Claiming the federal government's hands were tied by constitutional limitations on the power of the federal government, Menzies declared in August 1960 that the entire question of state aid to denominational schools was "outside the jurisdiction of this government."[5]

Despite Menzies' assurances that he had no plans to reintroduce state aid, this is precisely what occurred. After narrowly winning reelection in 1961 in a campaign where education had been a major issue, the Liberal Party and its coalition partner, the Country Party, began to rethink their positions on state aid. At about the same time, as I discuss below, the issue of state aid was dramatically thrust onto the political agenda in New South Wales by Catholic protests in the city of Goulburn. As Catholic unrest grew, the ALP descended into chaos over the issue of state aid. Menzies, sensing political advantage, called an early election for December 1963. In a surprise move, Menzies announced plans in his pre-election policy speech to set aside five million pounds for enhanced science laboratories, which would be made "available to all secondary schools, government or independent, without discrimination."[6] This announcement put direct state aid on the agenda for the first time, and instantly turned the 1963 election into a referendum on state aid. When Menzies decisively won the election, it cleared the way for a full-scale reevalaution of state aid policy.

With the Liberal Party – long the party most implacably opposed to state aid – on board, and (as I discuss below) with sectarian tensions declining in an increasingly ecumenical atmosphere, the political dynamics of state aid decisively shifted. Indeed, Menzies' science laboratories proposal proved to be merely the opening salvo in a decade in which state aid was reintroduced in ever-larger amounts and ever-diversifying formats. From 1964 onward, Liberal politicians in the Australian states cautiously began to experiment with their own state aid policies. In Queensland and Western Australia, secondary scholarship schemes were expanded and made payable directly to the schools, while

[3] Kim Beazley. 1983. "The Australian Labor Party and State Aid, 1950–1980 [Part I]." *Education Research and Perspectives* 10(2): 52–56, pp. 53, 55.

[4] Wilkinson et al., *History of State Aid*, pp. 24–25.

[5] Australia. House of Representatives. 1960. *Commonwealth Parliamentary Debates* 28. Canberra: Government Printer, p. 514.

[6] R.G. Menzies. 1963. *Federal Election, 1963: Policy Speech of the Prime Minister*. Sydney: Government Printer, p. 22.

loans for school construction were introduced in New South Wales and Victoria in 1966.[7] A more significant breakthrough occurred in 1967, when Victoria introduced direct per capita grants to denominational schools – a major concession that committed the government to paying religious schools' ongoing costs.[8] Inspired by the Victorian example, within a year, governments in every Australian state had introduced or were poised to introduce some form of per capita grant to independent schools.[9]

ALP politicians watched these developments with envy and trepidation. For reasons I elaborate below, the ALP leadership had been controlled since the mid-1950s by the socialist trade unions, which were unremittingly hostile to state aid. However, three straight disastrous elections between 1963 and 1965, in which their losses were most pronounced in heavily Catholic areas, drove home to ALP leaders the need to reconsider their stance on state aid.[10] In 1965, the Deputy Party Leader, Gough Whitlam, declared that state aid was an accomplished fact and opined that the ALP should develop a new policy recognizing that fact.[11] At a pair of Federal Conferences in 1965 and 1966, Whitlam and his reformist allies narrowly defeated the old guard, allowing the ALP to run on a platform favoring state aid in the 1966 election and beyond.[12]

By 1966, therefore, the stage was set for what political scientist Michael Hogan has termed an "electoral auction," wherein Australia's political parties competed with one another for Catholic votes by proposing ever greater amounts of state aid.[13] In 1968, the federal government introduced grants to fund the construction of school libraries in both government and nongovernment secondary schools.[14] The following year, federal Liberal leaders followed the lead of their state counterparts and introduced recurrent annual grants to both government

---

[7] Henry S. Albinski. 1966. *The Australian Labor Party and the Aid to Parochial Schools Controversy.* Pennsylvania State University Studies 19. University Park: Pennsylvania State University, pp. 31–32; L.J. Blake. 1973. "Free, Compulsory, and Secular." Pp. 167–238 in *Vision and Realisation: A Centenary History of State Education in Victoria*, edited by L.J. Blake. Vol. 1. Melbourne: Education Department of Victoria, p. 233; Wilkinson et al., *History of State Aid*, p. 36.

[8] Wilkinson et al., *History of State Aid*, p. 36.

[9] Australia. Senate. 1968. *Commonwealth Parliamentary Debates*, 13 June. Canberra: Government Printer, pp. 1740–43.

[10] Albinski, *Australian Labor Party*, p. 33; B. Bessant and A.D. Spaull. 1976. *Politics of Schooling*. Carlton, Vic.: Pitman Publishing, p. 123.

[11] Bessant and Spaull, *Politics of Schooling*, p. 123.

[12] Albinski, *Australian Labor Party*, pp. 34–36; Kim Beazley. 1985. "The Australian Labor Party and State Aid, 1950–1980: Part II." *Educational Research and Perspectives* 12(2): 40–49; Helen Praetz. 1982. *Public Policy and Catholic Schools*. Hawthorn, Vic.: Australian Council for Educational Research, p. 14.

[13] Michael Hogan. 1984. *Public versus Private Schools: Funding and Directions in Australia.* Ringwood, Vic.: Penguin Books, p. 3.

[14] Don Smart. 1974. "Origins of the Secondary Schools Libraries Scheme." Pp. 105–27 in *Influences in Australian Education*, edited by D.A. Jecks. Perth: Carroll's.

and nongovernment schools on a per capita basis.[15] Meanwhile, the ALP formulated its own state aid policy. It proposed the creation of an independent Schools Commission to administer a greatly expanded program of funding for both government and nongovernment schools, which would be impartially distributed on a per capita basis according to the "needs" of the schools.[16]

Whitlam's election as Prime Minister in 1972 signaled the arrival of a new, durable secular settlement that permitted greater financial entwining between church and state in education. Whereas the state aid concessions of the mid-to-late 1960s had been granted in a somewhat ad hoc manner, Whitlam's Schools Commission, instituted in 1974, formalized and rationalized the federal presence in education funding, and placed it on a more permanent footing. Although the "needs" formula was progressively watered down over the course of the 1970s, religious schools continued to receive copious amounts of government funding from both state and federal sources.[17] This policy continued even after the Schools Commission was folded into the Commonwealth Department of Education in 1987. Religious schools currently receive more than eight billion dollars in federal funding to pay for general expenditures, capital expenses, and targeted programs.[18] Australia's religious schools now rely on these subsidies for more than half of their annual income.[19]

THE NEW DYNAMICS OF RELIGIOUS CONFLICT AT MIDCENTURY

The emergence of a new secular settlement in Australia in the 1960s was driven by changes in the dynamics of religious conflict. To an even greater extent than in the United States, the Protestant–Catholic divide in Australia had begun to weaken by the late 1950s. A new ecumenical climate, nourished by the reforms of the Second Vatican Council, helped soften Protestants' opposition to state aid, and opened the door to a new secular settlement featuring greater church–state collaboration.

---

[15] Wilkinson et al., *History of State Aid*, p. 41.

[16] Lindsay Tanner. 1983. "The Policy Formulation Process of an Australian Political Party in Opposition: A Case Study of the Australian Labor Party's Schools Commission Proposal." Pp. 44–75 in *Melbourne Studies in Education, 1983*, edited by Imelda Palmer. Melbourne: Melbourne University Press, p. 46.

[17] Craig Campbell and Helen Proctor. 2014. *A History of Australian Schooling*. Sydney: Allen & Unwin, p. 212.

[18] Marilyn Harrington. 2013. "Australian Government Funding for Schools Explained: 2013 Update." Parliamentary Library Background Note. Canberra: Commonwealth of Australia, pp. 1, 6. Available online at http://parlinfo.aph.gov.au/parlInfo/download/library/prspub/366868/ upload_binary/366868.pdf;fileType=application/pdf#search=%22library/prspub/366868%22 (accessed 28 March 2016).

[19] Australian Curriculum, Assessment, and Reporting Authority. 2011. *National Report on Schooling in Australia 2011*. Sydney: ACARA, Table 55. Available online at http://www.acara .edu.au/verve/_resources/National_Report_on_Schooling_2011_Additional_Statistics.pdf (accessed 28 March 2016).

The Decline of the Protestant–Catholic Divide

The longstanding divide between Protestants and Catholics persisted into the early 1960s. Ensconced in largely separate religious and social worlds, Protestants and Catholics continued to engage in sectarian sniping throughout the 1950s.[20] Between 1945 and 1970, however, this divide weakened dramatically. Suburbanization and upward socioeconomic mobility among Catholics eroded the social and geographic barriers that separated them from Protestants.[21] Yet the three factors that most contributed to the weakening of this divide were the sharp demographic changes brought about by the relaxation of immigration policy after World War II, a vigorous ecumenical spirit among the Christian churches, and the ritual and doctrinal changes that occurred in the Catholic Church as a result of the Second Vatican Council.

In the wake of World War II, Australia significantly relaxed its immigration policy. Until the postwar era, the Australian Catholic Church was decidedly Irish, and Protestant anti-Catholicism was interlaced with ethnic anti-Irish sentiment.[22] But the arrival of Catholic "New Australians" from Poland, Hungary, Italy, Spain, and Yugoslavia dramatically diversified Catholic congregations.[23] Catholic leaders simultaneously took steps to "Australianize" the Catholic Church, reducing the ties between Catholicism and Ireland.[24] On the Protestant side, postwar changes in immigration policy were emblematic of a broader cultural divorce from the British Empire and the development of a new more purely "Australian" identity.[25] As Australia distanced itself from London, the association between Protestantism and Englishness similarly declined.[26] Thus, as Australian Catholicism became more internally diverse and less Irish, and the Protestant churches – including the Church of England – became less

---

[20] Edmund Campion. 1982. *Rockchoppers: Growing Up Catholic in Australia.* Ringwood, Vic.: Penguin; David Hilliard. 1998. "The Ties that Used to Bind: A Fresh Look at the History of Australian Anglicanism." *Pacifica* 11: 265–80, p. 274; Graham Wilson. 2003. "Error of Judgement or Outright Bigotry? The Colours Controversy of the 1950's." *Sabretache* 44(September): 15–22.

[21] David Hilliard. 1991. "God in the Suburbs: The Religious Culture of Australian Cities in the 1950s." *Australian Historical Studies* 24(97): 399–419, p. 409; David Hilliard. 1997. "The Religious Crisis of the 1960s: The Experience of the Australian Churches." *Journal of Religious History* 21(2): 209–27, p. 216.

[22] See, e.g., the conflict over conscription during World War I, in Russel Ward. 1977. *The History of Australia: The Twentieth Century.* New York: Harper and Row, p. 113.

[23] Michael Hogan. 1987. *The Sectarian Strand: Religion in Australian History.* Ringwood, Vic.: Penguin Australia, p. 238.

[24] John Luttrell. 2012. "'Australianizing' the Local Catholic Church: Polding to Gilroy." *Journal of Religious History* 36(3): 335–50, pp. 343–50.

[25] Stuart Ward. 2001. *Australia and the British Empire: The Demise of the Imperial Ideal.* Melbourne: Melbourne University Press.

[26] Michael Hogan. 1984. "Whatever Happened to Australian Sectarianism?" *Journal of Religious History* 13(1): 83–91, p. 88.

English, the "tribal" dimension of the Protestant–Catholic divide ceased to fan the embers of sectarian conflict.[27]

A second factor contributing to the weakening of the old sectarian cleavage was the rise of an ebullient ecumenical spirit among the Christian churches. Inspired by the need to coordinate social programming and resist the twin threats of communism and secularism, the Protestant churches increasingly began to pursue a platform of "Christian unity." Over the course of the 1950s, Protestants joined forces in the fields of education, evangelism, politics, and worship.[28] While lingering sectarian divisions and doctrinal restrictions on interfaith efforts initially kept Catholics out of this ecumenical blossoming, they were inexorably drawn into it. Over the course of the 1950s, Catholics and Protestants collaborated on a variety of initiatives, such as a Week of Prayer for Christian Unity in Melbourne, and an ecumenical Christmas pageant in Sydney.[29]

These nascent Catholic–Protestant ecumenical ventures accelerated rapidly after the summoning of the Second Vatican Council in 1959. Vatican II revolutionized the Catholic Church by ushering in drastic liturgical changes; relaxing dietary, ritual, and vestment requirements; relinquishing the claim to being the one true church; and endorsing religious freedom and ecumenical contacts.[30] These changes dissolved the remaining social and theological barriers separating Catholics and Protestants, and from 1959 onwards, the spirit of ecumenism brought Catholics and Protestants ever closer. Even before the first Council meetings were officially called to order in 1962, excitement among Protestants and Catholics alike led to an increasing number of "ventures of pragmatic ecumenism," such as the construction of nondenominational chapels, the creation of interdenominational religious services on Anzac Day, and the exchange of Catholic and Protestant speakers at denominational meetings.[31] After official restrictions on ecumenical cooperation were relaxed in 1964, Catholics moved to join the various inter-Protestant ecumenical bodies already in existence, such as the Australian Council of Churches.[32] As Catholics grew less distinctive in belief and practice, and as ecumenical dialogue expanded, the last vestiges

[27] Geoffrey Bolton. 2006 [1996]. *The Oxford History of Australia*. Vol. 5, *The Middle Way, 1942–1995*. New York: Oxford University Press, p. 113.

[28] Benjamin Edwards. 2008. *WASPS, Tykes, and Ecumaniacs: Aspects of Australian Sectarianism, 1945–1981*. Brunswick East, Vic.: Acorn Press, pp. 77, 81–84; Frank Engel. 1993. *Christians in Australia*. Vol. 2, *Times of Change, 1918–1978*. Melbourne: The Joint Board of Christian Education, pp. 230–31, 238–39, 246, 251; New South Wales Council on Religious Education Minutes, 10 July 1922. Uniting Church Archives, North Parramatta, NSW, Box 70327.

[29] Douglas Dargaville. 1997. "Ecumenical Life in the Diocese of Melbourne." Pp. 179–94 in *Melbourne Anglicans: The Diocese of Melbourne, 1847–1997*, edited by Brian Porter. Melbourne: Mitre Books, p. 187; Edwards, *WASPS*, p. 150.

[30] Melissa J. Wilde. 2007. *Vatican II: A Sociological Analysis of Religious Change*. Princeton: Princeton University Press, p. 1.

[31] Edwards, *WASPS*, pp. 152–53.

[32] Hilliard, "Religious Crisis of the 1960s," p. 216.

of the Protestant–Catholic divide withered away. As the result of Vatican II, Australian sectarianism had virtually "evaporated overnight."[33]

Ecumenism and the Religious Politics of State Aid

This ecumenical rapprochement had important implications for the dynamics of state aid. In brief, it weakened the passion behind Protestant opposition to state aid, thereby creating room for a new, favorable Protestant attitude to develop. Until the early 1960s, the Protestant churches remained steadfast in their opposition to state aid. Between 1956 and 1962, each of the major Protestant churches issued resolutions opposing state aid, in sometimes florid terms.[34] The Methodist Conference of New South Wales, for instance, resolved that it would "resist with every means at its disposal this baneful, segregationist, and anti-social measure."[35] Throughout the early 1960s, prominent Protestant leaders led rallies loudly and visibly opposing any aid to denominational schools.[36]

However, after state aid was reintroduced in 1964, Protestant opposition rapidly waned. Although many churches initially denounced the proposal,[37] their complaints decreased over the ensuing five years. Methodists, for instance, who protested in 1963 that "there is no justification for the State to provide State aid to denominational schools,"[38] had changed their tune by 1966, opposing only those forms of state aid that might "require the beliefs or teaching of the Church to be subservient to any government direction."[39] Although, as I discuss below, the allure of money for their own denominational schools certainly contributed to the rapid breakdown of Protestant opposition, the promising atmosphere of Vatican II also made the Protestant churches sensitive to the charge of sectarianism. Even while opposing state aid in 1963, Methodists clearly stated that they "would not willingly be a party to arguments based

---

[33] Stuart Piggin. 1996. *Evangelical Christianity in Australia: Spirit, Word, and World.* New York: Oxford University Press, p. 173.

[34] Letter, ACWCC General Secretary to Sir Arthur Fadden, 20 August 1956. National Library of Australia Manuscripts Collection [hereafter NLA], Australian Council of Churches Papers, MS 7645/Box 69/Folder "State Aid 1961, 1956"; and "Official Pronouncements of the Churches in Australia Regarding 'State Aid.'" No date [1962?]. Unpublished manuscript. NLA, Australian Council of Churches Papers, MS 7645/Box 69/Folder "State Aid 1961, 1956," p. 4.

[35] "State Aid to Church Schools." 1962. *The Methodist,* 21 July 1962, p. 2.

[36] Edwards, *WASPS,* pp. 168, 174, 177.

[37] See P.N. Gill. 1965. "The Federal Science Grant: An Episode in Church and State Relations, 1963–1964." Pp. 271–354 in *Melbourne Studies in Education, 1964,* edited by E.L. French. Melbourne: Melbourne University Press, pp. 286–98.

[38] Methodist Church of Australasia. 1963. *Minutes of the Twentieth General Conference of the Methodist Church of Australasia, May 1963.* Adelaide: Gillingham & Co., p. 77.

[39] Methodist Church of Australasia. 1966. *Minutes of the Twenty-First General Conference of the Methodist Church of Australasia, May 1966.* Redfern, NSW: Epworth Printing and Publishing, p. 214.

on denominational prejudices, particularly at a time when there are signs of growing mutual understanding between the divisions in Christendom."[40] Just as ecumenism softened the attitudes of Protestant leadership, the dissolving of religious boundaries contributed to declining opposition to state aid among the Protestant laity. By 1964, majorities of Anglicans, Presbyterians, and Methodists were expressing support for grants to denominational schools.[41] In short, as Protestant hostility to Catholics weakened, so too did their hostility to state aid. And since this weakening occurred just as Catholics were intensifying their demands for state aid, the religious politics shifted rapidly in favor of the Catholic campaign. What had been a standoff became a one-sided struggle.

The decline of anti-Catholicism had more irenic effects in Australia in part because the Protestant churches were less sharply divided internally in Australia than in the United States.[42] In part, this reflects the weaker position of evangelical Protestantism in Australia. Just one in six Australians is an evangelical, a figure approximately half that in the United States.[43] As in the United States, some of these conservative Protestants rejected ecumenical overtures toward Catholics, refusing to attend ecumenical services and withdrawing from interdenominational bodies in protest.[44] These Protestants were among the most likely to maintain their opposition to state aid, forming an important part of the Defence of Government Schools (DOGS) coalition that challenged state aid in the High Court.[45] But there were simply far fewer of these Protestant resisters than there were in the United States during the crucial 1960s.[46] And

[40] Methodist Church of Australasia, *General Conference Minutes, 1963*, p. 326.

[41] Gill, "Federal Science Grant," p. 352; Roger C. Thompson. 1994. *Religion in Australia: A History*. New York: Oxford University Press, p. 120.

[42] Fundamentalist–modernist controversies, for instance, tended to be smaller and more localized in Australia than they were in America. See, e.g., Ian Breward. 1993. *A History of the Australian Churches*. St. Leonard's, NSW: Allen & Unwin, pp. 113, 120, 128; and Malcolm D. Prentis. 2008. "The Presbyterian Church of Australia, 1901–1977: An Overview." *Church Heritage* 15(4): 227–43.

[43] On Australia, see Stuart Piggin. 1994. "The American and British Contributions to Evangelicalism in Australia." Pp. 290–309 in *Evangelicalism: Comparative Studies of Popular Protestantism in North America, the British Isles, and Beyond, 1700–1990*, edited by Mark A. Noll, David W. Bebbington, and George A. Rawlyk. New York: Oxford University Press, p. 290. Surveys peg the American evangelical population as low as twenty-five percent and as high as forty-five percent. For low estimates, see Mark A. Noll. 2001. *American Evangelical Christianity: An Introduction*. Malden, Mass.: Blackwell Publishers, p. 33; for high estimates, see Christopher D. Bader, F. Carson Mencken, and Paul Froese. 2007. "American Piety 2005: Content and Methods of the Baylor Religion Survey." *Journal for the Scientific Study of Religion* 46: 447–63, p. 458. These proportions have been roughly stable since the mid-twentieth century in both countries.

[44] Edwards, *WASPS*, pp. 154, 213, 218; Engel, *Times of Change*, p. 252.

[45] See Chapter 5.

[46] At midcentury, for instance, conservative and mainline Protestants had roughly equal constituencies in the United States, but Australian liberal Protestants outnumbered evangelicals by more than three to one.

even these dissenters quickly warmed to state aid as they saw its potential to strengthen their own evangelical Christian schools.[47]

Finally, the decline of Protestant opposition to state aid was not counterbalanced by the emergence of strong new voices against it. Although the number of Australians professing no religion and disbelieving in God began to grow substantially after 1960,[48] these unchurched Australians played only a supporting role in the DOGS coalition.[49] More importantly, the Jewish community, which staunchly opposed any public aid to religious schools in the United States, was studiously quiet on the matter of state aid in Australia. Postwar immigration tripled the Australian Jewish population, generating fierce internal conflicts and destabilizing the organization of Jewish communal life. Accordingly, the Jewish community was divided on state aid and remained silent in the political debates on the matter.[50] Once state aid became available, Jewish day schools also eagerly accepted it, and protested against any attempts to reduce their allotted amounts.[51] With few other voices arguing against state aid, therefore, the transformation in Protestant attitudes proved particularly consequential.

ELECTORAL INSTITUTIONS AND POLITICAL OPPORTUNITY: CATHOLICS AND PARTY POLITICS

While the ecumenical atmosphere of the 1960s was a boon to the Catholic state aid campaign, Catholics also succeeded thanks to unprecedented political opportunities generated by specific features of Australia's electoral institutions. In particular, the preference-voting system that governed Australian elections permitted minor parties to redirect their votes in ways that could hurt their opponents and reward their allies. This ultimately enhanced the electoral power of well-organized minorities by reducing the political costs of leaving unfavorable party coalitions. During the 1950s and 1960s, Catholics took advantage of these institutional features to advance their campaign for state aid. In 1954, a split in the ALP led to the creation of a new, overwhelmingly Catholic third

---

[47] Brian Fletcher. 2008. *The Place of Anglicanism in Australia: Church, Society, and Nation.* Mulgrave, Vic.: Broughton Publishing, p. 194; David Hilliard. 2002. "Pluralism and New Alignments in Society and Church, 1967 to the Present." Pp. 124–48 in *Anglicanism in Australia: A History,* edited by Bruce Kaye. Melbourne: Melbourne University Press, p. 130.

[48] Hugh McLeod. 2007. *The Religious Crisis of the 1960s.* New York: Oxford University Press; and Hans J.J. Mol. 1971. *Religion in Australia: A Sociological Investigation.* Melbourne: Nelson, p. 41.

[49] Edwards, *WASPS,* p. 223.

[50] Damon Mayrl. 2015. "Minority Faiths and Religious Education Policy: The Case of Australian and American Jews, 1945–1980." Pp. 59–82 in *Issues in Religion and Education: Whose Religion?,* edited by Lori Beaman and Leo Van Arragon. Leiden: Brill, pp. 74–76.

[51] Daniel J. Elazar and Peter Medding. 1984. *Jewish Communities in Frontier Societies: Argentina, Australia, and South Africa.* New York: Holmes & Meier, p. 311; W.D. Rubinstein. 1991. *The Jews in Australia: A Thematic History.* Vol. 2, *1945 to the Present.* Port Melbourne, Vic.: William Heinemann Australia, p. 241.

party. In an era of close elections, Catholics' "second-preference" votes became a highly valuable commodity. The pursuit of Catholic votes gave Catholics extraordinary political leverage in the early 1960s that they skillfully wielded to advance their claims for state aid.

Catholics, Socialists, and the Australian Labor Party, 1901–1955

At the end of World War II, Catholics were an integral part of the Labor Party coalition. Roughly half of Labor voters and over half of Labor parliamentarians were Catholic.[52] Likewise, the majority of Catholics – around seventy percent – voted for Labor.[53] Yet while Catholics were one key component of the Labor coalition, they shared power in an uneasy alliance with socialists based in the trade unions. Because it was a true labor party, the ALP retained strong formal links with Australia's trade unions. Trade unions affiliated with the Labor Party and sent dues to state parties, and in exchange they were permitted to send delegates to party conferences. Trade unionists accordingly wielded substantial power within the ALP – in the 1950s and 1960s, seventy to eighty percent of delegates at state conferences were union representatives.[54] While, for the most part, Labor was generally anticommunist, the strong union presence in its ranks meant that there was a strong socialist contingent, and often substantial factional sympathy for communist goals, within the party.[55] Many Catholic party members, however, inspired by papal encyclicals, were suspicious of both communists and socialists, inside and outside the party.

During the decade following World War II, the issue of communism festered within the Labor Party, undermining and eventually destroying the alliance between Catholics and socialists. The social dislocations of the Great Depression were a boon to Australia's communists, and by the end of World War II, communists had attained leadership positions in a number of major Australian unions.[56] Catholics viewed these communist gains with dismay, and determined to try to turn them back. In January 1942, the Archbishop of Melbourne, Daniel Mannix, gave moral and financial backing to a group – the Catholic Social Studies Movement (or "the Movement" for short) – whose

[52] James Jupp. 1968 [1964]. *Australian Party Politics*. 2nd edn. Carlton, Vic.: Melbourne University Press, p. 33; Joan Rydon. 1986. *A Federal Legislature: The Australian Commonwealth Parliament, 1901–1980*. Melbourne: Oxford University Press, p. 142.

[53] Judith Brett. 2003. *Australian Liberals and the Moral Middle Class: From Alfred Deakin to John Howard*. Cambridge: Cambridge University Press, p. 35.

[54] Robert Murray. 2004. "Looking Back on Evatt and the Split." *Quadrant* 48(10): 20–25, p. 21.

[55] D.W. Rawson. 1966. *Labor in Vain? A Survey of the Australian Labor Party*. North Clayton, Vic.: Longmans, pp. 77–99.

[56] Jupp, *Australian Party Politics*, p. 91; Stuart Macintyre. 2004 [1999]. *A Concise History of Australia*. 2nd edn. Cambridge: Cambridge University Press, pp. 180–81, 183.

explicit goal was to wrest the unions back from communist control.[57] Under the leadership of a devout young lawyer, B.A. Santamaria, the Movement designed a plan whereby small, hand-picked cells of Catholic unionists would infiltrate the communist-controlled unions and organize to roust out the communist leadership.[58] In 1945, the Movement received the official blessing of the Australian Catholic hierarchy in its mission "to permeate the whole of society with [positive] ideals [of Christian social teaching]."[59]

The swelling power of the communists also alarmed some in the Labor Party. Communist control of trade unions had serious implications for Labor, since the unions' formal links to party conferences meant they had the potential to shape or even determine the party line on an array of issues.[60] Labor leaders concluded that their political survival required that they intervene in union elections to reduce communists' power.[61] They did this by creating "industrial groups" within the trade unions, which would openly campaign for Labor's preferred candidates in union elections.[62] Although the groups were formally separate from the Movement, their aims were the same, and Movement members quickly came to dominate the industrial groups.[63] With the industrial groups as cover, the Movement grew dramatically in the postwar years, claiming some five thousand "really active fighters against Communism" by 1947.[64] Ultimately, the Movement/Group strategy paid dividends within the trade unions: Between 1945 and 1949, the industrial groups regained control of nearly every trade union from the communists.[65]

Once the communist threat in the trade unions had been neutralized, however, the Movement did not disband. Instead, it turned its sights on the Labor Party itself, with the goal of weeding out those party members it found insufficiently committed to the anticommunist cause. Santamaria ultimately hoped that the Movement would "be able to completely transform the leadership of the Labor Movement," thereby allowing it to "implement a Christian social programme in both the Federal and State spheres."[66] The Movement made massive gains in the 1949 elections, especially in Victoria, where six of eight

[57] Bruce Duncan. 2001. *Crusade or Conspiracy? Catholics and the Anti-Communist Struggle in Australia.* Sydney: University of New South Wales Press, p. 58.

[58] Robert Murray. 1970. *The Split: Australian Labor in the 1950s.* Melbourne: Cheshire, pp. 53–54.

[59] Quoted in Ross Fitzgerald. 2003. *The Pope's Battalions: Santamaria, Catholicism, and the Labor Split.* St. Lucia: University of Queensland Press, p. 76.

[60] Rawson, *Labor in Vain*, pp. 91–92.

[61] Graham Freudenberg. 1991. *Cause for Power: The Official History of the New South Wales Branch of the Australian Labor Party.* Leichhardt, NSW: Pluto Press, pp. 211–12.

[62] Murray, *The Split*, pp. 16–17.

[63] Hogan, *Sectarian Strand*, pp. 245–46.

[64] Duncan, *Crusade or Conspiracy*, p. 106.

[65] Tom Truman. 1960. *Catholic Action and Politics.* Melbourne: Georgian House, pp. 155–56.

[66] Quoted in Phillip Deery. 2001. "Santamaria, the Movement, and the Labor Split of 1954–55." *Journal of the Australian Catholic Historical Society* 22: 47–58, p. 53.

new representatives were Movement-supporting Catholics.[67] By 1953, the Movement dominated the Labor Party in the two largest states, Victoria and New South Wales. These new Movement politicians were committed to aggressively pushing Catholic issues, including not just anticommunism but also state aid. In 1950, the Victorian Labor Party passed a resolution supporting state aid, and the following year, Movement supporters convinced the federal Labor Party to adopt a resolution "That financial aid be granted for the purpose of assisting all forms of education."[68]

This shift in Movement ambitions destabilized the Labor Party. The Movement's brazen advocacy of Catholic aims created enemies among the old guard of the Labor Movement, including many trade unionists who remained resentful of the Movement's incursions into union politics. When Labor, under the leadership of Herbert Evatt, lost the 1954 federal election, the smoldering divide exploded dramatically. Evatt blamed his loss on a conspiracy masterminded by Menzies and the anticommunist faction within the Labor Party. On 5 October, Evatt publicly denounced the Movement, accusing "a small minority group of members" of "subversion," and announcing his intention to discipline insubordinate members. The intraparty conflict quickly spiraled out of control. Over the ensuing months, the federal party leadership purged the Victorian leadership, dissolved the industrial groups, and expelled seven Victorian parliamentarians from the party.[69] The expelled parliamentarians in turn formed a new ALP (Anti-Communist), and ran candidates against Labor in the 1955 election.[70] The following year, the Victorian party merged with Movement-supporting defectors in New South Wales and Tasmania to form the new Democratic Labor Party (DLP).[71] Eventually, more than ten percent of the Labor membership left and joined the DLP.[72]

The Consequences of the Split: Catholics as Political Free Agents

In the short term, Catholics found the Labor Party (hereafter, the ALP[73]) far more hostile to their requests for state aid than it had been before "the Split." As conservative Catholics deserted the party in droves, power shifted to the socialists in the trade unions, who quickly moved to eradicate all vestiges of Movement influence, including the party's friendly state aid plank.[74] Yet

---

[67] Murray, *The Split*, pp. 66–67.
[68] Beazley, "Australian Labor Party and State Aid [Part One]," p. 53.
[69] Murray, *The Split*, pp. 32–35, 38–40, 129, 179–81, 243–62.
[70] Duncan, *Crusade or Conspiracy*, pp. 273–74.
[71] Peter Love. 2005. "The Great Labor Split of 1955: An Overview." Pp. 1–20 in *The Great Labor Schism: A Retrospective*, edited by Brian Costar, Peter Love, and Paul Strangio. Melbourne: Scribe Publications, pp. 14–15.
[72] Bolton, *Middle Way*, p. 143.
[73] Australian Labor Party.
[74] Beazley, "Australian Labor Party and State Aid [Part One]," p. 55.

in the long term, the Split fundamentally altered political dynamics in ways that helped bring about state aid. As historian Patrick O'Farrell has written, "the end of [Catholics'] slavish attachment to Labor changed the status of the political activities and votes of Catholics from those of prisoners to those of desirable, sought-after supporters."[75] While Catholics had been bound tightly to the Labor coalition, their prospects for gaining state aid remained dim. The creation of the Democratic Labor Party, however, effectively transformed Catholics into political free agents, increasing their ability to lobby for concessions, including state aid.

The DLP was, for all intents and purposes, a Catholic party.[76] Although the ALP retained the votes of a majority of Australian Catholics, a substantial minority, on the order of ten to twenty percent of Catholic voters, defected to the DLP.[77] However, even if only a modest number of Catholics joined the DLP, the vast majority of DLP voters – as high as eighty-eight percent in some surveys – were Catholic.[78] What was true of its mass base was also true of its politicians; in Victoria, all but two of the DLP's parliamentarians were Catholic, while in Queensland, seventy percent of DLP politicians were Catholic.[79] The party was strongest in those areas where it had the support of the hierarchy, particularly in Victoria, where Archbishop Mannix gave full-throated support to Santamaria and the DLP;[80] and it was strongest among those Catholics who were most committed to their faith.[81] As a party with such strong connections to the Catholic community, the DLP effectively functioned as a vehicle for Catholic interests. This was most evident in its continuing opposition to communism, but it was also true on the issue of state aid. From 1958 onward, the DLP consistently included state aid for all private school students as part of its federal election platform, making it "the one political force in Australia which consistently advocated state aid" even when the other parties refused to consider it.[82]

[75] Patrick O'Farrell. 1968. *The Catholic Church in Australia: A Short History, 1788–1967*. Melbourne: Thomas Nelson (Australia) Limited, p. 273.

[76] John Warhurst. 2005. "Was the DLP a 'Church' Party?" Pp. 301–10 in *The Great Labor Schism: A Retrospective*, edited by Brian Costar, Peter Love, and Paul Strangio. Melbourne: Scribe Publications.

[77] Robert R. Alford. 1963. *Party and Society: The Anglo-American Democracies*. Chicago: Rand McNally & Company, p. 205.

[78] Don Aitkin. 1977. *Stability and Change in Australian Politics*. New York: St. Martin's Press, p. 178.

[79] Warhurst, "Was the DLP a Church Party," p. 307.

[80] John Warhurst. 1979. "Catholics, Communism, and the Australian Party System: A Study of the Menzies Years." *Politics* 14(2): 222–42, p. 237; Warhurst, "Was the DLP a Church Party," p. 306.

[81] Aitkin, *Stability and Change*, p. 176.

[82] P.L. Reynolds. 1974. *The Democratic Labor Party*. Milton, Qld.: Jacaranda Press, pp. 43–45.

Preference Voting and Political Power

Although its continuous advocacy of state aid helped keep the issue on the agenda, the DLP was never in a position to enact its preferred policies. In pure electoral terms, the DLP was not terribly successful, never drawing even ten percent of the vote in any election.[83] Nevertheless, it wielded outsized influence thanks to a feature of the Australian electoral system which magnifies the influence of third parties: preference voting. Under the preference-voting system,[84] voters rank candidates in numerical order. If no candidate attains an absolute majority, the least popular candidates are excluded, with their votes redistributed to voters' second-choice candidates. The process is repeated until one candidate obtains an absolute majority.[85] Preference voting increases the power of minor parties because it gives well-disciplined parties the ability to bargain their second-preference votes to the major parties in exchange for concessions.[86] In the annals of Australian political history, few minor parties have been more successful at manipulating the preference-voting system to enhance their power than the DLP.

Prior to 1955, second-preferences were primarily used by the non-Labor coalition partners, the Liberal and Country Parties, to run candidates in the same electorate without worrying that the competition between them would allow Labor to win the seat: Liberals directed their second-preference votes to the Country Party, and vice versa.[87] The DLP used its second-preference votes in a much different manner. By disciplining its voters to cast their second-preference votes for non-Labor candidates, it transformed second-preference votes into a weapon they could use to keep the ALP out of office. Even in electorates where the ALP candidate drew the most first-place votes, DLP second-preference votes could allow the Liberal or Country candidate to win the seat. In his memoir, B.A. Santamaria wrote that the disciplining of preferences was a major early focus of the DLP:

Above all, there was a most difficult educational task. What were originally about half a million voters had to be instructed that, in marking their ballot papers in federal and state elections, the second preference was as important as the first. Sufficient conviction had to be secured among the great majority, who had been traditional Labor voters,

---

[83] Reynolds, *Democratic Labor Party*, p. 50.

[84] In the United States, this system is known as "ranked-choice" or "instant runoff" voting, and is used in some municipal elections, such as elections for the San Francisco Mayor and Board of Supervisors.

[85] Scott Bennett and Rob Lundie. 2007. *Australian Electoral Systems*. Parliament of Australia Research Paper No. 5. Canberra: Parliament of Australia, pp. 4–6.

[86] Gwynneth Singleton, Don Aitkin, Brian Jinks, and John Warhurst. 2009. *Australian Political Institutions*. 9th edn. Frenchs Forest, NSW: Pearson Education Australia, p. 284.

[87] Paul Reynolds. 2005. "The Democratic Labor Party: A Retrospective." Pp. 290–300 in *The Great Labor Schism: A Retrospective*, edited by Brian Costar, Peter Love, and Paul Strangio. Melbourne: Scribe Publications, p. 294.

that they should mark their preferences in favour of the Liberal and against the Labor candidate.[88]

The DLP was incredibly successful in disciplining its second-preference votes. Between 1958 and 1969, nationwide, eighty-two percent of its second-preference votes were directed against the ALP.[89] DLP second-preference votes determined the outcome of at least one seat in every federal election between 1958 and 1972,[90] and clearly saved the Liberal coalition government from defeat (thereby keeping the ALP out of office) in 1961 and 1969.[91] As a result, the Liberal Party retained control of Parliament for an unprecedented twenty-three years between 1949 and 1972.

The Split thus had both direct and indirect consequences for the politics of state aid during the 1950s and 1960s. Directly, as the Liberals' position grew more tenuous and dependent on DLP second-preferences by the mid-1960s, the DLP began to make demands on Liberal politicians in exchange for their continued direction of second-preference votes. As I discuss below, on at least one occasion these demands included state aid. More indirectly, however – and perhaps more importantly – the very fact that an overwhelmingly Catholic third party had the ability to direct its second-preference votes in ways that could make or break parliamentary power made that party, and the issues it sponsored, enormously important. Even without any direct preference trading, politicians were incredibly cognizant of the "Catholic vote." No longer wedded to the ALP, and increasingly influential electorally, Catholic issues were suddenly of substantially greater interest to politicians. And after 1960, state aid would eclipse anticommunism to become the predominant Catholic issue, largely thanks to a highly visible and concerted campaign to regain state aid.

FROM OPENING TO REALIZATION: THE CATHOLIC CAMPAIGN FOR STATE AID, 1954–1972

While the Catholics' campaign was not the only factor leading to the return of state aid, Catholics were undoubtedly state aid's leading advocates and played an essential role in determining the form and timing of the new twentieth-century settlement. The Catholic campaign devised and disseminated new and more universal arguments for state aid, helping build popular support for the policy. It also forced the issue onto the political agenda through direct actions, such as the school "strike" in the city of Goulburn in 1962. Once initial concessions were made in 1964, the Catholic campaign convened a series of mass meetings that kept pressure on politicians to deliver ever-larger

---

[88] B.A. Santamaria. 1997 [1981]. *Santamaria: A Memoir*. Melbourne: Oxford University Press, p. 198.
[89] Reynolds, *Democratic Labor Party*, p. 49.
[90] Rydon, *Federal Legislature*, p. 41.
[91] Reynolds, "Democratic Labor Party," p. 295.

amounts of aid. Finally, the campaign provided direct electoral pressure that expanded the form of state aid from a limited concession to a large, recurrent program of general-purpose per capita grants. In short, between 1954 and 1972, the Catholic campaign created a viable public space for their demands, forced the issue to the top of the political agenda, and shaped the ultimate form that state aid eventually took.

The Catholic Campaign for State Aid: Genesis and Form

The Catholic campaign emerged out of a long string of largely fruitless and often subdued political activity stretching back to the late nineteenth century.[92] In the postwar era, this activity took on extra urgency because of increased financial pressures on the Catholic school system. These pressures had their roots in three trends: skyrocketing enrolments as a result of the baby boom and increased Catholic immigration, demand for more teachers and plant in response to the expansion of secondary schooling, and increased reliance on lay rather than religious teachers.[93] Catholics responded with a fragmented yet cohesive campaign for state aid that pursued multiple avenues of political influence. These included a quiet, behind-the-scenes negotiating strategy by Catholic bishops; loud and confrontational direct action by lay Catholics; and formal politicking by the DLP and the Movement's successor organization, the National Civic Council.

Although the Catholic hierarchy as a group did not push strongly for state aid, individual bishops contributed to the campaign by making low-key approaches to political officials. These ventures were important because Catholic bishops could negotiate on behalf of Catholics in ways that lay groups could not. In New South Wales, the bishops conducted a public relations campaign and coordinated negotiations with state officials throughout the 1950s.[94] Elsewhere, individual bishops took the initiative to press for state aid from time to time. In 1955, for instance, Eris O'Brien, Archbishop of Canberra-Goulburn, petitioned the Select Committee on the Development of Canberra for aid. He argued that the relocation of large numbers of public servants to the new capital had created a situation where the federal government was obligated to provide some sort of subsidies to private schools to enable them to expand to meet educational demand. Menzies recalled, in his memoir, that O'Brien was "one of the best-informed, mildest-mannered and persuasive of advocates,"[95] and his

92 Jeff Kildea. 2002. *Tearing the Fabric: Sectarianism in Australia, 1910 to 1925*. Sydney: Citadel Books; see also Hogan, *Sectarian Strand*, pp. 84–94.

93 Alan Barcan. 1993. *Sociological Theory and Educational Reality: Education & Society in Australia since 1949*. Kensington, NSW: University of New South Wales Press, pp. 92–93.

94 Michael Charles Hogan. 1978. *The Catholic Campaign for State Aid: A Study of a Pressure Group Campaign in New South Wales and the Australian Capital Territory, 1950–1972*. Sydney: Catholic Theological Faculty, pp. 38, 41, 155–56, 164.

95 Robert Gordon Menzies. 1970. *The Measure of the Years*. London: Cassell, p. 95.

personable and low-key approach appear to have helped convince Menzies to introduce interest subsidies for construction costs within the ACT in 1956.[96]

In contrast to the bishops' quiet campaign, more confrontational grassroots activism by lay Catholics emerged in the late 1950s in response to the crisis in the schools.[97] Rejecting the low-key style of the bishops, these lay groups specialized in direct action and publicity stunts designed to embarrass the government. Most dramatically, as I discuss below, they temporarily shut down Catholic schools in the city of Goulburn to draw attention to their cause. Their most consistently effective tactic, however, was the mass meeting. These events, which often drew thousands of attendees, brought political leaders face to face with the problems in Catholic schools as well as Catholics' demands. Lay groups were not particularly successful in extracting concessions from governments, especially early on, but their dramatic actions did force the issue of state aid onto the political agenda, expose the Australian public to the problems in the Catholic schools, and soften public opinion on the matter of state aid.

The third and final wing of the Catholic campaign consisted of formal partisan action. In 1957, Santamaria reconstituted the Movement as the National Civic Council (NCC), and for the next fifteen years, the NCC effectively acted as the organizational wing of the DLP. In some states, the NCC actually ran the party, financially and clerically, between elections.[98] The NCC's newspaper, *The News-Weekly*, was for all intents and purposes the "national organ of the DLP,"[99] and NCC leaders (including Santamaria) met regularly with DLP leaders to plot political strategy.[100] In his role as *de facto* leader of the DLP, Santamaria leveraged the party's electoral power to advocate for state aid. Between the 1961 and 1963 elections, for instance, Santamaria met with Menzies' Treasurer (and future Prime Minister) Harold Holt on at least three occasions to discuss how a state aid proposal could benefit both Catholics and the Liberal Party.[101] Santamaria warned Holt that "erosive factors" threatened the DLP's ability to guarantee that its voters would continue to direct their second-preference votes to the Liberal Party, and suggested that "some 'breakthrough' in the matter of education allowances, however meager the initiative might be," offered an excellent chance for the Liberals to secure DLP

[96] Anthony William Hannan. 1982. "The Catholic Campaign for State Aid in Victoria, 1939–63." Unpublished Ph.D. Thesis, Monash University, pp. 300–01.

[97] Hogan, *Catholic Campaign*, pp. 48–51; David Mossenson. 1972. *State Education in Western Australia, 1829–1960*. Nedlands: University of Western Australia Press, pp. 158–59.

[98] Patrick Morgan, ed. 2008. *B.A. Santamaria: Running the Show: Selected Documents, 1939–1996*. Carlton, Vic.: The Miegunyah Press and State Library of Victoria, p. 312.

[99] Jupp, *Australian Party Politics*, p. 86.

[100] Brian Costar. 2005. "Was the DLP a Labor or a Centrist Party?" Pp. 311–23 in *The Great Labor Schism: A Retrospective*, edited by Brian Costar, Peter Love, and Paul Strangio. Melbourne: Scribe Publications, p. 312.

[101] Ross McMullin. 1991. *The Light on the Hill: The Australian Labor Party, 1891–1991*. New York: Oxford University Press, p. 292.

second-preference votes.[102] While this was only one input into Menzies' eventual decision to enact the science laboratories scheme (see below), this inside game run by Santamaria and the NCC neatly complemented the outside pressure brought to bear by the bishops and lay groups.

Honing the Argument for State Aid: Ideological Work in the Catholic Campaign

In addition to making their case to politicians, Catholics also needed to craft an argument for state aid that was convincing to the broader Australian public. Catholic arguments for state aid were traditionally somewhat parochial, using arguments grounded in religious premises to make the case for aid to Catholic schools alone.[103] Beginning in the early 1950s, however, Catholic leaders repositioned their claims in nondenominational terms. Recognizing that a straightforward contest between Catholics and the rest of Australia meant sure defeat, they sought instead to portray religion as irrelevant to their argument. In a meeting of the Australian hierarchy in 1951, Archbishop Beovich of Adelaide suggested focusing on the "*Australian child*" rather than on Catholic schools. "By presenting our long-standing problem [as a Catholic one] … we emphasize inevitably the denominational side of the issue." Downplaying the religious aspect, he argued, would inhibit "irresponsible or bigoted talk about sectarian use of public funds."[104] Similarly, Catholics began to cast their arguments in terms of "independent," "private," or "nongovernment" schools, rather than Catholic schools.[105] In a petition to the New South Wales Premier in September 1962, for instance, Cardinal Gilroy presented his appeal on behalf of "the children enrolled at independent schools and their parents," rather than on behalf of Catholics alone.[106] This broader framing also enabled Catholics to reach out to potential allies among Protestant school headmasters and their supporters. Indeed, most of the Catholic lay organizations, including the Association for Educational Freedom (AEF) and Australian Parents Council, explicitly adopted a nondenominational framing and identity in the mid-1960s.[107]

In addition to casting their arguments in nondenominational terms, Catholics also developed a new set of justifications for state aid based on

---

[102] Santamaria, *Santamaria*, p. 217.

[103] Anthony William Hannan. 1973. "Victorian Catholics and the State Aid to Catholic Schools – Religion in State Schools Issues, 1901–1939." Unpublished M.Ed. Thesis, Monash University, pp. 346, 350, 367.

[104] Matthew Beovich. 1951. "The Social Service Analogy." Pp. 268–70 (Appendix A) in Hogan, *Catholic Campaign*, pp. 268–69. Emphasis in original.

[105] Ronald Fogarty. 1959. *Catholic Education in Australia, 1806–1950*. Vol. 2, *Catholic Education under the Religious Orders*. Melbourne: Melbourne University Press, p. 463.

[106] N.T. Cardinal Gilroy. 1962. "Cardinal Gilroy's 5 Point Petition, September 1962." Pp. 271–75 (Appendix B) in Hogan, *Catholic Campaign*, p. 271.

[107] Hogan, *Catholic Campaign*, pp. 124–26.

pluralism and economic efficiency. For instance, Catholics began to argue that facilitating educational pluralism would promote democratic values. "The freedom to be different is what constitutes a democracy, whereas conformity characterizes the totalitarian state," argued the AEF in one mid-1960s pamphlet.[108] Catholics also began to foreground the general economic benefits of supporting Catholic education. Cardinal Gilroy, for example, argued that Catholic schooling "concerns intimately the welfare of the whole community," and that state aid would allow Catholic schools to "maintain [their] present high standards."[109] Catholics coupled this positive argument with the threat of chaos in state schools if the Catholic system collapsed. The New South Wales AEF argued that "It is economically sounder for the government to help the independent schools to carry on," since "the cost of replacement would be colossal."[110] Both new kinds of argument allowed Catholics to argue that state aid was really about broader civic considerations, and that "religion really had nothing to do with it."[111] And their economic arguments proved especially persuasive to politicians, who adopted them in the late 1960s and early 1970s to justify their burgeoning state aid budgets. In a policy address in 1971, for instance, New South Wales Premier Robert Askin declared that "the economic argument is impossible to deny. The burden on the taxpayer as children leave the independent schools and enroll at State Schools is immeasurably heavier than if they had been assisted to stay at the independent schools."[112]

Finally, as the Catholic campaign began to score successes in the mid-1960s, it also strategically retreated on some of its claims. In the early 1960s, Catholics had demanded "equality" in education.[113] Yet as the campaign progressed, Catholics increasingly shifted to an argument based on equity – that is, on a fair share of government funding. According to Father Patrick Farrell, equity "would recognize the greater operational economy of the Catholic system; the devotedness of the parents who use it; the need to retain a proper independence and the injurious social effects probable with any greater claim. Equity, therefore, could be something less than financial equality."[114] The rise of the equity argument ceded the demand for full equality, but made the Catholic case appear more reasonable to the broader population. As the AEF stated,

---

[108] New South Wales Association for Educational Freedom. No date. *State Aid Means...* [Sydney]: Author, pp. 1–2. Copy available in Noel Butlin Labour Archives, Australian National University, Canberra, N111/1114.

[109] Gilroy, "5 Point Petition," pp. 271–72.

[110] New South Wales Association for Educational Freedom, *State Aid Means...*, pp. 2–3.

[111] Interview, Margaret Slattery, in John Luttrell. 2003. *Regaining State Aid: Interviews Relating to the Campaign for State Aid for Non-Government Schools, 1960–1980.* Sydney: Catholic Education Office, Sydney, pp. 109–10.

[112] Press Release, "Policy Speech by the Premier of N.S.W.," 28 January 1971. SRNSW, 12/1694, p. 8.

[113] See, e.g., B.A. Santamaria. 1960. *Equality in Education.* Kew, Vic.: Institute of Social Order.

[114] "State Aid for Independent Schools? – 2 Viewpoints." 1962. *Current Affairs Bulletin* 30(6): 82–96, p. 95.

hopefully, "A fair-minded people will agree that [Catholic children] deserve a fair share of public funds expended on education."[115]

Thus, over the course of the 1960s, the Catholic campaign honed new arguments for state aid in order to make their case more forcefully and compellingly to the broader Australian population. This ideological work downplayed the connections between state aid and Catholic schooling, ultimately yielding a stronger and more persuasive set of arguments for the political contests of the mid-to-late 1960s and early 1970s.

Direct Action and Agenda-Setting: the Goulburn School Strike

While the Catholic campaign crafted appeals to politicians and the public, it also used direct action to force state aid onto the political agenda. Most dramatically, Catholics temporarily closed all the Catholic schools in the New South Wales city of Goulburn in July 1962. The Goulburn school "strike" created an international media spectacle that forced politicians to respond to Catholic demands in a more sustained fashion.[116] For the decade after the Goulburn school strike, state aid became "one of the most important domestic issues in both State and Federal politics."[117] And this, in turn, ultimately led to a donnybrook over state aid in the ALP, which was the proximate cause of Menzies' science laboratories proposal in 1963.

In early 1962, the New South Wales Department of Education refused to certify one of Goulburn's Catholic schools because it failed to provide satisfactory toilet facilities. In response, the local bishop, John Cullinane, called a meeting of the Catholic community to discuss what to do. Although Cullinane had initially only contemplated closing the single school in question, the laymen who attended the meeting sought a more radical response, and overwhelmingly voted to close every Catholic school in the city as an act of protest.[118] At the end of the week, all six Catholic schools in Goulburn shut their doors, and on Monday morning Catholic schoolchildren showed up at the local public schools demanding admittance. The spectacle drew intense media coverage, and the strike dominated the headlines for the ensuing week. The Goulburn parents felt they had proved their point, and quickly ended the strike.[119]

In the wake of the strike, the campaign at both the lay and clerical levels expanded to take advantage of this attention. In cities around New South Wales, Catholics met to create an ongoing lay organization, which ultimately developed

---

[115] New South Wales Association for Educational Freedom, *State Aid Means…*, p. 2.

[116] Joshua Puls. 2004. "The Goulburn Lockout." *Australasian Catholic Record* 81(2): 169–83, p. 176.

[117] Hogan, *Catholic Campaign*, p. 72.

[118] J.N. Cullinane. 1989. *Goulburn School "Strike": The Inside Story*. Canberra: Catholic Education Office, Archdiocese of Canberra & Goulburn, pp. 15–32.

[119] Wilkinson et al., *History of State Aid*, p. 28.

into the New South Wales AEF.[120] Likewise, the New South Wales hierarchy ramped up its efforts.[121] In September, Cardinal Gilroy met with the Premier of New South Wales, Robert Heffron, and presented him with five specific requests for state aid, including secondary and teachers' college scholarships, capital grants for new schools in expanding suburbs, subsidies for teachers' salaries, and grants to construct science laboratories and train science teachers.[122] By stimulating Catholics to greater activity and organization, the Goulburn protest forced the issue of state aid onto the political agenda in an undeniable way.

The Fruits of Protest: ALP Conflict and the Science Laboratories Proposal

One result of Goulburn was a new focus on science education. In his petition to Heffron, Gilroy had indicated that "The needs of scientific education are so great" that he was compelled to make "a separate plea" for help building new science laboratories.[123] Heffron saw an opportunity to strengthen Labor's position with the Catholic community, and proposed both subsidies for science laboratories and scholarships for Catholic students in his budget later that year.[124] However, his proposal precipitated a ruinous faceoff with federal party officials. Although the ALP was organized around state parties, it was coordinated at the federal level by a Federal Executive that had the power to set binding party policy.[125] During the late 1950s and early 1960s, the Federal Executive was dominated – even more so than the party as a whole – by socialist trade unionists.[126] At its conference in August, the federal ALP reiterated its stance against direct state aid, insisting that aid to Catholic schools could extend to scholarships paid to the students, but no further. However, the New South Wales branch refused to back down, unanimously adopting a report at the end of the month that recommended aid to independent schools. The conflict between the state and federal branches came to a head about a month later, when the Federal Executive censured the New South Wales party for proposing a policy that was a "direct contravention of Federal ALP policy," and declared that in the future any proposal to extend aid to private schools would require Federal Executive approval.[127]

---

[120] Hogan, *Catholic Campaign*, pp. 92, 113.

[121] John Luttrell. 2008. "Come to Our Aid: Funding Catholic Schools in NSW since 1800." Unpublished manuscript, Catholic Education Office Sydney, p. 10.

[122] Gilroy, "5 Point Petition," pp. 273–74.

[123] Gilroy, "5 Point Petition," p. 274.

[124] Freudenberg, *Cause for Power*, p. 238.

[125] Joan Rydon. 1986. "The Federal Structure of Australian Political Parties." Working Paper No. 6, Australian Studies Centre, Institute of Commonwealth Studies, University of London, pp. 4–5.

[126] Clem Lloyd. 1983. "The Federal ALP: Supreme or Secondary?" Pp. 231–56 in *Machine Politics in the Australian Labor Party*, edited by Andrew Parkin and John Warhurst. Sydney: George Allen & Unwin, p. 235.

[127] Albinski, *Australian Labor Party*, pp. 17–21.

The showdown over state aid in 1963 was disastrous for the ALP. For many of those Catholics in New South Wales who had stood by the Labor Party through the Split, it signaled that the powers-that-be in the ALP were irredeemably arrayed against them.[128] More importantly, the chaos in the ALP over state aid convinced Menzies to call an election for December 1963, and contributed to his decision to introduce his own legislation providing state aid for science laboratories. The timing and content of Menzies' proposal strongly suggest that it was a direct reaction to the ALP conflict over state aid. The fact that Menzies proposed aid to science laboratories, the very form of state aid that Heffron had proposed and that the Federal ALP had rejected, was by no means coincidental; indeed, according to Liberal politicians, it was explicitly designed to "embarrass the Labor Opposition."[129]

At the same time, Menzies' proposal was also designed to consolidate the support of Catholic voters, which was seen as shaky in the wake of the 1961 election. The Liberal Party had only narrowly retained control of Parliament in 1961 thanks to DLP preference votes, and some party officials had begun to look to state aid as a means of securing DLP preferences.[130] Internal analyses in 1962 suggested that the party's opposition to state aid had hurt them among Catholics,[131] and the New South Wales Liberal Party's Policy Committee had recommended abandoning opposition to state aid as a means of wooing Catholic voters.[132] Thus, the chaos in the ALP provided the needed opening for Menzies to solidify the support of DLP voters, and therefore his own political future. But the opening and the issue were present thanks in large part to the direct action in Goulburn. By forcing the issue onto the political agenda in New South Wales, the Goulburn school strike set off a chain of events that ultimately contributed to the introduction of the science laboratories proposal.

Building Alliances: Protestant Schools and the Science Laboratories Scheme

Although Catholics were the driving force behind the campaign for state aid, they did not act entirely alone. Some Protestants had also begun to warm to state aid by the early 1960s. The leading edge of Protestant support for state aid came from the leaders of Protestant schools. Although Protestants had thrown their support behind state schooling in the late nineteenth century, they

[128] Freudenberg, *Cause for Power*, p. 239.

[129] Ken Jones, quoted in Wilkinson et al., *History of State Aid*, p. 31.

[130] John Roskam. 2005. "The Liberal Party's Response to the Split." Pp. 260–76 in *The Great Labor Schism: A Retrospective*, edited by Brian Costar, Peter Love, and Paul Strangio. Melbourne: Scribe Publications, p. 271.

[131] J.R. Willoughby to Robert Menzies, Preliminary Analysis of 1962 NSW State Election Returns, 3 March 1962. NLA Manuscripts Collection, Sir Robert Menzies Papers, MS 4936/Series 14(a)/Box 411/Folder 12.

[132] A.W. Martin. 1999. *Robert Menzies: A Life*. Vol. 2, *1944–1978*. Melbourne: Melbourne University Press, p. 470.

continued to support a system of elite secondary schools. Like the Catholic sector, these schools were reliant upon their own fundraising to remain operational, and from time to time the leaders of those schools looked covetously at state governments as a potential source of funding.[133] This was particularly true in rural areas, where state aid was seen as a promising means of expanding programs and facilities in areas where religious schooling was essential yet undersupported.[134]

As anti-Catholic feeling declined in the postwar years, Catholics began to find some allies among these Protestants. In 1950, Victorian Catholics joined forces with several members of the Protestant Headmasters Conference of Independent Schools in Australia (HMC) to form the Association of Independent Schools in Victoria (AISV), an organization dedicated to gaining state aid. The AISV successfully lobbied the federal government for income tax concessions in 1952. Yet despite these occasional collaborations, the Protestant campaign was largely independent of the Catholic campaign, since Protestants tended to favor more indirect forms of aid, such as tax credits for fees and gifts, over direct aid for construction and salaries.[135] Still, as the 1960s progressed, and as the Catholic campaign accelerated, Catholics maintained "cordial contacts" with Protestant groups as they mutually pursued state aid.[136]

In the late 1950s and 1960s, Protestant pressure groups increasingly warmed to more direct forms of state aid as the demographic pressures of the Baby Boom and rising costs put a squeeze on their operations. In 1959, the HMC released a public statement arguing that nongovernment schools should accept grants for capital improvements, so long as those improvements did not compromise their independence.[137] The fact that a prominent and influential Protestant voice was now on the record in support of direct state aid lent credence to Catholics' push to redefine state aid as a nondenominational issue. More importantly, the Protestant voices in favor of state aid likely helped persuade Menzies to introduce state aid in 1963. The vast majority of Liberal Party members (upwards of seventy percent according to one survey) had attended elite Protestant schools.[138] These politicians were often quite sympathetic to the problems of Protestant schools, and by the early 1960s, several of

---

[133] Breward, *History of the Australian Churches*, p. 161.

[134] Letter, Bishop of Riverina to ACC Assistant General Secretary, 1 August 1961. NLA, Australian Council of Churches Papers, MS 7645/Box 69/Folder "State Aid 1961, 1956"; Gill, "Federal Science Grant," p. 330; Keith Rayner. 2006. Interview with Rachel Kohn. "Faith in the Fifties." *The Spirit of Things*, 24 September. Australian Broadcasting Corporation Radio National. Available online at http://abc.net.au/rn/spiritofthings/stories/2006/1744520.htm (accessed 28 March 2016).

[135] Hannan, "Catholic Campaign," pp. 105–07, 154–56, 189–91, 605.

[136] Hogan, *Sectarian Strand*, p. 254.

[137] Don Smart. 1978. *Federal Aid to Australian Schools*. St. Lucia: University of Queensland Press, pp. 52–53; Wilkinson et al., *History of State Aid*, p. 26.

[138] Bessant and Spaull, *Politics of Schooling*, p. 116.

them, including members of Menzies' cabinet, were quietly expressing support for direct state aid.[139]

Although his decision ultimately owed more to political calculation and the pursuit of Catholic votes, Protestant support for state aid likely also influenced Menzies. Menzies had attended a private Protestant school as a teenager, and was a longstanding and vocal supporter of religious schools. Menzies believed that religion was an essential part of education, if schools were to turn out "Christian men and women, civilized men and women, and not merely ... clever pagans."[140] As early as 1943, he had expressed openness to state aid as a means of preserving religious private schools. Writing in response to an opponent of state aid, Menzies declared that since "the Church schools – of whatever denomination" offered a superior education, "If I found after the war that economic stringency in many homes threatened the continued existence of these schools, I would strongly advocate some State assistance to them."[141] Menzies' belief in the importance of religious schools thus predisposed him to sympathy for state aid, especially once the calls for state aid were supported by both Protestant and Catholic voices.

From Concession to Settlement: Keeping State Aid on the Agenda After 1963

The science laboratories legislation was a "breakthrough in political perception" about the electoral feasibility of state aid: "The dogma of a century that state aid was political suicide had been completely overturned. The new dogma was that state aid was a vote-winner."[142] Yet the new federal aid was small in real terms; although it provided needed assistance to Catholic schools, it did little to reduce the major costs burdening the Catholic system, including staff salaries, teacher training, and capital development.[143] In 1966, Santamaria expressed the feelings of many Catholics when he decried the existing concessions as "tiny" and "niggardly" and declared that "the process of reform has barely begun."[144] Accordingly, the Catholic campaign intensified its efforts to build support for state aid. Just as strict separationists kept pressure on the American courts to ensure that the new jurisprudence would be implemented in recalcitrant school districts, so too did Catholics press their advantage, extracting additional concessions from federal and state governments to turn the symbolic breakthrough into a durable settlement.

---

[139] Smart, *Federal Aid*, pp. 70–71.

[140] Robert Menzies, speech delivered to the Sydney Church of England Grammar School Old Boys' Union 75th Dinner, Menzies Hotel, Sydney, 1 May 1964. Transcript available in NLA Manuscripts Collection, Sir Robert Menzies Papers, MS 4936/Series 6/Box 279/Folder 199.

[141] Letter, Robert Menzies to H.P. Smith, 7 May 1943. NLA Manuscripts Collection, Sir Robert Menzies Papers, MS 4936/Series 14/Box 419/Folder 70.

[142] Hogan, *Catholic Campaign*, p. 87.

[143] Luttrell, "Come to Our Aid," p. 6.

[144] B.A. Santamaria. 1966. *"State Aid" in Perspective*. Melbourne: The Hawthorn Press, pp. 1, 3.

Catholics sought to build both public and political support for state aid. To shape public opinion, groups like the New South Wales AEF published journals and pamphlets presenting distillations of the Catholic argument, statements by non-Catholics in support of state aid, and statistics about the financial hardships faced by private schools. Supportive politicians made use of the information and arguments put forth in AEF literature to argue the case for state aid. To build political support, the Catholic campaign held an influential series of public meetings, of increasing size, which culminated in a mass meeting in Sydney in June 1969 that attracted more than five thousand people. Typically, these meetings combined elements of confrontation and propaganda. Politicians delivered speeches defending their party's educational policy, and Catholic spokesmen gave speeches highlighting the needs of Catholic schools. The meeting was then thrown open to allow politicians to respond to questions from the floor; cannily, the organizers typically planted questioners in the audience beforehand to ask pointed questions that clearly illustrated Catholic frustrations over state aid.[145] While politicians were usually happy to use the meetings as an occasion to plead their case to Catholic audiences, event organizers were not shy about issuing veiled threats to coerce attendance. Federal Treasurer and future Prime Minister William McMahon, for instance, was badgered into attending one meeting by an organizer who told him, "If you don't arrive on that night, I personally will stand on the platform and say that Mr. McMahon is not interested in the Catholic schools of this electorate."[146]

These meetings were important not only because they vividly illustrated the crisis in the Catholic schools and the passion of Catholic activists to political leaders, but because they helped to create a literal "auction" situation in which Labor and Liberal leaders competed to provide the most compelling promises for state aid to Catholic audiences. Gough Whitlam, who had only recently convinced the ALP to accept state aid, used the town hall meetings as an occasion to sell his new policies to suburban Catholics concerned about the future of their schools. Liberals, for their part, used the forums as occasions to remind voters about their contributions to state aid and promise them further concessions as a means of staying in power.[147] Through these direct competitions before Catholic audiences, state aid became solidified as an accepted policy in Australian politics, and the real concessions in terms of funding grew consistently over the late 1960s and early 1970s.

While the grassroots campaign kept public pressure on politicians through mass meetings, the campaign's clerical and partisan wings worked behind the scenes to obtain state aid in the form of recurrent per capita grants. Catholics sought per capita grants because they saw them as the optimal means of funding

---

[145] Hogan, *Catholic Campaign*, pp. 120–21, 135–36, 144–45.
[146] Interview, Monica Turner, in Luttrell, *Regaining State Aid*, p. 139.
[147] Hogan, *Catholic Campaign*, pp. 147–48.

the training and salaries of their teaching staff. Per capita grants were first introduced in Victoria in 1967, and the direct trading of DLP preference votes was central to this breakthrough. In that year, the state government, which the Liberal Party controlled outright without any coalition support, faced an election which threatened to force them into a coalition with the Country Party. Santamaria sensed an opportunity. Although the DLP refused to allocate its second-preference votes to the ALP, it had no compunctions about allocating them to the Country Party rather than the Liberals. Accordingly, they leaked a story to a Melbourne newspaper hinting that the DLP was planning on changing its second-preference votes from the Liberals to the Country Party. The Premier, Henry Bolte, fumed that the DLP was attempting to "blackmail" him, but ultimately agreed to introduce per capita grants to primary and secondary independent schools in exchange for DLP votes.[148] The breakthrough in Victoria quickly spread to other states; by June 1968, per capita grants had been enacted or were pending in every Australian state.[149]

At the federal level, the intensification of lobbying efforts by the Catholic bishops also helped secure aid in the form of per capita grants. In 1967, the bishops created a formal organization, the Federal Catholic Schools Committee (FCSC), to coordinate their negotiations on state aid. The FCSC developed an official policy statement calling for "not the whole, but a substantial proportion of operational costs," to be obtained by "per capita payments to the appropriate educational authority, based on the enrolments of the schools." They also requested capital supports for new buildings and ongoing maintenance costs, as well as subsidies for the cost of training teachers.[150] This statement of policy goals both reflected the focus on equity (rather than strict equality) that had developed in the campaign in the mid-1960s, and the desire for per capita grants as the preferred form of state aid. Armed with these goals, the FCSC entered into negotiations with the federal government. In 1969, the Liberal Party introduced a scheme of per capita grants at the federal level for the first time.[151] As political scientist Michael Hogan has argued, between 1967 and 1972, "Not only did State and Federal governments increase their aid to Catholic schools progressively ... but they also gave the aid very largely in ways which the Catholic negotiators demanded" – i.e., as per capita grants.[152]

---

[148] The exact details of this exchange are disputed. For various versions, see Costar, "Was the DLP," pp. 313–14; Santamaria, *Santamaria*, pp. 222–23; Wilkinson et al., *History of State Aid*, p. 36.

[149] See speech of Senator Wright, in Australia. Senate. 1968. *Commonwealth Parliamentary Debates*, 13 June. Canberra: Government Printer, pp. 1740–43.

[150] Hogan, *Catholic Campaign*, pp. 165–66, 171–72, 175.

[151] Wilkinson et al., *History of State Aid*, p. 41.

[152] Hogan, *Catholic Campaign*, p. 177. Catholics did not win every concession they asked for, however; teacher training subsidies were rejected at both state and federal levels.

ELECTORAL INSTITUTIONS AS CONTEXTS: STATE AID IN COMPARATIVE PERSPECTIVE

The Catholic campaign for state aid thus played a crucial role in forcing the issue onto the Australian political agenda and shaping the ultimate form that state aid took. In this regard, the campaign was instrumental in transforming a cynical political concession into a durable new secular settlement that brought church and state into closer alignment in education. That Catholics were able to do this reflected not simply their strategic capacity, however, but also the favorable institutional terrain that they encountered thanks to Australian electoral institutions and partisan coalitional politics. The importance of these institutional factors can be readily seen when the Australian experience is contrasted with American Catholics' parallel postwar campaign for public aid.

The Catholic Campaign for Public Aid in the United States

As in Australia, American Catholics never completely gave up the quest for public aid, though their efforts were typically locally oriented in the late nineteenth and early twentieth centuries. In the 1920s, however, statewide campaigns for public aid became more concerted. In a few states, most with large Catholic populations, Catholic pressure convinced state and local governments to extend health care, textbooks, or rides on public school buses to Catholic schoolchildren.[153] As discussed in Chapter 5, most of these indirect forms of public aid were challenged in the courts as violations of state constitutional provisions, with mixed results. However, in two cases that reached the Supreme Court, textbooks and transportation were upheld as constitutional under the so-called child-benefit theory. According to this theory, textbook loans were permissible because they were made to the schoolchildren "for their benefit and the resulting benefit of the state," not to the schools.[154] Similarly, transportation to parochial schools was held to be permissible as "public welfare legislation" akin to police protection and sidewalks.[155] These legal successes encouraged Catholics to step up their pursuit of public aid, especially for these "auxiliary services," at both the state and federal levels.

At the federal level, Catholics opposed any federal involvement in education until World War II.[156] However, in 1944, the Catholic bishops issued a

---

[153] "Catholic Schools and Public Money." 1941. *Yale Law Journal* 50: 917–27, p. 922 n.32; Richard J. Gabel. 1937. *Public Funds for Church and Private Schools*. Washington, DC: Catholic University of America, p. 761.

[154] *Cochran* v. *Louisiana State Board of Education*, 281 U.S. 370 (1930), p. 375.

[155] *Everson* v. *Board of Education*, 330 U.S. 1 (1947), pp. 16, 18.

[156] Patrick W. Carey. 2004. *Catholics in America: A History*. Westport, CT: Praeger, p. 96; see also Douglas J. Slawson. 2005. *The Department of Education Battle, 1918–1932: Public Schools, Catholic Schools, and the Social Order*. Notre Dame, IN: University of Notre Dame Press;

pastoral letter through their main organizational body, the National Catholic Welfare Conference (NCWC), in which they expressed openness to federal aid, provided that it were made "equitable to all children … without regard to color, origin, or creed," and that it not "impose in our country federal control of education either in law or practice."[157] Congressional leaders took note of the new Catholic attitude as the drive for a federal educational bill accelerated after World War II. Legislation that would have provided direct or indirect aid to Catholic schools was introduced in 1945, 1947, and 1949. Ultimately, however, all of these bills failed. Those bills providing aid to Catholic schools were sunk by opposition from national educational groups and Protestant separationists, who wanted federal aid to go only to public schools. Catholics, for their part, retaliated by refusing to support any legislation that *failed* to provide at least some support for Catholic schools; they, too, prevailed upon their supporters in Congress to block alternative public-school-only legislation that was sponsored in the two decades following World War II.[158]

This impasse was temporarily broken in 1958, with the passage of the National Defense Education Act (NDEA), which provided long-term low-interest loans to Catholic schools for the purchase of equipment for use in science, mathematics, and foreign language courses.[159] The passage of the NDEA, along with the election of Catholic John F. Kennedy as President in 1960, gave Catholics hope that further aid might be forthcoming. However, their hopes were dashed when Kennedy refused to countenance any aid to parochial schools. His 1961 federal education bill offered aid to public schools, but not to nonpublic schools, "in accordance with the clear prohibition of the Constitution."[160] After Catholics protested, Kennedy proposed a second bill to expand the NDEA loan program to cover the construction of additional classrooms. Yet both bills died in the House, which could not resolve Protestant–Catholic differences over which bill to bring up first for a vote.

and Gilbert E. Smith. 1982. *The Limits of Reform: Politics and Federal Aid to Education, 1937–1950*. New York: Garland Publishing.

[157] National Catholic Welfare Conference. 1984 [1944]. "Statement on Federal Aid to Education." Pp. 50–51 in *Pastoral Letters of the United States Catholic Bishops*. Vol. 2, *1941–1961*, edited by Hugh J. Nolan. Washington, DC: United States Catholic Conference, p. 50.

[158] On federal education legislation between 1945 and 1950, see generally Frank J. Munger and Richard F. Fenno, Jr. 1962. *National Politics and Federal Aid to Education*. Syracuse: Syracuse University Press; and Smith, *Limits of Reform*. During the 1950s, the religious conflict was subordinated to an escalating series of conflicts over segregation. On the effect of race, see Munger and Fenno, *National Politics and Federal Aid*, pp. 12–13, 68, 134.

[159] Wayne J. Urban. 2010. *More than Science and Sputnik: The National Defense Education Act of 1958*. Tuscaloosa: University of Alabama Press. Although the NDEA represented the first major federal concession to Catholic schools, it passed without controversy, largely because it was presented as an essential national security measure in the wake of the Sputnik crisis.

[160] John F. Kennedy. 1961. "Special Message to the Congress on Education, February 20, 1961." *The American Presidency Project*, edited by Gerhard Peters and John T. Wooley. Available online at http://www.presidency.ucsb.edu/ws/?pid=8433 (accessed 28 March 2016).

Ultimately, no legislation was passed in 1961, and an attempt to revisit the legislation the following year similarly failed.[161]

Catholics were finally able to score a victory in 1965, with the passage of the ESEA. The ESEA embraced the "child-benefit" theory, and used poor children as its primary funding mechanism, allowing some aid to parochial schools to flow through them.[162] Thus, the ESEA provided for a range of services to be provided by public school teachers in private school settings, library books which would be made available to all poor children irrespective of school, and the creation of "supplementary educational centers" that would offer assistance to both public and private school students after hours. However, the ESEA placed heavy restrictions on the services that were extended to religious schools, requiring all supplementary services, instructional materials, and library resources made available to religious schools to have their titles vested in public agencies in uncompromising language.[163] The ESEA was the last major Catholic success at the federal level;[164] in sum, their efforts had yielded some low-cost loans and indirect access to auxiliary educational supports.

Catholics had somewhat greater success in state legislatures during the 1960s. As in Australia, Catholic schools faced a crisis in the 1960s as enrolments skyrocketed and the proportion of lay teachers rose sharply.[165] Catholics responded by stepping up their demands for greater public subsidies. During the 1960s, seventeen states passed transportation legislation, four states passed textbook laws, and four states provided other auxiliary supports.[166] More significantly, eight states – all with large Catholic populations and high Catholic school enrolments – passed laws providing for direct financial aid to Catholic schools between 1968 and 1971.[167] These laws permitted the state to "purchase" the "secular services" of religious schools by paying them grants to cover

---

[161] Hugh Davis Graham. 1984. *The Uncertain Triumph: Federal Education Policy in the Kennedy and Johnson Years*. Chapel Hill: The University of North Carolina Press, pp. 20–22, 26–30.

[162] Gareth Davies. 2007. *See Government Grow: Education Politics from Johnson to Reagan*. Lawrence: University Press of Kansas, pp. 25, 35.

[163] United States Office of Education. 1965. *"The First Work of These Times...": A Description and Analysis of the Elementary and Secondary Education Act of 1965*. Washington, DC: United States Department of Health, Education, and Welfare, Office of Education.

[164] On the failure of further public aid campaigns from the late 1960s onwards, see Lawrence J. McAndrews. 2006. *The Era of Education: The Presidents and the Schools, 1965–2001*. Urbana: University of Illinois Press. For a discussion of successful voucher and scholarship tax credit programs in the states over the past two decades, see the Epilogue.

[165] Frank J. Sorauf. 1976. *The Wall of Separation: The Constitutional Politics of Church and State*. Princeton, NJ: Princeton University Press, pp. 14–15, 321–22.

[166] Joanne Golding. 1977. "State Aid to Nonpublic Schools: A Legal-Historical Overview." *Journal of Church and State* 19: 231–40, p. 235.

[167] Janet Shedd Foerster. 1971. "Public Aid to Nonpublic Education." Report to the President's Commission on School Finance, October 1971, pp. 11–12; Sorauf, *Wall of Separation*, pp. 327–28.

teacher salaries, textbooks, or instructional materials in secular subjects.[168] These forms of direct aid were decisively quashed in 1971, however, when the Supreme Court ruled Pennsylvania's and Rhode Island's direct aid plans unconstitutional. In *Lemon* v. *Kurtzman*, the Supreme Court weighed in definitively against direct public aid, and in a series of decisions over the following decade, against much indirect public aid as well.[169]

In short, the Catholic campaign for public aid in the United States succeeded in gaining only a limited array of indirect concessions from the federal government during the two decades after World War II. At the state level, they gained a considerable number of auxiliary supports in states with large Catholic populations, and even direct aid in some states before it was ruled unconstitutional in 1971. Yet overall, their successes were quite limited compared against their Australian counterparts. This was especially so at the federal level, where Australian Catholics enjoyed their most significant breakthrough in 1963. Why were Australian Catholics able to obtain state aid through legislative means while American Catholics were not? In the remainder of this chapter, I argue that the institutional terrain facilitated the Australian Catholic campaign but posed an obstacle for American Catholics. Specifically, I focus on the way that voting systems and political parties freed Australian Catholics from an unfavorable party coalition while trapping American Catholics in one; and the relative absence of constitutional limitations placed on Australian Catholics relative to their American counterparts.

The Catholic Campaign in the Electoral System: Voting Systems, Parties, and Coalitional Dynamics

One major reason why Australian Catholics had success in the legislative arena was that Australia's voting and party systems worked together to bolster their political opportunities. As discussed above, Australia's preference-voting system created space for third parties to succeed. This multiparty system, in turn, allowed Australian Catholics to escape the detrimental party coalition that had hampered their quest for state aid since the late nineteenth century, become a political free agent, and ultimately wield outsized influence in Australian politics, contributing to the reintroduction of state aid. By contrast, the first-past-the-post, plurality-voting system in the United States created strong institutional incentives toward a two-party system. The reduction of politics to two parties, in turn, reduced Catholics' political opportunities. Catholics were aligned with Southerners in the Democratic Party at midcentury, a coalition that

<hr>

[168] Joseph Richard Preville. 1992. "Constitutional Quarrels: Roman Catholics, Jews, and the Aftermath of *Lemon* v. *Kurtzman*." *Catholic Historical Review* 78(2): 217–31, p. 221.

[169] *Lemon* v. *Kurtzman*, 403 US 602 (1971); *Committee for Public Education and Religious Liberty (PEARL)* v. *Nyquist*, 413 US 756 (1973); *Meek* v. *Pittinger*, 421 US 349 (1975); *Wolman* v. *Walter*, 433 US 229 (1977).

was unfavorable to Catholics on the issue of public aid. Because Southerners regularly voted against public aid proposals, Catholics were unable to advance legislation despite Democratic control of Congress and the White House for much of the postwar era.

Catholics were a major piece of the Democratic Party's "New Deal" coalition that dominated American politics from 1933 through 1980. Catholics (and other non-Protestant immigrants) were first incorporated into the Democratic Party in the late nineteenth century through the political machines of major Northern cities.[170] The groundbreaking 1928 presidential candidacy of Catholic Al Smith helped to cement Catholic attachments to the Democratic Party.[171] By 1960, Catholics made up nearly one-quarter of the Democratic congressional delegation, and eighty-six percent of all Catholic congressmen were Democrats.[172] Yet Catholics were not the only component of the Democratic Party. The largest single Democratic constituency was white Southerners.[173] The "Solid South" moved en masse to the Democratic Party following the Civil War, and from 1876 to 1965 Southerners dominated the party.[174] Over the first three decades of the twentieth century, the Democratic Party was known informally as the "party of the South"; Southerners comprised nearly two-thirds of the party, and even after 1933 more than forty percent of Democrats hailed from the white South.[175]

This tenuous coalition of religious outgroups and an aggrieved regional minority created a particularly fractious partisan situation in the mid-twentieth century. While Southerners and Catholics could join forces on many economic and geopolitical matters, the coalition fell apart when faced with issues with a strong sectarian dimension. This was especially true on the question of public aid. Southern Democrats represented an overwhelmingly Protestant constituency that was strongly committed to the principle of separation of church and state as it was understood in the nineteenth century. Thus, even though Southern politicians were often vocal champions of federal aid to education, they were often "compelled by their Protestant constituencies to vote against

[170] See, e.g., Steven P. Erie. 1988. *Rainbow's End: Irish-Americans and the Dilemmas of Urban Machine Politics, 1840–1985*. Berkeley: University of California Press, *passim*.

[171] Michael Barone. 2003. "Franklin D. Roosevelt: A Protestant Patrician in a Catholic Party." Pp. 3–10 in *FDR, The Vatican, and the Roman Catholic Church in America, 1933–1945*, edited by David B. Woolner and Richard G. Kurial. New York: Palgrave MacMillan, p. 7.

[172] John H. Fenton. 1960. *The Catholic Vote*. New Orleans: The Hauser Press, pp. 87–89.

[173] Other important members of the New Deal coalition included the working class, blacks, and Jews. See Harold W. Stanley and Richard G. Niemi. 2006. "Partisanship, Party Coalitions, and Group Support, 1952–2004." *Presidential Studies Quarterly* 36(2): 172–88, p. 172.

[174] Nicol C. Rae. 1994. *Southern Democrats*. New York: Oxford University Press, p. 10; see also V.O. Key, Jr. 1949. *Southern Politics in State and Nation*. New York: Alfred A. Knopf, pp. 315–82.

[175] Ira Katznelson, Kim Geiger, and Daniel Kryder. 1993. "Limiting Liberalism: The Southern Veto in Congress, 1933–1950." *Political Science Quarterly* 108(2): 283–306, p. 284.

bills that included church schools."[176] These divisions help explain why, despite Democratic political dominance from 1933 to 1980,[177] the party was unable to pass any substantial federal aid to education until 1965, and no direct aid to Catholic parochial schools. In brief, Catholics were locked into an unfavorable partisan coalition with Southerners who were antagonistic to their public aid campaign.

Three features of the American electoral system helped to stabilize this fractious coalition: plurality voting, the electoral college, and an independent executive. In the American plurality-voting system, the top vote-getter wins an election irrespective of how many votes he or she receives. No fringe benefits accrue to runners-up, as can happen to minor parties in a preference-voting system, where second-preference votes can become a valuable political asset. This helps to create a perception among voters that votes for third parties are "wasted" votes. Moreover, while third parties might be able to win some local seats where their voters are particularly concentrated, they stand virtually no chance at the state or national level. The electoral college system of electing a president dilutes the potential power of geographic concentration, and strongly encourages the perpetuation of a two-party system for the purposes of national electoral competitiveness. Finally, because the American President is elected independently from the legislature and is thus not dependent upon its support, there is greater room within parties for disagreement and less incentive toward party discipline. Thus, as Lipset and Marks observe, "Because of the enormous pressure toward party consolidation exerted by the electoral system, factional coalitions have always taken place within, rather than between, political parties."[178]

Because the Republican Party remained the party of the Protestant Establishment, and the prospects for a third party were quite grim, Catholics had few options if dissatisfied with their political situation. However, Catholics were not particularly interested in leaving the Democratic Party at midcentury. Unlike Australia, where communism was the wedge that drove apart the Labor coalition, communism actually had a unifying effect on the Democratic Party. During the postwar decades, the Cold War catapulted anticommunism into a hegemonic position in American politics.[179] Accordingly, communism did not become a salient political issue that threatened to destabilize the Democratic coalition. On the contrary, it helped to strengthen it, because both Southerners

[176] Irving Bernstein. 1991. *Promises Kept: John F. Kennedy's New Frontier*. New York: Oxford University Press, pp. 221–22.

[177] Democrats controlled both houses of Congress for all but four years between 1933 and 1980 (excepting only 1947–1949 and 1953–1955), and controlled both Congress and the Presidency from 1933 to 1947, 1949 to 1953, and 1961 to 1969.

[178] Seymour Martin Lipset and Gary Marks. 2000. *It Didn't Happen Here: Why Socialism Failed in the United States*. New York: W.W. Norton & Company, pp. 45, 49, 65–66 (quote p. 49).

[179] M.J. Heale. 1991. *American Anticommunism: Combating the Enemy Within, 1830–1970*. Baltimore: The Johns Hopkins University Press, p. 167.

and Catholics were among the most ardent anticommunists in the country. Evangelical Protestants, who were strong in the South, had a long tradition of opposing political and economic radicalism. The Southern Baptist Convention declared in 1938 that there was "no room" for "radical Socialism" or "atheistic Communism" in the United States,[180] and many evangelical leaders were vocal opponents of communism during the postwar years.[181] Catholics, too, were among the most vigilant anticommunists in the country. Inspired by Pope Pius' 1937 encyclical *Divini Redemptoris*, which condemned communism as "intrinsically wrong" and prohibited any cooperation with communists, the Catholic hierarchy issued a continuous stream of pastorals decrying communism throughout the 1940s and 1950s.[182]

Communism also failed to play a disruptive role in the Democratic Party because labor was both less important to the party and less radical than it was in Australia. Whereas the ALP was a true labor party, the Democratic Party was not. Trade unions therefore did not have direct input into party decision-making in the United States. Further, socialism was relatively weak in American unions. The largest labor organization, the American Federation of Labor, was "conservative, loath to strike, respectable, and impervious to radicalism in any form."[183] Although communists made some inroads into the Congress of Industrial Organizations (CIO) in the 1930s, the advent of the Cold War quickly snuffed out any incipient radicalism in the unions. The passage of the Taft–Hartley Act, which required union officials to sign an affidavit declaring that they were neither Communist Party members nor sympathizers in order to receive the services of the National Labor Relations Board, alongside communist support for Henry Wallace's disastrous third-party Progressive presidential campaign in 1948, convinced the CIO to bar communists from its executive board, and purge any officials who failed to toe the line.[184] By 1949, radicalism had been successfully routed from the labor movement in favor of the Cold War's anticommunist orthodoxy.

[180] Quoted in Heale, *American Anticommunism*, p. 118.

[181] Daniel K. Williams. 2010. *God's Own Party: The Making of the Christian Right*. New York: Oxford University Press, p. 19.

[182] Pius XI. 1937. *Divini Redemptoris*. Papal encyclical, 19 March, paragraph 58. Available online at http://w2.vatican.va/content/pius-xi/en/encyclicals/documents/hf_p-xi_enc_19031937_divini-redemptoris.html (accessed 28 March 2016); Hugh J. Nolan, ed., *Pastoral Letters of the United States Catholic Bishops*. Vol. 2, *1941–1961*. Washington, DC: United States Catholic Conference.

[183] Douglas P. Seaton. 1981. *Catholics and Radicals: The Association of Catholic Trade Unionists and the American Labor Movement, from Depression to Cold War*. Lewisburg, PA: Bucknell University Press, p. 21.

[184] Ellen Schrecker. 2004. "Labor and the Cold War: The Legacy of McCarthyism." Pp. 7–24 in *American Labor and the Cold War: Grassroots Politics and Postwar Political Culture*, edited by Robert W. Cherny, William Issel, and Kieran Walsh Taylor. New Brunswick, NJ: Rutgers University Press, pp. 8–11; Heale, *American Anticommunism*, pp. 141–48.

If Catholics felt ideologically at home in the Democratic Party thanks to its rejection of communism, they were further drawn to it by the nomination of John F. Kennedy for President in 1960. Catholic support for their fellow Catholic, Kennedy, meant that – far from becoming a political free agent – Catholics voted Democratic at an unusually high rate in the 1960 election.[185] However, Kennedy was unable to champion public aid to parochial schools precisely *because* he was a Catholic.[186] Kennedy feared that the fate of future Catholic candidates hinged on his performance in office. He was particularly concerned that granting concessions to the Catholic Church would confirm the worst suspicions Protestants harbored about Catholic politicians, and be held against any future Catholic candidate.[187] Accordingly, Kennedy so adamantly opposed any concessions to Catholic schools that the Commissioner of Education, Francis Keppel, remarked that Kennedy "was the most Protestant president I ever saw on this issue."[188] Although Kennedy's obdurate defense of separation successfully helped to defuse Protestant fears of Vatican control,[189] it nevertheless came at the price of public aid for Catholic schools.

Thus, the way parties sorted Catholics into and out of political coalitions made their demands more or less attractive to politicians. In Australia, anti-communism split the Labor Party, transforming Catholics into a swing constituency whose votes and issues the major parties competed over. In the United States, by contrast, Catholics remained tightly linked to a party whose internal composition served as a continual drag on Catholic ambitions regarding funding for their schools. The Cold War and the election of John F. Kennedy strengthened Catholics' attachment to the Democratic Party, but at the price of weakening their ability to obtain funding.

The Constitutional Context of the Catholic Campaign

While electoral institutions posed the greatest institutional obstacle, the courts acted as a further set of institutional constraints that hampered American but not Australian Catholics. Because there was no High Court jurisprudence on Section 116, the question of constitutionality played only a minor role in discussions of state aid in Australia before 1963. Accordingly, Catholics were typically able to ignore or dismiss constitutional concerns respecting establishment in the early 1960s.[190] The DOGS case did move the constitutional

---

[185] Jeff Manza and Clem Brooks. 1997. "The Religious Factor in U.S. Presidential Elections, 1960–1992." *American Journal of Sociology* 103(1): 38–81, pp. 65–67.

[186] Leo R. Ward. 1964. *Federal Aid to Private Schools*. Westminster, MD: Newman Press, p. 2.

[187] Theodore C. Sorensen. 1965. *Kennedy*. New York: Harper and Row, p. 358.

[188] Quoted in Bernstein, *Promises Kept*, p. 244.

[189] Thomas J. Carty. 2004. *A Catholic in the White House? Religion, Politics and John F. Kennedy's Presidential Campaign*. New York: Palgrave Macmillan, p. 159.

[190] E.g., Santamaria, *Santamaria*, p. 217.

question to the center of the debate from the late 1960s through the 1970s.[191] However, this constitutional turn occurred after the crucial breakthrough had already been accomplished. Consequently, the issue of constitutionality did not encourage Catholics to place limits on their claims. It did, however, encourage them to support particular formulations for funding; part of the reason that Catholics strongly favored per capita grants was their belief that per capita grants were better positioned to survive any potential constitutional challenge under Section 116.[192]

In the United States, by contrast, constitutional issues loomed large over the Catholic campaign, shaping both the demands and the prospects for aid in the postwar years. The Supreme Court's 1947 *Everson* decision supercharged longstanding arguments about "separation of church and state" with weighty constitutional significance. Yet *Everson*, even as it affirmed a strict separationist interpretation of the Establishment Clause, also ruled that a transportation program in New Jersey passed constitutional muster. Accordingly, the implications of the new jurisprudence for public aid remained ambiguous throughout the 1950s and 1960s. Although the majority of legal scholars understood, along with eminent constitutional scholar Anson Phelps Stokes, that "laws permitting ... grants [to parochial schools] if passed would be declared unconstitutional,"[193] Catholic jurists and other scholars were quick to develop arguments that interpreted *Everson* in a much more permissive light. Supporters of public aid argued, *inter alia*, that "child benefit" and "public welfare" arguments could be extended to a variety of other appropriations, including grants, scholarships, and tuition subsidies; that Justice Black's famous "No tax" proclamation was simply "dicta" not binding upon the Court; and that the actual findings in favor of textbooks and transportation suggested that the Court was, in practice, open to public aid.[194] By the early 1960s, many

[191] See above, Chapter 5.

[192] See, e.g., The Central Commission of the Catholic Bishops of Australia, "Statement on Government Financial Assistance to Independent Schools," 30 May 1973. SRNSW, K283933–73/47084; and Interview, Margaret Slattery, in Luttrell, *Regaining State Aid*, p. 111.

[193] Anson Phelps Stokes. 1950. *Church and State in the United States*. Vol. 2. New York: Harper & Brothers, p. 729. For other prominent analyses that reached similar conclusions, see also Fred F. Beach and Robert F. Will. 1958. *The State and Nonpublic Schools, with Particular Reference to Responsibilities of State Departments of Education*. Washington, DC: United States Department of Health, Education, and Welfare, p. 15; Virgil C. Blum. 1958. *Freedom of Choice in Education*. New York: Macmillan, p. 23; Leo Pfeffer. 1948. "Religion, Education, and the Constitution." *Lawyers' Guild Review* 8: 387–99, p. 387; and Allanson W. Willcox, "Memorandum on the Impact of the First Amendment to the Constitution upon Federal Aid to Education," 28 March 1961. Reprinted in United States. House of Representatives. 1961. *Congressional Record*. Washington, DC: Government Printer, 87th Congress, First Session, 107(4): 5382–89, p. 5382.

[194] See, e.g., National Catholic Welfare Conference. 1962. "The Constitutionality of the Inclusion of Church-Related Schools in Federal Aid to Education: The Roman Catholic Viewpoint." *Journal of Church and State* 4(2): 159–65; James M. O'Neill. 1951. "Address of Dr. James M. O'Neill." Pp. 32–41 in *Public Aid to Parochial Education: A Transcript of a Discussion on*

constitutional scholars viewed the constitutionality of public aid as an open question. As University of Chicago Law Professor Philip Kurland concluded in 1962, "Anyone suggesting that the answer, as a matter of constitutional law, is clear one way or the other is either deluding or deluded."[195]

Ultimately, of course, the *Lemon* decision resolved this constitutional ambiguity by firmly outlawing direct aid in 1971. Yet in the two decades before *Lemon*, the intense debate around constitutionality indirectly shaped how Catholics approached their pursuit of state aid, in ways that ultimately proved detrimental to their efforts. For one thing, the *Everson* decision encouraged Catholics to scale back their claims for public aid. Seeing that the Supreme Court had assented to transportation and textbook subsidies, Catholics focused their efforts on these "auxiliary services" rather than aggressively pursuing more general programs of aid.[196] In 1949, the chair of the NCWC's education department (and Archbishop of Baltimore), Francis P. Keough, declared, "All we want for our children are just the necessary services where they are now difficult to get – a textbook, a bus ride, some medical and dental aid. We don't want anyone to build our schools. We don't want a penny for the salaries of our teachers."[197] Catholic officials made similar statements throughout the 1950s.[198] Only as the crisis in the parochial schools deepened in the early 1960s did Catholics again begin to demand more substantial concessions.[199] Thus, the American Catholic campaign made considerably more qualified demands than did the Australian campaign, especially during the debates over federal aid between 1947 and 1961.

The constitutional question also directly affected the position taken by America's first Catholic president, John F. Kennedy. Kennedy's Catholicism was a major issue in the 1960 campaign, and many Protestants were deeply suspicious that a Catholic president would undermine the separation of church and state.[200] Accordingly, Kennedy was obliged to tread a firm separationist

a *Vital Issue.* Cambridge: Harvard Law School Forum; Arthur Sutherland, in United States. House of Representatives. 1961. *Congressional Record.* Washington, DC: Government Printer, 87th Congress, First Session, 107(50): A2026–29; Speech of Senator Keating, 24 April 1961, in United States. Senate. 1961. *Congressional Record.* Washington, DC: Government Printer, 87th Congress, First Session, 107(5): 6591–94.

[195] Philip B. Kurland. 1962. *Religion and the Law: Of Church and State and the Supreme Court.* Chicago: Aldine, p. 111. For a review of other contemporary experts who saw public aid as potentially constitutional, see the testimony of Lawrence X. Cusack in United States Senate. 1963. *Education Legislation – 1963.* Subcommittee on Education, Committee on Labor and Public Welfare, Report 98–466, 88th Congress, First Session, Vol. 3. Washington DC: Government Printer, p. 1799.

[196] Smith, *Limits of Reform,* p. 175.

[197] Quoted in *New York Times.* 1949. "Advised to Recast Catholic Curricula." 18 February, p. 18.

[198] See, e.g., William E. McManus. 1955. "A Catholic View on Aid to Schools." *U.S. News and World Report* 39 (16 December): 121–22; and Neil G. McCluskey. 1959. *Catholic Viewpoint on Education.* Garden City, NY: Hanover House, pp. 168–76.

[199] E.g., National Catholic Welfare Conference, "Constitutionality of the Inclusion."

[200] Carty, *Catholic in the White House,* pp. 58–63; Williams, *God's Own Party,* pp. 51–52.

line. He repeatedly met with Protestant audiences in an attempt to prove his separationist bona fides,[201] most famously in a September 1960 speech to the Greater Houston Ministerial Association, where he flatly declared, "I believe in an America where the separation of church and state is absolute ... where no church or church school is granted any public funds or political preferences."[202] Opposing public aid was the price Kennedy paid to become the first Catholic president, but it created great difficulties for the Catholic campaign for public aid during his presidency. Thus, while their Australian counterparts faced few constitutional obstacles, American Catholics ran into constitutional difficulties both directly (in terms of the *Lemon* decision), and indirectly (in terms of the way the Establishment Clause affected their goals and political prospects in the years before *Lemon*).

CONCLUSION

Australian Catholics successfully obtained state aid through legislative means in the 1960s and 1970s for a number of reasons. The timing was right, thanks to ecumenical trends in the religious field that softened resistance to state aid. But Catholics were also successful because they were able to leverage electoral institutions – especially parties and voting rules – to their advantage. The Labor Party split freed Catholics from an unfavorable partisan coalition and transformed their votes into a sought-after commodity. That Catholic votes were so valuable owed much to Australia's preference-voting system. Despite its small size, the DLP, through the disciplining of its second-preference votes, could nevertheless wield outsized influence. Shrewd politicians like Robert Menzies and Henry Bolte granted state aid in calculated bids to gain Catholic votes, but Catholics put themselves in a position to benefit through their sustained campaign for state aid and their savvy manipulation of Australia's electoral institutions. The Catholic campaign for state aid which developed in the 1960s acted strategically to maximize their position and to take advantage of the remarkable political opportunity that the Labor schism and ecumenical zeitgeist provided them.

---

[201] Shaun A. Casey. 2009. *The Making of a Catholic President: Kennedy vs. Nixon 1960*. New York: Oxford University Press, p. 17.

[202] John F. Kennedy. 1960. "Speech of Senator John F. Kennedy, Greater Houston Ministerial Association, Rice Hotel, Houston TX," 12 September. *The American Presidency Project*, edited by Gerhard Peters and John T. Wooley. Available online: http://www.presidency.ucsb.edu/ws/index.php?pid=25773 (accessed 28 March 2016).

PART IV

IMPLICATIONS

7

Conclusion

By 1975, the new twentieth-century settlements had solidified in each country. Australia's system of public funding for religious schools, and America's strictly secular public schools, were largely accepted as the law of the land, despite ongoing legal and administrative challenges. Yet, as taken for granted as these arrangements may seem today, they reflect the sedimentation of multiple and longstanding political processes, as well as the unmistakable imprint of each country's peculiar political institutions. While this study has presented a novel interpretation for the emergence of these two secular settlements, it has also highlighted a number of dynamics whose relevance extends beyond these two cases. In this conclusion, therefore, I consider some of the broader implications of this study, both for secularization theory, and for our understanding of American political culture more generally.

RETHINKING SECULARIZATION

Secularization takes multiple forms, engages multiple actors with multiple motives, occurs in multiple contexts, and leads to multiple outcomes. In this book, I have attempted to develop an approach to studying secularization that embraces this multiplicity. Current theories of secularization provide important yet ultimately partial insights into the dynamics of religious change. They suggest we look to modernity, established churches, self-interested politicians, or intellectual elites to explain the secular settlements we see around us. Each captures part – but only part – of a much more complex and contingent story. I have attempted to develop an approach that allows us to put these insights into dialogue with one another and with the historical record, to see how these factors can work with or against one another, with greater or lesser force, in which patterns, and why. To appreciate this complexity, we need to approach secularization as a contingent and politically mediated outcome. And this means beginning with the political conflicts that lie at its core.

Politics and Contingency

Recent approaches to secularization have rightly emphasized its political dimension. Ultimately, secularization is driven by political conflicts, such as whether religious actors will be granted control over important social functions, whether religious ideas will define the contours of thought and action within social domains, and in what form religion will be recognized in public life. Different groups take different stances on these issues, and in so doing introduce the political dynamism that drives religious change. Rather than treating these conflicts as discrete or dissociated events, I have argued that we should understand them in terms of general causal processes, defined by their stakes, which recur across settings in recognizable patterns. There is no single conflict driving secularization in every case. While I have highlighted three processes in this book – state-building, professionalization, and religious conflict – these are not necessarily the only conflicts relevant to secularization. They have, however, played essential roles in the United States and Australia, and in identifying them, I have sought to provide a starting point and model for thinking about how to capture and study the recurrent political dynamics of secularization.

Although the political processes driving secularization are general, this does not mean that we should expect their ultimate effects to be uniform. Rather, those effects will ultimately be contingent upon how they interact with other political processes and institutional settings. While the political processes driving secularization are analytically distinct, they are frequently interdependent in practice. Sometimes they interact with other processes in ways that alter the dynamics of the processes themselves. Thus, for example, the state-building process in both the United States and Australia was intimately intertwined with religious conflict in ways that shaped both the kind of state that each country built, and how different religious groups related to the new educational systems. At other times, one process informs the development of other processes in a more sequential fashion. Because it fostered a decentralized administrative structure, for instance, the state-building process helped generate a particularly strong professionalizing dynamic in the United States. In Australia, by contrast, state-building yielded a centralized state that inhibited the professionalization process.

Similarly, the ultimate effects of these processes depend on how those processes interact with their institutional contexts. Despite increased interest in the political dimension of secularization in recent years, the role of political *institutions* (as opposed to political *actors*) has been largely neglected by scholars. Yet as this study has shown, administrative systems, legal procedures, and electoral systems can amplify, generate, or constrain the secularizing impulse. In this way, taken-for-granted political structures have powerfully shaped the fate of religion in modern societies. Existing theories of secularization have not paid sufficient attention to these contextual effects. To understand the construction of the modern secular order, we need to holistically examine how political actors, processes, and institutions interact. It is in these interactions that we should expect to find answers to why different countries adopt such different secular settlements.

The Role of Institutions

Political institutions play mediating and constitutive structuring roles in secularization. Institutions mediate secularization by shaping the terrain of political contestation in ways that advantage some actors and disadvantage others. Political institutions in the United States and Australia varied considerably in the extent to which they were accessible to groups outside the Protestant establishment, creating divergent opportunities for those actors to pursue and obtain their goals. The localized administrative system in the United States allowed concentrations of religious minorities to make credible claims on these smaller administrative bodies that they could not have made in a more centralized system. Similarly, the American legal system provided both more resources and more points of entry for litigants than did the more restricted Australian legal system. More accessible political institutions permitted more challenges to the nineteenth-century secular settlement, and generated a greater number of opportunities to mobilize localized pockets of opposition, both of which ultimately sped secularization. Political institutions also shaped the dynamics of political coalitions in ways that affected the course of secularization. Perhaps most notably, they bundled Catholics in the two countries into or out of coalitions with hostile partners, thereby affecting their ability to pursue their interests. Variations in electoral institutions, therefore, enhanced the power of Catholics in Australia, while limiting it in the United States.

However, political institutions are more than just a black box processing the demands of political actors. They can also help to constitute actors with secularizing interests. This is clearly evident in the United States, where professional educators, civil libertarians, and Jews – all of whom were among the most important advocates of more secular policies – in many respects formed their interests in response to dynamics unleashed by America's political institutions. America's weak state-level administrative bodies and strong local school boards created strong personal career incentives that encouraged educators to develop a professional orientation. As a result, they devoted substantial attention to curricular and pedagogical reforms. In Australia, where those administrative positions had different degrees of authority or did not exist, professionalization was much weaker. Accordingly, Australian educators focused on working conditions and did not develop into an important, autonomous force in policy-making in Australia until the 1960s. In this respect, the institutional structure of the state helps to explain variation in teachers' *interests*, and ultimately why educators played such starkly different roles in the negotiation of secular settlements in the two nations. Similarly, the positions taken by civil libertarians and Jews were shaped by the strong belief that the American constitution required the "separation of church and state." That civil libertarians were a negligible force in Australia, and that Jews there were not ardent defenders of strict separation, speaks to the importance that America's constitutional culture had upon the development both of secularizing groups and the motives and position-takings of already-existing collectivities.

The constitutive aspect of institutions is important because analyses that take the existence of secularizing groups for granted miss an important part of the story. It is true that professional educators, civil libertarians, and Jews were strong proponents of strict separation in the United States. But their interests had been molded by administrative and legal institutions in unique ways that did not preexist those institutions. These groups were not a purely exogenous force. They were to a real extent the creatures of those political institutions themselves.

Stability and Change

Because secular settlements result from the interaction of political processes and political institutions, their durability is intimately linked to the political and institutional dynamics that helped to bring them into existence. Secular settlements are relatively stable arrangements, but this stability is always a tenuous achievement that rests upon mutable political and institutional foundations. When these political and/or institutional foundations shift, a settlement may become destabilized. Accordingly, there are multiple routes to settlement change.

On the one hand, political changes can destabilize a settlement. These shifts may occur thanks to the rise of new groups, demographic transformations, or changes in actors' interests. In the United States, the nineteenth-century settlement endured so long as Protestants were relatively united and maintained a dominant position relative to other religious groups. Yet that settlement also began to erode because the expansion of education created new actors motivated to transform the knowledge base of the educational domain; and because immigration brought increasing numbers of Catholics and Jews who dissented from the Protestant establishment. In this way, a new professionalizing impulse was introduced, and the dynamics of religious conflict shifted, in ways that destabilized the nineteenth-century settlement and prepared the ground for its transformation in the 1960s.

On the other hand, settlements may become destabilized when their institutional foundations change. This may occur thanks to changes in the rules internal to an existing political institution, through the creation of new institutions, or the weakening or obsolescence of existing institutions. In Australia, changes within existing institutions helped destabilize the nineteenth-century settlement in the mid-twentieth century. The decentralization of administrative authority allowed new dynamics of professionalization and religious conflict to partially secularize the curriculum there, while a change in the number of political parties created an opening for Catholics to pursue desecularization through the reintroduction of state aid. In the United States, similarly, the rise of legal realism within the courts made them more favorable institutional terrain for strict separationists in the immediate postwar years.

Given the dependence of secular settlements upon these political and institutional foundations, we should expect change to be the rule rather than the exception. There is little reason to expect any given secular settlement to be permanent, for its foundations are always apt to change. The analysis of religious change should therefore start by looking for sources of stability and instability within the politics and institutions that sustain a settlement.

Agency and Motive

Thinking about secularization as a contingent political project reminds us that secular settlements are always connected to actors and movements who advocate for particular policies governing religion. Although attention to the agents behind secularization and their motives has grown in recent years, scholars have developed a fairly limited picture of who those actors are and what has motivated them. Existing approaches typically focus on elites, either political or intellectual, who are motivated primarily by some combination of self-aggrandizing or anticlerical motives.[1] Yet this is too narrow a picture of the actors and motives behind secularization. While elites can play an important role, they often work in tandem with important grassroots sources of support. And while some actors are motivated by pure self-interest or anticlericalism, they exist alongside religious minorities motivated by community defense or theological interests, professional administrators grappling with the pragmatic demands of their bureaucratic environments, evangelical ministers trying to usher in the Millennium, and many others. The spectrum of secularizing actors is broad and deep, and their social location, motives, and ultimate goals are remarkably diverse.

Consequently, scholars must resist the temptation to draw a sharp, binary distinction between "secularists" and "religion," to conflate the policy goals that actors pursue with their ideological motivation, or to assume that those

---

[1] Anthony Gill 2008. *The Political Origins of Religious Liberty.* Cambridge: Cambridge University Press; Ahmet T. Kuru. 2009. *Secularism and State Policies Toward Religion: The United States, France, and Turkey.* Cambridge: Cambridge University Press; Christian Smith. 2003. "Introduction: Rethinking the Secularization of American Public Life." Pp. 1–96 in *The Secular Revolution: Power, Interests, and Conflict in the Secularization of American Public Life.* Berkeley: University of California Press.

who argue for more secular policies must also be acting against religious interests. A sharp binary between religious and secular leaves no space for those "religious secularists" who advance secularizing reforms out of religious motivations. Yet many of the most important "secularists" in this book were motivated by deeply held religious beliefs. In the United States, sincere believers were among the most important advocates for a more secular educational system. Evangelical ministers seeking to build the "kingdom of God" pressed the case for public, rather than denominational, education in the mid-nineteenth century; Catholics and Jews fought Protestant devotionals in the late nineteenth and early twentieth centuries; and religious organizations were core members of the legal campaign for strict separation in the postwar era. While "religious secularists" were less common in Australia, they nevertheless played important supporting roles; dissenting clergy led the campaign for government schools and the abolition of state aid in the nineteenth century, for instance. And just as "religious secularists" exist, so too do "secular accommodationists"; as Marion Maddox has observed, desecularization in Australia has at times been promoted most fiercely by "secular" actors.[2] Secularization stories do not fit neatly in a religious–secular binary, and our theories of secularization need to be adjusted accordingly.

Other motives matter as well. Some secularizing actors may be animated by practical motives orthogonal to the question of religion's role in public life. Some administrative actors, for example, both in late-nineteenth-century America and in late-twentieth-century New South Wales, altered policies respecting religion in the public schools, not out of any pro- or anti-religious motivations, but out of concern for the smooth and successful functioning of their school systems. For these actors, religious conflict was first and foremost a practical obstacle to governance, and it is not surprising that some sought to remove that obstacle by diluting or eliminating religious content. Yet these prosaic and mundane acts are not equivalent to the strategic secularization evoked by the idea of a "secular revolution."[3]

Further, this diversity of motives means that secularizing actors are dispersed widely throughout society, not just concentrated among elites. Accordingly, secularization should be understood as (at times) a grassroots phenomenon, not just an elite project. In countries like the United States, elite and grassroots secularization campaigns worked together. While educational professionals and judges promoted secular policies from above, religious actors also promoted them from below. Catholics and Jews protested Protestant devotionals through school boards and state courts beginning in the nineteenth century, and Jews, Protestants, and civil libertarians continued to agitate for

---

[2] Marion Maddox. 2014. *Taking God to School: The End of Australia's Egalitarian Education?* Crows Nest, NSW: Allen & Unwin, pp. 182–83.

[3] For elaboration of this idea, see Damon Mayrl. 2011. "Administering Secularization: Religious Education in New South Wales since 1960." *European Journal of Sociology* 52(1): 111–42.

strict separation through the courts in the twentieth century. Secularization can have multiple trajectories, in other words, and these trajectories offer an important starting point for theorizing how secularization interacts with the institutional terrain.

Administrative Centralization

The observation that secularization has both elite and grassroots variants help to make sense of one of the more surprising findings of this study: that administrative decentralization can be advantageous to secularization. This finding is somewhat unexpected, because some recent scholarship suggests that centralized states are more conducive to secularizing campaigns. David Martin, for instance, has argued that secular elites have gained influence in Britain in recent years by taking advantage of centralized media and other institutions.[4] This finding also appears to run counter to familiar examples of very centralized states that are also highly secular, such as France.

One way of making sense of the role of administrative centralization is to distinguish between "top-down" and "bottom-up" secularization. Studies showing that centralized states abet secularization tend to focus on cases of top-down, elite-driven secularization, where elites capture or use centralized institutions to disseminate their preferred secular policies. Centralized states present definite advantages for elite campaigns. While centralized institutions tend to be less accessible, they may also more efficiently impose policies across space in a uniform manner. This creates a "capture-the-flag" dynamic where small groups who gain control of the administrative machinery may use it to advance their preferred policies. Elites, being fewer in number but more politically connected, may be able to use centralized institutions to disseminate secularizing reforms that they could not enact through normal democratic channels.

At the same time, however, decentralized administration offers advantages to grassroots secularizing campaigns. When multiple smaller bodies are given policy-making authority, the number of potential venues in which secular policies may be promoted increases. Although these venues do not provide the same scope as centralized institutions, they are more accessible to popular campaigns and protests. Grassroots campaigns for secularization may benefit from the local influence they can muster in decentralized institutions, and from the ancillary effects (e.g., administrative fatigue) that derive from seemingly perpetual conflict in permeable institutional bodies. By allowing grassroots actors to mobilize local strengths to bring about piecemeal policy change, decentralized administration may abet secularization from below.

---

[4] David Martin. 2005. *On Secularization: Toward a Revised General Theory*. Burlington, VT: Ashgate, p. 67.

Thus, we should not expect to find any absolute relationship between administrative centralization and secularization. Instead, we should expect the relationship to depend on how administrative structures interact with political conflicts. To the extent that political institutions are permeable (which often, but not always, means decentralized), they will be more conducive to bottom-up campaigns for secularization. To the extent that they are insulated, they will be less conducive to bottom-up, and more conducive to top-down, campaigns.

RELIGION, THE STATE, AND AMERICAN CULTURE

In addition to its implications for secularization theory, this book also suggests new insights into a number of exceptional features of American political culture. By focusing on the interaction of political conflict and political context, this study helps to explain why the United States has adopted such an unusual approach to religious education. And by comparing the American experience against the Australian, this study also sheds light on why religious conflict seems to be such a perennial feature of American public life.

Why is American Education so Secular?

One of the puzzles I posed at the beginning of the book was why American education was so extraordinarily secular in comparative perspective. In light of the history presented here, familiar explanations for America's remarkable educational secularity appear unconvincing. America's strong constitutional provisions separating church and state were no guarantee of strict separation throughout most of American history, and parallel provisions have been effectively interpreted out of existence in Australia. Similarly, America's extensive religious diversity has not always implied the exclusion of ties between religion and education, while in Australia those ties have grown stronger even as its society has grown more religiously diverse. Instead, I have shown that the decentralized, democratic, accessible American state made the difference. It was not religious pluralism alone that led to American secularity, but where and how that pluralism found political expression. And it was not just America's strong constitutional protections, but how those protections shaped American culture and provided opportunities for controversies to make their way into the courts. America's strict separation in education thus reflects the democratic, permeable character of the American state as much as its demographics or Constitution.

But we can go further still. The secularization of American education was more of a bottom-up process than we typically admit. In the popular imagination, the decline of religious devotionals in the public schools is often laid at the feet of "activist judges" or professional educators like John Dewey. These actors played important roles, but they did not act alone. Instead, they acted in dialogue with restive religious outsiders and administrators grappling with the practical problems thrown up by religious pluralism.

This suggests that, ironically, American education is as secular as it is today precisely *because* the country is so religious. Because religion matters so much, the symbolic stakes attached to religion are higher. The accessibility and permeability of American political institutions has meant that deep theological disagreements have more easily been translated into political disagreements. Although professionalization and state-building both played important roles in secularizing American education, religious conflict was in many respects the key to the ultimate profundity of its secularity. In the United States, battles over secularization have been shot through with religious conflict to a degree unseen in Australia, reflecting the deeply religious motivations of many of its most prominent "secularists." Taken as a whole, these observations suggest that the exceptionally secular character of American education has its roots not only in its permeable state institutions, but also in the public piety of its population. Ironically, the very strength of American religion likely contributed to its absence from education today – and some of the most intensely public religious groups, who today agitate most strongly for desecularization, played important (if now conveniently forgotten) roles in bringing that settlement about.

There is a certain paradox in this combination of public piety and institutional secularity, but it should not come as a great surprise. Scholars in the sociology of religion's "new paradigm" have long argued that societies that are institutionally secular will be more energetically religious because disestablishment unleashes mechanisms of institutional competition that promote religious vitality.[5] The converse, however, also appears to be true – religious vitality can promote institutional secularity. The same mechanisms of religious competition – and conflict – that strengthen religious identities may also make it harder for religious groups to come together behind a consensual institutional arrangement governing religion. In such circumstances, the exclusion of religion from public life may be one solution.

Why is there so Much Conflict Over Religion in the United States?

Although there was substantial religious conflict in Australian education, especially over the issue of state aid, religious conflict played a more prominent and consequential role in the United States than in Australia. However, the important role religious conflict plays in American policy-making is not unique to the educational sphere. In fact, recurrent and frequently intense religious conflict

---

[5] Gill, *Political Origins*; Steven Pfaff. 2008. "The Religious Divide: Why Religion Seems to Be Thriving in the United States and Waning in Europe." Pp. 24–52 in *Growing Apart? America and Europe in the Twenty-First Century*, edited by Jeffrey Kopstein and Sven Steinmo. Cambridge: Cambridge University Press; Rodney Stark and Roger Finke. 2000. *Acts of Faith: Explaining the Human Side of Religion*. Berkeley: University of California Press.

is a widespread feature of American public life that has drawn attention across the academy. According to comparative sociologist Robin Archer, American political culture has long been "a cauldron of religious conflicts."[6] Similarly, historian David Sehat recently observed that American religious history is best understood as "a history of religious conflict."[7] It might be stated, with only limited exaggeration, that religious conflict appears to be a structural condition of American politics. What accounts for this agonistic dynamic?

Part of the reason, I argue, has to do with the structure of the American state. Institutional arrangements in the United States create a system in which religious and political dynamics generate bitter, ongoing fights. While the American state does not possess a classic European bureaucracy, it nevertheless possesses substantial "infrastructural power" that reaches deep into civil society and gives it immense power to regulate social life – including aspects of social life that implicate religion.[8] Yet, while decentralized, local political administration is a key channel for infrastructural power, it also provides citizens with ample opportunities to resist those regulations. Every school board election becomes an opportunity to contest religious policy, and every perceived infraction can be taken into the courts relatively easily thanks to democratic standing rules and multiple layers of constitutional protections. This easy access to the instruments of policy formation encourages perpetual conflict.

Permeable institutions readily allow religious differences to enter into the policy-making process. Because administration is decentralized, decisions are not concentrated among a distant policy-making elite. Instead, authority is fragmented, and it is relatively easy for a wide array of actors, sometimes with widely divergent religious views, to engage in the policy-making process. Similarly, America's democratic standing rules and multiple constitutional religious protections invite disaffected citizens of all religious stripes to pursue litigation. Once initiated, the dynamics of adversarial legalism encourage a cycle of litigation and relitigation. Because courts are weak mechanisms for ensuring compliance, ongoing litigation is often necessary to ensure that decisions are implemented. Even when decisions are enforced, clever statute-drafting can allow policies to be continued under the letter of the law, if not its spirit, which may in turn spur further litigation and ongoing conflict.[9]

If decentralized administration makes it easy to bring religious differences into the policy-making process, it also promotes ongoing politicization by multiplying the number of venues where claimants may pursue redress and policy

[6] Robin Archer. 2007. *Why Is There No Labor Party in the United States?* Princeton: Princeton University Press, p. 242.

[7] David Sehat. 2011. *The Myth of American Religious Freedom.* New York: Oxford University Press, p. viii.

[8] William J. Novak. 2008. "The Myth of the 'Weak' American State." *American Historical Review* 113(3): 752–72, pp. 763–64.

[9] Leo Pfeffer. 1984. *Religion, State, and the Burger Court.* Buffalo, NY: Prometheus Books, pp. 37–38.

change. As sociologist Monica Prasad observes, "a fragmented [political] structure can make small minorities disproportionately powerful."[10] The promise of being able to obtain one's goals, even on a relatively limited scale, may encourage disaffected religious groups to challenge policies in those areas where their numbers are greatest, thereby promoting further religious conflict. Further, the fact that there are multiple venues in which religious issues can be taken up may make it harder to resolve these issues. In fragmented and decentralized states, there is always a temptation to seek out new venues which might provide a more favorable setting for policy challenges. As a result, "Instead of leaving the battlefield, losers simply seek new ones."[11] Given these institutional dynamics, it is unsurprising that religious differences are rarely resolved; instead, they give rise to a never-ending and inconclusive series of small skirmishes.

In fact, the close relationship between America's permeable democratic institutions and its ongoing religious controversies can be understood as part of an amplifying cycle, whereby participatory governance begets controversy, which in turn heightens the salience of (and thereby perpetuates) the religious issues that precipitated the conflict in the first place. Tocqueville long ago observed that one of the most visible effects of American democracy was its tendency to animate civil society with a participatory democratic spirit. Because Americans are in close proximity to government and participate in governing themselves, "a confused clamor rises on every side, and a thousand voices are heard at once, each expressing some social requirements." As a result, he observed, "An American does not know how to converse, but he argues."[12] The very fact that policy-makers were so readily accessible to America's diverse and frequently discordant religious groups meant that the constant churn of politics was particularly likely to spill over into the religious realm. But it is also the case that the opportunity to forge policy through local and accessible institutions heightened the salience of those religious conflicts. By placing governance close to the people, and allowing them to readily turn to the courts to address their grievances, the structure of American democracy promotes the politicization of religion.

It is not like this in other countries, such as Australia, where access to courts and to the levers of educational administration is more restricted. There, centralized control of education at the state level encourages top-down decision-making. The strong centralized state insulates administrators from popular demands, while the absence of local administrative bodies functionally enhances the power of majorities. Change is thus much more difficult to come by.

---

[10] Monica Prasad. 2012. *The Land of Too Much: American Abundance and the Paradox of Poverty*. Cambridge: Harvard University Press, pp. 43–44.

[11] Drew Halfmann. 2011. *Doctors and Demonstrators: How Political Institutions Shape Abortion Law in the United States, Britain, and Canada*. Chicago: University of Chicago Press, p. 26.

[12] Alexis de Tocqueville. 1988 [1835–40]. *Democracy in America*, edited by J.P. Mayer. New York: Harper Perennial, pp. 242–43.

When it comes to religion, therefore, I argue that American political institutions should be understood as *engines of conflict*, whose very structure encourages regular contestation. The issues may change, but the structure of the conflict has remained consistent since the late nineteenth century: conflict is channeled through those institutional vehicles most open and accessible to political actors – courts and local government. Those venues act as innumerable combustion chambers in which diverse and divergent religious, irreligious, professional, and political groups battle over the appropriate role of religion in public life. Even today, school boards and courts continue to be sites for conflict; religious conservatives actively strategize to take over local boards to implement policies more to their liking, while separationists dutifully challenge those actions in the courts.[13] If anything, these venues have become more dialogically related: court decisions are imposed on local boards, and local transgressions of those decisions are taken up into the courts, in a cycle of perpetual controversy. The structure of the state encourages religious conflict in American public life.

In the end, the politicization of religion cannot be understood apart from the institutional conditions that make it possible. Religion is always a potentially potent source of conflict because it is intrinsically important to people. But if religion has become an ongoing matter of public controversy in the United States, it is because our political institutions make it so easy for Americans to take it up in public forums.

---

[13] See, e.g., Melissa M. Deckman. 2004. *School Board Battles: The Christian Right in Local Politics.* Washington, DC: Georgetown University Press; Lauri Lebo. 2008. *The Devil in Dover: An Insider's Story of Dogma* v. *Darwin in Small-Town America.* New York: The New Press.

Epilogue

Toward a Twenty-First-Century Settlement?

One of the advantages of a political-institutional approach is that it can help us make sense of the current flux in American church–state jurisprudence. While strict separation remains the law of the land, it has been challenged on multiple fronts in recent years. The Supreme Court has offered increased protection to religious speech,[1] and has shown a willingness to permit some public displays of religious symbols – though it has not yet endorsed them in the public schools.[2] More dramatically, the Court has steadily retreated from its longstanding prohibition on public aid to religious schools. Increasingly, the Court now holds that indirect supports, such as tax credits and vouchers, may be justifiable.[3] While aid paid directly to the school, of the type provided in Australia, remains unconstitutional, funding schemes that provide benefits indirectly to religious schools are no longer forbidden. These decisions do not require states to instantiate public aid programs, but they do give them the freedom to construct programs that could potentially provide extensive indirect support for religious schools.[4]

Thus, to an important – though still somewhat limited – extent, the Supreme Court has denationalized policy on public aid. Today, voucher programs – nearly

---

[1] *Rosenberger* v. *Rector and Visitors of the University of Virginia*, 515 U.S. 819 (1995); *Good News Club* v. *Milford Central School*, 533 U.S. 98 (2001).

[2] *Lynch* v. *Donnelly*, 465 U.S. 668 (1984); *Van Orden* v. *Perry*, 545 U.S. 677 (2005); *Salazar* v. *Buono*, 559 U.S. 700 (2010). Other decisions on religion in the public square, however, have hewed to a more separationist line, e.g., *County of Allegheny* v. *ACLU*, 492 U.S. 573 (1989); *McCreary County* v. *ACLU*, 545 U.S. 844 (2005).

[3] *Widmar* v. *Vincent*, 454 U.S. 263 (1981); *Mueller* v. *Allen*, 463 U.S. 388 (1983); *Witters* v. *Washington Dept. of Services for the Blind*, 474 U.S. 481 (1986); *Zobrest* v. *Catalina Foothills School District*, 509 U.S. 1 (1993); *Agostini* v. *Felton*, 521 U.S. 203 (1997); *Mitchell* v. *Helms*, 530 U.S. 793 (2000); *Zelman* v. *Simmons-Harris*, 536 U.S. 639 (2002).

[4] Douglas Laycock. 2006. "Church and State in the United States: Competing Conceptions and Historic Changes." *Indiana Journal of Global Legal Studies* 13(2): 503–41, p. 524.

all of which include religious schools as eligible voucher recipients – are in place in fourteen states and the District of Columbia.[5] But in returning the voucher question to the states, the Supreme Court has unleashed a torrent of litigation in the state courts. Nearly every existing voucher program is being or has been challenged in state constitutional courts, and in many cases voucher initiatives have been struck down as violations of state constitutional provisions.[6] Further complicating matters, some states have begun to experiment with novel means of financing and organizing education that complicate and undermine traditional understandings of strict separation. In light of these trends, some legal scholars have begun to anticipate a profound transformation in church–state policy. Recent decisions, they claim, may portend "a major substantive departure from existing … Establishment Clause doctrine."[7]

These changes are explicable in terms of the political-institutional theory advanced in this book. Just as the rise of strict separation as a legal principle during the mid-twentieth century was premised upon favorable political coalitions and a variety of institutional supports that made the development of that doctrine possible, so too is separation's current precarious position attributable to changing political and institutional dynamics. Understanding how the supportive political and institutional conditions of the mid-twentieth century have changed in recent years is essential to understanding the changing fortunes of strict separation, and to understanding the challenges it faces in the early twenty-first century.

THE CHANGING DYNAMICS OF RELIGIOUS CONFLICT

Strict separation was the product of particular midcentury dynamics of religious conflict that no longer hold today. Just as the dynamics of religious conflict at midcentury provided an opening for separationists, they have shifted again

---

[5] National Conference of State Legislatures. 2015. "School Voucher Laws: State-by-State Comparison." Available at http://www.ncsl.org/research/education/voucher-law-comparison.aspx (accessed 28 March 2016).

[6] *Chittenden Town Sch. Dist.* v. *Vermont Dept. of Education*, 738 A.2d 539 (Vt. 1999); *Owens* v. *Colorado Congress of Parents, Teachers, and Students*, 92 P.3d 933 (Colo. 2004); *Bush* v. *Holmes*, 919 So. 2d 392 (Fla. 2006); *Cain* v. *Horne*, 202 P.3d 1178 (Ariz. 2009); *Federation of Teachers et al.* v. *State of Louisiana*, 2013-CA-0120 (La. Sup. Ct., 2013). As discussed below, other state courts have upheld voucher programs, e.g., *Jackson* v. *Benson*, 578 N.W. 2d 603 (Wis. 1998); *Meredith* v. *Pence*, 984 N.E.2d 1213 (Ind. 2013).

[7] Mark C. Rahdert. 2012. "Court Reform and Breathing Space under the Establishment Clause." *Chicago-Kent Law Review* 87: 835–65, p. 841. For parallel assessments, see Kern Alexander and M. David Alexander. 2012. *American Public School Law*. 8th edn. Belmont, CA: Wadsworth, p. 177; Douglas W. Kmiec. 2008. "Standing Still: Did the Roberts Court Narrow, but Not Overrule, *Flast* to Allow Time to Re-Think Establishment Clause Jurisprudence?" *Pepperdine Law Review* 35: 509–22, pp. 514, 522; Ira C. Lupu and Robert W. Tuttle. 2008. "Ball on a Needle: *Hein* v. *Freedom from Religion Foundation, Inc.* and the Future of Establishment Clause Adjudication." *BYU Law Review* 2008: 115–68, p. 167.

to provide an opening for today's "accommodationists" who favor closer ties between church and state in education. First, the flux that characterized denominational relationships at midcentury has resolved into a restructured religious divide between religious conservatives and religious liberals that transcends denominations.[8] Second, demographic shifts within American Protestantism have enhanced the relative power of evangelicals and reduced the influence of liberal and mainline Protestants. Although mainline Protestants constituted twenty-eight percent of the American religious scene in the 1970s, they made up just thirteen percent of the American population by 2008. Evangelicals, accordingly, have seen their share of white Protestants rise from less than half to nearly two out of three over the past forty years.[9] Finally, this religious realignment has been accompanied by a significant dealignment. The unchurched portion of the population has skyrocketed over the past twenty-five years, rising from seven percent in 1987 to twenty percent in 2012.[10]

These changes are linked to important transformations within the religious schools sector. Catholic schools, which once constituted an overwhelming majority of private schools, have declined dramatically as a proportion of all private schools. In 1971, three out of five private schools was a Catholic school, and Catholic schools educated eighty percent of all private school students. By 2012, however, only twenty-two percent of private schools were Catholic schools, and they educated just forty-three percent of private school students.[11] In their stead, conservative Christian schools have experienced dramatic growth. Whereas probably fewer than three hundred Christian schools existed nationwide in 1960, today nearly ten thousand conservative Christian schools (around thirty-one percent of all private schools) educate over a million American students (around twenty-three percent of all private school students).[12] Jewish day schools, favored by many Orthodox Jews, further

[8] James Davison Hunter. 1991. *Culture Wars: The Struggle to Define America.* New York: Basic Books; Robert Wuthnow. 1988. *The Restructuring of American Religion.* Princeton: Princeton University Press.

[9] Robert D. Putnam and David E. Campbell. 2010. *American Grace: How Religion Divides and Unites Us.* New York: Simon & Schuster, pp. 104–05.

[10] Michael Hout and Claude S. Fischer. 2014. "Explaining Why More Americans Have No Religious Preference: Political Backlash and Generational Succession, 1987–2012." *Sociological Science* 1: 423–47, p. 423.

[11] United States Bureau of the Census. 1974. *Statistical Abstract of the United States: 1974.* 95th edn. Washington, DC: GPO, Table 204, p. 126; Stephen P. Broughman and Nancy L. Swaim. 2013. *Characteristics of Private Schools in the United States: Results from the 2011–12 Private School Universe Survey: First Look.* Washington, DC: National Center for Education Statistics, p. 6.

[12] Figures from 1960 are for "fundamentalist" schools. See Donald A. Erickson. 1986. "Choice and Private Schools: Dynamics of Supply and Demand." Pp. 82–110 in *Private Education: Studies in Choice and Public Policy*, edited by Daniel C. Levy. New Haven: Yale University Press, p. 89. Contemporary figures are estimates derived from denominational information in Broughman and Swaim, *Characteristics of Private Schools in the United States*, p. 7.

diversify the private school sector; day schools now make up about five percent of all private schools.[13]

These changes have destabilized the politics of strict separation, particularly around questions of funding for religious schools. While mainline Protestants and most Jews (along with liberal Catholics) continue to support strict separation, these groups have seen their influence wane. Thanks to the fractionalization of denominational interests and the rise of competing religious organizations, groups like the AJC and National Council of Churches can no longer claim to speak for all Jews or Protestants as they did at midcentury.[14] By contrast, the unchurched have become a more prominent part of the strict separationist coalition. Many of these unaffiliated Americans have dropped their religious affiliation as a reaction against the prominence of conservative religious activism,[15] and unsurprisingly the unchurched are among the least supportive of religious devotionals in the public schools.[16]

At the same time, however, a new conservative coalition now favors accommodations both for religion in the public schools and for public aid to private schools. The diversification of the private school sector has led many evangelical Protestants and Orthodox Jews to become supporters of aid to religious schools – with schools of their own to support, public aid is increasingly attractive as a practical matter.[17] Similarly, strict separation drew conservative Catholics and evangelicals together in support of religious devotionals: for Catholics, nondenominational school prayer seemed less dangerous than a naked public square, while for many evangelicals, "secular humanism" seemed more threatening than aid to parochial schools.[18]

[13] Broughman and Swaim, *Characteristics of Private Schools in the United States*, p. 7. On Orthodox Jews and Jewish day schools, see Lawrence Grossman. 2002. "Mainstream Orthodoxy and the American Public Square." Pp. 283–310 in *Jewish Polity and American Civil Society: Communal Agencies and Religious Movements in the American Public Sphere*, edited by Alan Mittleman, Jonathan D. Sarna, and Robert Licht. Lanham, MD: Rowman and Littlefield, pp. 293–95.

[14] Joseph F. Kobylka. 1995. "The Mysterious Case of Establishment Clause Litigation: How Organized Litigants Foiled Legal Change." Pp. 93–128 in *Contemplating Courts*, edited by Lee Epstein. Washington: CQ Press, p. 116.

[15] Hout and Fischer, "Explaining Why More Americans Have No Religious Preference."

[16] Philip Schwadel. 2013. "Changes in Americans' Views of Prayer and Reading the Bible in Public Schools: Time Periods, Birth Cohorts, and Religious Traditions." *Sociological Forum* 28(2): 261–82.

[17] John C. Jeffries, Jr. and James E. Ryan. 2001. "A Political History of the Establishment Clause." *Michigan Law Review* 100: 279–370, pp. 358–61; see also Axel R. Schäfer. 2012. *Piety and Public Funding: Evangelicals and the State in Modern America*. Philadelphia: University of Pennsylvania Press.

[18] Noah Feldman. 2005. *Divided by God: America's Church–State Problem—and What We Should Do about It*. New York: Farrar, Straus, & Giroux, pp. 196–97; Sarah Barringer Gordon. 2010. *The Spirit of the Law: Religious Voices and the Constitution in Modern America*. Cambridge: Belknap, pp. 141–57.

Accommodationist Countermobilization and Separationist Reorganization

Just as the rise of strict separation was advanced through the courts by organized separationist interests, so too has its erosion been advanced by a countermobilization among religious conservatives. Groups such as the Christian Legal Society, Concerned Women of America, and the Rutherford Institute pioneered accommodationist litigation in the early 1980s.[19] They were joined in the 1990s by several more sophisticated organizations. The American Center for Law and Justice, founded by Pat Robertson, was designed to act as a counterpart to the ACLU, and has effectively promoted student religious speech in public schools.[20] On the libertarian side, the Institute for Justice (IJ) has played a central role in litigating cases on vouchers and tax credits,[21] and after splitting from the Baptist Joint Committee in 1991, the Southern Baptist Convention began conducting its own church–state advocacy through its Christian Life Commission (now the Ethics and Religious Liberty Commission), arguing tirelessly in favor of aid to religious schools and recognition of public Christianity.[22] Other organizations, such as the Liberty Counsel, the Center for Law and Policy, the Becket Fund, and the Thomas More Law Center, round out a robust ecology of accommodationist public interest law.[23]

These accommodationist legal groups have conducted a counterattack on separationist jurisprudence, using many of the same tactics that separationists pioneered in the mid-twentieth century. Like the ACLU and AJC, accommodationist firms seek out test cases whose facts seem likely to yield new and influential accommodationist precedents.[24] Accommodationist groups also seek out sympathetic plaintiffs; the IJ, for instance, strategically selects low-income minority parents for its public aid cases to maximize sympathy – a tactic the IJ's founder states he deliberately borrowed from the ACLU.[25] They also work to enforce their legal victories by threatening nonconforming schools with litigation, and conducting educational campaigns, such as mailing every principal in America news about favorable court rulings.[26] In short, just as the strict

[19] Lisa Shaw Roy. 2011. "The Evangelical Footprint." *Michigan State Law Review* 2011: 1235–91, pp. 1244–48; Gordon, *Spirit of the Law*, p. 148.

[20] Hans J. Hacker. 2005. *The Culture of Conservative Christian Litigation*. Lanham, MD: Rowman & Littlefield, pp. 17–45.

[21] Steven M. Teles. 2008. *The Rise of the Conservative Legal Movement: The Battle for Control of the Law*. Princeton: Princeton University Press p. 220.

[22] Andrew R. Lewis. 2014. "Abortion Politics and the Decline of the Separation of Church and State: The Southern Baptist Case." *Politics and Religion* 7: 521–49, pp. 525, 540–41.

[23] Hans J. Hacker. 2005. "Defending the Faithful: Conservative Christian Litigation in American Politics." Pp. 365–84 in *The Interest Group Connection: Electioneering, Lobbying, and Policymaking in Washington*. 2nd edn. Washington, DC: CQ Press, p. 369.

[24] Hacker, "Defending the Faithful," p. 371.

[25] Teles, *Rise of the Conservative Legal Movement*, pp. 238, 244–45.

[26] Steven P. Brown. 2002. *Trumping Religion: The New Christian Right, the Free Speech Clause, and the Courts*. Tuscaloosa: University of Alabama Press, pp. 46–58, 128–34.

separationists had done in the mid-twentieth century, accommodationists have
fashioned an organized campaign to undo strict separation, using strategic litigation to attain their goals.

By contrast, the separationists' organizational infrastructure has come
under increasing strain. Prior to 1980, the separationist cause prominently featured multiple groups with a distinctively religious orientation, such as the
AJC, the Baptist Joint Committee on Public Affairs, and Protestants and Other
Americans United for Separation of Church and State. Since 1980, however,
these groups have reduced their activity, thanks to declines in membership,
dwindling resources, personnel turnover, and intraorganizational conflicts.[27]
In their stead, strict separation is increasingly defended by groups that value
strict separation for its own sake, apart from any religious rationale – groups
like American Atheists, People for the American Way, and the Freedom From
Religion Foundation. As some of their names suggest, these new groups are
often aggressively and outspokenly antireligious in character and membership.
These nonreligious secularists tend to be uncompromising when it comes to
strict separation, which has at times led to conflict with the AJC, ACLU, and
National Council of Churches, who are more open to compromises and alternative solutions.[28]

The ascent to leadership of a stridently separationist constituency has
altered the dynamics of litigation. These new organizations have tended to be
more indiscriminate in their attacks on all forms of contact between church
and state – filing unsuccessful lawsuits challenging the phrase "under God" in
the Pledge of Allegiance, presidential prayer proclamations, and a memorial
cross at the World Trade Center, for instance.[29] Legal historian John Witte has
usefully distinguished between using separation as a shield to protect free exercise, and as a sword with which to wage cultural warfare.[30] In many respects,
these newer cases adopt a more "swordlike" approach to separationism, moving further afield of those earlier challenges on which separationist jurisprudence was originally built. Mid-twentieth-century separationists would have
been reticent to take on such cases, because they risk overextension and the

[27] On declining mainline Protestant advocacy, see Derek H. Davis. 2002. "From Engagement to
Retrenchment: An Examination of First Amendment Activism by America's Mainline Churches,
1980–2000." Pp. 317–42 in *The Quiet Hand of God: Faith-Based Activism and the Public
Role of Mainline Protestantism*, edited by Robert Wuthnow and John H. Evans. Berkeley,
CA: University of California Press; on declining Jewish advocacy, see Gregg Ivers. 1995. *To
Build a Wall: American Jews and the Separation of Church and State*. Charlottesville: University
Press of Virginia, pp. 192–205.

[28] See, e.g., Stephen Bates. 1993. *Battleground: One Mother's Crusade, the Religious Right, and
the Struggle for Our Schools*. New York: Poseidon, pp. 282–84.

[29] *Elk Grove Unified School District* v. *Newdow*, 542 US 1 (2004); *Freedom from Religion
Foundation* v. *Obama*, 641 F.3d 803 (7th Cir. 2011); *American Atheists Inc.* v. *Port Authority
of New York and New Jersey*, 936 F.Supp.2d 321 (S.D.N.Y. 2013).

[30] John Witte, Jr. 2006. "Facts and Fictions about the History of Separation of Church and State."
Journal of Church and State 48: 15–45, p. 43.

creation of negative precedents that could contribute to the development of a new, accommodationist jurisprudence.

THE ERODING INSTITUTIONAL FOUNDATIONS OF STRICT SEPARATION

The declining fortunes of strict separation reflect changes in the process of religious conflict: the growing strength of an interdenominational accommodationist coalition, the decline of core separationist constituencies, and the rise and mobilization of the unchurched. But at the same time, these political changes have been magnified because they have been accompanied by a weakening of strict separation's institutional foundations. In particular, the sharp public–private divide, "no-aid" provisions in state constitutions, and taxpayer standing have all faced challenges in recent years.

The Public–Private Divide

Strict separation is legally predicated on a sharp public–private divide, where public and religious schools are clearly distinguished in terms of organization, content, and funding patterns. Increasingly, however, these divisions are being undermined by the development of new hybrid educational institutions such as charter schools and scholarship tax credits. Charter schools combine elements of public and private education – although they are created by public agencies and funded by state and local governments, they are privately governed. They are thus usually considered public schools under private management.[31] Religion holds an ambiguous position in many charters. Because charters are permitted to adopt curricula and programs that are culturally distinctive, some religious groups have taken advantage of this feature to open "faith-based," "culturally religious," or "religiously themed" charter schools. Unsurprisingly, the boundaries between "culture" and "religion" are quite murky in many of these religious charter schools.[32] Even more severe blurring occurs in

---

[31] Diane Ravitch. 2010. *The Death and Life of the Great American School System: How Testing and Choice Are Undermining Education*. New York: Basic Books, p. 121.

[32] For instance, students at one Hawaiian charter school chant a traditional native Hawaiian prayer before entering the school building, a religious charter school in Texas teaches creationism and intelligent design, and a Muslim charter school in Minnesota faced a lawsuit after its staff organized voluntary prayers during the school day. See Robert A. Fox, Nina K. Buchanan, Suzanne E. Eckes, and Letitia E. Basford. 2012. "The Line between Cultural Education and Religious Education: Do Ethnocentric Niche Charter Schools Have a Prayer?" *Review of Research in Education* 36: 282–305, p. 296; Thomas Maeglin. 2010. "Minnesota Islamic Charter School Blurs the Line: The Case of the Tarek ibn Ziyad Academy (TiZA)." Pp. 57–72 in *Blurring the Lines: Charter, Public, Private, and Religious Schools Coming Together*, edited by Janet D. Mulvey, Bruce S. Cooper, and Arthur T. Maloney. Charlotte, NC: Information Age Publishing; Jessica Meyers. 2010. "Charter Schools with Ties to Religious Groups Raise Fears about State Funds' Use." *Dallas Morning News*, 22 November.

"homeschooling charters" or "cyber charters" which cater to homeschoolers. In such schools, staff primarily act as consultants to parents, who continue to teach their own preferred curriculum at home, including, in some instances, Bible reading and devotionals. In this case, it is parents rather than school staff who do the teaching, in a setting – their home – that is not typically seen as part of the school.[33] Such an arrangement creates serious problems for legal standards premised upon straightforward definitions of schools and teachers, public and private.

If the distinctions between public and private, religious and cultural are blurry in practice, they are also blurry legally. Although most courts have classified charter schools as state actors when the question has come before them, not all of them have.[34] In 2010, the Ninth Circuit Court of Appeals found that charter schools could "be designated a state actor for some purposes but still function as a private actor in other respects." Importantly, the Court ruled that the fact that state law characterized charters as "public" schools was not "controlling" – whether charters were public or private was, to some extent, context dependent.[35] In effect, charters may be both public and private simultaneously. This has potentially large implications for religious education policy. Because strict separation depends upon stark distinctions between public and private, and state and society, it becomes difficult to apply the law in situations where this distinction becomes blurry.[36]

While charter schools blur the boundary between public and private, scholarship tax credits obviate it by creating new institutional intermediaries. Under scholarship tax credit programs, which currently operate in sixteen states, businesses and individuals receive tax credits for donating money to scholarship funds managed by nonprofit scholarship foundations.[37] The nonprofit then provides scholarships directly to parents of students to cover the costs of attending a private school. As private entities, these organizations can provide scholarships to students irrespective of whether a school is religious or not. In fact, in some states, dozens of specialized scholarship foundations exist that provide scholarships for particular educational subsectors, such as

---

[33] Belinda M. Cambre. 2009. "Tearing Down the Walls: Cyber Charter Schools and the Public Endorsement of Religion." *TechTrends* 53(4): 61–64; Luis A. Huerta. 2000. "Losing Public Accountability: A Home Schooling Charter." Pp. 177–202 in *Inside Charter Schools: The Paradox of Radical Decentralization*, edited by Bruce Fuller. Cambridge: Harvard University Press, p. 188.

[34] Preston C. Green III, Bruce D. Baker, and Joseph O. Oluwole. 2013. "Having It Both Ways: How Charter Schools Try to Obtain Funding of Public Schools and the Autonomy of Private Schools." *Emory Law Journal* 63: 303–37, p. 326.

[35] *Caviness* v. *Horizon Community Learning Center, Inc.*, 590 F.3d 806 (9th Cir. 2010), pp. 75, 78.

[36] Aaron Saiger. 2013. "Charter Schools, the Establishment Clause, and the Neoliberal Turn in Public Education." *Cardozo Law Review* 34: 1163–225, p. 1178.

[37] National Conference of State Legislatures. 2015. "School Choice: Scholarship Tax Credits." Available at http://www.ncsl.org/research/education/school-choice-scholarship-tax-credits.aspx (accessed 28 March 2016).

Christian, Catholic, or Lutheran schools.[38] These programs effectively establish public subsidies for religious schools through the vehicle of personal charitable contributions. Accordingly, they exist largely beyond the purview of constitutional restrictions. Because the government makes no direct appearance at any point in the process, the funding mechanism – though subsidized by the state – is effectively not a public expenditure for legal purposes. As a recent guide coauthored by the IJ observes, "Since forgone tax revenue does not constitute public money, most state supreme courts do not or should not regard tax-credit-funded scholarships as subject to [constitutional] limitations."[39] The Supreme Court has recently refused to disallow such programs.[40]

State Constitutional Provisions

As federal restrictions on public aid have diminished, state constitutional restrictions on public aid have come under fire. Because state constitutional provisions provide a second line of defense for strict separation, opponents of strict separation have undertaken a concerted campaign to undermine, delegitimize, and outright eliminate them. At the center of this campaign is an effort to recast these state constitutional provisions as illegitimate "Blaine amendments." This term links no-aid provisions to the failed effort, led by Maine Senator James Blaine, to pass a federal constitutional amendment forbidding public support for religious schools in an atmosphere of anti-Catholic hysteria in 1876.[41] These efforts contribute to a broader critique that the concept of "separation and church and state" has its roots in nativist, anti-Catholic prejudice.[42] This argument has found a receptive audience among certain Supreme Court justices; Justice Clarence Thomas, for instance, has opined that the

[38] Stephen D. Sugarman. 2014. "Tax Credit School Scholarship Plans." *Journal of Law and Education* 43: 100–59, p. 131.

[39] Richard D. Komer. 2007. *School Choice and State Constitutions: A Guide to Designing School Choice Programs*. Washington, DC: Institute for Justice and American Legislative Exchange Council, p. 5.

[40] *Arizona Christian School Tuition Organization* v. *Winn et al.*, 131 S.Ct. 1436 (2011). As I discuss further below, the Supreme Court did not reach the merits of the case, dismissing it instead for lack of standing. However, by exempting tax expenditures from First Amendment review, the Court effectively made scholarship tax credit programs unreviewable for the foreseeable future at the federal level.

[41] See above, Chapter 2.

[42] For the most sustained version of this argument, see Philip Hamburger. 2002. *Separation of Church and State*. Cambridge: Harvard University Press, pp. 335, 483. For scholarly critiques of this thesis, see Tracy Fessenden. 2005. "The Nineteenth-Century Bible Wars and the Separation of Church and State." *Church History* 74(4): 784–811; Steven K. Green. 2010. *The Second Disestablishment: Church and State in Nineteenth-Century America*. New York: Oxford University Press; and T. Jeremy Gunn. 2012. "The Separation of Church and State versus Religion in the Public Square." Pp. 15–44 in *No Establishment of Religion: America's Original Contribution to Religious Liberty*, edited by T. Jeremy Gunn and John Witte, Jr. New York: Oxford University Press.

separation of church and state is a "doctrine born of bigotry" that "should be buried now."[43]

From a constitutional perspective, the payoff to associating state no-aid provisions with anti-Catholicism is potentially tremendous. If no-aid provisions were enacted as a form of discrimination against Catholics, then they violate the Constitution and must be overturned.[44] Accordingly, it is not surprising that accommodationist legal scholars have regularly evoked the ghost of James Blaine and anti-Catholic nativism in discussing state no-aid provisions.[45] From the pages of law journals, they assert that the "Blaine amendments" facilitate "religious persecution,"[46] constitute "state-sponsored discrimination" and a "legacy of hate,"[47] and are nothing more than "weapons of religious bigotry forged in the fires of nineteenth-century anti-Catholicism."[48] The argument has been put forward in accommodationist litigation as well. In 2004, the Becket Fund filed an amicus brief with the Supreme Court in which it argued that the Court should "tear out, root and branch, the state constitutional provisions that have enforced religious discrimination in the funding of education for well over a century."[49]

These legal efforts to delegitimize state no-aid provisions have been complemented by political efforts to repeal them outright. In Florida, voters narrowly defeated a proposal to amend the state constitution to eliminate its no-aid clause in the 2012 election.[50] The proposed amendment would have stricken Florida's no-aid clause and replaced it with a new clause stating "No individual or entity may be discriminated against or barred from receiving funding on the basis of religious identity or belief."[51] A similar attempt by Alaskan

---

[43] *Mitchell* v. *Helms*, p. 829.

[44] Toby J. Heytens. 2000. "School Choice and State Constitutions." *Virginia Law Review* 86(10): 117–62.

[45] The use of the term "Blaine amendments" was scarce in law journals before the late 1990s. A search of law journals on Hein Online reveals that, of 229 articles using the phrase since 1968, all but seven have been published since 1998. Similarly, all usages of "baby Blaine" have occurred since 1996.

[46] Kyle Duncan. 2003. "Secularism's Laws: State Blaine Amendments and Religious Persecution." *Fordham Law Review* 72: 493–593.

[47] Brandi Richardson. 2003. "Eradicating Blaine's Legacy of Hate: Removing the Barrier to State Funding of Religious Education." *Catholic University Law Review* 52: 1041–79, pp. 1041, 1046.

[48] Robert William Gall. 2003. "The Past Should Not Shackle the Present: The Revival of a Legacy of Religious Bigotry by Opponents of School Choice." *NYU Annual Survey of American Law* 59: 413–37, p. 414.

[49] Brief of Amici Curiae, the Becket Fund for Religious Liberty et al. in Support of Respondent, *Locke* v. *Davey*, No. 02-1315, 8 September 2003, p. 6. Though noting the argument in a footnote, the Court ultimately declined to rule on the question; see *Locke* v. *Davey*, 540 U.S. 712 (2004), p. 724 n.7.

[50] Lizette Alvarez. 2012. "Voters in Florida Are Set to Weigh in on Two Contentious Ballot Questions." *New York Times*, 7 October, p. A24; Brittany Alana Davis and Toluse Olorunnipa. 2012. "Most Florida Amendments Rejected." *Miami Herald*, 7 November.

[51] Florida. House of Representatives. 2011. "Joint Resolution 1471," 6 May, available at http://www.flsenate.gov/Session/Bill/2011/1471/BillText/Filed/HTML (accessed 28 March 2016).

legislators to replace Alaska's no-aid clause with text reading "nothing … shall prevent payment from public funds for the direct educational benefit of students as provided by law" was ultimately withdrawn before being sent to voters in 2014.[52] Attacks on state constitutional provisions have become part of political campaigns as well. In Virginia, 2013 Republican gubernatorial candidate Ken Cuccinelli included repeal of his state's no-aid amendment in his educational platform.[53] Both in courtrooms and on the campaign trail, therefore, state no-aid provisions are increasingly embattled.

Taxpayer Standing

Whereas state constitutional provisions have thus far managed to withstand most of the assaults directed toward them, the same cannot be said for taxpayer standing – that is, the ability for individuals to challenge public expenditures in the courts on the basis of being a taxpaying citizen. In recent years, the Supreme Court has made a concerted effort to roll back federal taxpayer standing and make challenges to public expenditures more difficult. In 2008, the Court restricted federal taxpayer standing to legislative appropriations, thereby placing funds dispensed through executive orders beyond the reach of litigation.[54] Three years later, it followed up with a potentially more wide-ranging decision disallowing challenges to tax credits.[55] The suit, which involved a challenge to Arizona's scholarship tax credit program, was rejected on standing grounds. The Court held that because the state did not expend any money, but instead only reduced the taxes of those who donated to the scholarship organizations, the tax credit system did not "implicate individual taxpayers in sectarian activities." "When Arizona taxpayers contribute to [scholarship funds]," the Court continued, "they spend their own money, not money the State has collected from respondents or other taxpayers."[56] The decision effectively immunizes all tax-credit-based programs from federal constitutional scrutiny.[57]

Such decisions radically alter the incentive structure for government actors. By denying standing to taxpayers challenging administrative appropriations and tax expenditures, the Court's decisions considerably restrict the kinds of federal

---

[52] Alaska State Legislature. 2014. "Bill Text 28th Legislature: Senate Joint Resolution No. 9." Available at http://www.legis.state.ak.us/basis/get_bill_text.asp?hsid=SJR009A&session=28 (accessed 28 March 2016); Pat Forgey. 2014. "School Voucher Bill Pulled from Senate Floor, Avoiding Fatal Vote." *Alaska Dispatch News*, 12 March. Available at http://www.adn.com/article/20140312/school-voucher-bill-pulled-senate-floor-avoiding-fatal-vote (accessed 28 March 2016).

[53] Ken Cuccinelli. 2013. "Ken's Education Plan." Available at http://web.archive.org/web/20131114194039/http://www.cuccinelli.com/apples/ (accessed 28 March 2016).

[54] *Hein* v. *Freedom from Religion Foundation*.

[55] *Arizona Christian School Tuition Organization* v. *Winn*.

[56] *Arizona Christian School Tuition Organization* v. *Winn*, p. 1447.

[57] Isabel Chou. 2011. "'Opportunity' for All? How Tax Credit Scholarships will Fare in New Jersey." *Rutgers Law Review* 64: 295–332, p. 312.

programs that are subject to review, raising the likelihood that challenges to public aid programs could be rejected for lack of standing.[58] Legal historian Steven Green predicts that the "slow death of taxpayer standing" will "keep otherwise qualified plaintiffs out of court."[59] Indeed, a number of taxpayer challenges were dismissed or abandoned in the immediate wake of the Court's decision.[60]

This would still leave state courts as potential venues for challenges to public aid, but in an ominous sign for strict separation, some state courts have also begun to roll back taxpayer standing. Most dramatically, in *Duncan* v. *New Hampshire*, the New Hampshire Supreme Court in 2014 overturned a lower court ruling invalidating that state's scholarship tax credit program by severely restricting all taxpayer standing in that state. Although New Hampshire had granted citizens taxpayer standing since the Civil War era, the Court disallowed it, ruling that it required judges to interfere in legislative politics in violation of the state constitution's separation of powers.[61] In many respects, *Duncan* epitomizes the challenges facing strict separation – not just because of its outcome, but because of how it unites the institutional challenges facing separationists: the increasing irrelevance of the public–private distinction, the weakening of standing law, and the faltering power of state constitutions as a backstop for strict separation.

TOWARD AN "AUSTRALIAN" SETTLEMENT?

If accommodationists were to succeed in forging a new secular settlement, what might it look like? In pondering this possibility, we can again draw lessons from Australia, because there is a good chance that a new twenty-first-century settlement might look something like the current Australian settlement: Religious and public schools would both be equally eligible for public funding, and religious speech and devotionals would be permitted (though not required) within the public schools. Some advocates have in fact pointed to Australia as an appropriate model (among others) for a new secular settlement in the United States.[62] In light of Australia's experience with such a system, what might we expect were the United States to move in that direction?

---

[58] Lupu and Tuttle, "Ball on a Needle," p. 120.

[59] Steven K. Green. 2011. "The Slow, Tragic Demise of Standing in Establishment Clause Challenges." *Advance: The Journal of the ACS Issue Groups* 5: 117–29, pp. 117–18.

[60] Lupu and Tuttle, "Ball on a Needle," pp. 117–18.

[61] *Duncan* v. *New Hampshire*, 102 A.3d 913 (N.H. 2014).

[62] See, e.g., Veit Bader. 2003. "Religious Diversity and Democratic Institutional Pluralism." *Political Theory* 31: 265–94, pp. 271–72; Stephen V. Monsma and J. Christopher Soper. 1997. *The Challenge of Pluralism: Church and State in Five Democracies*. Lanham, MD: Rowman & Littlefield, pp. 12, 218; United States Department of Education. 2008. *Preserving a National Asset: America's Disadvantaged Students and the Crisis in Faith-Based Urban Schools*. Washington, DC: United States Department of Education, pp. 74–76.

First, we might expect the position of public education to weaken significantly. The reintroduction of state aid has transformed the Australian education sector. Australian nongovernment schools – the overwhelming majority of which are religious – have seen dramatic growth since the reintroduction of state aid.[63] Overall, the proportion of Australian students attending private schools is now approaching thirty-five percent, up from approximately twenty percent in 1970.[64] We might expect the lowering of barriers to public aid in the United States to have a similar effect. With government funds supporting capital and recurrent expenditures, more religious schools with lower enrollment fees could be established. As in Australia, we might expect the primary beneficiaries of these changes to be members of the upper and middle classes.[65] And as private enrollments grow, we might expect to see public schools continue to weaken, as enrollments and resources shift to the private sector.[66]

Second, we might expect that formally neutral programs to reincorporate religion in the public schools will, in practice, disproportionately benefit Christian groups. In Australia, large Christian groups have accrued outsized influence within religious education programs. Conservative Protestants are overrepresented among special religious education (SRE) volunteers in Australia, for instance.[67] In some states, evangelical organizations have exclusive contracts with state governments to provide SRE.[68] Smaller religious groups, meanwhile, are often excluded. In recent years, Sikhs, aboriginal religions, and humanists have either faced administrative obstacles or been outright prevented from providing SRE in New South Wales and Victoria.[69] Accordingly, we might expect large Christian organizations to benefit most from the reintroduction of religious education in the public schools, and for many smaller groups to be excluded from such programs.[70] Indeed, in the United States, where a

---

[63] Jennifer Buckingham. 2010. *The Rise of Religious Schools.* St. Leonards, NSW: Centre for Independent Studies, pp. ix, 2–3, 8.

[64] Australian Bureau of Statistics. 2013. "4221.0 – Schools, Australia, 2013." Available at: http://www.abs.gov.au/ausstats/abs@.nsf/Previousproducts/4221.0Main%20Features42013?opendocument&tabname=Summary&prodno=4221.0&issue=2013 (accessed 28 March 2016).

[65] Louise Watson and Chris Ryan. 2009. "Choice, Vouchers and the Consequences for Public High Schools: Lessons from Australia." Unpublished manuscript, Faculty of Education, University of Canberra.

[66] Diane Ravitch. 2014. *Reign of Error: The Hoax of the Privatization Movement and the Danger to America's Public Schools.* New York: Vintage.

[67] Catherine Byrne. 2014. *Religion in Secular Education: What, in Heaven's Name, Are We Teaching Our Children?* Leiden: Brill, pp. 71–72, 168.

[68] Anna Halafoff. 2013. "Education about Religions and Beliefs in Victoria." *Journal for the Academic Study of Religion* 26(2): 172–97.

[69] Byrne, *Religion in Secular Education*, pp. 74–75, 106–07, 112, 243–44; Marion Maddox. 2014. *Taking God to School: The End of Australia's Egalitarian Education?* Sydney: Allen & Unwin, pp. 143–44.

[70] This dynamic has been observed in other countries with similar religious education programs, such as Germany, Belgium, and the Netherlands. See Alfred Stepan. 2011. "The Multiple Secularisms of Modern Democratic and Non-Democratic Regimes." Pp. 114–44 in *Rethinking*

comparably "neutral" program already exists for military chaplains, Protestants are overrepresented among the chaplaincy.[71]

Therefore, third, we might expect that adopting an "Australian" settlement in the United States would do little to stem religious conflict in education. This might seem a curious conclusion, considering that religious education has precipitated relative little controversy in Australia since the 1970s. By creating programs open to, and which benefit, most major denominations, the system has effectively won over many of those who might have objected to a system that did not include them. Today, most Australian denominations are united in supporting state aid, and in substantial agreement on the merits of SRE. At the same time, however, this lack of controversy likely reflects the continuing insulated nature of Australian government. In a telling trend, a number of high-profile controversies have recently begun to break out over the form and propriety of religious education.[72] Many of these controversies involve legal challenges, which take advantage of new anti-discrimination boards and human rights statutes that have been introduced in the Australian states since 2000.[73] This suggests that conflicts over religious education have not disappeared, but may instead have simply been stymied by a lack of institutional opportunities.

The United States, as this book has shown, has not historically lacked venues in which religious conflict may permeate the policy-making process. The return of religious content to public education, and the enticement of public dollars to religious schools, would invite further contestation over content and distribution. The likeliest outcome, then, would be that the adoption of an Australian-style solution might shift the specific parameters of conflict over religion, but would not reduce that conflict more generally.

Fourth, we might expect some realignment in the religious alliances and coalitions around religious education. Since the Supreme Court nationalized American religious education policy, debates over religion and education have been dominated by conflicts between religious and nonreligious actors. We should not expect these conflicts to disappear; on the contrary, the unaffiliated will retain a substantial organizational infrastructure on church–state matters

Secularism, edited by Craig Calhoun, Mark Juergensmeyer, and Jonathan VanAntwerpen. New York: Oxford University Press, p. 139.

[71] Lee Marsden. 2014. "Faith-Based Diplomacy: Conservative Evangelicals and the United States Military." *Politics and Religion* 7: 475–98.

[72] E.g., *Hoxton Park Residents' Action Group Inc.* v. *Liverpool City Council* (2010) 246 FLR 207; *Williams* v. *Commonwealth of Australia* [2012] HCA 23; *Aitkin & Ors* v. *The State of Victoria's Department of Education and Early Childhood Development*, [2012] VCAT 1547. See also Byrne, *Religion in Secular Education*, pp. 112, 177–79; Bridie Jabour. 2012. "Mother Rails against Religion in Schools." *Brisbane Times*, 9 July; Maddox, *Taking God to School*, pp. 124, 144, 178.

[73] Carolyn Evans. 2012. *Legal Protection of Religious Freedom in Australia*. Sydney: Federation Press, pp. 98–99, 142–43; Denise Meyerson. 2009. "The Protection of Religious Rights under Australian Law." *Brigham Young University Law Review* 2009: 529–53, pp. 531, 544.

even should America's secular settlement shift. Indeed, if the unchurched population continues to grow, we might expect to see nonreligious secularists playing a still larger role in contemporary conflicts over American religious education. At the same time, however, the difficulty of creating truly religiously neutral policies would heighten the salience of issues of equal access and the content of religious programming, reawakening long-dormant conflicts among religious groups in the process. Groups that today join forces in pursuit of a less secular settlement may part ways on these questions, just as obscure and politically unpopular religious voices may be encouraged to make new claims on the state. Consequently, older dimensions of the debate would once again return to prominence – namely, *whose* religion, and in what form, should be recognized. Under the new settlement, therefore, religious conflict would both be more fragmented, and potentially wider in scope.

Finally, we can expect the institutional settings for these conflicts to shift and diversify. Rather than being concentrated in the courts, these conflicts would return to America's permeable administrative institutions. There is an important caveat here, however. Over the past forty years, state and federal mandates have begun to play an important role in shaping the curriculum.[74] Although control of public education is still largely in the hands of local boards, local control is less absolute than it once was. This suggests that, while local boards will continue to be important sites where religious education policy gets hashed out, these local conflicts will be supplemented by battles at the state and federal levels. We might expect supporters of religious education, for instance, to attempt to incorporate religious education mandates into state and federal education policy documents, much as they did in the early twentieth century by campaigning for state Bible-reading legislation.[75] At the same time, however, we should not expect legal challenges to disappear entirely – unless state constitutional provisions are completely gutted as a secondary line of defense. Just as voucher challenges have been made on a variety of state constitutional grounds, so too may opponents of religion in education continue to find constitutional grounds to challenge religious education and aid to religious schools.

---

[74] Jeffrey Henig. 2013. *The End of Exceptionalism in American Education: The Changing Politics of School Reform*. Cambridge: Harvard Education Press; Ravitch, *Reign of Error*, pp. 278–89. While the Every Student Succeeds Act, passed in December 2015, promises to devolve some federal authority back to states and districts, its ultimate effect on educational policy remains to be seen. See, e.g., Alyson Klein. 2016. "New Law, Fresh Challenges." *Education Week*, 6 January.

[75] Indeed, in Australia, the incipient development of federal curricular standards has already drawn the attention of activists, who protest that the curriculum "belittles religion" and "fails to acknowledge the central role of Christianity in the nation's history." See Kevin Donnelly. 2013. "National Curriculum's Crusade against Christianity." *News Weekly*, 8 June. Available at http://newsweekly.com.au/article.php?id=5608 (accessed 28 March 2016).

These predictions, of course, are contingent on the demise of the strict separationist settlement in the United States and its conversion into a new secular settlement. This is not inevitable by any means, though the structural conditions, in my view, appear to be tilting against strict separation. The ultimate outcome, however, both in the courts and elsewhere, will depend, as always, on how political struggles play out in America's contentious institutional landscape.

Index